CRITICAL INSIGHTS

The Adventures of Tom Sawyer

THE ADVENTURES OF TOM SAWYER

BY MARK TWAIN.

ILLUSTRATED

CRITICAL INSIGHTS

The Adventures of Tom Sawyer

Editor
R. Kent Rasmussen

SALEM PRESS
A Division of EBSCO Information Services, Inc.
Ipswich, Massachusetts

GREY HOUSE PUBLISHING

Cover illustration: Designed and colorized by R. Kent Rasmussen from an illustration by True Williams, *The Adventures of Tom Sawyer*, 1876.

Frontispiece: The American Publishing Company's 1892 "cheap" edition of Tom Sawyer was the first US edition of the novel with a picture of Tom on its cover. Image courtesy of Kevin Mac Donnell. [Used with permission.]

Publisher's Cataloging-in-Publication Data
(Prepared by Parlew Associates, LLC)

Names: Rasmussen, R. Kent, 1943- , editor. | Twain, Mark, 1835-1910. Adventures of Tom Sawyer.
Title: Critical insights : the adventures of Tom Sawyer / R. Kent Rasmussen, editor.
Description: Ipswich, MA : Salem Press, a division of EBSCO Information Services, Inc. ; Amenia, NY : Grey House Publishing, [2022]. | Series: Critical insights. | Includes bibliographic references, appendices, and index. | Includes photos and illustrations.
Identifiers: ISBN 9781637003435 (hardback)
Subjects: LCSH: Twain, Mark, -- 1835-1910 -- Adventures of Tom Sawyer. | Twain, Mark, -- 1835-1910 -- Criticism and interpretation. | Adventure stories, American -- History and criticism. | BISAC: LITERARY CRITICISM / American / General. | LITERARY CRITICISM / Children's & Young Adult Literature. | LITERARY CRITICISM / Modern / 19th Century.
Classification: LCC PS1306.C77 R37 2022 | DDC 813 --dc23

First Printing

Contents

Resources

About This Volume

R. Kent Rasmussen

Mark Twain's *The Adventures of Tom Sawyer* has remained in print continuously since it was first published in 1876. One of the most widely read novels in American literature, it has been translated into scores of languages and republished in more than one thousand editions. Although its status as a classic work of literature is unquestioned, its reputation as a literary work worthy of serious study has always been shaky. As an essay in the present volume explains, the novel has been overshadowed by its sequel, Mark Twain's acknowledged masterpiece, *Adventures of Huckleberry Finn*. That book has monopolized so much scholarly attention that *Tom Sawyer* has been neglected to a degree far greater than it has deserved. Hundreds, perhaps even thousands, of critical articles and scores of books have been written about *Huckleberry Finn,* whereas only a tiny fraction of those numbers have been published about *Tom Sawyer.* It is a singularly remarkable fact that in the nearly century and a half since the novel first saw print, *Critical Insights: Adventures of Tom Sawyer* is the *first* collection of entirely original essays ever to be published about *Tom Sawyer*. The present volume brings more than a few fresh perspectives and novel approaches to the novel; perhaps they will help change how the book is regarded. Whether or not *Tom Sawyer* should be considered a "great" book, it is unquestionably an important book. It is also one with far greater depths than have previously been recognized, as this collection amply demonstrates.

The first section of this volume presents the editor's views on Mark Twain's life and *The Adventures of Tom Sawyer*—two fascinating subjects far more intimately related than is the case for most authors and their novels.

Critical Contexts

Essays in this section explore *Tom Sawyer* in its broadest historical and cultural contexts. The first essay is by Great Britain's leading Mark Twain authority, Peter Messent. "*Tom Sawyer*'s Evasion of History," considers the novel from two significantly different chronological perspectives: the mid-1870s, the time when Mark Twain wrote the book; and the pre-Civil War 1840s, the period in which the story is set. Messent shows how the two-way movement between those periods in American history led Mark Twain to transform the real Hannibal in which he had grown up during the same period as that in which the novel is set into a fictional St. Petersburg that is a "highly selective version" of historical reality, cut off from the fast-changing outside world. Messent goes on to argue that Tom Sawyer's St. Petersburg appears to exist outside the parameters of any real world. For this reason, he sees the novel as a profoundly *anti*-historical text. Messent's essay should forever alter readers' perceptions of *Tom Sawyer* as a simple "boy story."

What would *Tom Sawyer*'s literary reputation be today if Mark Twain had never written *Huckleberry Finn*? That is the compelling question veteran Mark Twain authority Alan Gribben addresses in "*Tom Sawyer*: A Classic Overshadowed by Its Successor." No one seriously questions the assertion that of those two literary classics, *Huckleberry Finn* is the greater work. Gribben examines the history of *Tom Sawyer's* critical reception in the broader context of the book's own place in nineteenth-century literature, calling attention to innovative and unique aspects that set it apart from other novels of its time. He points out, for example, that *Tom Sawyer* differs from Thomas Bailey Aldrich's once popular *The Story of a Bad Boy* by going beyond its author's recollections of his own tame boyhood experiences by adding startling scenes of pure fiction, such as the midnight murder in a graveyard. There are cogent reasons why *Tom Sawyer* is still being read, while boy books such as Aldrich's are now mostly forgotten. The fact that *Tom Sawyer* today stands alone among books of its genre says something about its importance. Gribben concludes by admonishing readers "to stop comparing *Tom Sawyer* to its companion novel" and instead see it on its own terms.

Who would have thought of *Tom Sawyer* as "environmentally insightful"? Joe B. Fulton, the editor of the *Mark Twain Journal*, offers a truly original perspective on the novel in "Thinking Like Jackson's Island; Or, Why *Tom Sawyer* Is Good for the Environment." As innovative as its enigmatic title, Fulton's essay explores the novel's abundant allusions to the natural world and shows how they enhance the kinds of nostalgic feelings the book evokes in readers, especially adults. He also shows how in invoking those feelings "*Tom Sawyer* helps revitalize perceptions of the natural world and, in so doing of the civilized world." His essay is like a wake-up call: While reading it, one constantly asks, "Why didn't I think of that before?"

The final essay in the "Critical Contexts" section will appeal especially to younger readers, but older readers should not overlook it. In "Tom Sawyer and Harry Potter: The Boys Who Live" Philip Bader compares the iconic nineteenth-century American boy Tom Sawyer with author J. K. Rowling's iconic twenty-first-century boy hero, Harry Potter, who, when he is about Tom's age, learns he is wizard with great magical powers who holds a key place in the nexus of the magical and non-magical ("muggle") worlds. Rowling herself has never publicly acknowledged a literary debt to Mark Twain, but Bader identifies so many parallels between the two fictional characters and the settings of their books it is difficult to imagine that *Tom Sawyer* did not influence her creation of Harry Potter, even if only unconsciously. He goes on to explore what it is about each character that has appealed to readers and points out that while Tom certainly has no magical powers he is clearly fascinated by magic. Drawing on evidence within *Tom Sawyer*, he explains why Tom would probably like to live in the magical world and even attend Hogwarts School of Witchcraft and Wizardry. He concludes with the intriguing suggestion that Harry Potter might be seen as the embodiment of Tom Sawyer's imaginative yearnings.

Critical Readings

This section contains eleven innovative essays examining more specialized themes and topics, many of which have not previously been studied. A central message running through all these essays is the value of reading texts closely. *Tom Sawyer* is such an entertaining book it is easy to read it repeatedly without noticing important things going on between the lines. One of the salutary effects these essays should have will be encouraging readers to go back and read the novel again more carefully.

Written by another seasoned veteran of Mark Twain studies, John Bird, "The *Tom Sawyer* Franchise: The Evolution (and Devolution) of a Character," is an iconoclastic survey of Tom Sawyer's history through *Tom Sawyer, Huckleberry Finn*, and Mark Twain's finished and unfinished sequels—*Tom Sawyer Abroad, Tom Sawyer Detective*, "Huck Finn and Tom Sawyer among the Indians," "Tom Sawyer's Conspiracy," and "Schoolhouse Hill." Bird looks at that history as if it were a Hollywood film franchise that Mark Twain kept going after realizing he had in the character of Tom both a literary gold mine and a financial one. Kept alive for two decades, Tom underwent positive and negative changes that reveal Mark Twain's understanding of human psychology and seem to mirror contradictory traits in his own personality. This essay will naturally be compelling reading for those already familiar with all the Tom and Huck stories. For others, the essay may well forever change the views of those who see Tom Sawyer as a hero.

Is *Tom Sawyer* a "boy book," a "coming-of-age" novel, or something else? That is a central question expert researcher Kevin Mac Donnell's addresses in "Tom Sawyer: From Boy-Book Hero to Coming-of-Age-Hellion." The essay is a thoughtful analysis of how *Tom Sawyer* reflects Mark Twain's efforts to exploit genre writing, contrasting the boy-book *Tom Sawyer* with the coming-of-age novel, *Huckleberry Finn*. It pays special attention to how the Tom in his own book differs from the Tom in *Huckleberry Finn* and helps illuminate the differences between the two novels themselves. Along the way, the essay also offers insights into why modern readers are apt to view Tom differently than how readers of earlier generations viewed him.

In 1980, Cynthia Griffin Wolff published an article arguing that *The Adventures of Tom Sawyer* offers such a "nightmare vision of American boyhood" that the book is inappropriate for children to read. Her article launched a debate about the nature of the novel that has lasted for four decades. In "Is *Tom Sawyer* an Idyllic Dream or a Boy's Nightmare?" K. Patrick Ober, a Mark Twain scholar and a distinguished physician known for his insights into medical and psychological issues, may have finally settled that debate. Drawing on his experience from working with children and his close textual analysis of *Tom Sawyer*, he addresses two questions: Is the book an idyllic dream or is it really a nightmare? Moreover, is it a book for children or a book for adults? His well-reasoned argument has a happy ending.

Tom Sawyer is typically perceived as a book for boys, so now it is time to consider feminist perspectives. Mark Twain has never been known for creating strong female characters, and those in *Tom Sawyer* have rarely been shown much respect. Becky Thatcher, in particular, has generally been dismissed as a passive, flat character typifying the stereotype of frilly little girls, and even the adult women in *Tom Sawyer* have not been highly regarded. Linda Morris's lively essay, "Becky Thatcher and Aunt Polly in Three Dimensions," should help to change such views. As another example of the importance of close textual reading, Linda finds persuasive reasons to regard Becky as a worthy counterpart of Tom by closely observing her words and her behavior, particularly in the frightening episode in which Tom and Becky get lost in the cave. After discussing the "original compositions by young ladies" at the school's "examination day," the essay turns its attention to Aunt Polly, whom it shows to be a far stronger and livelier character than even readers long familiar with the novel might suspect.

Next in the lineup is "Republican Motherhood and Tom Sawyer's Political Education" by Hannah J. D. Wells, a promising Baylor University graduate student who will soon earn her doctorate. Her essay explores family issues from a variety of perspectives, starting with Aunt Polly's struggle to discipline Tom and moving on to broader questions about how families are raised in St. Petersburg, a community in which Christian mothers dominate and strong father figures are rare. It also looks at how the absence of natural parents and full biological siblings in Aunt Polly's household affects Tom,

Sid, and Mary. Among the household's four members only Tom's surname, "Sawyer," is known. Hannah's surprising but persuasive argument for what the surnames of the others may be a powerful reminder of the need to read texts closely.

Just before killing Dr. Robinson in chapter 9 of *Tom Sawyer*, "Injun Joe"—whom even non-judgmental Huck calls a "murderin' half-breed"—tells the doctor, "The Injun blood ain't in me for nothing. And now I've got you, and you got to settle, you know!" That incident and others in the novel cry out for an analysis of the book's depictions of Native Americans. There is no greater authority on that subject than Kerry Driscoll, who has drawn on years of research to write "Injun Joe and Mark Twain's Attitudes toward Native Americans." Her stimulating essay examines the historical and cultural significance of Joe's role in *Tom Sawyer* and uses Joe as a lens for exploring Mark Twain's conflicted attitudes about Indigenous peoples through his extensive career. The essay addresses such concepts as "half-breeds," bloodlust, and revenge as Indian stereotypes, and considers the concept of race as a determinant of behavior.

The next four essays take another turn by looking at various kinds of reactions to and adaptations of *Tom Sawyer*. The first, "Tom Sawyer as an Enduring Icon of Boyhood," has the benefit of being written by *two* Mark Twain experts, John H. Davis and Hugh H. Davis, who also happen to be father and son. Although both have written about Mark Twain for many years, this essay is their first collaborative effort. Their essay continues its predecessors' focus on the boy of the novel and its sequels, it also steps outside the novel by examining how Tom has been appropriated in a wide variety of adaptations—books, films, television shows, games, and more. The result has been to transform Tom into "Everyboy"—a seemingly ageless and impish youth who represents the "rank rascalities" of a boy. The sheer variety of the ways Tom has been appropriated make this essay full of fascinating surprises that should remind readers of the breadth of the novel's influence in popular culture.

"*Tom Sawyer*'s Complicated Relationship with Mark Twain's Hometown," analyzes the extraordinary impact the novel, its title character, and its author have had on Hannibal, Missouri—Mark Twain's boyhood home and the model for the fictional St. Petersburg. There cannot be many people as well qualified to write on that subject as the essay's author, Cindy Lovell, a lifelong *Tom Sawyer* devotee and a former director of Twain's Hannibal Boyhood Home and Museum. Lovell is a first-hand source for much of what she writes. Her essay describes sites in and around Hannibal that are related to Mark Twain's life there and how they are connected to the novel and goes on to recount the history of the town's efforts to honor its most famous resident and to capitalize on tourist interest in Mark Twain and *Tom Sawyer*. As the essay's title suggests, the relationship between Tom Sawyer and Hannibal has not always been smooth, but the essay does not gloss over the rough patches. The result is a balanced and always fascinating exploration of a small midwestern town that is probably more closely associated with a single literary work than any other American town.

Barbara Schmidt is another Mark Twain scholar known for prodigious research skills, and she brings them to bear in her essay, "Illustrating Tom Sawyer." It surveys the considerable number of artists who have illustrated American editions of *Tom Sawyer* since the book's original publication nearly a century and a half ago. Starting with the very first illustrator, True Williams—about whom Schmidt wrote the first biography—she traces the sequence of illustrators chronologically, devoting at least a paragraph to each, with engaging observations about their individual styles and which aspects of the novel they chose to illustrate. As book illustration can be considered a form of literary interpretation, it is fascinating to see how artists' styles and choices have interpreted the novel over the years.

"The *Tom Sawyer* Movie That Hollywood Got (Almost) Right," the essay by the present volume's editor, R. Kent Rasmussen, is a product of his years of researching Mark Twain screen adaptations for another book. There have been dozens of *Tom Sawyer* adaptations, but rather than trying to survey all of them, Rasmussen has decided it would be more useful to discuss one film in depth. To that end, he chose producer David O. Selznick's 1938 film, *The Adventures of Tom Sawyer*, which is generally considered not only the best *Tom Sawyer* film but also perhaps the best of *all* Mark Twain adaptations. This essay covers the history of the film's production and discusses several earlier productions to provide comparisons, but its main focus is the 1938 film's relationship to Mark Twain's original novel. The essay argues that screen adaptations are another form of literary interpretation, so it poses the implicit question of what watching that film can contribute to one's understanding of the novel.

The volume's final essay is something quite different from the others: "Adventuring with Tom Sawyer in a Twenty-first-Century Classroom." The classroom in question is that of John Pascal, a long-experienced high school English teacher, who for seven years has had the unique experience of teaching a high school class devoted solely to Mark Twain. Each year's course has included *Tom Sawyer*, and his essay discusses teaching techniques he has developed for his students—virtually none of whom had already read the book before taking his class. Of particular interest in his essay are the remarks of the students themselves about both the book and his teaching methods. This is an essay teachers should not miss.

Resources

In order to make this volume as useful a reference tool as possible, it contains an unusually large selection of appendices. The section begins with something incredibly special—a first-hand description of what is now called the "Mark Twain Cave," which inspired Mark Twain's creation of McDougal's Cave in both *Tom Sawyer* and *Huckleberry Finn*. Because so much of what has been written about the relationship between Hannibal's cave and the novel's cave, it is useful to devote some space to clarifying what is real and what is fictional. The author of the article is a lifelong Hannibal resident, Danny Norman, who has worked as a guide in the cave and even served as one of the town's official "Tom Sawyer" ambassadors.

Other appendix items include a detailed Chronology of Mark Twain's Life and Legacy with special attention to events relevant to *Tom Sawyer*. Bibliographical information is presented in six lists:

- Works by Mark Twain
- Bibliography
- Notable Editions of *The Adventures of Tom Sawyer*
- Published Plays Adapted from *The Adventures of Tom Sawyer* and Its Characters
- Illustrators of American Editions of *The Adventures of Tom Sawyer*
- Filmography

Notes about the volume's editor and contributors contain a unique feature. With a few exceptions, the entries recall the moments when each person first encountered *Tom Sawyer*. Taken as a whole, these comments reveal a striking pattern: Almost every contributor first read the book as a child. For how many other classic works might the same thing be said? The contributor notes are themselves, therefore, a commentary on the importance of *Tom Sawyer* to both children and adults.

Editorial Notes

R. Kent Rasmussen

What to call Mark Twain can get confusing. He was born Samuel Langhorne Clemens and used that name throughout his life. He did not adopt the pen name "Mark Twain" until 1863 when he wrote for a Nevada newspaper. From that moment he signed his pen name to almost everything he published through the remainder of his life. At the same time, however, he also continued to use his real name and never hid the fact that "Mark Twain" and "Sam Clemens" were the same person. In fact, his real name appeared on the title or copyright pages of almost all his books while he was alive. *The Adventures of Tom Sawyer* itself says "COPYRIGHT BY SAMUEL L. CLEMENS" on its copyright page. In writing about the man, some scholars call him "Mark Twain," others call him "Clemens," and still others simply call him "Twain." All three forms are used in this volume, as the editor has made no effort to impose uniformity.

Questions about when certain words appearing in the novel should or should not be capitalized can also be confusing. When Mark Twain wrote *Tom Sawyer* he almost always wrote "aunt Polly" and "widow Douglas" lowercasing "aunt" and "widow." Modern convention has tended to uppercase such words when they appear directly before names as titles; that is how those words are rendered here.

The last chapters of *Tom Sawyer* introduce a character named Jones, who is known as the "old Welchman." As the character presumably derives from Wales, he should properly be called a "Welshman." In direct quotes from the novel, however, calling him a "Welchman" is technically correct.

The full title of *The Adventures of Tom Sawyer* begins with "*The.*" That should be obvious but is worth mentioning because the full title of the novel's sequel, *Adventures of Huckleberry Finn*, does not have the article.

One final note in that regard: Readers will find citations to many articles published in two similarly titled periodicals. The full title of one is *"The Mark Twain Annual"*; the other is simply *"Mark Twain Journal."*

On Mark Twain and *The Adventures of Tom Sawyer*

R. Kent Rasmussen

On the occasion of his seventy-second birthday in November 1907, Samuel Langhorne Clemens—better known to the world as Mark Twain—received a letter from a fourteen-year-old girl named Florence Benson saying she shared his birth date and adding, "I am writing to wish to you many happy returns of the day and to tell you that I think Tom Sawyer is the nicest boy I have ever known." In his brief reply, Clemens wrote,

> I have always concealed it before, but now I am *compelled* to confess that *I* am Tom Sawyer!
>
> Sincerely Your friend
> S. L. Clemens

That sounds like a definitive statement, but was Clemens being honest? Florence believed him. A typed memo she later composed has fortunately been preserved. In it she wrote, "It may be my imagination but I feel that he was telling the truth . . . when he said it was the first time he had ever 'confessed' it and that he thought it an amusing way to send the fact out into the world by way of an unknown little girl" (Rasmussen 247-48).

It is almost certain that Clemens was being playful when he replied to his young admirer, but it is also certain there were a few grains of truth in his claim to "be" Tom Sawyer. Questions about how much of himself he put in his most famous character dogged him throughout his life and have continued ever since. Such questions have been almost inevitable since he included this statement in his preface to *The Adventures of Tom Sawyer*:

> Most of the adventures recorded in this book really occurred; one or two were experiences of my own, the rest those of boys who were

schoolmates of mine. Huck Finn is drawn from life; Tom Sawyer also, but not from an individual—he is a combination of the characteristics of three boys whom I knew, and therefore belongs to the composite order of architecture.

It is impossible to pin down every "adventure" in the novel that actually occurred and which of them involved Clemens himself, but it is clear that there is enough of Clemens in the fictional Tom to make the relationship between him and his novel exceptionally intimate. Almost everything in *Tom Sawyer*—its time period, settings, characters, and themes—has a close, indeed, almost organic connection with its author. Like its equally famous sequel, *Adventures of Huckleberry Finn* (1885), it is a novel that only Clemens could have written, as he alone lived the life from which it sprang. One of the first questions that readers of *Tom Sawyer* might bring to the novel, therefore, is how the circumstances of its author's life influenced the way he wrote his book.

Samuel Langhorne Clemens was born in the obscure northeastern Missouri village of Florida on November 30, 1835. He would start using his famous pen name in 1863 but would never stop using his real name, which appeared on the title or copyright pages of almost all his books, including *Tom Sawyer*, which he wrote in the fortieth year of his life.

The sixth of seven children of parents who had migrated to rural Missouri from eastern Tennessee shortly before he was born, Clemens grew up in a home so strongly affected by his father's business failings that he would spend the rest of his life obsessed with avoiding making his father's financial mistakes. As things turned out, he eventually did experience massive business failures two decades after writing *Tom Sawyer*. He would, however, also recover financially, pay off all his debts in full, and go on to great public acclaim for that very reason. Meanwhile, he would also outlive all his siblings, his wife, and three of his four children. He died in his last home in Redding, Connecticut, on April 21, 1910—just under five months after turning seventy-four. To place his life in historical perspective, it may help to note that the famous American short story writer O. Henry, the great Russian novelist Leo Tolstoy, and Mary Baker Eddy, the founder of Christian Science, would also die later that same year.

Fig. 1. Luther D. Bradley's editorial cartoon, published in the *Chicago Daily News* the day after Mark Twain died, is a graphic expression of how closely the author was identified with Tom Sawyer. *Chicago Daily News*, April 22, 1910. [Public domain.]

In his later life, Clemens pointed out that when he was born the village of Florida "contained a hundred people and I increased the population by 1 per cent." That may have been true, but he jokingly added, "I could have done it for any place—even London, I suppose" (*Autobiography* 1:209). Florida, Missouri, still exists, but its twenty-first-century population has shrunk to zero. The main reason its name even remains on maps is the fact that "Mark Twain" was born there. Nearby, his name is preserved in Mark Twain

State Park, whose Mark Twain Birthplace Museum looks over the waters of the artificially made Mark Twain Lake. His name is also preserved in the much-fragmented Mark Twain National Forest. In fact, between the state park and national forest, three percent of the surface of the state of Missouri is named after him.

Youth in Missouri

In 1839, after Clemens's parents gave up hope of prospering in Florida they moved about thirty-five miles northeast to the Mississippi River port town of Hannibal, where Clemens spent most of his formative years. Clemens would later endow on that town a form of literary immortality by making it the fictional "St. Petersburg" in his writings about Tom Sawyer and Huck Finn. Those works would eventually include two published novels, two published novellas— *Tom Sawyer Abroad* (1894) and *Tom Sawyer, Detective* (1896)— and three unfinished stories that would be published posthumously. It is generally believed Clemens chose the name "St. Petersburg" for his fictional town to symbolize its being a "heavenly" place for children—especially boys. Whether or not he saw Hannibal as a heavenly place during his own boyhood, it is clear that many of the activities in which his fictional characters engaged were things he said his boyhood friends had done in Hannibal. For example, he later claimed to have based the famous episode in *Tom Sawyer* in which Tom and his sweetheart Becky Thatcher get lost in a labyrinthine cave on an incident that really happened to him.

Young Clemens did nothing during his youth that could have given anyone any reason to imagine the incredible life that lay ahead for him, but one of the hallmarks of his best writing would be his skill at converting experiences from his own life into poignant fiction. The grist he milled from his youth in Hannibal was extraordinarily bountiful. His life there and in the even smaller inland village of Florida— where he spent many summers while growing up—would provide the primary settings not only for *Tom Sawyer* and the opening chapters of *Huckleberry Finn* but also for parts of *The Gilded Age: A Tale of To-day* (1874), which he coauthored with Charles Dudley Warner, and *Pudd'nhead Wilson* (1894). The latter novel transforms Hannibal into "Dawson's Landing," which is located *south* of St. Louis. His fictional St. Petersburg, like the real Hannibal, is far north of that major river port city. However, while Dawson's Landing's name and location may differ from those of St. Petersburg, it is otherwise much the same place.

St. Petersburg's heavenly imagery has not been lost on modern Hannibal itself, which has built a healthy tourist industry around its ties to Twain and *Tom Sawyer* and used those ties to advertise itself as "America's Hometown." Although the town has long emphasized its connections with *Tom Sawyer*, it has had much less to say about *Huckleberry Finn*. Some reasons should be obvious. The earlier novel is set entirely within or near Hannibal's fictional clone of

Fig. 2. E. F. Ward's fanciful painting of young Sam Clemens overlooking the Mississippi River from a promontory above Hannibal for Albert Bigelow Paine's serialized biography of Mark Twain. *St. Nicholas*, November 1915, p. 3. [Public domain.]

St. Petersburg, while *Huckleberry Finn* merely begins there and soon moves down the river. *Tom Sawyer* also has more tangible connections with Hannibal, most notably in the form of Clemens's own boyhood home, on which Tom's fictional home is closely modeled, and the home of Laura Hawkins, the real-life girl on whom Clemens modeled Becky Thatcher. Both houses still stand as fully restored tourist attractions. Nearby are the island and cave that play important roles in *Tom Sawyer*, and a local promontory has been renamed "Cardiff Hill" after the similar fictional hill in the novels. (The latter is a true case of life imitating art.)

Although Clemens based St. Petersburg primarily on Hannibal, his fictional town also contains traces of the smaller village of Florida, which he remembered, not from the very early years when he had lived there, but from the summers he spent there while growing up. Indeed, apart from St. Petersburg's location on the Mississippi River and its prominent landmarks such as Cardiff Hill, the town is in many ways more similar to the Florida of Clemens's youth than it is to the Hannibal of the same period. Florida was more rural; it had fewer residents, businesses, and industries; and tombs in its graveyard—like those in St. Petersburg's graveyard in chapter 9 of *Tom Sawyer*—had no tombstones, only decaying wood grave markers. Moreover, much of the novel has the feel of a carefree summertime that was probably reminiscent of Clemens's happy summers on his uncle's Florida farm.

Transition to Adulthood

Located on what was then the edge of America's western frontier during Clemens's boyhood, Hannibal was a technologically primitive community, lacking either railroad or telegraph links with other regions at that time. Its main connections to the outside world were through the steamboat packets that regularly stopped at its docks. It was not a promising place to produce a writer who would one day be regarded as one of America's great authors, but the fact that it actually did so invites reflection on *why*. Clemens's experiences in Florida and Hannibal clearly planted many of the seeds that would later blossom in his writing. Had he grown up almost anywhere else, he almost certainly would never have written *Tom Sawyer*, *Huckleberry Finn*, and his other Mississippi River stories.

Because of the limited educational opportunities in his community as well as the impoverished condition of his family that required him to go to work at an early age, Clemens received little formal education. Nevertheless, he became and always remained a prodigious reader who would eventually become one of the great self-educated figures of his time. At an early age, he began working in Hannibal printshops that produced newspapers. His tasks included setting type for news stories taken from eastern newspaper. Reading those stories increased his awareness of the outside world. Between his newspaper work, reading adventure stories, daydreaming about traveling to faraway places, and watching steamboats ply the nearby river, he developed a lifelong thirst for travel and especially wanted to venture out on steamboats. A nostalgic passage in *Life on the Mississippi* (1883) recalls his boyhood longing:

> When I was a boy, there was but one permanent ambition among my comrades in our village on the west bank of the Mississippi River. That was, to be a steamboatman. We had transient ambitions of other sorts, but they were only transient. When a circus came and went, it left us all burning to become clowns; the first negro minstrel show that came to our section left us all suffering to try that kind of life; now and then we had a hope that if we lived and were good, God would permit us to be pirates. These ambitions faded out, each in its turn; but the ambition to be a steamboatman always remained (chapter 4).

Although written for *Life on the Mississippi*, that paragraph says a great deal about both *Tom Sawyer* and *Huckleberry Finn*. Modern film adaptations aside, neither Tom nor Huck ever works on a steamboat. Surprisingly, while steamboats play important roles in *Huckleberry Finn*, not a single one appears in *Tom Sawyer*! The closest thing to a steamboat in that novel is the "little steam ferry boat" used to search for Tom, Huck Finn, and Joe Harper when the boys are presumed drowned in chapter 14 of *Tom Sawyer*. The boat reappears in chapter 29 to convey picnickers to the cave. (It may even be the same boat used to search for Huck's body in chapter 8 of *Huckleberry Finn*.) Otherwise, the only allusion to steamboats in *Tom Sawyer* is Ben Rogers's "personation" of the "Big Missouri" while Tom is starting to whitewash the fence in chapter 2.

The circuses, minstrel shows, and pirate games Clemens enjoyed as a boy were clearly on his mind when he was writing his novels. Circuses and pirates are mentioned often throughout *Tom Sawyer*, and a minstrel show comes to St. Petersburg in chapter 22. Clemens himself eventually defied the long odds against fulfilling his boyhood dream by becoming a real steamboatman well before he would become "Mark Twain."

In 1853, Clemens left Hannibal permanently to begin several years of drawing on his printing experience to work as a journeyman printer in newspaper offices and print shops in the Midwest and East. The fact that he left home and traveled to the East Coast on his own before he even turned eighteen says much about both his desire to travel and his courage in striking out on his own. He would eventually become one of the most widely traveled authors of his time and would make homes in a staggeringly large number of American and European towns and cities. Meanwhile, after returning to the Midwest for a few years, the next major turning point in his life came in early 1857, when he persuaded a master steamboat pilot named Horace Bixby to take him on as an apprentice. He then spent the four years actually living out his dream "to become a steamboatman," by piloting steamboats between St. Louis and New Orleans. That career, however, ended for him with the start of the Civil War in 1861.

Bixby himself continued working on the river until his death at the age of eighty-six, and had it not been for the war, Clemens might also have continued in that profession to a ripe old age. "I supposed—and hoped," he wrote in *Life on the Mississippi*, "that I was going to follow the river the rest of my days, and die at the wheel when my mission was ended. But by and by the war came, commerce was suspended, my occupation was gone" (chapter 21). If that terrible war had any positive outcomes—besides the noble one of forcing an end to human slavery—they included redirecting Clemens to a career that would lead to his becoming "Mark Twain" and writing *The Innocents Abroad* (1869), *Roughing It* (1872), *Tom Sawyer*, *Huckleberry Finn*, and other great books. It is not an exaggeration, therefore, to suggest that without the Civil War, the world would never have heard of Tom Sawyer, Huck Finn, and a host of other memorable characters.

While Clemens's years in Missouri helped prepare him to write about his boyhood there, his years of piloting boats on the Lower Mississippi prepared him to write about the river, which he later did, and at length, in many books—most notably *Life on the Mississippi* and *Huckleberry Finn*. The river also figures prominently in *Tom Sawyer*, but what that novel says about it are things that almost anyone who grew up around a river town like Hannibal would have known from their daily experiences of observing the river, taking occasional swims, and boating or rafting to nearby islands.

Continuing Travels

Clemens's visits to St. Louis, Cincinnati, New York, Philadelphia, Washington, DC; and other places during the early 1850s and his years on the Mississippi satisfied part of his travel urge, but his wanderlust never stopped growing. In 1861, as the Civil War began, he went west with his older brother, Orion Clemens, whom recently elected President Abraham Lincoln appointed secretary of the government of the new federal territory of Nevada. In the first chapter of *Roughing It* (1872), the book Clemens later wrote about his experiences in the Far West, he reiterated his dream of traveling, in the words of a young and inexperienced naïf who had seemingly never been anywhere before:

> I was young and ignorant, and I envied my brother . . . especially the long, strange journey he was going to make, and the curious new world he was going to explore. He was going to travel! I never had been away from home, and that word "travel" had a seductive charm for me.

This was gross exaggeration, of course, as Clemens had already been far away from home, traveling almost continuously, over the eight years leading up to his journey to the West. It is, however, also an honest reflection of his deep desire to see the world at large. Some of that interest is hinted at in *Tom Sawyer*. In chapter 4, for example, when Becky's father, Judge Thatcher, is introduced to Tom's Sunday school class, Tom marvels at "the most August creation these children had ever looked upon. . . . He was from Constantinople, twelve miles away—so he had traveled, and seen the world. . . ." Tom's own travel hopes in the novel are modest;

he aspires only "to escape from hard usage and lack of sympathy at home by roaming abroad into the great world never to return" (chapter 13). He satisfies that desire by playing pirates with his friends on an island only a few miles down the Mississippi River from St. Petersburg. In the last chapters of *Huckleberry Finn*, Tom sails down the river and joins Huck in Arkansas, but it is not until the 1894 novella, *Tom Sawyer Abroad,* that Tom literally takes flight to see the world. Huck's narrative of that story opens by recounting how Tom's recent travels in *Huckleberry Finn* have made him want to go even farther:

> Some called him Tom Sawyer the Traveler, and that just swelled him up fit to bust. You see he laid over me and Jim considerable, because we only went down the river on a raft and came back by the steamboat, but Tom went by the steamboat both ways. The boys envied me and Jim a good deal, but land! they just knuckled to the dirt before TOM.

When Clemens wrote that story, he had already seen much of the United States, been to Europe several times, journeyed by caravan in the Holy Land, and even climbed a pyramid in Egypt. In *Tom Sawyer Abroad,* he had Tom, Huck, and Jim fly to North Africa aboard a mad inventor's marvelous balloon craft. Their adventures reach a dramatic conclusion at Egyptian landmarks Clemens himself had visited in 1867 and described in *The Innocents Abroad, or The New Pilgrims' Progress.*

Writing *Tom Sawyer*

It is difficult to pinpoint exactly when Clemens began writing *Tom Sawyer*, but the broad outlines of what led up to the book are fairly well established. While he was doing mostly journalistic writing during the early to mid-1860s, he occasionally wrote humorous stories. He achieved national attention for the first time in 1865 with his publication of a widely reprinted sketch about a jumping frog in a California mining camp. Most of his earliest fictional writings might be classified as "sketches," rather than short stories, because they lack the depth and character development of more fully fleshed-out stories. Among Clemens's early creative work are sketches about children, typically ones with behavioral quirks, such as "The Story of the Bad Little Boy Who Didn't Come to Grief" (1865) and "The Story of the Good Little Boy Who Did Not Prosper" (1870). Sketches such as those seemed to point toward *The Adventures of Tom Sawyer*, as they dealt with boys whose behavior—both good and bad—often led to unexpected consequences, just as things that Tom Sawyer also would later do—such as turning a punishment into a profit-making scheme. Others of Clemens's early essays and sketches also occasionally drew on his boyhood memories of such things as Sunday school, Hannibal's Cadets of Temperance that he had joined, school examination days, and childhood sweethearts—all of which he would eventually develop more fully in *Tom Sawyer*.

Around 1868—when he was finishing his first major book, *The Innocents Abroad* (1869)—Clemens completed a 7,500-word story that more clearly anticipated *Tom Sawyer* by drawing heavily on his childhood experiences. When Bernard DeVoto, a future editor of the Mark Twain Papers, first published the story in 1942, he called it the "embryo of *Tom Sawyer*" (Twain, *Huck Finn* 265). By then, the story's first two manuscript pages—along with Clemens's original title—had gotten lost, so DeVoto published it as "Boy's Manuscript," a title that stayed with it through later publications. (Albert Bigelow Paine, DeVoto's predecessor as editor of the Mark Twain Papers, had typed "Boy's Manuscript" on the envelope in which DeVoto found the story.) The protagonist in "Boy's Manuscript" is named "Billy Rogers," not "Tom." His story is in the form of several weeks of diary entries recording his lovesick obsession with an eight-year-old girl named Amy. Incidents in the story are similar to those in the first half of *Tom Sawyer* involving Tom and Becky. Eventually, Billy breaks up with Amy in favor of an older girl. It may be significant that Clemens wrote the story around the same time he was courting his future wife, Olivia (Livy) Langdon. Less clear is the question of whether there is any significance in Clemens's modeling *Tom Sawyer*'s Becky on the "Amy" in "Boy's Manuscript," while "Amy Lawrence" is the novel's name of Tom's girlfriend who "vanished out of his heart and left not even a memory of herself behind" the first moment he sees Becky in chapter 3.

The first novel Clemens published was *The Gilded Age* (1874), which he coauthored with his friend and Hartford neighbor Charles Dudley Warner. His portions of that book include its opening eleven chapters chronicling a family's relocation from Tennessee to Missouri that he modeled on the history of his own family's settlement in Florida, Missouri. He even modeled one of the family members, Clay Hawkins, on himself; however, nothing about Clay resembles Tom Sawyer. Meanwhile, it appears that Clemens may have begun writing his first solo-authored novel, *Tom Sawyer*, as early as 1872, even before he wrote *The Gilded Age*. After finishing that book, he returned to *Tom Sawyer* during the summer of 1874, which he spent with his family at his sister-in-law, Susan Langdon Crane's, Quarry Farm just outside Elmira, New York. That year, Susan had a detached study built for him that overlooked the Chemung Valley, away from household noises and distractions. During the 1870s and 1880s, the Clemens family spent almost all their summers at Quarry Farm, and Clemens himself did much of his most important writing there—not at his Hartford home.

After Clemens finished writing *Tom Sawyer* in mid-1875, he had his friend and distinguished writer and editor W. D. Howells read his manuscript. Clemens thought his book's primary audience should be adults who would appreciate being nostalgically reminded of their own childhoods. He even hoped to serialize the novel in the *Atlantic Monthly*, a literary magazine that Howells edited. He resisted Howells's suggestion that the novel be presented as a boys' book but eventually yielded after his wife agreed with Howells. A paragraph he wrote in the book's preface feels like a grudging concession to their judgment:

> Although my book is intended mainly for the entertainment of boys and girls, I hope it will not be shunned by men and women on that account, for part of my plan has been to try to pleasantly remind adults of what they once were themselves, and of how they felt and thought and talked, and what queer enterprises they sometimes engaged in.

That statement actually foreshadowed a debate about the book that has continued to the present day: Is it best suited for juvenile readers or for adults? A persuasive argument can be made for considering it appropriate for both.

In November 1875, shortly before he turned forty, Clemens delivered his completed manuscript to Elisha Bliss, president of the American Publishing Company (APC) of Hartford, Connecticut. That firm, which specialized in "subscription books" sold door-to-door and not in traditional bookshops, had already published his first four major books—*The Innocents Abroad, Roughing It, The Gilded Age*, and *Sketches New & Old* (1875). The subscription market catered to buyers who preferred hefty, lavishly illustrated volumes on nonfiction subjects, so a juvenile novel like *Tom Sawyer* was out of its normal line. Bliss accepted the book because of APC's success with Clemens's previous titles, and the firm eventually profited from it. The Hartford illustrator True W. Williams, who had contributed many illustrations to APC's first three Clemens books and all the illustrations for *Sketches New & Old*, was engaged to illustrate the novel. For various reasons, some of which remain murky, APC took more than a year to get *Tom Sawyer* in print. Meanwhile, Clemens had a friend help arrange a contract with the London firm Chatto & Windus for an unillustrated English edition, which was issued in June 1876—well before the APC edition appeared. A semi-authorized English-language edition was published in Germany several months later. To Clemens's great anger, a Canadian firm issued a pirate edition in July that hurt later American sales and paid him no royalties. APC's first American edition of the book finally appeared in December 1876, and the book has remained continuously in print ever since.

The Novel

It has already been shown how Clemens used the familiar locales of his childhood in *Tom Sawyer* and other writings. Geographical settings, however, were not the only memories that Clemens mined in his fiction. His own family members and Hannibal friends and neighbors would also provide models for many of his characters both in his Tom and Huck tales and in other writings. Matching Tom Sawyer with a real-life person has always proven tricky because of Clemens's own coyness on that subject, though—as has already been shown—he sometimes claimed *he* was Tom. Other characters are easier to connect with his real-life contemporaries. For example, he explicitly identified his younger brother, Henry Clemens, as the model for Tom's younger half-brother, Sid, though he also added that Henry was a finer person than Sid ever was. Sid figures prominently in *Tom Sawyer* but appears only momentarily in *Huckleberry Finn*—on the steam-ferry searching for Huck's presumably drowned body in chapter 8. Later, in chapter 32, when Tom reappears in the narrative, he finds Huck in the home of his own Aunt Sally and Uncle Silas Phelps, who mistakenly assumed Huck is Tom. Tom then pretends to be Sid from that point, and it is not until Aunt Polly arrives at her sister Sally's place that the boys' true identities are revealed.

Clemens clearly modeled Tom's Aunt Polly on his own mother, Jane Lampton Clemens. Aunt Polly is a major character throughout *Tom Sawyer*, makes an important appearance in the last chapters of *Huckleberry Finn*, and also appears in Clemens's other Tom and Huck sequels. Tom's cousin Mary—whose surname and precise relationships to everyone else are mysteries—is modeled on Clemens's sister Pamela Clemens. She appears frequently in *Tom Sawyer*, but like Sid, she makes only token appearances in *Huckleberry Finn* and its sequels. Tom's sweetheart, Becky, Clemens modeled on one of his own childhood sweethearts, Laura Hawkins, whose family for many years lived directly across the street from Clemens's own Hill Street home. Not long after Clemens left Hannibal, Hawkins married a physician and went west with him, but after he died in 1875, she returned and spent the remainder of her long life in Hannibal. In 1899, she recalled how Clemens had shown off for her the first time they met—as Tom shows off for Becky—but denied having ever been lost in the cave with him.

Of greatest interest, perhaps, is Clemens's model for Tom's comrade Huck. In contrast to uncertainty about his model for Tom, Clemens explicitly identified his boyhood friend Tom Blankenship as his Huck in a 1906 autobiographical dictation. He was speaking in reference to his *Huckleberry Finn* novel at that moment, but the same description applies equally to the Huck of *Tom Sawyer*:

> In "Huckleberry Finn" I have drawn Tom Blankenship exactly as he was. He was ignorant, unwashed, insufficiently fed; but he had as good a heart as ever any boy had. His liberties were totally unrestricted. He was the only really independent person—boy or man—in the community, and by consequence he was tranquilly and continuously happy, and was envied by all the rest of us. We liked him; we enjoyed his society. And as his society was forbidden us by our parents, the prohibition trebled and quadrupled its value, and therefore we sought and got more of his society than of any other boy's (*Autobiography* 2:172)

Compare that description of Blankenship to *Tom Sawyer*'s description of Huck when he first appears in chapter 6:

> the juvenile pariah of the village . . . son of the town drunkard. Huckleberry was cordially hated and dreaded by all the mothers of the town, because he was idle, and lawless, and vulgar and bad— and because all their children admired him so, and delighted in his forbidden society, and wished they dared to be like him. Tom was like the rest of the respectable boys, in that he envied Huckleberry his gaudy outcast condition, and was under strict orders not to play with him. So he played with him every time he got a chance. . . .
>
> Huckleberry came and went, at his own free will. He slept on doorsteps in fine weather and in empty hogsheads in wet; he did not have to go to school or to church, or call any being master or obey anybody . . . In a word, everything that goes to make life precious, that boy had. So thought every harassed, hampered, respectable boy in St. Petersburg.

During Clemens's lifetime and afterward, numerous men stepped forward claiming to have been the original Huckleberry Finn, but that honor belongs solely to Blankenship, whose eventual fate is not known. Like the fictional Pap Finn, incidentally, Blankenship's father was a notorious town drunk.

Success and Its Aftermath

By 1885, Clemens appeared to have reached a point at which his success was assured. He owned the New York firm Charles L. Webster & Co. that published *Huckleberry Finn* successfully, and its next publication, General Ulysses S. Grant's two-volume Civil War memoirs would prove to be one of the best-selling works of the nineteenth century. Clemens himself was at the height of his creative powers and was one of the highest-paid authors in the world. He lived in a magnificent custom-built home in Hartford, Connecticut, had a loving wife, and three adoring daughters. Some significant works still lay in his future—most notably *A Connecticut Yankee in King Arthur's Court* (1889) and *Pudd'nhead Wilson* (1894)—but by the 1890s, his creative powers were beginning to wane. During that decade, he and his wife, Olivia, closed down their Hartford house—to which they would never return—and took their family to Europe to cut down on household expenses. Over the next decade, the family moved from country to country, with a major interruption in 1895–96.

That interruption was caused by the collapse of Clemens's most costly business ventures. In 1894, the publishing company he had launched a decade earlier declared bankruptcy. Around the same time, a revolutionary automatic typesetting machine in which he had invested a fortune and had hoped would make him rich beyond his dreams was finally pronounced too unreliable to be marketable, causing him to lose his entire investment. Despite having reached a pinnacle of success as an author, he suddenly found himself a business failure, and on a far grander scale than his father's failure had been. To recover his fortunes and pay off his publishing firm's creditors, he left England in May 1895 to undertake an exhausting round-the-world lecture tour that started in North America and took him to Fiji, Australia, New Zealand, India, and South Africa. When he returned to England in August 1896, he wrote *Following the Equator* about his long trip. Meanwhile, he and his wife were shattered by the sudden death of their oldest daughter, Susy. With much of the joy sucked out of their lives, the family continued to move about in Europe until October 1900, when they returned to the United States. There Clemens found himself more admired and celebrated than ever before, in large part because of his success in paying off his bankrupt company's creditors in full when he could easily have satisfied most of them with much less.

Clemens continued to write through his last decade but little of what he published during those years matched the quality and interest of his earlier writings. On his death in 1910, he left a large body of unfinished writings that would keep editors busy publishing new Mark Twain books far into the future. In addition to volumes containing previously unpublished and uncollected stories such as "Tom Sawyer's Conspiracy" and "Huck Finn & Tom Sawyer Among the Indians," the posthumous volumes included collections of previously unpublished sketches, essays, letters, speeches, notebooks, unfinished novels, and even plays. His autobiographical writings have been published in at least a half-dozen different versions, culminating in publication of the first truly complete edition in three massive volumes in 2010–15. It is probably not an exaggeration to say that more words of his writing have been published for the first time since he died than were published during his lifetime. Moreover, as late as 2022, still more of his papers awaited publication.

Mark Twain's Legacy

In 1906, four years before Clemens died, he observed that over the course of the preceding century, 220,000 books had been published in the United States, but "not a bathtub-full of them are still alive and marketable." That statement may contain a modicum of exaggeration, but its essential point is as true now as it was in Clemens's time: Few books outlive their authors, then or now. Indeed, this may have been especially true for nineteenth-century American novelists, most of whom are utterly forgotten today. There are exceptions, of course, and of these, Clemens is the most outstanding example. In the year 2022—more than a century after his 1910 death—not only were most of his books still in print, some—including *Tom Sawyer*—had *never* gone out of print, even briefly, since their original publication. There may not be another American author of his time for whom the same can be said. That fact raises questions about what accounts for his enduring popularity and whether his popularity says anything about his greatness as a writer.

A simple but incomplete answer to the question of why Clemens's popularity has endured is that at least three of his books have entered the realm of immortal classics. The title characters and basic story lines of *Tom Sawyer*, *Huckleberry Finn*, and *The Prince and the Pauper* (1881) have become so deeply ingrained in American culture that many people who know these titles may not even know that it was Mark Twain who wrote them. Indeed, when the Disney Company used "The Prince and the Pauper" as the

Fig. 3. Toward the end of his life, Clemens dictated much of his autobiography to his biographer Albert Bigelow Paine (right) and a stenographer. E. F. Ward, *St. Nicholas*, October 1916, p. 1080. [Public domain.]

title for an animated Mickey Mouse film in 1990, it did not even bother to include the name "Mark Twain" in the film's credits—an omission that seemed to imply that Clemens's story has passed beyond the realm of a mere classic to become a timeless and anonymously created fairy tale. *Tom Sawyer* has not quite achieved that same status, but judging by the sheer number of plays, films, television productions, cartoons, and games adapted from it, it has come close.

Among scholars, the difference between literary works worthy of study and those that are not lies in the matter of their "interpretability"—or, in simpler language, how much can be read into them. A work such as Herman Melville's *Moby-Dick* (1851) may lend itself to nearly endless interpretations of its themes, symbols, and multiple levels and require multiple readings and close study to be fully understood. In contrast, another novel that is intelligently written, witty, beautifully crafted, and immensely entertaining may reveal all it has to say on its first reading, leaving nothing more to be interpreted. One of the things that makes Clemens a truly great writer is that many of his books—especially *Huckleberry Finn*—can be read both as high entertainment and as deep works of almost limitless interpretability. *Tom Sawyer* has always been recognized for its entertainment value but not so much for its depth. It would be foolish to suggest it is on the same literary level as its famous sequel, but perhaps essays in the present volume will help enhance its reputation as a serious literary work.

Clemens's writings are carefully read, reread, analyzed, reanalyzed, interpreted, and reinterpreted because they continue to have something fresh to say to each new generation. In an essay comparing Clemens to Ambrose Bierce, the distinguished scholar Lawrence I. Berkove called Clemens "an unaccountable literary genius, a giant for the ages" (Berkove 132). Berkove's description is apt, as it reflects the growing view that Clemens has depths that can never fully be plumbed, that scholars can go on forever studying and reexamining him and never fully explain his work. Many who study Clemens feel momentarily satisfied when they seem to have answered a question about him, only to find new questions emerging to take its place. Meanwhile, every year sees the publication of perhaps a half dozen new books and even more new articles about him. If all this makes studying Clemens sound like it should be wearing, it is not. In fact, exactly the opposite is the case. Most people who have spent years reading and studying Clemens—both scholars and "buffs"—relish sharing in the thrill of making new discoveries. Enough new research is being done to convene international conferences every two years—alternating between Elmira, New York, and Hannibal, Missouri. These conferences are always well attended, and the enthusiasm participants bring generates palpable excitement.

Some years ago, when Shelley Fisher Fishkin, one of the leading scholars in the field, was working on *Lighting Out for the Territory: Reflections on Mark Twain and American Culture*, she wondered why she never grew bored with Mark Twain and hit on a little epiphany: We cannot get bored with the man, she suggested, because he connects with *everything*. Like Clemens's own bathtub anecdote, her remark may contain a touch of exaggeration, but it also expresses an important truth. Clemens actually does connect with almost everything. During his nearly seventy-five years on this planet, he lived through one of the greatest periods of social, political, and technological change in human history. When he was born in 1835, fewer than thirteen million Americans were living in the nation's twenty-four states. By the time he died, in 1910, the country had grown to more than ninety-two million people living in forty-six states, and the percentage of them living in cities had more than doubled. Moreover, at the time of his birth, slavery was flourishing in the Southern states, steam-powered trains and vessels were still in rudimentary stages of development, medical practices had scarcely advanced beyond those of the Middle Ages, and inventions such as photography, telegraphy, and even typewriters still lay in the future. By the end of his life, American slavery had long since been abolished. Tens of thousands of miles of railroad lines were moving high-speed trains around the country, and gas-powered automobiles were beginning to appear everywhere, iron-hulled steamships were plying the world's seas, and airplanes were taking to the skies. Photography had advanced so far that color film was already being used and motion pictures were being made. The telegraph was carrying messages almost everywhere in the world, and telephonic and radio communication was rapidly spreading. Thanks to a new understanding of germs and other developments, medicine was moving into the modern age. Clemens himself was quick to adopt new technologies, such as typewriters, electrical lighting, modern plumbing, and telephones. He was one of the first people to be photographed in color, and he appears in a brief Thomas A. Edison movie that can be seen on YouTube.

Clemens was certainly not the only American to live through all those and other changes, but he was unusual in closely observing and writing about most of them. He was also unusual for his time in being exceptionally well traveled from a relatively young age.

He lived for at least a few months in almost every region of the present United States. He also crossed the Atlantic Ocean twenty-five times, visited every inhabited continent, and spent nearly twelve years living in other countries. During his widespread travels, he met many of the world's leading cultural, political, and scientific figures and had close relationships with more than a few of them. As a consequence, he has attracted almost as much attention from biographers as he has from literary scholars.

Clemens's interests were so broad and diverse that it is difficult to find a subject on which his writings do not touch. He had a rich imagination and incredibly inventive mind that allowed him to foresee future technologies and political and social developments. He left a large body of speculative fictional writings unpublished when he died. Had he finished and published more of those works, he might now rank alongside Jules Verne and H. G. Wells as a pioneer of science fiction.

For all those reasons and more, suggesting that Clemens connects with everything may not be as great an exaggeration as it first appears to be. There are, however, other dimensions to Clemens that keep readers and scholars returning to him. One of the most important—and perhaps most obvious—is his remarkable ability to make people laugh. Whatever else one thinks about his writing, he very frequently is funny and often in unexpected ways. Indeed, an ironic effect of his humor was that he enjoyed such a great reputation as a humorist during his lifetime that it got in the way of critics appreciating the profundity and his work. It would not be until decades after he died that the full greatness of his writing began to be appreciated.

Is Mark Twain the greatest writer American has yet produced? Whether it is even possible to answer such a question, it should be enough to say that Twain is, indeed, a great writer and that both *Tom Sawyer* and *Huckleberry Finn* are great books. Proof in support of this assertion lies in the fact that fully a century after his death, people continue to read both books avidly—even when they are not assigned in schools—and scholars continue to offer new and often exciting interpretations of his life and work—as the essays in the present volume amply demonstrate.

Works Cited

Berkove, Lawrence I. "Kindred Rivals: Mark Twain and Ambrose Bierce." *Critical Insights: Mark Twain*. Edited by R. Kent Rasmussen, Salem Press, 2011, pp. 110–36.

Fishkin, Shelley Fisher. *Lighting Out for the Territory: Reflections on Mark Twain and American Culture*. Oxford UP, 1997.

Rasmussen, R. Kent, editor. *Dear Mark Twain: Letters from His Readers*. U of California P, 2013.

Twain, Mark. *Adventures of Huckleberry Finn*. Chas. Webster, 1885.

_____. *The Adventures of Tom Sawyer*. American Publishing Co., 1876.

_____. *Autobiography of Mark Twain*. Vol. 1. Edited by Harriet Elinor Smith, et al., U of California P, 2010.

_____. *Autobiography of Mark Twain*. Vol. 2. Edited by Benjamin Griffin, Harriet Elinor Smith, et al., U of California P, 2013.

_____. *Huck Finn and Tom Sawyer Among the Indians and Other Unfinished Stories*. Edited by Dahlia Armon, et al., U of California P, 1989. (Includes "Boy's Manuscript")

_____. *The Innocents Abroad, or The New Pilgrims' Progress*. American Publishing Co., 1869.

_____. *Pudd'nhead Wilson and Those Extraordinary Twins*. American Publishing Co., 1894.

_____. *Roughing It*. American Publishing Co., 1872.

_____. *Tom Sawyer Abroad*. Chas. Webster, 1894.

_____, and Charles Dudley Warner. *The Gilded Age: A Tale of To-day*. American Publishing Co., 1874.

CRITICAL CONTEXTS

Tom Sawyer's Evasion of History

Peter Messent

Samuel L. Clemens wrote *The Adventures of Tom Sawyer* between the summers of 1872 and 1875. He set the story though in the pre-Civil War period, dating it in his 1876 preface "thirty or forty years ago." In thinking about history and the novel, therefore, both sets of dates, and the two-way movement between them, need to be kept in mind. But, if inevitably formed by and entangled with its historical contexts, *Tom Sawyer* is nonetheless a profoundly *anti*-historical text. This essay explores that paradox. It shows how St. Petersburg, Clemens's representation of his hometown Hannibal, is a highly selective version of actuality, shaped to emphasize its fictional status as a place cut off from the larger concerns of a fast-changing historical world. The essay also shows how the particular version of an American small-town frontier community given in *Tom Sawyer* cannot be seen in isolation from a larger American history as it unrolled both before and after the Civil War, even as that defining context goes unmentioned or unexplored in the novel itself. It is, then, not present-day or past history that concerns Clemens in *Tom Sawyer*, but rather the creation of a place, time, and community that appears to exist outside such parameters. His use of the Gothic mode toward the end of the novel also contributes to prompt the reader away from historical particularity and toward patterns of symbolic meaning that appear to transcend both time and place. As will be shown, such an appearance is, in fact, deceptive.

Antebellum Hannibal and St. Petersburg

The novel's fictional St. Petersburg of about 1836 to 1846 is based on history and is a thinly disguised version of Hannibal, Missouri, Clemens's real home through most of his childhood. His fictional town, however, reveals only selected parts of that historical past. St. Petersburg is a "poor little shabby village" (chapter 1) or, in Huck Finn's words, a "one-horse town" (chapter 27). So, too,

Clemens would describe the real Hannibal as "either a small town or a village, I hardly know which" (Twain 2013, 177). Both the incidents of Clemens's own Hannibal boyhood and the adults and the children he then knew figure significantly, in fictional form, in the novel. As the novelistic details of St. Petersburg are gradually laid out, its extended physical geography pivots around the Mississippi, Cardiff Hill, McDougal's Cave and Jackson's Island. These last three correspond with Holliday's Hill, McDowell's Cave (now known as "Mark Twain Cave"), and one of the several islands near Hannibal that could have served as the model for Jackson's Island. Some details are given of the religious, civic, and economic life of St. Petersburg, too. There are several churches in the village,

THE CHURCH.

Fig. 1. Among the few specific sites the novel mentions in "the poor little shabby village of St. Petersburg" are a school, the courthouse, and the church Tom attends. True Williams, *Tom Sawyer*, 1876. [Public domain.]

with one foregrounded. This evidently is Presbyterian, thus mirroring Clemens's own religious background, assuming the details of the minister's address and the singing of the "Old Hundred" can be seen as indicative. Also referenced are St. Petersburg's two taverns, its town pump, public square, small frame schoolhouse somewhat isolated from the main town, graveyard, tannery, little brick jail, slaughterhouse, court house, distillery or still-house, two taverns, quarry, and foundry.

All this forms a loose but recognizable fit with what is known about Hannibal in the 1830s and 1840s. Clemens himself started at Samuel Cross's school on Holliday Hill when he was about nine years old. Hannibal, too, had its village pump, slaughterhouses (as the pork butchering center for the region), tan yards, blacksmiths, distillery, two churches and three taverns. However, in setting the novel from around 1836 to 1846—that "thirty or forty years ago"—Clemens is actually referring to a time *before* most of his own relevant boyhood experience. Given Clemens's birth in 1835 and first schooling in roughly 1844, the novel's dating of Tom's boyhood actions and adventures precedes, for the majority part, the author's own. This pushing back in time is significant. For the dating connects with Clemens's overall depiction of St. Petersburg/ Hannibal life, what he chooses to leave out, and how he looks to represent his fictional town.

Hannibal grew fast in the period about which Clemens was writing. Its population in 1840 is variously estimated, somewhere between 450 and 1,000. This swelled to 2,020 in 1850 and 6,505 in 1860 (census figures). Its rapid growth was boosted by its role as a transportation center for both river traffic on the Mississippi and travel west. Indeed, by 1860, Hannibal was one of Missouri's largest cities and commercial centers. Clemens's depiction of the town does not completely ignore the industrial development that accompanied this growth. The door "sheathed with boiler iron" (chapter 32) that will finally bar entry and, more crucially, exit to the cave is telling in this respect. But, in essence, the St. Petersburg/Hannibal presented in the novel is pre-modern, small, and relatively undeveloped. So, in saying that Judge Thatcher was "from Constantinople, twelve miles away—so he had traveled, and seen the world" (chapter 4), the point is to emphasize St. Petersburg's parochialism and insularity. The population is still, it seems, small. Tom's church seats "about three hundred persons" (chapter 4). "All the village" (chapter 23) flock to the courthouse for Muff Potter's trial. Moreover, when the "whole town" is raised by the alarm over Tom and Becky's absence, there are "two hundred men" (chapter 30) who gather to search the cave.

This emphasis on the small and parochial nature of the village is helped by Clemens's decision, whether coincidentally or deliberately, to set 1846 (however loosely) as the end-date of the novel's time frame. This is just prior to the 1848 Californian gold rush and its expansive effect on the Hannibal scene and economy as the town became a stopping point and supply-center for eastern gold-rushers on their journey to St. Joseph, Missouri, and farther west. An even more significant development in Hannibal's growth was the building of the Hannibal and St. Joseph railroad soon after, with Hannibal as terminus of what was an important westward rail route. Construction started in 1851, with the road formally opened in 1859. It was this transport link to the West that confirmed Hannibal's connectedness with the larger American world, sealing its status as an important regional hub for east-west trade and traffic to add to the north-south link already existing via the Mississippi. But, regarding the latter, it is noticeable in *Tom Sawyer* that despite the importance of river traffic to Hannibal's early identity, and despite a popular association of the river steamboat with the book, there is no sign of a steamboat in the novel, merely Ben Rogers imitating one in chapter 2. All this helps to build an impression of St. Petersburg, Hannibal's fictional shadow, as a small community, almost completely untouched by larger national historical patterns and concerns.

Clemens's representation of his eponymous protagonist also differs significantly from his own Hannibal history. For Clemens's own childhood, in contrast to the apparent ease of Tom Sawyer's, was a hard one. His family was left in poverty after his father's death in March 1847 and a "hard-sledding" boyhood life followed, marked by "grinding poverty and privation" (Twain 2010, 454–55). In some ways, then, *Tom Sawyer* is a composite of Clemens's own childhood experiences. In others, it is a romanticized and nostalgic version of that past. In other ways still—with its murders, deaths, and gothic elements—it is the stuff of melodramatic nightmares, though nightmares that are finally contained as the book moves toward its conclusion. If the novel borrows from actual history, it crafts, edits, and changes that history toward its own dramatic and mythic ends.

The Post-Civil War Context for the Writing of *Tom Sawyer*

Clemens wrote and published *Tom Sawyer* in the 1870s. The historical experiences of that time strongly influenced the making of the book, but the book's success lies precisely in its fictional existence at an earlier period, before the Civil War, and before the proliferation of those anxieties and pressures brought about by a later modernizing society and economy. The appeal of the novel for its postbellum audience is, in fact, largely explained by the gap between the attractions of this antebellum boyhood past and a later set of historical circumstances necessarily unmentioned in the novel. For later readers, something of that same tension still applies.

In some ways a complete rupture exists between the antebellum and postbellum time periods, with the Civil War, "the most traumatic experience endured by any generation of Americans" (McPherson), lying in-between. A sense of profound dislocation and alienation, of a world shattered into two separate historical pieces was widely shared by Americans living after that war. Accordingly, the fact that Clemens represented St. Petersburg for the most part as a small, inward-looking, community-centered, pre-industrial antebellum village helps to account for his novel's enormous allure. Its picture of a simpler and coherent world, far removed from the pressures of postbellum modernization, struck a deep nostalgic chord then, and continues to do so now. On one side of the Civil War, then, *Tom Sawyer* is a celebration of childhood adventure and exploration, the free-spirited move beyond the fences and constraints of the adult world, and the appeal "to a mythic 'once upon a time' in the national past." On the other side are the divisive effects of acute internal national conflict, together with the massive transformations that Gilded Age America introduced. These included, most crucially, urbanization, industrialization, and wide-scale immigration, all "already beginning to transform the face of America even when [Clemens's] novel first appeared" (Railton).

Many Americans, including Clemens, suffered from the pressures and anxieties that came with the impact of the Civil War and the modernizing transformations that followed. There were widespread fears of a type of debility of the nervous system (neurasthenia) affecting the population in the years following the war. This was seen as a specifically American disease caused by the new industrial age, its mechanical repetitions, and the modern technology it represented. These latter were seen as together contributing to place intolerable pressures both on the human body and mind. Clemens's attitude to technological modernization was highly ambivalent (Messent 2001, 88–94) but repeatedly in his writing there are signs of its negative effects. So, for example, Clemens published his popular sketch, "A Literary Nightmare," in 1876, the same year as *Tom Sawyer*. "Mark Twain," Clemens's comic persona here, is harassed and eventually made into a "tottering wreck" as a set of "jingling rhymes" he reads in the newspaper act as an earworm, come to repeat themselves continually in his mind to discomposing effect. These rhymes describe the repeated and mechanical actions of a horse-drawn streetcar conductor using his punching machine on the tickets of passengers: "Punch, brothers! punch with care! / Punch in the presence of the passenjare!" (Twain 1992, 639–40).

Twain repeats the jingle to a valued friend, "the Rev. Mr.—," who likewise cannot get the rhymes out of his mind and, what is more, finds their words exactly matching the clacking of the wheels of a train he takes on his way to conduct a funeral. Finally and predictably, when at the funeral this same friend is asked by an elderly relative of the deceased about the latter's last words, he replies: "He said—he said—oh my head, my head, my head! He said—he said—he never said *any*thing but Punch, punch, *punch* in the presence of the passenjare" (Twain 1992, 643). This comic piece draws a connection between new technology (the punch machine), mechanical repetition (those clacking train wheels) and nervous exhaustion to suggest the wider impact of modernization on its hapless human victims.

The implicit antimodernist thrust in this sketch is repeated in Clemens's travel writing of the period. So, Bermuda in "Some Rambling Notes of an Idle Excursion" (1877–78) is associated with idleness, freedom, and a charming picturesqueness as "Mark Twain" and his companion leave behind the "millions of harassed people" (Twain 1882, 40) on the American mainland. In a notebook entry of the time, Clemens himself writes "Bermuda is free at present from the triple curse of railways, telegraphs & newspapers" (Twain 1975, 36). It is significant, in this respect, that in *Tom Sawyer*, too, these signs of the network of communication systems binding all citizens in the rush and hurry of modern life are absent, all except the telegraph that remains "as yet undreamed-of" (chapter 11).

In Clemens's 1880 travel book, *A Tramp Abroad*, the narrator-protagonist-traveler is affected by nervous agitation in his hotel room in Heilbronn in Germany, caused he thinks by "the rasping and grinding of distant machinery"—later discovered to be the sounds of a mouse (Twain 1880, 114–16). Again, he later describes his bad nerves, and how they are jangled even by the sound of the Swiss cuckoo clock (262). A raft trip on the Neckar River—anticipating the later more famous raft shared by Huck and Jim in *Huckleberry Finn*—allows an escape from modernizing pressures, its gentle motion and calming and silent movement the very opposite of "the dusty and deafening railroad rush" (126). The railroad here stands as the very sign and symbol of American modernity. All these examples, and the anti-modernism that drives them reflect on *Tom Sawyer*, in which Clemens's conjuring up of antebellum small-town American life acts as the same kind of imaginative escape from an anxiety-filled postbellum American historical reality. *Tom Sawyer*'s appeal and success vitally depends upon a later history, necessarily absent from the novel—all that was happening in America at the time of its writing and publication.

The anti-modernist impulse in Clemens's writing, then, is directly linked to the social and economic changes of the postwar period—and *Tom Sawyer* must be seen in this same light. Twain published his novel at a particularly resonant moment in American history, in 1876, the hundredth year of American independence and the year of the staging of the Centennial Exhibition in Philadelphia. *Tom Sawyer* complemented this note of national celebration in its nostalgic depiction of America's small-town past. At that exact time, however, the country was beset by problems. The 1873 financial panic commenced a five-year depression in the United States, with six thousand businesses closing the following year. The decade, too, was marked by increasing industrial turmoil, with more than one hundred thousand workers taking part in the nationwide conflict of the 1877 railroad strike, which raised fears of a second civil war over class difference at exactly the time when the country was still looking to recover from those earlier *sectional* divisions.

Marcia Jacobson's 1994 study of the popularity of boy books in this period (of which she identified *Tom Sawyer* as the most significant) is astute. She sees them as speaking to the "persistent and apparently insoluble needs" of its American readership in a period of "massive, disruptive social change," and allowing a "vicarious escape from . . . the culture that produced it" (Jacobson 4,7,13). *Tom Sawyer*'s immediate and lasting appeal lies exactly here, in the less complicated and less-regimented antebellum world it represents, an easy-going village society and often-idyllic natural surroundings where the sense of adventurous childhood possibility and individual freedom is potent. Clemens's own later words that the book "is simply a hymn, put into prose form to give it a worldly air" (unmailed letter to W. R. Ward, 8 Sept. 1887) emphasizes the dreamy, comforting, and reassuring qualities of the cultural space he represents, a space that comes to exist in a kind of historical vacuum.

Tom Sawyer, History, and Race

The St. Petersburg of Clemens's novel is a place that seems in many ways outside time. A knowledge of the history both of its own time and of the later postbellum period is, however, essential to that reading. *Tom Sawyer* must also be seen in both these historical contexts in its representation of slavery and of the American Indian, "Injun Joe." There is a lot of historical whitewashing in *Tom Sawyer*, most noticeably in the way slavery is virtually obliterated from St. Petersburg (Hannibal) life. The real Hannibal was a slave town operating according to a racist ideology and marked by numerous cruelties done to its slave population. Clemens's own father played a significant role in supporting that dominant system, enforcing in his sometime role as justice of the peace the laws concerning slavery in the town.

Tom Sawyer offers very few references to the all-important social and economic fact of slavery. Aunt Polly has, and presumably owns, a "small colored boy" called Jim (chapter 1). There are four references to "negroes" in the text, perhaps the most significant in terms of slavery to the "three negro men" belonging to the old Welchman (chapter 30). There are just two occasions when the rights and wrongs of slavery are implicitly and very briefly raised. One is a footnote about distinguishing a slave from a dog in the way they are named after their owner (chapter 10). The other is when Huck tells of Uncle Jake, the Rogers' slave, admitting: "Sometimes I've set right down and eat *with* him. But you needn't tell that. A body's got to do things when he's awful hungry he wouldn't want to do as a steady thing" (chapter 28). There is also one brief joke alluding to Josiah Wedgwood's anti-slavery medallion, "Am I not a man and a brother" (chapter 4). And nothing more.

Slavery was definitely on Clemens's mind at the time of writing *Tom Sawyer*, and it was still, even after Emancipation, a matter of major national concern and debate. The South, in theory, was learning to live without slavery. Too often, in practice, it effectively resisted the various changes to the antebellum racial order that the Civil War and its aftermath had brought. The 1875 federal Civil Rights Act, passed under Radical Republican pressure as the climax of Reconstruction legislation, may have granted African Americans equality in their use of public accommodation and transportation (but not schools). African American civil rights, however, were generally unenforced in the South with white-on-black violence commonplace. The act itself was subject to constitutional challenge from the time it was passed, to be declared unconstitutional just eight years later. Reconstruction dramatically waned in the latter decades of the 1870s. By 1876 only three southern states, Florida, Louisiana, and South Carolina, remained under Republican control. In the American South, the African American gains from the war and early postbellum period were accordingly demolished.

For Clemens himself the status of African Americans in his country was increasingly an issue. In 1874, two years before *Tom Sawyer*'s publication, he broke away from the comic straight-jacket that had previously defined him to write "A True Story." In this powerful short piece, the African American vernacular voice of "Aunt Rachel" carries the majority of the narrative and is—in a radical formal move—given full authority once the more conventional "framed" opening of the story is out of the way. Her story of family loss and partial recovery, pivoting around the Civil War, is a moving and serious testimony of slave and post-slave experience (Messent 2001, 59–66). Sherwood Cummings, indeed, claims it marks "a sea-change in the author's racial attitude" (Cummings 13).

Why then did Clemens turn so quiet on race, whitewash slave history from the picture, before once more focusing on the subject in *Adventures of Huckleberry Finn*, the companion book to *Tom Sawyer*? Mainly, one would assume, because any engagement with the subject would go against his dominant intentions in writing this boy-book. For if the novel is not quite that out-and-out celebration of life in small town America that many see it as being, it does nonetheless constantly push toward the nostalgic, the idyllic, and the lyrical. It certainly was not Clemens's intention to explore the dangerous subject of race in the book. That would wait for another day, and another boy protagonist, less committed than Tom to the values of the community around him.

As for the representation of the American Indian, Clemens does here reflect his times. He uncritically adopts the dominant perspective of both antebellum and postbellum periods in using the stereotype of the dangerous savage "other" in his depiction of "Injun Joe" as the melodramatic villain of the novel. Joe is a nightmare figure throughout the text—and one whose "halfbreed" status (chapter 26) further damns him, given the fear of miscegenation in the period. Kerry Driscoll takes Joe's appeal to "the great Sachem" (chapter 26) to indicate probable membership of the Sac and Fox tribe (Driscoll 43), removed from Missouri to Kansas and Nebraska following the 1830 Indian Removal Act. Long gone from the immediate Missouri area by the time Clemens was writing, the wider Indian "problem" was, however, still a work-in-progress but with one inevitable national result: shrinking Indian population and land use, and cultural suppression.

This larger historical process is reflected in *Tom Sawyer* but in an oblique way. Here, Tom and Joe are initially depicted as interrelated figures, with Tom's testing of the limits of village authority and regulation taken to savage extreme in Joe's attitudes and actions. It is Tom though, the young white protagonist, who finally re-enters village life as a hero, "courted, admired, stared at" (chapter 35). Joe, with his American Indian heritage, concludes the novel locked in the cave to meet his grisly death. As Robert Tracy succinctly describes the book's ending, "the Indian dies and the treasure disappears into a bank—a neat and accurate symbol of the fate of the trans-Mississippi frontier. Civilization's progress exorcizes the devils, exterminates the Indians, and banks the proceeds" (Tracy 110). Here again a knowledge of historical events and processes informs Clemens's novel even as no explicit recognition of that context is given.

Tom Sawyer, Indian Joe, and the Gothic

This essay has looked to put *Tom Sawyer* into its historical context but also to show how Clemens's representation of St. Petersburg works against that history—self-contained, islanded from a larger connecting world, existing by and large in a temporal and spatial vacuum. That representation, further, drives against any desire for larger historical understanding in its primary appeal to a separate childhood realm of adventure, mystery, and romance. When Louis Budd wrote of Clemens as "the magic flutist of nostalgia for childhood in a simpler, happier time" (Budd, 6), he captured something of this sense. Indeed, one might replace his word "childhood" with "America" to equally accurate effect. Clemens's book also encourages an ahistorical reading in the way he ends the "Indian Joe" part of the narrative, leading the reader away from history to symbol and archetype in his use of the Gothic. This forms the subject matter of the last section of this essay.

Revealingly, it is at this very point in the novel, with Joe found "starved to death" behind the newly installed locked door of McDougal's cave (chapter 33) that Clemens engages most explicitly with human history, but only immediately to cast any sense of day-to-day and year-to-year change and progression to one side. For the text makes an unusual digression at this point, moving away from its current time and place to refer to the passing of historical time— to the pyramids, the fall of Troy, the Roman Empire, Christopher Columbus, and more. This is only then to return to the regular fall of a drop of water from the stalagmite in the cave that first prompted the digression, the drop "still . . . falling when all these [named events] shall have . . . been swallowed up in the thick night of oblivion." History is effectively silenced here, swallowed up by the endless repetitions of nature and the vast expanses of time itself.

This silencing of history connects with the status of Indian Joe in the story. In his novel, Clemens implicitly recognizes the historical process of American Indian removal and suppression. Joe's death and disposal from the narrative occurs, however, outside this history—not in St. Petersburg and the events associated with it, nor in any direct action taken by the white populace against him, but in an episode heavy with symbolic weight: in the cave with its subterranean depths, a separate and labyrinthine space outside the village. Joe's disposal occurs, then, not as part of the day-to-day and mostly realistic episodes of St. Petersburg life but in a nightmare realm where the evil presence of this "bloody-minded outcast" is necessarily exorcized. This follows the near meeting with Tom Sawyer, the book's hero, that takes place there. Joe's body lies close to the previously mentioned stalagmite, which has provided him, until death, with the "priceless drops" of water (chapter 33) to slake his thirst. Joe's dying and dead body, and the stalagmite, symbol of the endless passage of time's passing, are linked in a scene of Gothic excess featuring the claws of the bats Joe had managed to catch and eat and the signs of his desperate efforts to hack through the foundation-beam of the cave's iron door. The gruesome death of Joe, Tom's dark shadow, fulfils a necessary logic in the text—and in both the America it represents and human history as it was then seen. For it symbolically rids the nation of its secret sharer, its disinherited outcast, in line with the logic of Manifest Destiny. On a larger scale, it also rids civilization of its primitive and savage past.

Not just Joe's death, though, but all the final episodes in the cave operate in the Gothic mode. The Gothic works by taking its readers to a liminal space, a separate, timeless and unreal world where the guilt, fears, and anxieties of a culture can be displayed and worked through at a safe distance and in an entertaining way. That is what happens here. Caves are traditionally associated with the unconscious and with repressed memory. Here, locked in that dark and apparently timeless space, Joe is safely dispatched from the (American) story, and Tom can re-emerge into the daylight world as community savior and hero.

This needs further explanation. First, one should note Tom Sawyer and Indian Joe's status as symbolically twinned figures. Their relationship can be seen in terms of different sides of the self—the conscious (civilized and rational) and the unconscious (primitive, irrational, and instinctive). This opposition as encoded here again leads the book's readers away from history and, in this case, toward psychology. For it points to a recurrent concern with the deep psychic division in the human personality, the conscious self in conflict with its hidden and darker impulses. It also takes one away from any immediate concern with the details of history toward larger issues of race and stereotype, whiteness and Indian-ness.

Fig. 2. Although True Williams's depiction of Tom's final confrontation with Injun Joe in the cave is not completely true to the text, it very much gets the symbolic point of a face-off between the two linked characters. *Tom Sawyer*, 1876. [Public domain.]

This helps to explain why Tom and Joe are twinned—Tom's night-time escapes from domesticity through his bedroom window, to give one example, mirrored in Joe's courtroom window flight. Indeed, literary critic Cynthia Griffin Wolff uses the term "shadow self" to describe their relationship, seeing Joe's anger and violence—and, one might add, his sexual threat—as the inherently hostile, dangerous, and antisocial side of Tom's rebellion against village authority and its comforting rituals, the unconscious part of Tom's conscious being. If this final statement might be a step too far for some readers, the term shadow self still makes sense here. It is, accordingly, highly significant that the last time the reader sees Tom and Joe together, it is when both are trapped in the cave, together with Becky, whose innocent girlhood, one might suggest, stands symbolically between them. Tom and Joe are positioned opposite each other here, on either side of some chasm or "jumping off point." Clemens's text avoids any direct visual confrontation between the two, and Becky is at the margins of the scene, but True Williams's original illustration of the episode very much gets the symbolic point, depicting a face-off between the linked characters, with Becky, shielded by Tom, also in the picture (chapter 31).

In the McDougal's cave episode, then, the story enters Gothic territory as Joe and Tom both navigate its underground symbolic realm of darkness and death, its "tangle of rifts and chasms . . . labyrinth underneath labyrinth, and no end to any of them" (chapter 29). Here, the main actor (Tom) undergoes a type of initiation fitting him for his return to village society in a more adult and responsible guise. Selflessly protective toward Becky, he puts his disruptive and antisocial (Injun Joe) side behind him, leaving Joe accordingly in the cave to perish. A type of rebirth and resurrection occurs that strongly echoes Christian myth. Tom is three days underground before his return to the daylight world when he "pushed his head and shoulders through a small hole and saw the broad Mississippi rolling by" (chapter 32). His ordeal, a form of symbolic death, is followed by the transformation that occurs as he re-enters the community, this time to take up his place within it and to accept its values rather than to disturb them, slated to become "a great lawyer or a great soldier someday" (chapter 35).

In moving his text into the realm of symbol and archetype, then, Clemens leaves the world of history—both antebellum and postbellum—behind, to immerse his readers in long-familiar symbols and archetypes. There are some ambiguities that remain, however. For there is a gap here between the notion of the unchanging passing of time and the shift from a savage and primitive past to the white and civilized present. This can be explained by Clemens's acceptance of the basic paradigm of racial evolutionary development, a type of "long" history that explains its slowly changing shape (like the effect of the stalagmite's drip); something seen as "natural" to the dominant values of the time. Clemens himself would later challenge beliefs in Darwinian evolution in essays such as "Was the World Made for Man?" (1903). He would further challenge the idea that so-called savagery precedes and is inferior to present-day civilization in *Following the Equator*, in which he writes: "There are many humorous things in the world; among them, the white man's notion that he is less savage than the other savages" (Twain 1897, 213). Indeed, it seems that it was the very reliance on conventional attitudes in *Tom Sawyer* that led Clemens to keep it as a boy-book and to end it where he did. As he famously wrote to William Dean Howells, "If I went on now, & took him into manhood, he would just be like all the one-horse men in literature & the reader would conceive a hearty contempt for him" (Smith and Gibson, 91–92). For the Gothic ending of the novel and what then follows seals off the text in a deeply conventional way, both in terms of Tom's final social positioning and in its use of the savage/civilized binary. In this respect, it is deeply suggestive that Tom's two symbolic rebirths lead to a joyous sense of his rejoining the village community and being folded in its arms. He is "restored . . ., smothered . . . with kisses . . . thanksgivings . . . poured out" (chapter 17) when he shows up at his own funeral. While Tom and Becky's safe return from the cave is "the greatest night the little town had ever seen" (chapter 32). In *Adventures of Huckleberry Finn,* things are very different. For when Huck, Clemens's new main protagonist, fakes his own death (chapter 7), this leads to no renewed integration in a safe St. Petersburg world but to the Mississippi, the leaving of Hannibal, his chance meeting with Jim, and (on Clemens's part) a radical engagement with the southern world and with race and its politics. *Tom Sawyer*, in this way, prepares the ground for Clemens's more challenging later great novel.

Works Cited

Budd, Louis J. "Mark Twain as an American Icon." *The Cambridge Companion to Mark Twain*. Edited by Forrest G. Robinson, Cambridge UP, 1995.

Cummings, Sherwood. "Afterword" to *Sketches, New and Old* by Mark Twain. Oxford UP, 1996.

Driscoll, Kerry. *Mark Twain among the Indians and Other Indigenous Peoples*. U of California P, 2018.

Jacobson, Marcia. *Being a Boy Again: Autobiography and the American Boy Book*. U of Alabama P, 1994.

McPherson, James M. "Out of War, a New Nation." *Prologue Magazine*, vol. 42, no. 1, Spring 2010.

Messent, Peter. *The Short Works of Mark Twain: A Critical Study*. U of Pennsylvania P, 2001.

Railton, Stephen. *Mark Twain in His Times*. twain.lib.virginia.edu/tomsawye/nostalgia/nostalgiahp.html.

Smith, Henry Nash, and William M. Gibson, editors. *Mark Twain-Howells Letters: The Correspondence of Samuel L. Clemens and William Dean Howells, 1872–1910*. Vol. 1. Belknap Press, 1960.

Tracy, Robert. "Myth and Reality in *The Adventures of Tom Sawyer.*" *Critical Essays on "The Adventures of Tom Sawyer."* Edited by Gary Scharnhorst, G. K. Hall, 1993, pp. 103–12.

Twain, Mark. *Autobiography of Mark Twain*. Vols. 1–2, U of California P, 2010 and 2013.

_____. *Following the Equator.* 1897. Oxford UP, 1996.

_____. *Mark Twain's Notebooks & Journals.* Vol. 2, 1877–1883, U of California P, 1975.

_____. *The Stolen White Elephant Etc.* 1882, Oxford UP, 1996.

_____. *Tales, Sketches, Speeches, & Essays.* Vol. 1, 1852–1890. Edited by Louis J. Budd, Library of America, 1992.

_____. *A Tramp Abroad.* 1880. Oxford UP, 1996.

Wolff, Cynthia Griffin. "*The Adventures of Tom Sawyer*: A Nightmare Vision of American Boyhood." *Massachusetts Review*, vol. 21, no. 4, Winter 1980, pp. 637–52.

Tom Sawyer: A Classic Overshadowed by Its Successor_____

Alan Gribben

The Adventures of Tom Sawyer (1876) remains perennially popular in the United States and is still a recognizable title around the globe. Publishers have kept the book in print throughout the decades. Nevertheless, critics, editors, historians, librarians, and Internet websites have long been confounded when categorizing and evaluating the novel that Mark Twain composed soon after he recounted his steamboat piloting days in a series of essays titled "Old Times on the Mississippi" (1875). *The Adventures of Tom Sawyer*, set in a small town in Missouri, sold well and received favorable book reviews. However, the author's reintroduction of these same characters into a new novel that followed nine years later permanently affected how people perceived the earlier work. The brilliant, groundbreaking *Adventures of Huckleberry Finn* (1885), in which a young comrade of Tom Sawyer leaves St. Petersburg for a picaresque journey on a raft accompanied by an adult escaping from enslavement, eclipsed *Tom Sawyer's* reputation. The previous book soon took second place to this subsequent masterpiece. Because that initial novel was obviously (and emphatically by the author) linked to *Huckleberry Finn*, the literary achievements of the second work continue to influence how commentators take stock of *Tom Sawyer*. Literary scholars and critics, rather than pausing to analyze its ingredients, habitually refer to *The Adventures of Tom Sawyer* in passing as a requisite but inconsequential preparation for a vastly more important artistic achievement. Reflecting this attitude, bookstores tend to shelve *Tom Sawyer* with juvenile literature or young adult fiction instead of according it a place among literary classics.

Fig. 1. First editions of *Tom Sawyer* and its successor, *Huckleberry Finn*, whose subtitle was designed to remind readers of its connection to *Tom Sawyer*. Image courtesy of Alan Gribben. [Used with permission.]

Setting *Tom Sawyer* Apart

Decades ago Louis D. Rubin, Jr. speculated that, had Mark Twain's difficulties with the plot of *Huckleberry Finn* prevented him from completing that manuscript, the "marvelous story" in *Tom Sawyer* ("Mark Twain," p. 171) would have guaranteed its status as "Mark Twain's best novel"("Mark Twain," p. 158) and "a classic if ever there was one" ("Mark Twain," p. 171). It is, indeed, intriguing to theorize what the literary stature of *The Adventures of Tom Sawyer* would be had the author *not* followed it up with any sequel. Critics would then have to acknowledge that Mark Twain had produced something here that no one else had done before him. They might very likely praise the detailed river village setting and tick off the many clever employments of autobiographical elements. The book's humor would be touted as refreshing and unforced, the boy characters drawn from life, the "adventures" promised by the title amply delivered. Tom Sawyer, unprejudiced commentators might say, mirrors realistic childhood tendencies in his showing off, his craving to play-act the classics he has explored in his ambitious, self-directed reading, and his courageous leadership in transporting the boys to an island and safely back again. More than that, his sympathy for Aunt Polly's fretting about his supposed drowning confirms his basically good impulses when he winds up his river excursion (and demonstrates adept stagecraft) by arranging a dramatic reappearance of the trio of missing boys in a church balcony during their own funeral service so that she and the other adults will not suffer further anxiety and grief. Injun Joe might be interpreted as a tragically abandoned figure, unfortunately left behind by the receding frontier and embittered by the prejudice he confronts. Joe's threats against the widow Douglas perhaps insinuate sexual assault but definitely foretell a planned mutilation and possible murder, so Huckleberry Finn's actions are, especially for his youthful age, resourceful and determined. The novel builds to a fulfilling resolution on several fronts. Perhaps, in the light of these various attributes, editors might deem the book worthy of an excerpt or two in high school and college textbooks. This is admittedly pure conjecture. The towering shadow cast over *Tom Sawyer* by the arrival of *Adventures of Huckleberry Finn* negated all of those potentially favorable judgments. When critics do condescend to look at *The Adventures of Tom Sawyer,* they usually express disappointment in its faults and shortcomings— compared to *Adventures of Huckleberry Finn*, they mean.

Challenges to Interpretation

The perplexing problems about gauging Mark Twain's authorial accomplishment in writing *The Adventures of Tom Sawyer* are partly traceable to the novel's predecessors and were, more crucially, portended in the creator's indecision about the chronological span and suitable narrative tone for this book. Readers seldom give much thought to the fact that Mark Twain's embroidered description of his Hannibal boyhood was not the first venture in depicting the trials besetting adolescents. Thomas Hughes's stiff-upper-lip account of an English boyhood, *Tom Brown's School Days* (1857) made an indelible impression on North American as well as British readers. Yet, it was arguably the immense popularity of Louisa May Alcott's

Little Women (published serially in 1868 and 1869) that stirred male authors to contemplate the possibilities of relating the far-less-prim-and-proper antics that their boy gangs were capable of contriving. Thomas Bailey Aldrich's *The Story of a Bad Boy* (1869) launched this subgenre, presenting a robust, risk-taking set of young characters who sneaked out at night, set off abandoned cannons on the seashore, and took an unauthorized voyage to Sandpeep Island.

Twain professed not to be impressed by Aldrich's book ("for the life of me I could not admire the volume much," he wrote to his fiancée Olivia Langdon on 27 December 1869), but his own exploration of boyhood experiences would bear unmistakable parallels to Aldrich's *The Story of a Bad Boy*. In virtually every respect, though, Twain's treatment of the escapades hatched by youths of the same age group left Aldrich's book behind in the dust. As evidence, history has neglected Aldrich's effort, whereas Twain's *The Adventures of Tom Sawyer* retains a lively pulse. To take one example, Aldrich's novel merely mentions the books of derring-do that fascinated Aldrich himself as a boy, but Twain cleverly introduces their titles and contents as the daily diet of the romance-addled Tom Sawyer. The sword fight between Tom Sawyer and Joe Harper on Cardiff Hill in chapter 8 is scripted stroke-by-stroke from Stephen Percy's *Robin Hood and His Merry Foresters* (1841), and the pages of a dime novel, Ned Buntline's *The Black Avenger of the Spanish Main; or, The Fiend of Blood* (1847), dictate Tom, Joe, and Huck's play during their decampment to Jackson's Island.

Twain's uncertainty about exactly what type of literature he had thought up became evident when he confided to the author and critic William Dean Howells, "I didn't take the chap beyond boyhood. . . . I perhaps made a mistake in not writing it in the first person. . . . It is *not* a boy's book, at all. It will only be read by adults. It is only written for adults." Twain's irresolution about his intended audience grew more apparent when he reversed himself after Howells read the manuscript. "Mrs. Clemens decides with you that the book should issue as a book for boys, pure & simple—& so do I. It is surely the correct idea." This vacillation that bedeviled the author—whether he had given birth to a book for younger readers or for older adults—would similarly haunt discussions of *Tom Sawyer* in the years to come.

A handful of distinguished commentators have undertaken impressive efforts to point out deeper implications below *Tom Sawyer's* sunny surface, but their arguments hardly prevail among the instructors of college and graduate school literature courses. For example, Joseph Csicsila, whose *Canons by Consensus: Critical Trends and American Literature Anthologies* (2004) studied the contents of literary anthologies assigned since 1919 in university English courses, found that "not even so much as a single episode from *The Adventures of Tom Sawyer* has *ever* been excerpted for a major collection of American literature marketed specifically for college students. . . . Initially stigmatized as a work of juvenile fiction, [it] remains largely neglected by scholar-editors and their college textbooks." In public libraries, too, the two novels are generally separated—*The Adventures of Tom Sawyer* is relegated to the juvenile or young adult sections, whereas *Adventures of Huckleberry Finn* sits amid distinguished company in the adult fiction or classic literature spheres.

Mark Twain had neither foreseen nor desired this bifurcation of his two narratives about Tom Sawyer and Huckleberry Finn. As a matter of fact, the second novel opens with Huckleberry Finn notifying the readers (and thus explicitly plugging the author's previous book), "You don't know about me, without you have read a book by the name of 'The Adventures of Tom Sawyer.'" When the long-lost original manuscript for this page turned up in 1990, we could see that Mark Twain tinkered with the phrasing of that sentence, seeking to establish Huck's folk speech diction. Later on, perhaps concerned that readers might be discouraged from proceeding any farther in the text by this admonition that familiarity with the earlier work was necessary, the author went back and added a reassuring concession at the end of the sentence, "but that ain't no matter." Twain even made an effort to have the two novels resemble each other in size and bindings, despite their having issued from two different publishers. His efforts were in vain, however. *Adventures of Huckleberry Finn*—when the book is not banned from classrooms owing to its 215 usages of the detested n-word racial slur in the first edition—is nearly always taught without its predecessor, leaving students to try to make sense out of an unnamed village situated on an unnamed river and (for the first three chapters) the novel's title character chaffing under restrictions imposed by a woman called Widow Douglas and her sister Miss Watson, while he is engaging with other boys in horseplay orchestrated by someone named Tom Sawyer.

Tom Sawyer's Achievements

In the face of this academic neglect of *The Adventures of Tom Sawyer* one should not overlook a monumental contribution the novel made to the possibilities of American literature. Thomas Hughes's "Tom Brown" character and Thomas Bailey Aldrich's "Tom Bailey" essentially adhered to their creators' actual boyhood experiences. Mark Twain, by contrast, inserted startling scenes of pure fiction—a midnight graveyard murder, a killer whom the witnesses to this crime fear is stalking them, a funeral for three boys thought to have drowned in the river, a buried treasure left behind by a vicious robber, a spooky cave in which a boy and a girl become lost—that far outdid the tamer events described by his predecessors. In short, as the title of his novel made clear with the word "Adventures," Mark Twain borrowed the blood-and-thunder features of the widely read dime novels of the mid-nineteenth century and wove those lurid components into the threads of his own Hannibal boyhood, giving *Tom Sawyer* a jolting advantage over the efforts of the dozen prominent authors who would follow the model of Aldrich's *The Story of a Bad Boy* by dutifully (and too often boringly) chronicling the phases of their actual juvenile lives. Only Mark Twain in his era had the audacity and imagination to blend his childhood memories with themes and situations that would engage younger readers as well as adults. In recent decades *The Adventures of Tom Sawyer* has received insufficient acclaim for inventing this powerful mixture of autobiographical recollections and fantasized adventures, which would ultimately enable twentieth-century authors—having forsaken the scruples of fidelity to absolute truthfulness—to convey readers on riveting journeys into blends of memory and imagination.

While combining these elements, Mark Twain took great liberties with the actual circumstances of, and the people he knew in, his Hannibal days. Tom Sawyer is an orphan, a traditional literary disadvantage that appeals to readers' sympathies, who is being reared by an indulgent aunt; Samuel Clemens's father died when his son was in his early teens, but he still had the care of an attentive at-home mother, Jane Clemens. The setting of St. Petersburg—a fictional name alluding to the (then) capital of Russia but more importantly evoking the gateway to Heaven associated with the biblical disciple St. Peter—bears resemblances to Hannibal, since the wharves of both jut into the Mississippi River, but in many respects Mark Twain heightened or altered details. For instance, he gave Judge Thatcher the appearance of a towering authority that probably no single legal figure possessed in early-day Hannibal. He vilified and distorted the Native American from an Osage tribe on whom he modeled the character "Injun Joe," in part to suggest (and benefit from) the stereotype of the ferociously vindictive "Indians" then appearing on stage in nineteenth-century melodramas. He elevated the geographical dimensions of the summit he called Cardiff Hill, increased the width of the river, enlarged and moved downriver the boys' refuge he named Jackson's Island, and devised labyrinthian tunnels and recesses within the interior of a simple limestone cave. There really was an outlaw named John Murrell (or a criminal having a close variant name) who had operated along the Mississippi River. Several biographers of this robber probably exaggerated his exploits, and Mark Twain embellished them even further. Whether that real river pirate actually buried any unclaimed booty is doubtful, but Mark Twain took the suggestion that not all of his loot was ever accounted for and inflated the idea into treasure hunts as a pastime for boys. Comparable departures from the factual environs of real-life Hannibal and its region can be detected in many chapters.

Spotting Supposed Flaws

Literary critics have complained about a number of things that, in their opinion, obliterate even the diminished significance and rank sometimes accorded *The Adventures of Tom Sawyer*. One can discern why they raise these cavils, but in almost every case an explanation can be offered or a counterargument mounted. For instance, it has been pointed out that the narrator's tone is erratic, occasionally shifting from the third person to address the reader directly. Yet, this was a common practice in the works of Charles Dickens, William Makepeace Thackeray, and other novelists of that period; Mark Twain should not be scolded for employing one of the conventions in wide usage during the period when he wrote.

Critics have also found the book to be unduly nostalgic, as though the author were pining for antebellum Sunday schools, community picnics, and innocent social customs. Let it be noted that Mark Twain was hardly the only United States author displaying a sense of regret for bygone days. Like him, a large number of writers, including, Thomas Bailey Aldrich, William Dean Howells, Charles Dudley Warner, Hamlin Garland, and Stephen Crane, had migrated from farmlands or small towns to large cities such as San Francisco, Chicago, Boston, Hartford, and New York. Having made their mark in the literary world, they could never consider returning to the rural or village life they left behind, yet their fiction and memoirs betrayed tender yearnings for the simpler world in which they grew up. This tendency would disappear within another decade or two upon the arrival of a harsh, condemnatory revolt against the village that twentieth-century United States literature ushered in and fostered.

Becky Thatcher, some commentators allege, is merely a petulant, two-dimensional, overly emotional stick figure. Recently several novelists have creatively, justifiably rectified and enriched her characterization. Yet, any insistence that a girl of the 1840s could evince in *Tom Sawyer* modern-day attitudes and a range of mature responses seems unwarranted. Young girls then were hardly encouraged to be anything but decorous, and Mark Twain would have been false to the times and the locale if he had expanded her role very vigorously. For that same reason—historical verisimilitude—those objecting to the narrative's ethnic identifications (the "Welchman," "Injun" Joe, enslaved African Americans, the "Spaniard") appear to require Mark Twain to go against the customs of that day. In those decades of mass immigration to North America there was much emphasis on one's racial or ethnic origins, and the author was being accurate in referring to characters by the identifying labels that clung to citizens in St. Petersburg.

Far more serious is the charge that human slavery is mentioned, if incidentally, without condemning the reprehensible practice. Indeed, the first edition of *Tom Sawyer* contained nine usages of the n-word. There is no getting around this merited objection and no perfect solution. In school classrooms and college lecture halls instructors have the choice of either assigning the readily available editions of *The Adventures of Tom Sawyer* in which this racial insult is replaced with the word "slave" (a loaded word itself, but at least a historical reality rather than a repulsive flash word) or else being careful not to read aloud or discuss those passages in which the derogatory n-word occurs. Individual readers should bear in mind Mark Twain's courage in reminding his audience of what most of his fellow writers were hiding—that a hideous system of enslavement had persisted in the plantation states decades after England, Europe, and the northern states of the Union had repudiated it as barbaric and contemptible. Few post-Civil War works of fiction had the nerve even to refer to slavery. Most authors in the 1870s and 1880s who set their narratives in the American South chastely alluded to "servants" in the house and delicately referred to the "hands" working in the fields. Twain should get credit for treating enslavement as a fact in antebellum Missouri during an era when the entire nation, North and South, seemed eager to undergo a gigantic memory lapse about the issue that had brought about the Civil War—a tragic conflict that killed more than 600,000 soldiers.

The majority of artistic quibbles about *The Adventures of Tom Sawyer* revolve around the bullying, scheming, and grandstanding of its principal character. Certain commentators defending the boy-protagonist have valiantly attempted to make the case that, viewing *Tom Sawyer* and *Huckleberry Finn* as composite novels, one can detect a certain degree of maturation in Tom Sawyer's thinking and actions. A preponderance of those who discuss Tom, however, are less charitable about his demeanor and behavior. One detractor, Robert Bray, devoted most of a witty essay in 1981 to scoffing at the boy's tomfoolery. An eminent scholar remarked in 2002 that "Tom deserved a good shooting" and regretted that Mark Twain had not fatally wounded the illogical, maddening, trouble-causing young character in the second novel (Steinbrink, "Who Shot Tom Sawyer?"). Does it really matter whether Tom makes any progress toward maturation? Readers only glimpse a few months of this fictional character's boyhood. He is what he is—a boy who plays hooky from school; challenges a St. Louis newcomer to a scrap; uses his wits to evade hard work on a Saturday; pretends to be the hero of books he has been absorbing; absconds to a river island with boys over whom he has a dominating influence owing to his precocious literacy; returns to relieved hugs from his aunt and friends; gets whipped by a frustrated, ill-natured schoolmaster; explores parts of a cave he is not supposed to enter without a group; recovers stolen money, and ends up restored to good standing with his fellow townspeople. Reading over the predominating criticism of Mark Twain's first boy book, one begins to ponder how we have become such a solemn society. Fictional juvenile characters in a short novel are judged as though they were real-life adults. In the nineteenth century these huffy moral analysts would assuredly have slammed the door on the salespeople whom the American Publishing Company had recruited to sell a new kind of novel filled with humorous incidents, comical drawings, and chilling moments.

A Long-Recognized Prototype

One of the things literary critics find especially irritating is Tom Sawyer's apparently insufferable reliance on outmoded romantic reading like Sir Walter Scott's novels and poems. The idea that Twain is burlesquing the works against which the Age of Realism had set itself appears to be lost on those who have little sense of humor. They seem to want Huckleberry Finn to be the master presence rather than a subsidiary figure in a novel titled *The Adventures of Tom*

Sawyer. The evolution of literary genius proceeds in increments. One must be patient and wait for Huck Finn to find his own voice in a subsequent work. Despite that delay for his central role, in both novels Huckleberry Finn serves a crucial function, and Mark Twain's literary model has long been known. His admiration for Miguel de Cervantes' *Don Quixote* (1605, 1615) is so well established that Olin H. Moore wrote about the subject in 1922 in one of the first scholarly articles to study Mark Twain. As early as 1861 Samuel Clemens (before he adopted the pen name "Mark Twain") declared *Don Quixote* to be one of his two "*beau ideals* of fine writing." Eight years later he called it "one of the most exquisite books that was ever written." In 1877 he referred to Don Quixote's "library of illustrious shams," and in 1883 he praised the way Cervantes' work "swept the world's admiration for the mediaeval chivalry-silliness out of existence." As late as 1896 he predicted that Cervantes' "romance . . . would exist as long as language endured" (*Mark Twain's Literary Resources*). Just as Don Quixote required his commonsensical Sancho Panza as a companion, so the pragmatic Huckleberry Finn needs the deluded Tom Sawyer as a foil. It would take Mark Twain an entire boy book before he had the inspirations to develop Huckleberry Finn as the hero of his own narrative and to keep Tom Sawyer around to counterbalance and complicate Huck's direct approaches to easily remediable situations. The fact that these characters are mere boys was supposed to be funny in itself.

The ingenuity behind this evenly matched team infuriates modern critics, who solely value the portions of *Adventures of Huckleberry Finn* that take place on the drifting raft and only applaud Huck's gradual, grudging recognitions of the enslaved Jim's humanity and generosity. These commentators who disparage Tom Sawyer's interferences might do well to look up the innovative and "corrected" *The True Adventures of Huckleberry Finn* that John Seelye published amid much fanfare in 1970. Seelye acceded to and implemented the objections that contemporary critics had been making about Tom Sawyer's presence toward the end of that novel; he reduced that character's role, enlarged Huck Finn's, and assigned Jim the doomed fate that his enslaved status demanded. Yet, who hears of Seelye's *The True Adventures of Huckleberry Finn* today? Its existing copies sit dusty and unread on the library shelves. The public (and even the academics) have voted their preference for the original version, Tom Sawyer's antics and all.

Critics are principally disappointed in the ending of *Adventures of Huckleberry Finn* because the conclusion seems to them a steep descent from the preceding raft chapters with their sharp portraits of early-day river life. To them, this decline shares the problem with the entirety of *The Adventures of Tom Sawyer* and, in their view, that book's absurdly happy ending. A tremendous misconception is discernable in their approach to these works. They pick up the two novels expecting and hoping to encounter bold ethical lessons about chicanery, cruelty, complacency, hypocrisy, and inequality in every chapter. They are bound to be disillusioned in those anticipations, because Mark Twain made his financial living in three ways—as a travel writer, a performer on the lecture circuit, and a published literary humorist. Inasmuch as Mark Twain's books were sold by canvassers going door-to-door, the literature he offered had to be highly marketable and precisely as amusing as advertised. In the two conjoined novels, *Tom Sawyer* and *Huckleberry Finn*, he elected to derive comedy by sketching the purported "adventures" of two adolescent boys. This fictional strategy had not been attempted previously. A portion of the burlesque effect stems from focusing on immature, inexperienced boys, relatively powerless and dependent upon the protection of adults, who hardly possess the set of qualifications for the usual strong, vital characters in a novel. Part of the humor that Mark Twain predicted would appeal to his subscribing readers would be the emergence of serious topics perceivable within the accounts of these frivolous boys' activities. Applying a magnifying glass to the tribulations of pint-sized protagonists, Mark Twain obliquely treated thought-provoking topics such as the fine distinction between work and play (Tom's fence-painting ruse), the effects of bondage on the enslaved and on the society that demanded they work without compensation or basic human rights, the dangers to children playing around treacherous water currents (the toll of the Mississippi River), charlatans who visit towns (mesmerizers and their ilk), religions that teach rote memorization rather than principles, body snatchers, patent medicine hazards, schoolroom lessons inflicted rather than motivated, cruel corporal punishment, alcoholism (Muff Potter's plight), and unrealistic, fanciful literature that misleads young people about the true nature of the world (sensational dime novels, chivalric romances, accounts of daring prison escapes).

Other Ways to Think About These Works

All of the problems that critics deplore would vanish or at least largely dissipate if they opted to read the two books as the companion novels that Mark Twain intended. In that way *Tom Sawyer* prepares the reader for the first three chapters of *Huckleberry Finn*, whose raft journey can be seen as an exciting bonus segment—a series of chapters in which the author no doubt exceeded even his own expectations—and then the Phelps farm chapters ease the narrative back into the comfortable boy book form within which Twain had launched his twin novels. Somber subjects such as devout religious services and compulsory elocution performances are related lightly, whereas superficial, transient topics like puppy love are given elaborate, sober treatment. Readers should keep reminding themselves that both books were the creations of a professional humorist, not (especially in the 1870s and 1880s) an inveterate social reformer. Later, when his literary standing was secure, Mark Twain would venture opinions about political, military, and scientific misdeeds and take positions about international causes, but in mid-career he was more typically obsessed with monetary possibilities.

Furthermore, *Tom Sawyer* offers a number of original and memorable moments. For example, in a gripping incident in chapter 26, Tom and Huck, having been interrupted in their search for a hidden treasure, watch in paralyzed consternation as the knife-wielding Injun Joe mounts the stairs of a deserted house to look for them—only, to the boys' immense relief, to crash through rotten wooden timbers. In chapter 31, after Tom and Becky have nearly given up on ever finding their way out of McDougal's cave, Tom sees "a human hand, holding a candle," protrude around a rock. Tom instantly presumes that they are saved and cries out, just a moment before realizing to his horror that the light is held by the murderous villain whom he most fears. Nothing matching these frightening scenes for trapped juveniles would take place in literature until seven years later in Robert Louis Stevenson's *Treasure Island* (1883), when a mutinous cutthroat on a ship reaches into the barrel of apples in which Jim Hawkins is hiding.

One would do well to stop comparing *Tom Sawyer* to its companion novel and acknowledge that Mark Twain's feat in writing this first book was of a different order than what he accomplished later. *Tom Sawyer* will never challenge the irrevocable place that *Huckleberry Finn* holds among literary critics and the public. Still, it has outperformed the legacy of all other boy books written by Mark Twain's contemporaries, including those produced by the next generation of authors such as Booth Tarkington's once-popular *Penrod* (1914), never yielding its place as the most dynamically vigorous and best of that subgenre. It succeeded in capturing as in a photograph an antebellum village that served pausing travelers on the major waterway of the United States. Human enslavement would be abolished, the gaps delineating social strata become more pronounced and consequential, naïve superstitions and home remedies give way to advances in medical science, political and financial corruption (in Mark Twain's opinion) increase drastically following a calamitous Civil War, racial segregation scar the society, railroads render the gaudy steamboats obsolete relics, telegraph wires transform the nation by uniting it, the American South pay a long-lasting price for seceding from the government formed by the American Revolution, and streetcars, streetlights, and (within the lifetime of Mark Twain) ubiquitous automobiles alter the appearance and pace of formerly sleepy towns. The society etched forever in *The Adventures of Tom Sawyer* should be, as it is, condemned for its practice of enslavement, but Mark Twain wanted to evoke eternal and universal emotions—the delights and fears, the victories and disappointments that are inescapable in childhood. He reached across the intervening decade since the American Civil War to remind his readers that some things stay the same; only the surroundings shift around us in swiftly modifying configurations.

Tom Sawyer Tomorrow

What does the future hold for Mark Twain's first boy book? If the past is any indication, academic scholars and critics are not likely to warm up to *Tom Sawyer*. As the nation becomes ever more urban and less rural (even the creek that ran behind Mark Twain's Hartford house that once had ducks swimming on it has been sealed off and covered over), it seems probable though lamentable that readers, especially younger ones, will have greater and greater trouble entering an imaginary world in which children swarm from small clapboard houses, their slates in tow, and walk to classes held in a wooden schoolhouse presided over by a single tyrannical teacher. Impressions of the surrounding forest, meadow, river, and other natural scenery will likewise grow dimmer and harder to picture. The shape of Cardiff Hill will be difficult to conjure up. What will endure are the many passages reproducing the joys and pains of living under the supervision of others and having relatively little notion of what lies ahead in one's life. That perennial dilemma of the adolescent is likely to prove durable enough to preserve this fast-paced, hard-to-categorize, pioneering little novel in the unpredictable, technologically chaotic world that lies ahead.

Works Cited

Bray, Robert. "*Tom Sawyer* Once and for All," *Review*, vol. 3, 1981, pp. 75–93.

Csicsila, Joseph. *Canons by Consensus: Critical Trends and American Literature Anthologies*. U of Alabama P, 2004.

Fischer, Victor, and Michael B. Frank, editors. *Mark Twain's Letters*. Vol. 3, 1869. U of California P, 1992.

Gribben, Alan. *Mark Twain's Literary Resources: A Reconstruction of His Library and Reading*. Two Vols., NewSouth Books, 2019, 2022.

Moore, Olin H. "Mark Twain and Don Quixote." *PMLA*, vol. 37, no. 2, June 1922, pp. 3,234–346.

Rubin, Louis D., Jr. "Mark Twain: *The Adventures of Tom Sawyer*," *Landmarks of American Writing*. Edited by Henning Cohen, Basic Books, 1969, pp. 157–71.

Seelye, John. *The True Adventures of Huckleberry Finn*. Northwestern UP, 1970.

Steinbrink, Jeffrey. "Who Shot Tom Sawyer?" *American Literary Realism*, vol. 35, no. 1, Fall 2002, pp. 29–38.

Thinking Like Jackson's Island; Or, Why *Tom Sawyer* Is Good for the Environment

Joe B. Fulton

Deeming himself "a forsaken, friendless boy," Tom Sawyer summons his friends Joe Harper and Huck Finn to join him in escaping to Jackson's Island, an uninhabited locale free from preachers, teachers, aunts, and other such pests. In chapter 13 of *The Adventures of Tom Sawyer*, Mark Twain's narrator describes how the boys commandeer a log raft and cross the "mighty river" in the "starlight." The chapters that follow, with the boys cavorting and frolicking on the island, surviving on turtle eggs they dig up and fish they catch, are some of the most memorable in the book and help to explain why generations of readers return to *Tom Sawyer*.

Readers praise the language of the book, the famed whitewashing scene, the hunt for treasure, and the village shenanigans of the young characters—and rightly so— but these are surely not the only reasons readers have delighted in the book. They also delight in the book because of the natural world that is so much a part of the setting; the action that takes place in that world is the life readers collectively long for. In her study of nostalgia in nineteenth-century literature, Jennifer Ladino has analyzed the American preoccupation with "nostalgia that takes nature as its object of longing," noting the

THE PIRATES' EGG MARKET.

Fig. 1. Collecting turtle eggs to eat is one way the "pirates" live off nature. True Williams, *Tom Sawyer*, 1876, p. 135.
[Public domain.]

etymology of the word as homesickness (Ladino 8). The delight readers take in *Tom Sawyer* has much to do with homesickness for childhood freedom, and Twain knew this. After all, he announces in the book's preface that he hoped "to pleasantly remind adults of what they once were themselves." But the book also works because of the nostalgia adult readers feel for the natural world and the close relationship children have with it. By drawing on these feelings, *Tom Sawyer* helps revitalize perceptions of the natural world and, in so doing, of the civilized world. Twain shows characters engaging in a close and humble relationship with Nature, gaining not only delight in the natural world but also a cleansed attitude toward human nature.

The Nature of Twain's Realism

Many have argued over the years about the nature of Twain's realism, with most writers concluding that if Twain was a realist, he was not a realist of the Henry James or W. D. Howells stripe, both of whom very publicly participated in what has been called "the realism war." Realism, as an aesthetic movement, arose in mid-nineteenth-century America partly as a response to the excesses of Romanticism. In *Criticism and Fiction*, Howells called for the truthful treatment of material, depicting people "as they are" (Howells 328). Twain's realism does include this, along with quite a bit of caricature at times, but more important is the nature of his realism, or the nature in it. Laurence Buell in *The Future of Environmental Criticism: Environmental Crisis and Literary Imagination* rejects the notion of "a one-to-one correspondence between text and world," advocating instead "a certain kind of environmental referentiality as part of the overall work of the text" (Buell 32). An ecocritical reading of *Tom Sawyer*, one that pays attention to the role of the environment in the book, reveals that Twain's novel does present "dense, accurate representations of actual natural environments," and Nature plays a vital, active role in many of its major scenes, conflicts, and interactions among characters (Buell 40). One critic, Barbara Eckstein, has faulted Twain, contending that the boys in *Tom Sawyer* "are not curious about other species" and the book as a whole embodies a shallow response to the natural world (Eckstein 23). Such a reading ignores the pervasive role of Nature both as a source of delight for the characters as well as a force that changes perceptions.

Indeed, such mischaracterizations of the book are easily dispelled by considering only one class of references: the many entomological features of the story. Consider, for example, the dramatic role played by the pinch-bug during the church service that turns the dog into a "wooly comet" (chapter 5). A tick becomes an object of admiration in the school scene in chapter 7, where Tom and Joe Harper share a kind of joint custody of the creature. Interestingly, Huckleberry Finn himself had traded the tick to Tom in the previous chapter, placing a high valuation on it because it is "a pretty early tick, I reckon." Huckleberry, whose name shows his bond to the landscape, rejects Tom's assertion that "I could have a thousand of 'em if I wanted to," by pointing out it was simply too early in the season for ticks. While this might seem like a small point, it illustrates that both boys know the truth about the tick, that it is an "early" tick, and they know that fact the only way one can know it, by knowing their landscape thoroughly. In chapter 8, Tom consults a doodle-bug, often called an ant lion, to find the location of a lost marble. Readers chuckle at his superstition but should also take note that he demonstrably knows the habits of doodle-bugs and how they kick dirt out of their conical dens. One memorable paragraph in chapter 14 features an inchworm, a ladybug, and a "procession of ants." *Tom Sawyer* is not the work of a naturalist, let alone an entomologist, but it is the work of a writer who knew the smallest details of the landscape and felt they were important enough to include in his best work. *Tom Sawyer* is a work in which Nature is central to the world the characters inhabit; moreover, it is a work that reminds adult readers what Nature once gave them as children and what good it may still do them.

Thinking Like Jackson's Island

The Jackson Island chapters as well as those involving McDougal's Cave foreground the question of what a person's relationship to the natural world and each other should be. One of the main points made about Jackson's Island early on is that, while it might bear the name of a person, no one lives there. "It was not inhabited," the narrator declares, and then proceeds to observe that even on the further shore loomed a "dense and almost wholly unpeopled forest" (chapter 13). Later in the chapter, these characterizations are repeated, where the landscape is described as "the virgin forest of an unexplored and uninhabited island, far from the haunts of men." The language describing the forest promotes a particular kind of attitude readers ought to have toward it, and by extension to all of the earth, for Twain characterizes the surrounding land as a "forest temple," intimating that a worshipful attitude would be appropriate.

Shifting away from the usual human ways of looking at a landscape requires a particular kind of attitude change, declares Aldo Leopold in *A Sand County Almanac*. Leopold's chapter "Thinking Like a Mountain" introduces the idea that natural sites and systems contain logic not obvious to the casual observer. He uses the example of hunters recklessly shooting wolves, thinking that such actions will increase the deer population. In fact, by removing predators and increasing prey population, deer soon denude the mountain to the last blade of grass, leaving the deer to starve. In such a world "lies a deeper meaning, known only to the mountain itself" (Leopold 114). Leopold provides examples of the hubris of those, often motivated by safety and certainty, who fail to think like a mountain and so destroy the land they rely on and profess to love, while "only a mountain has lived long enough to listen objectively to the howl of a wolf" (Leopold 114). What Leopold is calling for is essentially a change in perception from one that looks *at* the landscape to one that looks from *within* it.

Such a transformational change in perspective occurs on Jackson's Island in chapter 14, with Tom slowly awakening in the "cool gray dawn" as the "marvel of Nature shaking off sleep and going to work unfolded itself" before him. The word choice "unfolded" is important, for the idea of an event "unfolding" before Tom is at other points in the book somewhat alien to his personality. Rather than letting events unfold, Tom usually takes the lead in whatever events he participates in. What he is getting from Nature is a change in vision to one of humility. An early ecocritic, Lynn White, famously argued that St. Francis of Assisi preached the "virtue of humility—not merely for the individual but for man as a species" (White 1206). Readers see a humble Tom on the island. Ordinarily a person who makes things happen, here he is described as "musing" as he allows Nature to materialize in all of its glory large and small. The inchworm is one example, for the narrator states that "the worm approached him of its own accord" and Tom reacts by becoming "still as a stone," at that point becoming one with the landscape. To St. Francis's "Brother Ant" one might add Tom's "Brother Inchworm."

Fig. 2. When Tom awakens on the island in chapter 14, he senses "a delicious sense of repose and peace in the deep pervading calm and silence of the woods. Not a leaf stirred; not a sound obtruded upon great Nature's meditation." True Williams, *Tom Sawyer*, 1876, p. 121. [Public domain.]

In *The Reign of Wonder: Naivety and Reality in American Literature,* Tony Tanner has contrasted this scene on Jackson's Island with Huck's first-person description of a similar scene in chapter 19 of *Adventures of Huckleberry Finn.* "Clemens could never have achieved such a vibrant, alive, and luminously rendered verbal reincarnation of the seen-world without looking through Huck's eye," he argues, citing *Tom Sawyer* as proof, which he criticizes as "a book about youth, but not a book by a youth" (Tanner 122). There is no need to quarrel with Tanner here, or with Huck, for that matter; *Tom Sawyer* has a third-person narrator, and *Huckleberry Finn* has a first-person narrator. The insinuation, though, that the narrator is out of place in *Tom Sawyer* rather misses the point about the important role the adult perspective offers. Nineteenth-century American Realism included attentiveness to the natural world because, increasingly, writers were becoming aware that the world they were describing was disappearing, not just the way it always had, with the cycles of death and birth in populations and landscapes, but with the flora and fauna of the land disappearing, too. Examples of such early environmental concern from the nineteenth century include James Fenimore Cooper's *The Pioneers*, T. B. Thorpe's "The Big Bear of Arkansas," and Sarah Orne Jewett's "The White Heron." Twain saw the changes in the environment, too, and wrote about them with his many comments about the "tamed" Mississippi that had succumbed to levies and dredging. The stories based on his youth in the small town on the Mississippi River represented nostalgia for his childhood but also nostalgia for a lost world, the so-called "new world" that, like him, had grown older and not always gracefully. Twain's narrator, older than his protagonist, plays an important role in making *Tom Sawyer* not just a good book, but a great one. The book is fundamentally about remembering a younger America and about having a closer relationship to the natural world.

Nature's Power

One might argue that it is really the adult narrator that makes this book so environmentally insightful. In his book *The Environmental Imagination: Thoreau, Nature Writing, and the Formation of American Culture*, Buell identifies one trait of environmental literature as the *"sense of the environment as a process rather than as a constant or a given"* (Buell 8). This is certainly true of these scenes on Jackson's Island, as well as everything Twain wrote with the Mississippi River in it. Twain spends much time in this scene describing the process by which Tom becomes part of the landscape and begins thinking like an island. But Twain's art is part of this process, too. He makes the point that a gray squirrel and a fox squirrel come to "inspect and chatter at the boys" because "the wild things had probably never seen a human being before and scarcely knew whether to be afraid or not" (chapter 14). The boys, and Twain the writer himself, however, are more like the cat-bird that is described as producing "imitations of her neighbors in a rapture of enjoyment." That is part of the realism of Nature in Twain's writing, as he is imitating, reproducing in some sense a scene in the natural world, but unlike the squirrels, these are not things he is seeing for the first time. The same is true of the boys. They experience on the island things they have experienced before; yet somehow, it is all fresh and new as Nature is a process one can see unfolding. This is the essential attribute of realism, that it does not deal with the unusual, the extraordinary, the otherworldly, but draws attention back to what readers have already seen but perhaps have not noticed.

One line in chapter 14 stands out in this regard. As the boys explore the island, the narrator states that "they found plenty of things to be delighted with but nothing to be astonished at." Tom and the boys see nothing new, nothing to astonish them that would be the stuff of a romantic story: no volcanoes erupt, no tigers crouch ready to leap, no cannibals play their drums preparing for a feast on the shore. Indeed, asked to describe what actually happens in this chapter, one would be forced to say, not much. But that is the nature of Twain's realism here, the focus on the natural world as an important part of what the book is about, as the text pays attention to the songs of birds, the chattering of squirrels, and the activities of inchworms and ants. The book makes that point so well, in part, because it emphasizes the recognition that the characters and readers have seen this world before and consequently are not astonished but delighted. Being part of that history, literally having a history with the landscape, the narrator, like Tom, revels in the landscape, delights in it. But he is not astonished by it, for he has been there before.

Moreover, the island's power to delight relates to the readers' recognition that Nature is always new and full of delight. Readers may not be astonished by something exotic in this book, but the newness here is the type that is the result of constant creation. That creation is powerful, as wild as the natural process readers see always at play in the book. The island setting is both a place set apart from civilization and a place that is being constantly created by the elements. The Mississippi River, not a tame river at this point, is the God of creation and destruction in the story. Jackson's Island lives and dies and changes according to the natural processes of water and geology. As Twain put it in *Life on the Mississippi*, the river is "always changing its habitat bodily," constantly recreating itself (chapter 1). While the boys are on the island, they experience other natural forces, even experiencing the terror a thunderstorm creates for those exposed to the elements. Nature awes them by its sheer power.

Twain spends a great deal of time describing the process of the thunderstorm. Climate activist Bill McKibben's claim in *The End of Nature* might be extreme, but it is sobering: "By changing the weather, we make every spot on earth man-made and artificial. We have deprived Nature of its independence, and that is fatal to its meaning. Nature's independence *is* its meaning; without it there is nothing but us" (McKibben 58). Indeed, in an era where global warming has become an issue of global concern, it is impossible to have quite the same reaction to the comment, sometimes attributed to Twain, that everybody talks about the weather, but nobody ever does anything about it. Humans obviously have done something about the weather, and it has not been good. Yet, what the boys experience in the thunderstorm scene in chapter 16 is awe at the independence of Nature. Twain provides the same attention to detail as in the morning scene, but present, too, is the humility in a more profound way. The boys on the island experience the process of the thunderstorm, from the gradual approach of a "quivering glow that vaguely revealed the foliage for a moment" to the "sweep of chilly air" and the arrival of "roaring wind and the booming thunder-blasts" that "drowned their voices utterly." The details of the storm's process, that is, Twain's attention to the details of this natural phenomenon, show the power of Nature and also its power to inspire awe and art. The boys survive the "wild night" and regroup around the fire, where they "expanded and glorified" their adventure in each retelling. Two aspects of this scene seem preeminently important: the amount of space Twain lavishes on describing the realistic particulars of the storm and the boys' reaction to their experience of it. These attributes of the book promote a particular point of view about what a person's relation to the natural world ought to be: awe, humility, and delight. As the boys tell and retell the story, readers witness the creation of a realistic art.

Natural Perception

Participating in that constant newness of Nature and recognizing its importance is how Twain shows us to think like a river or to think like Jackson's Island in *Tom Sawyer*. Tom's reaction to the place illustrates the perception necessary to appreciate Nature. One thinks of the nineteenth century environmental writer John Burroughs, who said, "I do not propose to attempt to tell my reader how to see things, but only to talk about the art of seeing things, as one might talk of any other art" (Burroughs 146). Such a change in perception should not imply that people must leave no trace at all, that Nature is something that happens to humans, as in the storm, and that humans do not happen to it. Indeed, the boys in Twain's novel participate in the storm by telling of it and readers participate by reading of it. Later, readers see the boys leaving a trace, one might say, as Tom, Huck, and Joe enjoy a "famous" feast of fried turtle eggs on two occasions (chapter 16). What the change in perception does mean is meeting Nature on its own terms, with humility and wonder at its power. Watch the inchworm. Listen to the birds. Experience the storms. Let "Nature," capitalized by Twain in several places in these chapters, unfold before us and transform us.

At the same time, Twain's realism in *Tom Sawyer* has much in common with the work of earlier nature writers like Henry David Thoreau or later ones like Aldo Leopold. One might consider the ways in which Twain's realism involved Nature itself as a touchstone for every aspect of the life his characters lead. The nature of realism in Tom Sawyer is as much Thoreauvian or Leopoldian as it is Howellsian or Jamesian, particularly in its focus on perception. In his chapter "Conservation Esthetic," Leopold talks about the importance of "a search for perception" and of "building receptivity in the still unlovely human mind" (Leopold 150–51). The new receptivity aims at nothing less than the regeneration of the adult human mind, to re-create while engaging in recreation in the natural world, so that one might think like a river, think like an island, and adopt the "land ethic" that considers "what is ethically and esthetically right, as well as what is economically expedient. A thing is right when it tends to preserve the integrity, stability, and beauty of the biotic community. It is wrong when it tends otherwise" (Leopold 188). The shift in perception that *Tom Sawyer* illustrates with its protagonist and fosters for its readers relates to the "usefulness" Howells describes in *Criticism and Fiction* (1891): "Let fiction cease to lie about life . . . let it speak the dialect, the language, that most Americans know—the language of unaffected people everywhere—and there can be no doubt of an unlimited future, not only of delightfulness but of usefulness, for it" (Howells 328). The "delightfulness" he references is an interesting point because Howells spends a great deal of time talking about aesthetic delight and how it can be useful. Twain's realism in *Tom Sawyer* involves delighting in a world readers remember, so while they may not be astonished by it, they are engaged by it, and drawn into its world. When Howells spoke of the ethical attributes of realistic fiction that make it useful, he may not have been thinking about ethical interactions with the environment. That, however, is exactly what ecocriticism does when analyzing works like *Tom Sawyer*. Twain's idea of usefulness is hidden in plain sight, for it is taking notice of and delighting in the simple, natural facts of the world, and in doing so changing perceptions of the world.

Wild by Nature

The change in perception *Tom Sawyer* fosters is not just toward Nature, but also toward human nature. Just as Twain presents readers with an uncharacteristically humble version of Tom on Jackson's Island, many of the book's scenes imply that an appreciation for the natural world fosters a greater humility in appraising human nature, too. When the boys leave the island and return to town, they attend their own funeral. In his funeral sermon for the boys, the pastor tells only the good things about them. In fact, he seemingly portrays them as the town's most promising young people, despite the fact that earlier the townspeople had a very low opinion of their behavior. Twain's irony in the scene indicates that perhaps children should be viewed more realistically—as neither reprobates nor paragons of virtue, but as kids.

When the minister exhorts the congregation, "Praise God from whom all blessings Flow–Sing!—and put your hearts in it!" he knows they know the Doxology because they sing it every Sunday. He also knows they know its second line: "Praise Him all creatures here below." Mixing talk about God and talk about "creatures" is by no means an isolated moment in the story. Another scene suggesting a change toward a more realistic assessment of people based on human nature as naturally wild, as "creatures," occurs when the Widow Douglas asserts that Huck "has good spots in him" because "that's the Lord's mark. He don't leave it off. He never does. Puts it somewhere on every creature that comes from His hands" (chapter 30). This relates even more directly to the idea that all people are creatures, yet all have good spots. Twain consistently depicts human nature as neither all good nor all bad, and this fact argues that an attitude of humility toward one's fellow human beings is as important as having a humble attitude toward ticks, doodlebugs, and inchworms.

An important change in perception toward the character Injun Joe takes place when Tom mourns his death, a dramatic change in perception provoked by a shared experience of the natural world. Joe is, of course, a dangerous person in the story. He kills Dr. Robinson in the graveyard in chapter 23. After Tom testifies that Joe killed Dr. Robinson, Joe escapes punishment. Tom is then naturally fearful, for the felon has a grudge against him and reason to target him. At the same time, Joe is the stock villain of the story and is characterized in negative and even racist ways that implicate the attitudes of the village of St. Petersburg. Joe is referred to as a "hapless half-breed," for instance, who is not just a murderer but is inherently murderous because of *who* he is, because of his "Indian blood," as Osage Indian poet and critic Carter Revard has argued, who also takes exception to the very name "Injun Joe" (Revard 645). The point is that the character in the book has done things that justify fear, but the social attitudes in St. Petersburg toward Joe were demeaning and racist to begin with; Tom, therefore, has no reason at all to mourn the death of this person. But he does. When Tom and Becky are lost in the cave, Tom is disturbed to discover that Joe is also in the cave.

Like the thunderstorm scene, the scene in the cave is one that highlights the power of Nature to instill humility. Twain's narrator describes McDougal's Cave as "walled by Nature with solid limestone" (chapter 29). As for the independence of Nature, readers are assured that "no man 'knew' the cave. That was an impossible thing" (chapter 29). Like what the boys experience on the island, Tom and Becky see the "familiar wonders" of the cave, a slightly different way of saying that the children in the cave found, as the boys did on the island, "much to delight in but nothing to be astonished at." After all, what is the natural world but a collection of "familiar wonders"? Familiar or not, the cave, like the storm on the island, is dangerous. Despite its familiarity, despite the names smoked on its walls with candles, it remains independent, nonhuman, and threatening. Just as Jackson's Island has a name but no owner, the cave has a name and its walls are festooned with the names of those who have visited, but it has no owner. No one can claim to "know" the cave.

The cave's danger is not relieved by Tom and Becky's escaping from it, for when Tom discovers that Judge Thatcher has sealed the door to the cave, he instantly sounds the alarm that Joe has been locked in the cave. They arrive too late, finding his body by the door. In the scene that follows, Twain's narrator describes many responses to "Injun Joe," from those who, before his death, had ignored his crimes and tearfully petitioned the governor for his pardon, to those on the other extreme who celebrate his death, confessing "they had had almost as satisfactory a time at the funeral as they could have had at the hanging" (chapter 33). The narrator tells us that Tom felt a great sense of relief knowing that Joe was dead, yet "Tom was touched, for he knew by his own experience how this wretch had suffered" (chapter 33). Tom's reaction is striking. He is the only character who sees Joe for who he really was, both a very dangerous person and also a fellow human being. It is a remarkable moment of humanity in the book.

However strange it might seem, the reason Tom can empathize with a man who sought to kill him is that he experienced the cave as Joe did. The change in perception is provoked by their shared experience as vulnerable human beings living in a dangerous environment in which they could easily die. Tom and Becky believe that they will die in the cave, and Joe does actually die. Readers are told that no one knew the cave, but it is also true that the cave does not know—or care about—the people who enter it. Far from it. In a lengthy passage reflecting on Joe's death, the narrator refers to many points in human history, including references to the ancient pyramids, Christ, the American Revolution, only to observe that the slow drip of water from a stalactite "will still be falling when all these things shall have sunk down the afternoon of history and the twilight of tradition" (chapter 33). "Did this drop fall patiently during five thousand years to be ready for this flitting human insect's need?" the narrator asks. The larger point of the scene is that *all* people are flitting human insects compared to the cave's geological time. Whether one is the village scamp, the daughter of a judge, or a murderer seeking a safe hideout, it is all one to the cave. Thinking like McDougal's Cave means realizing insignificance in relation to the forces of Nature, and that change in perception brings people together. That experience can change the perceptions and ideas people inherit from civilization. Because he himself has been trapped in the cave, Tom experiences not only humility toward the natural world but also toward another human being. Perhaps the most important lesson Nature teaches Tom involves shared humanity. Tom sees that "Injun Joe," saddled with a racist epithet in his name, characterized throughout as an outcast and a half-breed, has the good spots the Widow Douglas sees in Huck.

Tom Sawyer is nothing if not a hopeful book. The boys return from the island to find that the villagers have a more realistic and more charitable assessment of their worth, Tom and Becky get out of the cave safely, and Tom is freed from worrying about Injun Joe's vengeance and has a more realistic and charitable assessment of Joe's worth. The story argues that immersing oneself in the natural world creates a greater appreciation not just for the earth, but for fellow human beings. Tom provides a model for what a change in perception toward Nature and human nature can accomplish. That is what it means to think like the Mississippi River, to think like Jackson's Island, or even to think like McDougal's Cave. That is why generations of readers return to the book, and that is why the book is good for them—and just possibly why *Tom Sawyer* is good for the environment.

Works Cited

Buell, Lawrence. *The Environmental Imagination: Thoreau, Nature Writing, and the Formation of American Culture*. Harvard UP, 1995.

_____. *The Future of Environmental Criticism: Environmental Crisis and Literary Imagination*. Blackwell, 2005.

Burroughs, John. "The Art of Seeing Things." *American Earth: Environmental Writing Since Thoreau*. Edited by Bill McKibben, Library of America, 2008, pp. 146–59.

Eckstein, Barbara. "Child's Play: Nature-Deficit Disorder and Mark Twain's Mississippi River Youth." *American Literary History*, vol. 24, no. 1, 2012, pp. 16–33.

Howells, William Dean. *Criticism and Fiction. Selected Literary Criticism*. Vol. 2, *1886–1897*. Indiana UP, 1993.

Ladino, Jennifer K. *Reclaiming Nostalgia: Longing for Nature in American Literature*. U of Virginia P, 2012.

Leopold, Aldo. *A Sand County Almanac and Other Writings on Ecology and Conservation*. Library of America, 2013.

McKibben, Bill. *The End of Nature*. Random House, 1989.

Revard, Carter. "Why Mark Twain Murdered Injun Joe—and Will Never Be Indicted." *Massachusetts Review*, vol. 40, no. 4, Winter 2000, pp. 643–70.

Tanner, Tony. *The Reign of Wonder: Naivety and Reality in American Literature*. Cambridge UP, 1965.

White, Lynn. "The Historical Roots of Our Ecologic Crisis." *Science*, vol. 155, no. 3767, 1967, pp. 1203–207.

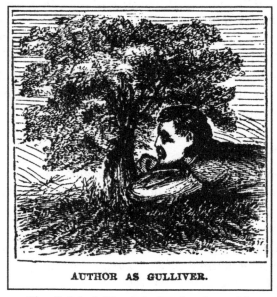

AUTHOR AS GULLIVER.

Fig. 3. Mark Twain's fascination with nature is also evident in *Roughing It*, which describes him lying before a sagebrush, studying insects and imagining them to be Liliputian birds and beasts and himself a giant Brobdingnagian.
True Williams, *Roughing It*, 1872, p. 33.
[Public domain.]

Tom Sawyer and Harry Potter: The Boys Who Live

Philip Bader

In 1876, Mark Twain introduced one of the most famous and beloved boys in world literary history in his novel *The Adventures of Tom Sawyer*. Nearly a century and a quarter later, in 1997, novice British author J. K. Rowling introduced a boy named Harry Potter in what would expand into a seven-novel series set in a world in which real magic exists. Since then, Rowling's young wizard has reigned unchallenged as the most famous boy in twenty-first-century literature, if not of all time. The iconic status of these two characters almost inevitably invites questions about possible connections between them.

Rowling herself has never publicly acknowledged a literary debt to Mark Twain or even hinted that Tom Sawyer may have helped inspire her Harry Potter novels. Significant parallels between the two boys, however, strongly suggest that connections between them may exist. Is it unreasonable to think that one beloved book might have contributed in at least a small way to the creation of another? And is it not possible that readers of both might discern connections that escape the notice of the books' creators?

Literary comparisons have been drawn between the Potter novels and works as varied as William Shakespeare's *Macbeth* (1606), T. H. White's *The Once and Future King* (1958), and even the novels of Jane Austen. Although Rowling may not have directly acknowledged the influence of such works, authors may be familiar with literary antecedents without consciously drawing on them for inspiration. Rowling has carefully avoided making explicit references to any of her literary influences, preferring instead to say that she has no idea "where my ideas come from, or how my imagination works" (Rowling, "Mr. Darcy" 4). Even if clear lines cannot be drawn between literary figures as famous as Tom Sawyer and Harry Potter, exploring the issue may place both in a new light.

Children's Stories and Adult Readers

Children love stories, particularly those featuring characters with whom they can easily identify. Stories provide important pathways for young people to understand the world in which they live and to develop empathy for others. They also help children escape to realms that they could not imagine on their own and give them templates—both good and bad—for the types of people they will become. The best stories pull young readers in so deeply that their fabricated reality feels as genuine as their readers' everyday lives and, in some ways, more meaningful. The hold such stories have on children might relax in later years as they mature, but it never disappears altogether.

Adults can be as enthralled with stories as children, not simply on the stories' individual merits or the worlds they depict, but often because of the memories they evoke of childhood years long past, or even worlds they would have loved to encounter themselves when they were children. Indeed, reminding adults of this enduring connection to stories seems to have been at least part of Mark Twain's motivation in writing *Tom Sawyer*. Admitting in its preface that he wrote the book mainly to entertain boys and girls, he hoped nonetheless that the story would serve as a reminder of what adults "once were themselves, and how they felt and thought and talked, and what queer enterprises they sometimes engaged in."

In 2001, more than a century after Twain wrote those words, film legend Charlton Heston made a similar but more oblique observation when he appeared at the American premiere of the much-anticipated film adaptation of *Harry Potter and the Sorcerer's Stone* (1998), the first of Rowling's seven books about the unassuming boy who discovers not only that he is a wizard but an extraordinarily powerful one. "Think of *Tom Sawyer*; think of *Treasure Island*," Heston told the *Hollywood Reporter*. "Any story involving a major character that's a boy is going to be pretty good" (Kit, "Harry" 10). On the surface, in connecting Tom Sawyer with Harry Potter, Heston could not have selected two more different boys to make his point. Tom Sawyer exists as something of an everyman, or "everyboy," figure who stands in for his author as a guide through a distinct time and place in American history that most readers, young and old, find familiar. Harry, in contrast, is an epic figure, whose seeming ordinariness masks a much more exalted role in both magical and non-magical worlds. In fact, the fates of both those worlds eventually rest squarely on his shoulders.

Despite obvious differences in their characters and circumstances, Tom and Harry have managed to capture the imaginations of generations of readers of all ages across the world in ways that few other literary figures have. When Southern California's Disneyland opened in 1956, it unveiled an attraction personally designed by Walt Disney himself—"Tom Sawyer's Island." Visitors reached the island on canoes and rafts, and there they explored Injun Joe's Cave, Tom's Landing, and Smuggler's Cove. Disney loved Mark Twain's novels and wanted to pay homage to the fictional world surrounding Tom Sawyer and Huckleberry Finn in a place guaranteed to make an indelible mark—the very heart of what he called the "Happiest Place on Earth." In 2007, the island underwent renovations. After the success of Disney's *Pirates of the Caribbean* films, it was renamed "Pirate's Lair on Tom Sawyer's Island" but has still retained some of its original charms.

At the Universal Studio parks in both Southern California and Florida, visitors can experience "The Wizarding World of Harry Potter." Its attractions recreate key locations from Rowling's novels, including Diagon Alley, Hogwarts Castle, and the village of Hogsmeade. Children and adults alike can pretend to cast spells with special wands that interact with stations located throughout the park. In Hogsmeade, for example, one can visit the Three Broomsticks and enjoy food and beverages that characters consume in the Potter novels, such as butterbeer and pumpkin juice. These attractions provide fully immersive experiences for Potter fans by bringing the imaginative sights, sounds, and even tastes of Rowling's magical world to life. The worlds that Twain and Rowling create have a gravitational pull that affects both children and adults, much as the novels do. The books clearly depict places that are both familiar and fantastical—worlds recognizable as parts of the natural landscapes of real lives that still offer escapes to very different realms.

Twain and Rowling are not unique in this respect. Other authors have created similarly compelling imaginative worlds. C. S. Lewis's *The Chronicles of Narnia* series and J. R. R. Tolkien's *The Hobbit* (1937) and *Lord of the Rings* (1954–55) trilogy are among the most famous examples. More recent works include the *His Dark Materials* series by Philip Pullman, who holds the distinction of being the only author of so-called children's or young-adult literature who has been long-listed for the prestigious Booker Prize for Fiction. Like C. S. Lewis before him, Pullman does not differentiate between children's and other types of literature. "There must be some sort of continuity here," he said, "surely we should all be interested in books for every age, since our experience includes them all" (Pullman 114).

Literature—High and Low

Although *Tom Sawyer* was neither Twain's first bestseller nor the most popular book he published during his lifetime, it eventually became his best-known and most-beloved work of fiction, and it has never gone out of print. It did, however, find an uneven reception during its early years. In 1865, after he had published some of his earliest sketches, he wrote a letter to his family in which he acknowledged having a "'call' to literature of a low order—*i.e.,* humorous" (Branch 322). *Tom Sawyer* first appeared in an English edition in mid-1876, and some early British critics seemed to agree with that assessment. One unsigned review, for example, suggested that Twain's literary range "does not extend beyond the sporting newspapers, the Racing Calendar, and the 'Diseases of Dogs'" (Welland 99).

The subsequent popularity of *Tom Sawyer* in the decades following Twain's 1910 death has demonstrated clearly enough that he was, in fact, capable of a much higher order of literature, and that he could enthrall and entertain readers of any age. Part of that success might be attributed to the growing popularity of a literary genre that came to be known as "boy books." This "curious stepchild of American fiction" (Gribben 127) is thought to have originated in America with the publication of Thomas Bailey Aldrich's *Story of a Bad Boy* in 1870. Boy books, sometimes called "bad boy books," are generally episodic in nature, semi-autobiographical, and represent "a conscious reaction against the sentimental and pious child literature" (Trensky 505). It is interesting to note that while *Tom Sawyer* owes a debt to Aldrich, Twain had earlier anticipated this genre with his publication of "The Story of the Bad Little Boy" in 1865 and "The Story of the Good Little Boy" five years later (Trensky 506).

Aldrich's novel was a literary successor to a still earlier work written in the tradition of British boarding school fiction. *Tom Brown's Schooldays* by Thomas Hughes enjoyed immense popularity in both Great Britain and America after its publication in 1857 and may well have inspired Aldrich's *Story of a Bad Boy* (Gribben 128). Hughes's novel recounts the coming of age of its titular hero, from his childhood in rural Berkshire to his education at Rugby School, one of England's oldest and most prestigious public academies. There, he excels at sport, overcomes the brutal bullying of Harry Flashman, and acquires the courage and understanding to become an effective leader. Just as Hughes's novel influenced the work of Aldrich and Twain, it also has obvious parallels to the Harry Potter novels, all of which are set mostly in or near Hogwarts School of Witchcraft and Wizardry, one of the magical realm's most elite boarding schools. Settings in boarding school fiction play a crucial role in shaping the destiny of the heroes of these stories.

Both Hughes's Tom Brown and Rowling's Harry Potter benefit from friendships they forge at their schools under the attentive mentorships of wise and benevolent headmasters. Each boy excels in sports—Tom in rugby, and Harry in Quidditch, the delightfully quirky game in which players compete on flying broomsticks. In an annotation Rowling wrote in a rare first edition of *Sorcerer's Stone* in 2013, she revealed she had invented the sport after "pondering the things that hold a society together, cause it to congregate and signify its particular character and knew I needed a sport" ("J. K. Rowling"). In *Tom Sawyer*, Tom and his comrades do not play sports in any conventional sense but are nevertheless bound together in the way Rowling describes by their imaginative Robin Hood adventures in Sherwood Forest and high seas as adventurers as fearsome pirates. Though clearly influenced by boarding school literature, Rowling transforms the genre in several important ways. She makes Hogwarts accessible to both male and female students, without regard for wealth, class, or ethnicity. Instead, admission to Hogwarts is based primarily on merit. Rowling also addresses subjects far weightier than those commonly found in her literary antecedents, such as the enslavement of elves, racism, and blood-purity myths–all of which are frequently recurrent themes in the Potter novels.

Fellow Adventurers

One might not immediately see direct connections between either *Tom Sawyer* and the Harry Potter novels or between their eponymous heroes. A brief sidebar in R. Kent Rasmussen's *Mark Twain for Kids* offers useful insights. Rasmussen points out that Tom and Harry are both around eleven years of age when their stories begin, although Tom's exact age is uncertain. Both boys are also orphans being raised by maternal aunts, and their home lives are often disturbed by the cruelty and meddling of other family members. Tom has an insufferable half-brother named Sid. While not at Hogwarts, Harry is frequently tormented by his spoiled and bullying cousin Dudley. Tom and Harry are both outwardly ordinary in nearly every respect. What makes Harry extraordinary emerges when he learns of his deep connection to a magical realm that was previous unknown to him. Tom experiences a broadly similar elevation in stature by transforming his humble surroundings through the power of his imagination. Further, both boys share adventures with boy and girl companions, and each is as capable of mischief as of courage. Finally, both boys confront murderous villains in dark and dismal places. After testifying against Injun Joe for murdering Dr. Robinson and going through most of his book fearing retribution, Tom encounters Joe deep inside the pitch-black cave in which he and Becky are lost. Most of the Potter novels reach their climaxes in dark dungeons and other dismal places, where Harry has showdowns with the Dark Lord Voldemort (Rasmussen, *Mark Twain* 10).

Tom lives with his Aunt Polly, a kindly woman who is warm and loving despite her often stern demeanor. She loves Tom deeply and punishes him only reluctantly—sometimes, not at all—because she feels a duty to raise him right. "I'm laying up sin and suffering for us both, I know," she says. "He's full of the Old Scratch, but laws-a-me! he's my own dead sister's boy, poor thing, and I ain't got the heart to lash him, somehow" (chapter 1). In contrast, Harry lives with his Aunt Petunia Dursley and her husband Vernon. Petunia's ambivalence about Harry's welfare is matched only by her indulgence of her spoiled son Dudley's every whim. She turns a blind eye to Dudley's physical and emotional abuse of Harry and makes only minimal efforts to look after Harry's welfare. Though wildly different in most respects, these guardians of the boys share one interesting similarity. Each has no use for the imagination and sense of adventure enlivening the boy in her care. Polly, for example, is more interested in seeing Tom excel in school, say his prayers, and grow up to be respectable. The Dursleys want nothing to do with Harry's magical life—a point driven home in the opening lines of the first Potter book: "Mr. and Mrs. Dursley, of number four, Privet Drive, were proud to say that they were perfectly normal, thank you very much. They were the last people one would expect to be involved in anything strange or mysterious, because they just did not hold with such nonsense" (Rowling, *Sorcerer's Stone* 1). The Dursleys take their fetish for normalcy a step further. They forbid all mention of Harry's life at Hogwarts or his parents. Harry's dead mother and Petunia's sister, Lily, had embarrassed the family by being a talented witch and by marrying gifted wizard James Potter. In the second novel in the series, *Harry Potter and the Chamber of Secrets* (1998), Harry's casual use of the phrase "say the magic word" as a euphemism for "say please" sends his uncle into an apoplectic rage. Harry's connection to the magical world is an abnormality that must never be mentioned, even metaphorically.

Tom's half-brother Sid and Harry's cousin Dudley both appear to the adults around them to be good, when, in fact, they are quite the opposite. *Tom Sawyer* describes Sid as "a quiet boy" who had "no adventurous, troublesome ways" (chapter 1). Sid enjoys Sunday school, says his prayers each night, and does his chores and schoolwork diligently. In many ways Sid is a "model boy" in the eyes of St. Petersburg's adult residents. His private behavior, however, is driven largely by pettiness and jealousy over the fact that Tom frequently escapes the punishments Sid thinks he deserves. Dudley's attentions to Harry are marked more by physical violence. In *The Sorcerer's Stone*, for example, Harry endures routine beatings at the hands of the larger Dudley and his friends before he departs for Hogwarts. Harry's magical powers could make him unassailable, but he is prohibited from using them outside Hogwarts, leaving him an easy target for Dudley's aggression. On a few occasions, however, both Sid and Dudley show signs of sympathy and even caring in their treatment of Tom and Harry. Sid, for example, is visibly affected by Tom's apparent drowning in chapter 15 of *Tom Sawyer*. In *Order of the Phoenix*, Harry saves Dudley from a fate worse than death: the dementor's kiss, which leaves recipients in permanent states of soulless despair. In that book, several ghostly dementors, whose very presence removes all hope and joy from anyone nearby, attack the boys before Harry is due to leave for Hogwarts. The terrifying incident seems to soften Dudley's feelings about his cousin. When the two later part company for the last time in the final Potter book, they do so with a rather stiff but comradely handshake.

Both Tom and Harry also enjoy the companionship and support of close male and female friends who play important roles in their adventures. In the Potter books, a deep bond develops among Harry, Hermione Granger, and Ron Weasley. Each has unique strengths and weaknesses that dramatically affect the outcomes of key events. A fitting example comes in the closing chapters of *Sorcerer's Stone*. When Harry learns that the Hogwarts gamekeeper Hagrid might have inadvertently given away the secret of how the magical stone is protected, he and his companions act to secure it before it can be stolen. In doing so, they face challenges that play to each child's strengths, thereby enabling Harry to triumph over the villains opposing him.

Tom's relationships with Huck and Becky may lack the depth and substance that binds Harry, Ron, and Hermione, and the three never operate as a team. Nevertheless, Huck and Becky are with Tom during his most perilous moments. Huck is with Tom in the terrifying graveyard scene when the boys witness Injun Joe killing

Dr. Robinson and afterward provides a willing and sympathetic ear when Tom wrestles with his conscience over revealing the truth about who really killed the doctor (chapters 9–10). Toward the end of the novel, after learning of Joe's death in the cave, Huck returns with Tom to the cave to retrieve Joe's hidden treasure, despite his crippling fear of encountering the murderer's ghost (chapter 33). Becky also plays a role in Tom's development. Her character remains largely undeveloped throughout the novel, while she serves as the focus of Tom's romantic attention and occasionally inspires him to courageous acts most notably when Tom takes her punishment for tearing a page of their teacher's anatomy book in chapter 20. Moreover, Becky may also be said to serve as an important source of inspiration for the courage Tom displays in evading Injun Joe and ultimately finding a way safely out of McDougal's Cave in chapters 31 and 32.

Readers of the Potter stories may notice that some members of Ron Weasley's family might be equally at home in St. Petersburg and among Tom's compatriots. Ron himself shares Tom's thirst for glory. He envisions himself as captain of his house Quidditch team as well as Head Boy at Hogwarts. Like Tom, who is steeped in the lore of pirate adventures and Robin Hood stories, Ron has grown up reading thrilling adventure stories from his own world. Ron's older twin brothers, Fred and George, also share Tom's love for mischief and rule breaking. They are never happier than when they use magic to stir up innocent trouble. After the nefarious Ministry of Magic official Dolores Umbridge seizes control of Hogwarts in *Order of the Phoenix*, they exit the school in a spectacular fashion, leaving an enormous mess in their wake (chapter 29). They later move to London's Diagon Alley and open a magical joke shop.

Familiar and Fantastical Worlds

Tom Sawyer has long occupied a place in literature and in America's national consciousness that few other books have ever rivaled. Twain may well have conceived and written it merely "to excite the laughter of God's creatures," as he had said in his 1865 letter to his family (Branch 323). The novel, however, has evolved into something much more substantial. Twain displays an ability to penetrate "the child's mind with a much greater depth than preceding writers" (Hunter 433). In his introduction to the Oxford Mark Twain edition of *Tom Sawyer*, novelist E. L. Doctorow describes Tom as a boy conjured from the author's genius as "the carrier of our national soul" (Doctorow xxxii). A readers guide to the novel prepared by the National Endowment for the Arts' Big Read program described the novel's significance in even grander terms. *"The Adventures of Tom Sawyer* is not merely a literary classic. It is a part of the American imagination. More than any other work in our culture, it established America's vision of childhood" (Kipen). Since 1956, Twain's hometown of Hannibal has hosted a National Tom Sawyer Days festival that has featured Tom and Becky look-alike contests and fence-painting competitions. The town's festival now takes place on July 4, a clear indication of just how close to the national soul Twain's fictional hero resides.

Rowling's wizarding world may have not yet penetrated any nation's soul, but it has already permanently altered the cultural landscape of childhood for many young people. It has also had a dramatic effect on children's reading habits. Beginning with the fourth book in the series, *Harry Potter and the Goblet of Fire* (2000), bookstores, such as the Barnes and Noble chain, began hosting release parties for each new Potter book as it came out. Children and adults dressed up as favorite characters and waited eagerly in long lines on Friday nights for each new title to be released at the stroke of midnight. Much like Hannibal's National Tom Sawyer Days events, such parties had the air of festivals, replete with face paint, handmade costumes and crafts, food, games, and trivia contests (Amatulli). Children and more than a few adults gathered to discuss already published Potter books and share theories about where the new books might go. With their new books finally in hand after midnight, they then read together long into the morning. As the series progressed, and the books grew in word count, readers had ever more pages to read. *Harry Potter and the Order of the Phoenix*, for example, contains 257,000 words–three and a third times as many as in *Tom Sawyer*. The commercial success of the lengthy

Potter books has encouraged other publishers to increase the sizes of their own books for young readers significantly.

Part of what makes Tom's and Harry's fictional worlds so compelling for readers of all ages is that they remain so accessible. Tom's St. Petersburg, a sleepy riverside village in an era of American history to which few readers today have any direct connection or knowledge, is less a real location and more a background for readers' collective childhood memories. Against this backdrop, readers identify with a young and mischievous boy who finds creative ways to avoid his chores, brawls with other boys, leads imaginary armies in battle, and wants nothing more than to be a pirate or a "high-toned" robber. This is not a magical world in any conventional sense, though Twain imbues it with an otherworldly air. In chapter 58 of *Life on the Mississippi* (1883), he recalled the villages that lined the river as being "as tranquil and reposeful as dreamland," and as having "nothing this-worldly about it—nothing to hang a fire or a worry upon." The second chapter of *Tom Sawyer* says much the same thing about St. Petersburg as Tom emerges one fine Saturday morning "when the summer world was bright and fresh, brimming with life" and all was right with the world. "Cardiff Hill, beyond the village and above it, was green

MOTHER HOPKINS.

Fig. 1. If Huck Finn is to be believed, the sleepy village of St. Petersburg contains at least one witch, old mother Hopkins, who "witches" people when she looks at them "stiddy" and mumbles the Lord's Prayer backwards. True Williams, *Tom Sawyer*, 1876, p. 67. [Public domain.]

with vegetation and it lay just far enough away to seem a Delectable Land, dreamy, reposeful, and inviting." One suspects that nostalgia contributes as much to the portrait Twain paints as any concrete memory. He did, after all, once call *Tom Sawyer* "simply a hymn, put into prose form to give it a worldly air" (Paine 477).

Tom and Magic and Witchcraft

It is intriguing to consider what Tom Sawyer might make of Hogwarts, what grand schemes he might devise, and what mischief he might muster with the help of a real magic wand. Tom and Huck both have a deep and pervasive fascination with folk superstitions—some of them quite elaborate. The two boys conduct something of a Socratic dialogue on the question of whether a dead cat or spunk-water provides the most effective cure for warts (chapter 6). In fact, it is their testing of the dead cat hypothesis that lands them in the graveyard where they witness Dr. Robinson's bloody murder in chapter 9. The boys also believe unequivocally in the existence of witches, devils, and ghosts. Tom's faith in the mystical workings of an unseen world remains unshaken even in the face of incontrovertible evidence of the failure of a well-known incantation that promised to restore every marble he has ever lost in chapter 8. He chalks the failure up to the interference of a witch and uses another magical incantation to conjure a doodlebug to confirm his suspicion.

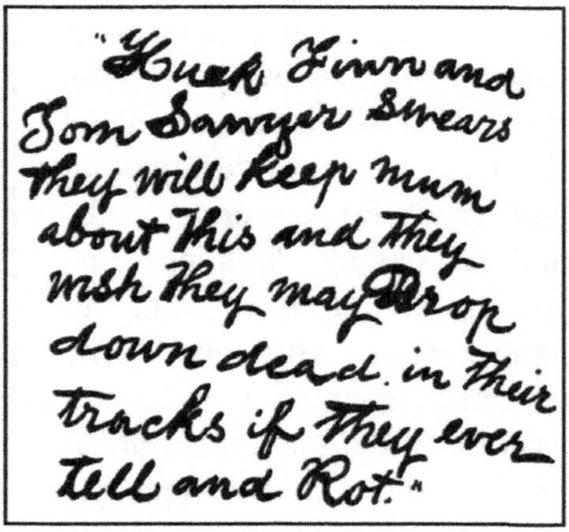

" Huck Finn and Tom Sawyer Swears they will keep mum about this and they wish they may drop down dead in their tracks if they ever tell and Rot."

Fig. 2. This picture of the oath Tom and Huck sign in blood in chapter 10 was originally written in Mark Twain's own deliberately sloppy handwriting. *Tom Sawyer*, 1876, p. 95. [Public domain.]

After the events in the graveyard, Huck suggests that he and Tom make a solemn oath, sealed in blood, never to reveal what they have witnessed, for fear of divine retribution. Using a piece of "red keel," Tom carefully scrawls the terms of the oath on a pine shingle, and both boys prick their fingers and add their bloody signatures. When Huck asks if the oath will really prevent them from ever revealing what they have witnessed, Tom tells him earnestly that "they may drop down dead in their tracks if they ever tell and rot." One might see in Tom's oath shades of the unbreakable vow that Hogwarts professor Severus Snape makes with Narcissa Malfoy to keep her son Draco from harm in carrying out his mission for Lord Voldemort in *Harry Potter and the Half-Blood Prince* (2001). Breaking the terms of this kind of vow promises precisely the same deadly consequences that Tom's vow spells out in *Tom Sawyer*. Indeed, Snape's vow proves to have serious consequences. Precisely because of it, Snape must kill Albus Dumbledore when Draco cannot bring himself to do it in chapter 27 of *Half-Blood Prince*.

Both Tom's St. Petersburg and Harry's wizarding world blend reality and magic in similar ways. Tom and Harry alternate episodically between the real world of their daily experience and a more imaginative and magical one that creates the foundations for their adventures. In the end, those adventures bring the two worlds together and fuse them. Tom ultimately has no need to imagine what it would be like to be a hero. After testifying against Injun Joe and leading Becky safely out of the cave he becomes one. Hogwarts gives Harry a sense of purpose and belonging. There he finds the family, the friends, and the love that transform him into the hero he is destined to be. These transformations remain as compelling for adults as they are for children, even though members of each generation doubtless read and interact with the stories differently.

For young readers, Tom Sawyer provides "a sense of recognition for the feelings of childhood truly rendered" (Doctorow xxxiii). Twain's friend Howells said much the same thing in his 1876 review of the novel for the *Atlantic Monthly*. He described Tom's occasional cruelty and mischievousness, among other traits, as evidence that he is little more than an "ordinary boy on the moral side . . ." His behavior is instantly recognizable and authentic for most young readers. It is Tom's indomitable thirst for adventure, as Howells continues, that makes him something more than simply an authentically conceived boy. "What makes him delightful to the reader is that on the imaginative side he is very much more, and though every boy has wild and fantastic dreams, this boy cannot rest till he has somehow realized them" (Howells 126). Tom's limitless imagination and resistance to anything that attempts to rein it in appeal directly to experiences common among most children, both in Twain's day and in our own. For adult readers, however, he is "more a pastiche of boyhood qualities" that "confer upon Tom an unnatural vividness rather than a human character" (Doctorow xxxv).

Readers of all ages engage with the Harry Potter novels in much the same way. Adults see themselves in the faithful depictions of children who experience the same sorts of emotional and physical hardships that they did at that age. They can also appreciate the creative ways that Rowling depicts Harry's epic journey, from powerless orphan to triumphant hero, and how she handles questions of morality. The popular science-fiction writer Brian Stableford notes that a remarkable feature of the Potter books is their "continual blurring of moral boundaries." Rowling's characters and the conflicts they face appeal so broadly because they are not binary. No single character is absolutely good or irredeemably evil. Professor Snape embodies this moral ambiguity, perhaps, better than any other. Throughout the series, Snape goes out of his way to make life as difficult as possible for Harry, stopping just short of doing him actual harm. Snape remains connected with Lord Voldemort and his Death Eaters while also being allied with Professor Dumbledore. Readers only fully understand the complicated nature of Snape's motives as Harry's adventures draw to a close (Stableford 2453).

Even readers only casually familiar with Tom Sawyer and Harry Potter might spot interesting parallels. For example, the settings of the boys' adventures share some characteristics. Each boy spends most of his time in a largely circumscribed environment. Tom lives in an isolated village from which he rarely wanders too far afield. Descriptions of his village mention homes, a church, a school, a tanyard, the riverfront, and not much more. In Harry's first novel, he spends most of his time at the Dursley home in a nondescript Surrey suburb and at Hogwarts. Neither character has much contact with an outside world. They spend as much time as they can in the magical or imaginative worlds where they find the most contentment. In his preface to *Tom Sawyer*, Twain addresses older readers, explaining that his youthful characters behave in ways intended to remind them of how they once behaved—if only they could remember. His meticulous memory of boyhood is part of what makes Tom such a compelling character for children and adults alike. In a 2000 BBC Radio interview, Rowling recalled how the nineteenth-century author Edith Nesbit had once said that she was lucky enough to remember "exactly how she felt and thought as a child." Rowling added that Nesbit's 1899 novel *The Story of the Treasure Seekers* could serve as the principal exhibit in a case for "the prohibition of all children's literature by anyone who cannot remember exactly how it felt to be a child" (Rowling, "Mr. Darcy" 4). The same thing could easily be said about *Tom Sawyer*.

Tom Sawyer and the Harry Potter books continue to fuel the imaginations of readers of every generation, and it is difficult to imagine a time when that would not be true. The deep connection that readers share with both authors is perhaps a more important consideration. In his introduction to the Penguin Classics edition of *Tom Sawyer*, R. Kent Rasmussen suggests that regardless of whether Tom Sawyer had a direct influence on Rowling's creation of Harry Potter, "the millions of modern young readers who relish her books find in them many of the same pleasures readers have always found in Mark Twain's book" (Rasmussen, Introduction xiii). In some ways, Harry Potter can be seen as the embodiment of Tom Sawyer's imaginative yearnings. The latter has only folklore and superstition at his disposal. Harry leads a thoroughly unenjoyable and commonplace existence until his eleventh birthday. At that time, he discovers he is a powerful and famous wizard, and that an entire magical world full of wonder and enchantment exists alongside his own nonmagical "Muggle" world. Each of Rowling's seven Potter novels unveils new details about Harry's past, his own magical strengths, and a looming evil that hangs over both realms. Each book also brings him closer to the fulfillment of his destiny—

his final confrontation with a powerful dark wizard that will decide the fate of magical and non-magical worlds alike. That is a dark adventure story worthy even of a connoisseur of the genre like Tom Sawyer, the would-be Black Avenger of the Spanish Main.

Works Cited

Amatulli, Jenna. "A Retrospective on Harry Potter Midnight Release Parties." *HuffPost*, 26 June 2017.

Branch, Edgar Marquess, et al., editors. *Mark Twain's Letters*. Vol. 1: *1853–1866*. U of California P, 1988.

Doctorow, E. L., Introduction to *The Adventures of Tom Sawyer*, by Mark Twain. Oxford UP, 1996.

Gribben, Alan. "Tom Sawyer, Tom Canty, and Huckleberry Finn: The Boy Book and Mark Twain." *Mark Twain Journal*, vol. 55, no. 1/2, Spring-Fall, 2017, pp. 127–44.

Howells, W. D. "The Adventures of Mark Twain." *My Mark Twain: Reminiscences and Criticisms*. Harper & Brothers, 1910.

Hunter, Jim. "Mark Twain and the Boy-Book in Nineteenth-Century America." *College English*, vol. 24, no. 6, 1963, pp. 430–38.

"J. K. Rowling, Harry Potter and the Philosopher's Stone—with Annotations." *The Guardian*, 18 May 2013, www.theguardian.com/books/interactive/2013/may/18/jk-rowling-harry-potter-philosophers-stone-annotations.

Kipen, David. "The Adventures of Tom Sawyer." National Endowment for the Arts, www.arts.gov/initiatives/nea-big-read/adventures-tom-sawyer.

Kit, Borys. "Something about 'Harry' (About Town)." *The Hollywood Reporter*, vol. 370, no. 47, Nov. 2001.

Paine, Albert Bigelow, editor. *Mark Twain's Letters*. Two Volumes. Harper & Brothers, 1917.

Pullman, Philip. *Daemon Voices: Essays on Storytelling*. Alfred A. Knopf, 2017.

Rasmussen, R. Kent. Introduction to *The Adventures of Tom Sawyer*, by Mark Twain. Penguin, 2014.

_____. *Mark Twain for Kids: His Life & Times*. Chicago Review Press, 2004.

Rowling, J. K. "From Mr. Darcy to Harry Potter by Way of Lolita." *Sunday Herald*, 21 May 2000.

_____. *Harry Potter and the Chamber of Secrets*. Scholastic, 1998.

_____. *Harry Potter and the Goblet of Fire*. Scholastic, 2000.

_____. *Harry Potter and the Half-Blood Prince*. Scholastic, 2005.

_____. *Harry Potter and the Order of the Phoenix*. Scholastic, 2003.

_____. *Harry Potter and the Sorcerer's Stone*. Scholastic, 1997.

Stableford, Brian. "J. K. Rowling." *Critical Survey of World Literature*. Edited by Robert C. Evans, Salem Press, 2018.

Trensky, Anne. "The Bad Boy in Nineteenth-Century American Fiction." *The Georgia Review*, vol. 27, no. 4, 1973.

Welland, Dennis. "A Note on Some Early Reviews of 'Tom Sawyer.'" *Journal of American Studies*, vol. 1, no. 1, 1967.

CRITICAL READINGS

The *Tom Sawyer* Franchise: The Evolution (and Devolution) of a Character_____

John Bird

Movie franchises have dominated Hollywood for decades. Film series such as *Star Trek* and *Star Wars*, *Batman* and *Spiderman*, *Jaws* and *Jurassic Park*, *Toy Story* and *Shrek*—the originals and sequels attract huge audiences, make a great deal of money, and provide reliable if repetitive entertainment before eventually fizzling out in creative exhaustion. Mark Twain employed his own literary franchise in his repeated use of the character Tom Sawyer. From 1876 to 1902, he published four novels and wrote three unfinished stories that exploited Tom's adventures and misadventures. Like Hollywood producers, Mark Twain knew immediately that he had struck a literary gold mine with this character and also a financial one. He used this character for decades, amusing and entertaining readers, but also counting on their familiarity with and affection for Tom as a way to raise money. Whatever Mark Twain's motivation, Tom Sawyer is a fascinating character study in his evolution and devolution over the course of seven texts. Tom embodies positive and negative personality traits, revealing the importance of narrative stance, showing Mark Twain's understanding of human psychology in general and adolescent psychology in particular, and perhaps mirroring the contradictory character of the author himself. Tracing Tom Sawyer's character over the course of these works shows the power as well as the weakness of the franchise and provides a study of audience response to a character who has become an American icon.

The Adventures of Tom Sawyer: The Franchise Begins

In his 1876 novel, *The Adventures of Tom Sawyer*, Mark Twain chose to write in the third person, with an omniscient narrator looking back at boyhood in 1840s Missouri, partially his own boyhood, but also incorporating that of his friends, as he notes in his preface:

> Most of the adventures recorded in this book really occurred; one or two were experiences of my own, the rest those of boys who were schoolmates of mine. Huck Finn is drawn from life; Tom Sawyer also, but not from an individual—he is a combination of the characteristics of three boys whom I knew, and therefore belongs to the composite order of architecture. (Preface)

Readers first see Tom through the eyes and thick spectacles of his Aunt Polly, reinforcing the narrative position of an older person looking at Tom. Mischievous Tom is punished for playing hooky and lying, and in an iconic scene, tricks all his friends into whitewashing the fence, not only avoiding work, but also getting rewarded for it. This scene sets up a recurring theme in the novel: Tom as rule breaker, rebel, rapscallion, and scamp who is continually rewarded for his "bad" behavior. He is what Judith Fetterley in a seminal article on the novel calls a "sanctioned rebel." He transgresses society's norms, but his society, rather than punishing him, finds relief and entertainment in his antics (Fetterley 287).

Tom is an orphan. His mother has died, and the narrator tells readers nothing about his father. His orphan status is one clue to his psychology, with no strong male role model and a surrogate mother in his Aunt Polly. Tom's characterization is a triumph of Mark Twain's understanding of child psychology. Tom is a mixture of elements, his personality not yet fully formed, a person still exploring to find himself. He is by turns confident, yet unsure. He is smart, but often with only half knowledge. Outwardly, he is happy, but with an inward melancholy. He is both brash and introspective, an apparent extrovert, but also with the traits of an introvert. He is childish, as befits his age, but he also takes on adult responsibility. He is a charismatic leader, a person who attracts followers and admirers, but he is also a loner. He appears bold, but he is inwardly insecure. In public, he is cocksure, but in private he is troubled by an overactive conscience. He is lazy when it comes to schoolwork, household chores, and Sunday school lessons, but he is industrious, indefatigable, and imaginative at play. He shuns school assignments but is a voracious reader of the kind of books he likes—although he often only half understands them. Mark Twain's characterization of Tom Sawyer captures the contradictions of a boy who is on the verge of adulthood, and the result is a character who has captured the imagination of generations of readers, both children and adults, in America and around the world.

The effect of this contradictory characterization results in contradictory reactions from readers: amused by some of his antics, but annoyed by others; sympathetic with his loneliness, but repelled by his mawkish self-pity; laughter at his childishness, but admiration for his bravery and occasional adult behavior.

An aspect of Tom's characterization that evolves and then devolves over the course of the Tom Sawyer franchise is his devotion to books and stories. In *The Adventures of Tom Sawyer*, this devotion leads to imaginative play, with Tom enacting what he has read, leading his friends like Joe Harper and Huckleberry Finn in games as pirates, "Indians", and Robin Hood. Although Tom only half understands what he has read, he internalizes the fictions and makes them central to his imaginative play. As his character progresses in the several sequels, Tom's infatuation with books and stories ossifies into rule-bound and irritating legalism. But that is to come. In his own book, stories bring freedom, a release from humdrum reality, and the unlocking of a vivid imagination.

Tom's play also prepares him for real-life adult events. After Aunt Polly mistakenly punishes him for something he did not do, he sulks and imagines her sorrow if he were sick, and, even better, drowned:

> He pictured himself lying sick unto death and his aunt bending over him beseeching one little forgiving word, but he would turn his face to the wall, and die with that word unsaid. Ah, how would she feel then? And he pictured himself brought home from the river, dead, with his curls all wet, and his poor hands still forever, and his sore heart at rest. How she would throw herself upon him, and how her

tears would fall like rain, and her lips pray to God to give her back her boy and she would never abuse him any more! But he would lie there cold and white and make no sign—a poor little sufferer whose griefs were at an end (chapter 3).

Tom's self-indulgent fantasy, so true to child psychology, becomes a reality when Aunt Polly and the whole town think that he, Huck, and Joe have drowned. The boys gleefully watch as the adults search for their bodies in the Mississippi River, then even more gleefully attend their own funeral, observing the real grief that Tom had so lugubriously imagined.

Tom's play at pirates and robbers and hidden treasure becomes real with Injun Joe's murder of the grave-robbing Dr. Robinson and the subsequent finding of treasure in the cave. Tom's imagination of himself as a hero comes true at the trial of Muff Potter, wrongly accused of the murder, when Tom takes on the very adult role of witness and names the real killer. As the narrator says, with some concluding humor: "Tom was a glittering hero once more—the pet of the old, the envy of the young. His name even went into immortal print, for the village paper magnified him. There were some that believed he would be President, yet, if he escaped hanging" (chapter 24).

This theme of Tom's imagination becoming reality continues when the narrator says, "There comes a time in every rightly constructed boy's life when he has a raging desire to go somewhere and dig for hidden treasure" (chapter 25). Tom knows of buried treasure from books, and he talks Huck Finn into joining him in the search. After several fruitless searches, real treasure appears. Injun Joe has found a box full of gold coins, but he hides it in a secret place.

TOM SAWYER'S BAND OF ROBBERS.

Fig. 1. E. W. Kemble's depiction of Tom showing his leadership and his delusion when he organizes "Tom Sawyer's Gang" in the second chapter of *Adventures of Huckleberry Finn* (1885). [Public domain.]

The culmination of Tom's imaginative fantasy of himself as a hero comes true in the cave scene when he both rescues Becky Thatcher and finds the treasure: $12,000. Tom is now an actual hero in the town, celebrated by the adult community: "Judge Thatcher hoped to see Tom a great lawyer or a great soldier some day. He meant to look to it that Tom should be admitted to the National military academy and afterwards trained in the best law school in the country, in order that he might be ready for either career or both" (chapter 35). Lest the story become the common narrative of the boy maturing into a man, Mark Twain ends his novel with a reversion to Tom's imaginative play. Tom resolves to form "Tom Sawyer's Gang," with an initiation at midnight, allowing Huck Finn to join along with the respectable boys. Mark Twain had originally intended to continue the narrative, to show Tom growing up, but he stops, with the narrator explaining in his conclusion, "So endeth this chronicle. It being strictly a history of a *boy*, it must stop here; the story could not go much further without becoming the history of a *man*" (Conclusion). That seemingly abrupt decision not only arrests Tom on the cusp of adulthood, but it also allows Mark Twain to establish his franchise. However, the Tom Sawyer of the sequels is a very different character.

Adventures of Huckleberry Finn: Tom Strikes Back!

As Mark Twain was nearing completion of *The Adventures of Tom Sawyer* in July 1875, he wrote to his friend and fellow writer William Dean Howells about his decision to end the book with Tom still a boy:

> I have finished the story & didn't take the chap beyond boyhood. I believe it would be fatal to do it in any shape but autobiographically— like [Alain-René Lesage's] Gil Blas. I perhaps made a mistake in not writing it in the first person. If I went on, now, & took him into manhood, he would just be like all the one-horse men in literature & the reader would conceive a hearty contempt for him. It is *not* a boy's book at all. It will only be read by adults. It is only written for adults (Smith and Gibson 91).

Mark Twain's comment about readers' "hearty contempt" was to prove somewhat prescient, and his idea about a first-person narrative was to bear fruit, as well as bring a big change to the character of Tom Sawyer. As *Tom Sawyer* was being readied for publication in August 1876, he began that sequel. He wrote to Howells, "[I] began another boys' book—more to be at work than anything else. I have written 400 pages on it—therefore it is very nearly half done. It is Huck Finn's Autobiography. I like it only tolerably well, as far as I have got, & may possibly pigeonhole or burn the MS when it is done" (Smith and Gibson 144). He did not burn the manuscript, but he did pigeonhole it, several times, over the next eight years. When *Adventures of Huckleberry Finn* was finally published in 1885 (1884 in England), it bore the subtitle "Tom Sawyer's Comrade," advertising for readers the connection and continuing the franchise.

Tom Sawyer is a prominent character in the beginning of *Huckleberry Finn* and an enduring presence throughout. The action of the narrative begins on the very night *Tom Sawyer* ends, with Huck sneaking out of the Widow Douglas's house to meet Tom and join Tom Sawyer's Gang. The shift to first-person voice causes a dramatic transformation in Tom's characterization. Readers now see Tom only through Huck's eyes, which results in a magnification of Tom's outward qualities and a loss of Tom's inner life. Gone are the glimpses of Tom's tortured conscience, his guilt, his melancholy, his self-pity, and his doubts. Instead, readers see only Tom's actions and hear only his words. Both are manifestations of his vivid imagination, fueled by his reading and his partial understanding of romantic literature. The Tom who had seemed playful and creative in his own narrative is replaced by a Tom who is rule bound, stiff, dictatorial, and often cruel. His flawed reading has turned him into a pedantic tyrant.

The boys' play as Tom Sawyer's Gang comes to a head in chapter 3. As Huck says,

> One time Tom sent a boy to run about town with a blazing stick, which he called a slogan (which was the sign for the Gang to get together) and then he said he had got secret news by his spies that next day a whole parcel of Spanish merchants and rich A-rabs was going to camp in Cave Hollow with two hundred elephants, and six hundred camels, and over a thousand "sumter" mules, all loaded down with di'monds, and they didn't have only a guard of four hundred soldiers, and so we could lay in ambuscade, as he called it, and kill the lot and scoop the things.

Ever practical, Huck says he "didn't believe we could lick such a crowd of Spaniards and A-rabs, but I wanted to see the camels and elephants, so I was on hand the next day, Saturday, in the ambuscade; and when we got the word, we rushed out of the woods and down the hill." But all they find is a Sunday school picnic, which they bust up until the teacher runs them off. When Huck tells Tom he did not see any diamonds, Tom will not admit he was only imagining. Instead, he doubles down, telling Huck if he had read *Don Quixote*, he would see "it was all done by enchantment." Instead of admitting that he was only playing, Tom spins a wider fantasy, involving magicians, genies, and a palace forty miles long, built of diamonds. Huck argues at every turn, using practical logic to counter Tom's book-bound fantasy, until Tom tells him, "'Shucks, it ain't no use to talk to you, Huck Finn. You don't seem to know anything, somehow—perfect sap-head.'". Where before Tom had seemed to recognize that he was only playing, acting out what he had read and what his imagination created, he has now become prisoner and victim of his own imagination, turning what had been play into something akin to psychosis. Huck finally concludes "that all that stuff was only just one of Tom Sawyer's lies." Huck sees through Tom's delusions—and so do readers. Perception of Tom Sawyer will never be the same.

Tom is physically present in only the early and late chapters of the novel, but his presence lingers throughout the long middle section of the narrative. Huck constantly invokes Tom's name, wishing he were there for one of the adventures, or comparing what he had just done to what Tom would have done, with Huck seeing Tom as superior. In Huck's arguments with Jim, Huck takes on Tom's previous role, based on reading he only half understands and on logic that is only half formed, repeatedly shot down by Jim's more realistic stances. Where Tom's adventures are mostly imaginary, Huck is experiencing real adventures, often dangerous ones, nearly deadly ones. Huck's ultimate real and dangerous adventure is setting Jim free from captivity and slavery. But in this most important adventure, Tom Sawyer returns in chapter 33, intervening in ways that are maddening, further revealing the negative aspects of Tom's character.

Tom's return is a remarkable coincidence, if not an actual miracle. Mark Twain clearly wanted to bring the ending back to the beginning, so he has Tom show up, hundreds of miles down the river, bound for the very farm where Jim is being held captive. Huck is surprised to see his friend, and even more surprised that Tom Sawyer is willing to join Huck in attempting to free Jim. Tom does not *join* Huck, however, he takes control, in a convoluted, crazy, and cruel plan that has annoyed generations of readers, coloring their perceptions of Tom Sawyer forever. Rule-bound Tom is now even worse, determined to free Jim according to books like *The Man in the Iron Mask* and *The Count of Monte Cristo*, books he takes as how-to-do-it manuals rather than as romantic, escapist entertainment. In the beginning of the book, his play is not serious, but now he is playing games with peoples' lives, especially Jim's. Huck tries to fight back against Tom's foolishness, but he ultimately gives in as Tom puts Jim through a series of indignations: making Jim grow a flower with his tears; making Jim scribble messages on the wall, then on a grindstone; making Jim eat a pie that contains torn up bed sheets to use for his escape; and most alarmingly, filling Jim's "prison cell" with spiders, rats, and snakes. Tom's outlandish plans become even more dangerous when he writes anonymous letters about the impending escape, warning that a gang of abolitionists is coming to liberate Jim, which arouses neighbors to form an armed guard. Tom's fantasies become deadly real when he himself is shot in the leg—which only makes him happy. His delusions have brought him perilously close to death.

As the story concludes, Tom makes a startling revelation, one that that makes his antics all the more maddening: Jim's owner, Miss Watson, had died and set Jim free in her will. Huck and Jim's journey was thus needless, but even worse, Tom's cruel torture of Jim was just play gone insane. A talkative old woman, commenting on the events of the "Evasion," remarks that Jim is "plumb crazy" (chapter 41)—but the plumb crazy person is Tom Sawyer.

Without the glimpses into Tom's inner life that a third-person narrator provides, readers see a Tom Sawyer emerge who is nothing less than a monster. Many readers who were entranced by Tom's characterization in his own story can no longer see him in any positive light. That negative perception continues through the rest of the Tom Sawyer franchise.

"Huck Finn and Tom Sawyer among the Indians": The Failed Attempt at Trilogy

In the summer of 1884, while *Huckleberry Finn* was being set in type, Mark Twain began another sequel–just as he had begun *Huckleberry Finn* itself when he was finishing *Tom Sawyer* eight years earlier. Also as he had done before, he based his new story on comments at the end of his recently completed book. This time, he used Huck's end-of-the-novel wish to "light out for the Territory" as the inspiration for Tom's suggestion that he, Huck, and Jim light out for the Indian territories to have further adventures. From his reading of James Fenimore Cooper's Indian stories, such as *The Last of the Mohicans* (1826), and dime novels, Tom has garnered a romantic view of Indians. As he tells Jim in chapter 1 of his new story, "they're the noblest human beings that's ever been in the world." The five Oglala Sioux they encounter satisfy Tom's romantic notions, but when the Indians attack the family that Huck, Tom, and Jim are traveling with, killing several of the party, taking Jim and the girls prisoner, Tom's ideals are shattered. Huck asks him, "'Tom, where did you learn about Injuns—how noble they was, and all that?'"

Tom's response is telling:

> He give me a look that showed me I had hit him hard, very hard, and so I wished I hadn't said the words. He turned away his head, and after about a minute he said "Cooper's novels," and didn't say anything more, and I didn't say anything more, and so that changed the subject. I see he didn't want to talk about it, and was feeling bad, so I let it just rest there, not having any disposition to fret or worry any person (chapter 4).

His illusions shattered by grim reality, Tom becomes little more than an accessory for the remainder of the narrative. Gone is the lively Tom of his own story and of Huck's, replaced by a wooden character who is little more than an automaton. The leader becomes Brace Johnson, an experienced frontiersman who leads Tom and Huck on a hunt for Jim and for Brace's sweetheart, Peggy. Their trail leads them to the remains of an Indian camp. Evidence of foul play includes a piece of Peggy's dress with blood on it, her footprint, and four stakes driven into the ground. The unmistakable implication is that Peggy has been tortured, raped, and killed, a gruesome fact of Indian tactics Mark Twain had read about in his background study for the story. The scene demanded a frank and brutal ending he could not publish, so he abandoned the narrative in mid-sentence. More years would pass before he would return to the story of Tom.

Tom Sawyer Abroad: Tom Takes Flight

With a mad professor, a futuristic balloon, and a voyage across the Atlantic Ocean to Africa, Mark Twain uses Tom, Huck, and Jim in a science-fiction novel, a return more to the tone of *Tom Sawyer* than of *Huckleberry Finn*. Again, Huck narrates, so readers again see Tom only from the outside, as he argues with Huck and Jim, showing off his book knowledge and his knowledge of geography. Tom revels

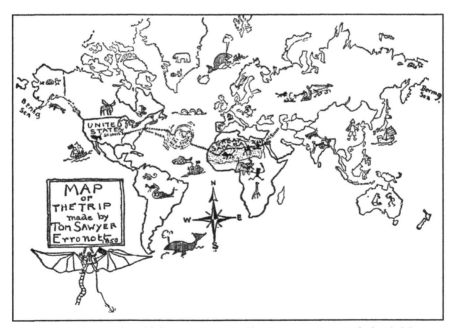

Fig. 2. Tom's fanciful map of his balloon voyage reveals both his imagination and his massive ego. Daniel Beard, *Tom Sawyer Abroad*, 1894, p. 214. [Public domain.]

in his status as a traveler and an "errornort" in this whimsical 1894 short novel. In several passages, Tom becomes a mouthpiece for Mark Twain's satire, and in a particularly cruel passage, Tom (and Huck) laugh themselves silly over Jim's ignorance of fractions as Jim takes on the bulk of the work of shoveling Sahara Desert sand from the balloon. Despite some good humor and some hair-raising adventures, the novel is little more than a diversion, with not much other point. The narrative has neither the focus on the development of character and inner consciousness of *Tom Sawyer* nor the seriousness of *Huckleberry Finn*. By this point in the franchise, Tom has become little more than a function. Mark Twain was clearly writing more for money than for art.

Tom Sawyer, Detective: The Boy Returns

By 1896, Mark Twain was in even greater need of money: he and his publishing firm had declared bankruptcy in 1894. He turned once again to his familiar characters, this time setting another short novel, *Tom Sawyer, Detective*, back at Phelps farm, where *Huckleberry Finn* had ended. In a spoof of detective fiction, a genre Mark Twain enjoyed lampooning, he employs a number of his familiar themes: twins, identity changes, a fake deaf and dumb character, and a murder trial. Tom again gets to show off as star witness, exonerating his uncle Silas Phelps from a false murder charge. As Huck says, Tom works up the scene for effect, and when the people in the courtroom yell, "Tom Sawyer! Tom Sawyer! Tom Sawyer! Shut up everybody, and let him go on! Go on Tom

" WHICH MADE HIM FEEL UNCOMMON BULLY "

Fig. 3. A. B. Frost's depiction of Tom feeling "uncommon bully" after again playing the hero in *Tom Sawyer, Detective* (1896). [Public domain.]

Critical Insights

Sawyer!," Huck notes it "made him feel uncommon bully, for it was nuts for Tom Sawyer to be made a public character that way, and a hero, as he calls it" (chapter 11). Just as in his own story, Tom earns the admiration of the adults and is again rewarded with a treasure. Tom is a showoff and a spectacle for the adult community, a remarkable boy, as the judge calls him. Less the despicable character than in *Huckleberry Finn*, he is nonetheless a shell of the character he had been in *Tom Sawyer*. As is common with most franchises, Mark Twain was running out of steam. But he was not through trying.

"Schoolhouse Hill" and "Tom Sawyer's Conspiracy": The Franchise Abandoned

Mark Twain attempted to use Tom and Huck in two more narratives that he never finished and did not publish himself. "Schoolhouse Hill" (1898) is the second of his *Mysterious Stranger* manuscripts, the shortest, and curiously, the only one written in the third person. A stranger comes to St. Petersburg who is gradually revealed to be an angel. Huck barely appears, and Tom appears only in a passage in which he puzzles the mysterious stranger with his slang. Mark Twain made notes suggesting that Tom and Huck would play a larger role later on, but he abandoned the narrative before that could happen. The franchise might have ended with that failed attempt. Mark Twain made one more try, however.

Between 1897 and 1902, Mark Twain intermittently worked on one final Tom Sawyer story, which was first published in 1969 as "Tom Sawyer's Conspiracy." A direct sequel to *Tom Sawyer, Detective*, the narrative has Tom, Huck, and Jim back in St. Petersburg, again narrated by Huck. Purely for adventure, Tom wants to start a civil war, an idea Jim rejects, then a revolution, then an insurrection, before finally settling on an absurd "conspiracy." To arouse fears among local abolitionists, Tom proposes to wear blackface and disguise himself as a slave, so Huck can sell him to a slave dealer, from whom Tom would then escape. After posting mysterious handbills to arouse the townspeople (an echo of events in the ending of *Huckleberry Finn*), the plan goes awry when, even more absurdly, the same faked scenario is carried out for real, ending in a murder. In an echo of *Tom Sawyer, Detective* (as in most franchises, Mark Twain resorts to reusing plots), Jim is accused of the murder. Tom promises to save Jim, but also as in *Huckleberry Finn*, in a convoluted and dangerous way, once again revealing Tom's megalomania:

> "I'm going to save you—that's all right, and perfectly easy. But where's the glory of saving a person merely from jail. To save him from the gallows is the thing. It's got to be murder in the first degree—you get the idea? You've got to have a *motive* for killing the man—*then* we're all right! Jim, if you can think up a rattling good motive, I can get you put up for murder in the first degree just as easy as turning your hand over" (chapter 6).

At the trial, an echo of both *Tom Sawyer* and *Tom Sawyer, Detective*, Tom testifies, but this time he also serves as a lawyer, allowing him to show off one last time. But in a telling moment, when he is called to take the stand, the adults in the courtroom mumble, "Course, couldn't happen 'thout *him* being in it; couldn't do an eclipse successful if Tom Sawyer was took sick and couldn't superintend" (chapter 10). The town is finally on to him, seeing what readers have been seeing in all the narratives of the franchise. Curiously, Mark Twain ended his story just at the moment Tom is about to solve the case, prove who the murderers are, and exonerate Jim. Instead, he abandoned both the story and his Tom Sawyer franchise.

Even more curious is that, despite the absurdity of the plot, "Tom Sawyer's Conspiracy" has more potential and artistic merit than several of the published works. Although it is similar to *Tom Sawyer, Detective*, it contains more depth: the stakes are higher, with echoes of the serious issues raised in *Huckleberry Finn*. Further, Tom shows more humanity than in any of the stories since his own: he shows real remorse for the trouble he has caused Jim, and recognizing the calamity caused by his out-of-control fantasy play, he cries three times. Perhaps Mark Twain intended to finish the story someday, or perhaps he just did not need the money at this time in his life. Whatever the reason, the franchise was ended.

Conclusion: Mark Twain as Tom, Tom as Mark Twain

Why did Mark Twain write about Tom Sawyer so often? The obvious answer is money. He knew that a book with "Tom Sawyer" in the title would sell. But a deeper reason lies in his biography and his psychology. Mark Twain and Tom Sawyer share many experiences, actions, attitudes, and attributes. In many ways, both positive and negative, Tom Sawyer is a projection of Mark Twain's personality.

Mark Twain's preface to *Tom Sawyer* notes that "one or two were experiences of my own," but that is an understatement, and when he writes that Tom "is a combination of the characteristics of three boys whom I knew," he obscures the fact that he himself is one of the main models. Samuel Clemens was a mischievous boy, often punished by his mother, who, like Aunt Polly, held a firm belief in patent medicines. He was an avid reader but an indifferent scholar, apt to play hooky to go swimming or fishing. He had a vivid imagination, but he also suffered from a tortured conscience. The death of his father when he was eleven robbed him of his most important male role model.

In his adult years, Mark Twain exhibited Tom Sawyer-like qualities, for good and for ill. His wife called him "Youth," a testament to his child-like demeanor. Like Tom, he could be a showoff, wearing outlandish clothes, early on a fur coat reversed, and near the end of his life, white suits, no matter what the season, a fashion faux pas at the time. He was proud of the gaudy academic gown he received from Oxford University in 1907, which he wore to his daughter Clara's 1909 wedding, upstaging the bride. He reveled in public attention, becoming the center of attention at the many dinners and events he attended, stealing the show repeatedly. Like Tom, he took disappointment and failure hard, but like Tom, he recovered quickly and pressed on to his next adventure or misadventure. On a decidedly positive note, like Tom, he was a creator, his voluminous writing a testament to his drive, his vitality, his humor, and his rich inner life. Like Tom Sawyer, Mark Twain himself has become an American icon.

After encountering Tom Sawyer in *Huckleberry Finn* and the other sequels in the Tom Sawyer franchise, readers may never

---

recover the image of Tom in his original story—his cruelty and megalomania are apt to destroy that sense of wondrous boyhood so prevalent in the first novel. It is worthwhile, and possible, however, for one to go back to that story with fresh eyes and experience once again the character of Tom Sawyer in his first and best presentation.

Works Cited

Fetterley, Judith. "The Sanctioned Rebel." Mark Twain, *The Adventures of Tom Sawyer*. Edited by Beverly Lyon Clark, Norton Critical Edition, W. W. Norton, 2007, pp. 279–90.

Smith, Henry Nash, and William M. Gibson, editors. *Mark Twain-Howells Letters*. 2 vols., Belknap Press, 1960.

Twain, Mark. *Adventures of Huckleberry Finn*. U of California P, 2003.

_____. *The Adventures of Tom Sawyer*. The Mark Twain Library, U of California P, 1982.

_____. *Huck Finn and Tom Sawyer among the Indians and Other Unfinished Stories*. U of California P, 1989.

_____. *Tom Sawyer Abroad; Tom Sawyer, Detective*. The Mark Twain Library. U of California P, 1982.

Tom Sawyer: From Boy-Book Hero to Coming-of-Age Hellion

Kevin Mac Donnell

For readers of the boy book *The Adventures of Tom Sawyer* who never get around to reading its sequel, the coming-of-age novel *Adventures of Huckleberry Finn*, Tom is the lovable embodiment of the all-American boy. The Tom of *Tom Sawyer* is, however, not the same as the Tom of *Huckleberry Finn*. Those two Toms are as different as the two books, the first being Mark Twain's contribution to the then popular boy-book genre, the second a proto-coming-of-age novel, the genre that would supersede boy books. To understand Mark Twain's twain Toms [sic] requires an understanding of those two genres and Twain's life-long efforts to succeed as a writer.

Mark Twain's literary efforts began early. At the very beginning of his career in the 1850s, he had styled his own humor after the popular southwestern humor then in vogue and imitated the style of the "Phunny Phellows" who dominated American humor at that time. He very likely even snatched his pen name itself from a sketch that was written or edited by Artemus Ward, the most successful of the Phunny Phellows (Mac Donnell, "Mark Twain Did Read" 152–54). Twain had a keen eye for what kind of writing was popular and would sell, and chased those markets his entire life, and although not all of his forays into genre writing were bestsellers, most of them were successful because he did not follow the rules but instead loosed his own creative genius, his own brand of humor brimming with parody and satire, written in colloquial language, molding the style and subject matter that defined other books in a given genre into his own—exactly as he would do in *Tom Sawyer* (Stone 63–72).

Most of Twain's own books fit into one of the major literary genres of his era. His first bestselling book, *The Innocents Abroad* (1869), was a travel book. It was followed by other travel books and books that used travel as a central theme: *Roughing It* (1872), *A Tramp Abroad* (1880), *Life on the Mississippi* (1883), *Adventures of Huckleberry Finn* (1885), *A Connecticut Yankee in King Arthur's Court* (1889), *Tom Sawyer Abroad* (1894), *Following the Equator* (1897), and finally, *Extract from Captain Stormfield's Visit to Heaven* (1909), in which Twain transports its protagonist much farther than any of his previous characters. He also wrote detective fiction, beginning with *The Stolen White Elephant* (1882), and continuing with *Pudd'nhead Wilson* (1894), *Tom Sawyer Detective* (1896), "Tom Sawyer's Conspiracy" (written ca. 1897), *A Double Barrelled Detective Story* (1902), and even *Is Shakespeare Dead?* (1909), in which Mark Twain himself plays detective as he gathers evidence and prosecutes his case against William Shakespeare as a playwright.

The major attraction of genre writing was financial. Genre books sold well—and the popularity and sale of his books was a lifelong preoccupation of Mark Twain. His letters to publishers are filled with concerns about his royalty rates, contractual terms, earnings, payments, and unauthorized printings. He filed lawsuits against copyright infringers, recorded word counts of nearly everything he wrote, supported international copyright, and even trademarked his pen name. Wishing to exploit his own books on stage, Twain wrote to his lecture agent, James B. Pond, asking him to obtain royalty figures for the stage version of George Peck's wildly successful boy book, *Peck's Bad Boy* (*UCCL* 13566, Clemens to Pond, Feb. 9, 1884). Twain would gain his most enduring success when he entered the boy-book genre.

The Boy-Book Genre

Boy books are not merely books written for boys who will enjoy the adventures (and miss much of the humor). They are written also to appeal to adults, who will value the humor over the adventures. Instead of being pedantic, they are accounts of boys being boys. As critics Beverly Lyon Clark, Alan Gribben, and Marcia Jacobson have pointed out, boy books are defined by several elements. They are almost always autobiographical in whole or in part; this is usually made explicit by the author. They are often inspired by some triggering event in the author's adult life and are typically narrated by an adult recalling the past. They are invariably episodic and usually unfold in a matriarchal social setting with an ineffectual or absent father and few adult male role models and are confined to a single locale writ large. A river or lake often plays a prominent part in the adventures. Boy books often involve gangs of boys, are frequently nostalgic, and nearly always include a boy's crush on an older or otherwise unattainable girl. There are always incidents involving injustices taking the form of boys being punished for other people's misdeeds. There are comic disruptions of the adults' peace and order. Most of them feature a best friend or buddy and include a fight with a newly encountered boy that reinforces a pecking-order. At some unexpected moment, a situation arises that presents a test of courage. Almost all boy books include a tragic death or serious illness, sometimes a father or father figure, but just as often a boy. They typically conclude with adults reasserting control.

Besides those elements of plot and structure, boy books focus on the untamed character of the boys themselves. The boys in them are often regarded as "bad boys" who are really nothing worse than scamps and rascals who inflict no genuine harm and are portrayed as lovable "boys being boys" who pull pranks, show off, fantasize about improbable escapades, and break rules for which they are often caught and punished—or at least learn lessons. These "bad" boys in boy books were a response to the romantic literary tradition that all children, both boys and girls, were spiritually pure innocents "trailing clouds of glory" as the poet William Wordsworth famously expressed it, and there were both boy books and girl books (Hunter 432, 438; Stone 24). Girl books, exemplified by Louisa May Alcott's *Little Women* (1868–69), are beyond the scope of this discussion (Clark 102–27; Jacobson 14, 163.n.12). However, if the fan mail Twain preserved is any indication, girls were a very large and vocal percentage of the readers of *Tom Sawyer*, some of whom wished to know what sort of man Tom became (Rasmussen 86, 99). Unlike girl books, boy books embraced the notion, popular in psychological theory of the day, that little boys passed through a "savage" phase on their way to manhood (Mailloux 115–16; Jacobson 85, 155).

Unhappily for two of the girls who wrote to Twain, a key element is that these formulaic narratives never follow a boy beyond his childhood years into his adult life. While the boys in these books are sometimes a bit older and wiser at the end of their stories, they rarely seem more mature—merely less savage. Although boys in these books are often on the cusp of manhood—preparing to return home, return to school, or enter the workforce—their stories invariably end before the next phase in their path to adulthood begins. Boy books are not coming-of-age stories, a genre that would evolve out of boy books and overtake their popularity in the early twentieth century with writings by Booth Tarkington, Sherwood Anderson, Ernest Hemingway, Katherine Anne Porter, and Richard Wright. (Jacobson 150, 159). Perhaps the best exemplars showing the evolution of boy books into coming-of-age novels are those written by an author who wrote one of each. Edgar Lee Masters wrote *Mitch Miller* (1920), a boy book about two buddies who travel to Hannibal expecting to meet Tom Sawyer in the flesh, and its sequel, *Skeeters Kirby* (1923), a coming-of-age story about Skeet as a young lawyer after the gruesome accidental death of his buddy Mitch at the end of the first book.

Mark Twain the Boy-Book Author

Twain himself was writing sketches about boys before *Tom Sawyer*, and he knew his good boys from his bad boys. Although a brief sketch, his "Story of a Bad Little Boy Who Did Not Come to Grief" (1865) defined what made a boy bad according to the Sunday school books, lampooning the absurdities of those preachy texts. Likewise, Twain's "Story of the Good Little Boy Who Did Not Prosper" appeared in *The Galaxy* in May 1870, and left no doubt where Twain stood on the matter of good and bad boys. Twain's readers probably winced knowingly (and guffawed) when Twain's bad boy became successful and rich, but no doubt relished seeing the irksome good little boy (known in contemporary fiction of the era as The Model Boy) getting blown to smithereens. To make his point, Twain retitled and paired these stories when they first appeared in book form in *Sketches New and Old* (1875).

That same May 1870 issue of *The Galaxy* includes Twain's "Disgraceful Persecution of a Boy," a scathing satiric sketch about a "well-dressed boy on his way to Sunday school" in San Francisco who was arrested for stoning some Chinese adults. Twain mockingly defends this bad boy on grounds he was following the racist example of white Christian American adults, whose social norms "conspired to teach him that it was a high and holy thing to stone a Chinaman." Twain would revisit that very same theme in chapter 54 of *Roughing It*. In "Just 'One More Unfortunate'," a short newspaper character sketch published in June 1865, Twain describes his encounter with a teenage bad girl (a prostitute) in San Francisco who pretends to be a sweet innocent girl led astray but reveals her true self after she thinks Twain is out of earshot. The following month Twain published two sly and very funny newspaper sketches, instructing good little girls and boys how to be bad (Branch and Hirst 236–45). Mark Twain was quite conscious of good and bad boys (and girls), and boy books in particular, well before he wrote *Tom Sawyer* (Gribben, *Literary Resources* 160–61).

Mark Twain met his greatest success when he crashed the boy-book genre with *Tom Sawyer* (1876). He had read Thomas Bailey Aldrich's *The Story of a Bad Boy* (1870) but did not think much of it initially. Two days after Christmas in 1869, he wrote to his wife-to-be that "for the life of me I could not admire the volume much" (*UCCL* 00394, Clemens to Olivia Langdon, Dec. 27, 1869). Two years later, however, he began work on his own boy book. When first published, *Tom Sawyer* sold slower than expected, but it would become one of Twain's most commercially successful books. He would follow it with another boy book, *The Prince and the Pauper* (1882), and the coming-of-age novel, *Adventures of Huckleberry Finn* (1885), and would write several less successful sequels featuring Tom Sawyer: *Tom Sawyer Abroad* (1894), *Tom Sawyer Detective* (1896), and the unfinished "Huck Finn and Tom Sawyer among the Indians" (written ca. 1884; published 1968) and "Tom Sawyer's Conspiracy" (written ca. 1897; published 1969).

THE STORY OF A BAD BOY.

CHAPTER I.

IN WHICH I INTRODUCE MYSELF.

HIS is the story of a bad boy. Well, not such a very bad, but a pretty bad boy; and I ought to know, for I am, or rather I was, that boy myself.

Lest the title should mislead the reader, I hasten to assure him here that I have no dark confessions to make. I call my story the story of a bad boy, partly to distinguish myself from those faultless young gentlemen who generally figure in narratives of this kind, and partly because I really was *not* a cherub. I may truthfully say I was an amiable, impulsive lad, blessed with fine digestive powers, and no hypocrite. 1

Fig. 1. First page of Thomas Bailey Aldrich's *The Story of a Bad Boy*, 1869. [Public domain.]

There is a consensus among critics that Aldrich's *Bad Boy* was Twain's model for *Tom Sawyer*, but the boy-book genre was evolving before Aldrich's book (Clark 96; Stone 31). Well before boy books, there were books *for* boys by Jacob Abbott, Benjamin P. Shillaber, and Charles Dickens containing elements of the boy-book genre, but Thomas Hughes's *Tom Brown's School Days* (1857) is generally thought to have been the model for Aldrich and was among the first books that could accurately be described as a boy book. Twain was familiar with all of these authors and had most of their writings in his personal library. As several critics have noted, parts of *Tom Sawyer* can be traced to some of these other authors, especially Shillaber's long-suffering but loving Mrs. Partington, who raises her orphaned prankster nephew Ike much like Aunt Polly raises Tom (Gribben, *Literary Resources* passim).

The "Bad Boy" of the Boy-Book *Tom Sawyer*

When *Tom Sawyer* appeared, it displayed nearly every element of a boy book. Twain's preface is explicit that the adventures he describes are largely autobiographical: "Most of the adventures recorded in this book really occurred; one or two were experiences of my own, the rest those of boys who were schoolmates of mine." Some authors, including William Dean Howells, wrote their own boy books in the aftermath of losing a child; the triggering event that provoked Twain to write *Tom Sawyer* was the death of his infant son (Jacobson 71; Csicsila 64–68). Twain is the narrator. A glance at the chapter headings makes clear that the book will be episodic, promising one adventure after another—which it delivers. The setting is St. Petersburg, the small Mississippi River town where Tom lives without a father, under the supervision of his Aunt Polly. The river plays a major role in the story when the boys cross its dangerous waters to an island, where they linger until the village thinks they have drowned (chapters 13–14). Tom has a crush on Becky Thatcher (chapter 3). He is the victim of an injustice when he is swatted by Aunt Polly for the sugar bowl his brother Sid broke (chapter 3) and when he is whipped by his teacher for an ink spot left in his spelling book by another boy (chapter 20), but he also saves Becky from punishment when he falsely confesses to tearing the page she has torn in the schoolmaster's anatomy book (chapter 20). He has a habit of disrupting church services (chapters 5 and 17). He meets a test of courage by keeping a cool head and rescuing himself and Becky after they get lost in the cave where Tom sees the murderous Injun Joe lurking (chapters 31–32). He challenges a boy he has just met to a fight and flattens him (chapter 1), and his buddy is the town's pariah, Huck Finn, who is considered "idle, and lawless, and vulgar and bad" by the mothers of the other boys in the village (chapter 6).

Like the boys in other boy books, Tom is a juvenile trickster when he inveigles other boys to paint the fence (chapter 2) and swaps trinkets to obtain the tickets needed to acquire a prize Bible (chapter 4). There is the murder of the doctor in the graveyard (chapter 9), followed by the death of his killer, Injun Joe, who dies trapped in the cave (chapter 33). Tom displays an active if self-pitying fantasy life when his feelings are hurt, and he imagines himself dead and others grieving over him (chapter 8). Examples of boy-book elements—or satiric inversions of them—can be found on nearly every page, and one can almost imagine Twain checking them off a hit-list as he writes the book. Eventually, the adults indeed assert control once again, and Tom capitulates to their authority while Huck questions it (Wolff 158–59). True to the boy-book formula that prohibits boys from ever coming of age, Twain famously steps in, adding the novel's final (unnumbered) chapter to abruptly shut down the narrative with his declaration that "It being strictly a history of a *boy*, it must stop here; the story could not go much further without becoming the story of a *man*."

After those slow initial sales and becoming a bestseller, and long after the last reprints of the most popular nineteenth century boy books thinned out by the late 1930s, *Tom Sawyer* had been filmed and staged, and continued to be reprinted with new illustrations. Tom himself would be featured in various games, crayons, paint sets, dolls, comic books, toys, a harmonica, a clothing line, a US postage stamp, and even a brand of root beer well into the twenty-first century. Tom and Becky continue to play a central role in the image of Mark Twain presented to Hannibal tourists.

The reason for this perpetual popularity of *Tom Sawyer* is the character of its protagonist. As his Aunt Polly describes him after she thinks he has drowned, "he warn't *bad*, so to say—only mischeevous. Only just giddy and harum-scarum, you know. He warn't any more responsible than a colt. *He* never meant any harm, and he was the best-hearted boy that ever was . . ." (chapter 15). Tom is a "bad" boy going through his "savage" phase, but not a bad boy like the young criminals featured in dime novels who were thought to inspire impressionable readers to become criminals, creating a national hysteria in the 1880s and 1890s (Mailloux 110–29). In sharp contrast, only one instance has been discovered in which Twain stood accused of inspiring some of his young readers to form a gang and go on a crime spree (Mac Donnell, "Mark Twain Kills" 17–20). But Tom would go from "bad" to worse when he reappeared in the final chapters of *Huckleberry Finn*. Tom would break bad.

Breaking Bad in *Huckleberry Finn*

Picking up where *Tom Sawyer* ends, and advertised as its sequel, *Huckleberry Finn* is a coming-of-age story, the genre that would replace the boy-book genre in the early twentieth century. Although *Tom Sawyer* contained nearly all of the classic elements that nineteenth century readers had come to expect in a boy book; not so with *Huckleberry Finn*. Readers of *Tom Sawyer* would look in vain for the tell-tale markers of a boy book in *Huckleberry Finn*. From the beginning, it is narrated by the boy himself, not the boy who has grown into a man and now looks back fondly on his childhood years. In fact, key boy-book elements get turned inside-out in *Huckleberry Finn*. Huck's relationship with Mary Jane Wilks is not based on antics or puppy-love, but on mature responsible judgment. Instead of a fight with a new boy, Huck makes friends with Buck Grangerford. Like Tom, boys in other boy books are avid readers of romantic adventures stories, but not Huck, who, while impressed by Tom's knowledge of such fantastical lore, increasingly resists Tom's schemes when he cannot see some practical benefit. Unlike the adventures in most boy books, and those of Tom Sawyer in particular, Huck's repeated encounters with dangerous surroundings, and his entanglements with menacing adults and life-threatening violence are not always imaginary or exaggerated or merely witnessed but are quite genuine. Critics have debated whether *Huckleberry Finn* meets the criteria of a boy book and reached no firm consensus (Clark 77–101; Gribben *Mark* 178–79).

The chief difference between boy books and coming-of-age narratives is that the boy in a coming-of-age story becomes a young man through his experiences, matures, and is usually (but not always) followed into early adulthood. Rather than a gang of boys or a buddy, Huck is accompanied by an unconventional father figure, a runaway slave, during most of the adventures that prepare him for adulthood. As countless critics have agreed, Jim replaces Huck's drunken and abusive (and eventually dead) father as his paternal role model. Critics also agree that the turning point in the story is the dramatic moment when Huck tears up his letter to Jim's owner, Miss Watson, and accepts that he will go to Hell for doing it. That scene is also significant as the moment when Huck rejects the "morality" imposed upon him by his boy-book matriarchs. Huck's experiences leave him wiser, even cynical, and ultimately more humane and mature than his childish previous self or his friend Tom. The fact that Huck is not followed into adulthood may cause some to bar his book from full admission to the shelf of coming-of-age novels, but it is clear at the end of the story that he has survived a series of truly traumatic events that would defeat many adults, has matured, and is in many ways no longer a boy. Unlike the boys in the boy books, he does not prepare to return to "civilization," or to his family, or go off to school, or embark upon a career, or otherwise conform in any way to the expectations of the adults in the story. Rather, he rejects the "civilized" (that is, white society) of his childhood when he declares that he expects to light out for the Territory. No reader of the book can doubt that Huck will do exactly that and enter his adult life in another place far from home and on his own terms. This is certainly not the ending found in any boy books before or after *Huckleberry Finn*.

Exactly how Huck arrives at that momentous decision has everything to do with Tom. Early reviewers of *Huckleberry Finn* frequently indicted Huck as the bad boy in the story (Mailloux 124–29; Budd 259–65). Huck was a "Bad Boy" according to the headline over a review in the *New York World*. Even Twain's "hometown" *Hartford Evening Post* called Huck a bad boy but conceded that his decision not to betray Jim's location to Miss Watson also made him a "sharp" boy who would be well-remembered for that heroic act. There were comparisons to other bad-boy books, and one reviewer considered Huck so bad that he deserved to be killed by "indignant citizens" at the end of his odyssey. Most reviewers were kinder, but none went so far as to label Tom the truly bad boy of the story. One astute reviewer did praise the satire behind Tom's antics because they ridiculed the romantic adventure tales to which readers were accustomed (Budd 261–80).

Despite escaping the wrath of the critics who attacked Huck, Tom is no longer the sympathetic "bad" boy of *Tom Sawyer* in those final evasion chapters of *Huckleberry Finn* that have confounded modern critics for decades. Tom's behavior far exceeds the harmless, sometimes thoughtless pranks played by the "bad" boys in boy books. Although he knows Jim was set free by the death of Miss Watson, he keeps this a secret so he can keep a human being enslaved for his own entertainment. Soon after Tom arrives at the Phelps plantation, he and Huck each propose ways to rescue Jim, who is imprisoned in a cabin awaiting his return to slavery. Huck's plan is logical and likely to succeed quickly without unnecessary risks, but Tom hatches an elaborate series of ruses (his "evasions") and convinces a perplexed Huck to go along with him. Jim and Huck are impressed by Tom's knowledge of the supposedly proper way such things are done in adventure books of the day, but the evasions reach the height of the ridiculous when Tom puts Jim, Huck, and himself in mortal danger and gets himself shot in the leg. At that moment Huck rejects Tom's juvenile nonsense and finds a doctor, who saves Tom's life, but Jim is drawn out of hiding and back into bondage. Not until after Jim is threatened with being lynched does Tom confess that Jim had been free the whole time (chapters 34–42).

Unlike their nineteenth-century counterparts, modern critics have not always had kind words for Tom's actions in those final chapters of *Huckleberry Finn*. He has been described as an "unattractive know-it-all," a "little con man," a "self-deceiver," a "creature of delusion," and of "living a constant lie of style and substance" (Jacobson 70). However, other critics have argued that "in many cases, the vilification of Tom Sawyer's traits and role have proceeded too far" and that Tom "is hardly . . . a candidate for despising" (Gribben, "Tom Sawyer" 306; Hill 194). Despite the critical animosity directed at both Tom and those evasion chapters, they are essential to the story: They crystalize the profound differences between Tom and Huck. Tom is no more aware of just how bad a boy he really is than Huck is aware of just how good a boy he has become. Self-awareness is not a hallmark of boyhood. Yet, while Tom plans to return home and resume his boyhood, Huck envisions broader horizons. The difference in the character and maturity of the two boys is something Twain took pains to delineate. Twain spelled out those differences after watching a rehearsal of Lee Arthur's musical, *Huckleberry Finn,* which blended scenes from that work with scenes from *Tom Sawyer*. Shortly before it debuted in Hartford in November 1902, he wrote the producer, Charles Dillingham, with advice for the actor playing Huck:

> I believe it will improve the performance for Huck to study his character from my book. He will see that it is sharply differentiated from Tom's, & gains a good deal, with its unconscious depth & long-headedness & sobriety, as contrasted with Tom's rattle-brained vivacities. However, it may be that he can't see the deeps & the dignity of Huck's character. . . . (*UCCL* 11679, Clemens to Dillingham, Nov. 9, 1902)

Fig. 2. Tom's "rattle-brained vivacities" as Mark Twain himself witnessed them in a Hartford production of Lee Arthur's play in 1902. Image courtesy of Kevin Mac Donnell. [Used with permission.]

Mark Twain's characterization of the two boys is more clearly stated than in any subsequent literary critic's analysis. In *Huckleberry Finn* Tom functions as a foil to showcase Huck's maturity. As if further proof were needed of Tom's incorrigible immaturity, Twain supplies it in two of his sequels when Tom attempts yet another evasion episode in *Tom Sawyer Detective* (chapter 10) and actually carries out an elaborate evasion in nine of the ten unfinished chapters of "Tom Sawyer's Conspiracy" (chapters 2–10).

Thanks, Tom

By the end of *Huckleberry Finn*, Huck has grown to a point where, if he does not fully know what kind of man he wants to be, he knows what he does not wish to be—a boy like Tom Sawyer who, despite his antics, accepts the cant that is part of the romantic literary tradition of the "civilized" society that beckons to them both. Huck famously and utterly rejects that society, something the boys in boy books never dared, and Huck's readers are confident that he has the "long-headedness & sobriety" to survive when he lights out for the Territory and escapes into adulthood. Readers also have no doubt that Tom's "rattle-brained vivacities" will render him an eviction-proof inhabitant of the romantic world of boyhood. At best, Tom is Twain's eternal "bad" boy who never comes of age, the very boy Huck would have to become if he did not light out for the Territory. The Tom of *Huckleberry Finn* is the same Tom as the Tom in *Tom Sawyer*; his personality and behaviors are no different. He is the same boy but in new surroundings—a boy book "bad" boy who is out of place in a coming-of-age narrative—an immature boy who is utterly unfit to comprehend Jim's humanity. Tom's fate is overshadowed by Huck's declaration of independence, and has been ignored by most critics, but by the end of *Huckleberry Finn* Tom's role has degenerated from that of a typical boy-book hero.

Read at another level, the character of Tom in *Huckleberry Finn* is reduced to functioning as a physical manifestation of the childish impulses Huck must overcome on his way to adulthood, or more darkly, he is elevated to the status of a symbol of the deplorable treatment of black Americans after the Civil War, in particular, as some critics have pointed out, the convict lease system (Nilon passim). Tom behaves as badly as Mark Twain's Sunday school boy who stoned the Chinaman. This contrast between Tom and Huck reflects Twain's conception of bad and good boys. Twain's "Story of the Bad Boy Who Prospers" and "Story of the Good Boy Who Comes to Naught" are not the stories of a Bad Boy and a Good Boy, but rather the stories of a Bad Boy and a Model Boy. Twain did not conceive of a truly Good Boy until Huck met Jim.

Past readers have celebrated Tom as a nostalgic symbol of boyhood—just a boy being a boy—as if the full measure of his character had been presented in the boy book *Tom Sawyer*, but twenty-first century readers tend to dislike him when viewing him through the lens of modernity. It might still be possible to have some affection for Tom if not for his thoughtless cruelties toward Jim in *Huckleberry Finn*, and his dreaming up more juvenile evasions in

Tom Sawyer Detective and "Tom Sawyer's Conspiracy." But Tom functions as something more than a bedeviling annoyance or literary symbol when he resurfaces in those final chapters of *Huckleberry Finn*. The little hellion unwittingly joins forces with Jim, Aunt Polly, and the others to shape Huck into a coming-of-age hero. Modern readers may not hold Tom in the same affectionate regard as his earlier readers, but he deserves their gratitude. As for those unfortunate readers of the boy book *Tom Sawyer,* who never get around to reading its sequel, the coming-of-age novel *Huckleberry Finn*, Tom will forever flourish as the lovable embodiment of the "rattle-brained" all-American boy.

Works Cited

Budd, Louis J., comp. *Mark Twain: The Contemporary Reviews*. Cambridge UP, 1999.

Branch, Edgar Marquess, and Robert H. Hirst, editors. *Early Tales and Sketches* by Mark Twain, Vol. 2: *1864—1865*. U of California P, 1981.

Clark, Beverly Lyon. *Kiddie Lit: The Cultural Construction of Children's Literature in America*. Johns Hopkins UP, 2003.

Clemens, Samuel L. Manuscript letters. *UCCL*. marktwainproject.org/xtf/search?category=letters.

Csicsila, Joseph. "Langdon Clemens and *The Adventures of Tom Sawyer*." *Mark Twain and Youth: Studies in His Life and Writings*. Edited by Kevin Mac Donnell and R. Kent Rasmussen, Bloomsbury, 2016.

Gribben, Alan. "Boy Books, Bad Boy Books, and *The Adventures of Tom Sawyer*." *The Adventures of Tom Sawyer*. Edited by Beverly Lyon Clark, W. W. Norton, 2007.

_____. *Mark Twain's Literary Resources: A Reconstruction of His Library and Reading*. Vol. 1, NewSouth Books, 2019.

Hill, Richard. "A Beautifully Crafted Ending." *Readings on "The Adventures of Huckleberry Finn."* Edited by Katie de Koster, Greenhaven Press, 1998.

Hunter, Jim. "Mark Twain and the Boy-Book in Nineteenth-Century America." *College English*, vol. 24, no. 6, 1963, pp. 430–38.

Jacobson, Marcia. *Being a Boy Again: Autobiography and the American Boy Book*. U of Alabama P, 1994.

Mac Donnell, Kevin. "Mark Twain Did Read *Vanity Fair*—in Nevada." *Mark Twain Journal*, vol. 58, no. 1, Spring 2020, pp.146–56.

_____. "Mark Twain Kills a Boy." *Mark Twain Journal*, vol. 54, no. 1, Spring 2016, pp. 17–32.

Mailloux, Steven. *Rhetorical Power*. Ithaca & London: Cornell UP, 1989.

Nilon, Charles H. "The Ending of *Huckleberry Finn*: *Freeing the Free Negro*." *Mark Twain Journal*, vol. 22, no. 2, Fall 1984, pp. 21–27.

Rasmussen, R. Kent, editor. *Dear Mark Twain, Letters from His Readers*. U of California P, 2013.

Stone, Albert E. *The Innocent Eye: Childhood in Mark Twain's Imagination*. Yale UP, 1961.

Wolff, Cynthia Griffin. "*The Adventures of Tom Sawyer*: A Nightmare Vision of American Boyhood." *Critical Essays on "The Adventures of Tom Sawyer."* Edited by Gary Scharnhost, G. K. Hall, 1993.

Is *Tom Sawyer* an Idyllic Dream or a Boy's Nightmare?

K. Patrick Ober

A child's life is never static. Every day brings a continuous stream of new lessons. Some lessons must be learned. Other lessons are better ignored. "Growing up" is not a passive process. Parents often have the delusion that they are in control of their children's development. In truth, the children themselves choose many of their most influential experiences. Children are particularly adept at creating fantasy worlds as appealing alternatives to the sometimes incomprehensible world of adults. In the simplified sanctuaries of their own making, children retreat from the complexities of the adult world, avoid the confusing barrage of inconsistent adult expectations, and (most importantly) escape from the boredom that seems so pervasive in the land of adults. During these escapes from adult oversight, children develop many of the skills they will need in the future. The act of fantasizing allows children to explore alternative versions of their own identity that are discouraged by the rules of the adult world. Well into his adult life, Samuel Clemens still remembered some of the greatest forbidden aspirations of his childhood, including the hope that "if we lived and were good, God would permit us to be pirates" (*Life on the Mississippi*, chapter 4).

The Quintessential Book of Childhood

All of that should make *Tom Sawyer* the quintessential book of American childhood. It is loaded with unimaginable liberty (sneaking out of the house in the dark of night, at will), imaginative play (searching for buried pirate treasure), victorious sibling rivalry (getting revenge on Sid), schoolhouse heroics (taking the punishment for Becky), public exhibits of cleverness (amassing Bible verse tickets without ever touching a Bible), joyful retaliation (plucking headmaster Dobbins's toupee right off his head for all to see), and creative moments of unpunishable sassiness (shaming Aunt Polly with guilt because she almost "roasted [Tom's] bowels out of him" with Pain-killer). *Tom Sawyer* is a boy's idyllic dream, a life almost too good to be true. It has become an American icon. Norman Rockwell captured its essence in his painting of Tom's fence whitewashing episode (a painting later immortalized on an eight-cent U.S. postage stamp in 1972). Sentimentalists portray *Tom Sawyer* as nothing less than a heartwarming story of a perfect American childhood: a spunky boy in frontier America takes on childhood's challenges with imagination, inventiveness, and humor as he prepares himself to become an accomplished adult. This vision is even embraced within the book itself by Becky

Fig. 1. Tom Sawyer's childhood also has nightmarish features such as his fear of Injun Joe that haunts his dreams. True Williams, *Tom Sawyer*, 1876, p. 190. [Public domain.]

Thatcher's father as he foresees Tom's courage and ingenuity as predictors of the boy's future accomplishments: "Judge Thatcher hoped to see Tom a great lawyer or a great soldier some day. He said he meant to look to it that Tom should be admitted to the National military academy and afterward trained in the best law school in the country" (chapter 35).

A Nightmare Vision of American Boyhood

Not everyone accepts this idyllic vision of *Tom Sawyer*. Some writers take a closer look at the book's more disturbing events and are led to vehemently disagree with the idea that *Tom Sawyer* is a glorious and sublime dream. Cynthia Wolff is one of the novel's more outspoken challengers. In her opinion, the Norman-Rockwell-painting-on-a-postage-stamp vision of a Tom Sawyer childhood is an oversimplification of a world that never really existed. She sees a lot of trouble in the St. Petersburg of Tom Sawyer. Wolff is appalled by the patterns of unsupervised risk-taking by children throughout the novel, and she is alarmed by the repeated exposures to mortal danger that recur throughout the book. For her, Tom's saga is steeped in an atmosphere of unalloyed fear; the story is a sinister "nightmare vision of American boyhood," a world that should not be allowed (much less be praised), and the book a terrible literary failure (Wolff 637).

Wolff criticizes the book's unbalanced perspectives. For her, it lacks a true sense of place, and she cites the failure to include commonplace downtown buildings in St. Petersburg as an example. She characterizes the place as "a phantom town inhabited largely by ghostly presences . . . No stores are mentioned in the novel. No blacksmiths. No livery stable. No bank." Wolff is chagrined that the only downtown buildings in the book are the taverns, the courthouse, the jail, and a deserted slaughterhouse (the town's "grisly emblems of crime and punishment") (Wolff 638).

Those criticisms are easily countered. For a child, the familiar structures of everyday life are rarely more than a background blur. A boy's attention is always drawn to the most emotionally intense places, the locations where attendance and participation are required (or forbidden), and where a boy's presence or absence will be noted and rewarded (or possibly punished) by authorities. A boy's interest is pulled to the places where opportunities to excel or fail are abundant (school competitions); to the spaces declared off-limits by adults, with their attractiveness further intensified if they might be places of risk or trouble (the haunted house); and to the places that possess their own intrinsic mystery (the graveyard and the cave). Wolff misses the point when she objects to the book's lack of attention to the commonplace. Tom and Huck have no interest in the mundane. They have no reason to notice the shops and stores of St. Petersburg as they sneak over to the jailhouse in the middle of the night to visit Muff Potter. They have weightier things on their minds as they give him tobacco and matches through his jailhouse window. They are trying to allay their own guilt for not getting Muff out of his predicament, even as they are trying to avoid being discovered by Injun Joe.

The jail episode in *Tom Sawyer* is a watered-down version of an emotionally intense event from Samuel Clemens's childhood, an occurrence that created tremendous guilt for Clemens far exceeding Tom Sawyer's guilt for remaining silent about Muff's innocence. In 1853, a "whisky-sodden tramp" was harassed by a roving gang of Hannibal boys. Sam Clemens, in an act of kindness, gave the drunken man some matches he requested. Later that night, the tramp was thrown into the local jailhouse. During the night, he ignited the straw bedding and dry timbers of his cell, and he burned to death while trapped in the jail as helpless onlookers (including Sam Clemens) watched. Clemens could not erase the image of the perishing man from his mind: "I saw that face, so situated, every night for a

Fig. 2. (At left) In *Life on the Mississippi* Clemens recalls having nightmares about a vagabond to whom he gave matches who burned himself to death in jail. *Life on the Mississippi*, 1883, p. 554; (At right) *Tom Sawyer* offers a less disturbing variation of that incident when Tom and Huck give Muff Potter tobacco and matches while he is in jail. True Williams, *Tom Sawyer*, 1876, p. 184. [Public domain.]

Critical Insights

long time afterward; and I believed myself as guilty of the man's death . . . the impressions of that time are burnt into my memory." His self-inflicted guilt for the situation anticipates the guilt that Tom Sawyer would experience during Muff Potter's imprisonment: "I knew more about his case than anyone else; I knew too much of it" (*Life on the Mississippi,* chapter 56). Clemens was victimized by recurring nightmares about the man's death. The man's death "lay upon my conscience a hundred nights afterward and filled them with hideous dreams—dreams in which I saw his appealing face as I had seen it in the pathetic reality, pressed against the window-bars, with the red hell glowing behind him." In Clemens's nightmares, the dead man accused him of murder: "If you had not given me the matches, this would not have happened; you are responsible for my death" (*Autobiography* 157). Wolff's criticism of *Tom Sawyer* as a "nightmare vision of American boyhood" loses some traction when we contemplate the parallel jailhouse experiences of Clemens's and Tom Sawyer's boyhood and realize how much Sam Clemens had to tone down his own nightmare vision at the jail to create a far milder version for Tom Sawyer.

Wolff also criticizes the book's lack of adult male role models. "There are no available men in it—no men whom Tom can fancy himself imitating." She describes an environment that "is not normal, certainly not congenial to a boy's coming of age." Instead, it is "a matriarchy . . . a world that holds small boys in bondage," a world "saturated with gentility, that is, with women's notions" (Wolff 641). As with Wolff's criticism of place, this condemnation misses the reality that a boy will have limited interest in the storekeeper or blacksmith who has a bland, repetitive daily routine. A boy is prone to devote most of his attention to monitoring authority figures (for example, the schoolmaster, Dobbins) and mysterious and frightening individuals (for example, Injun Joe) in his immediate vicinity. Wolff's chagrin at an apparent lack of adult males can be contested by the observation that trustworthy men (for example, Judge Thatcher and the "Welchman") always seem to appear when they are needed. When not needed, they seem invisible (at least to Tom), and their invisibility is a great advantage (at least to Tom).

Being unencumbered by adult influence is the perfect way for a boy to establish his identity in the world. It is an uncommon freedom for most boys. It made Huck Finn the most envied of all the children in town. Unlike the others, Huck is free to be "idle, and lawless, and vulgar and bad." With the limitless opportunities arising from Huck's unsupervised life, "children admired him so, and delighted in his forbidden society, and wished they dared to be like him" (chapter 6).

Even with the obvious rebuttals, though, Wolff's concerns about *Tom Sawyer* deserve attention. The book has its ghoulish components. Is it emotionally healthy for a boy to worry about being murdered in his sleep by an Injun Joe, or trapped in a cave to die of starvation? The story without question has nightmarish features, but are they sufficient to disparage *Tom Sawyer* in its entirety? Might there even be redeeming components of the nightmare events? To resolve this dichotomy, idyll vs. nightmare, it may be helpful to further compare Samuel Clemens's own childhood experiences in Hannibal to the modifications he created for Tom's experiences in St. Petersburg. The relationship of the two boyhoods is complex; it would be foolish to think that *Tom Sawyer* is simply a whitewashed recounting of Sam Clemens's childhood. The single critical question remains: Is Tom Sawyer's story an idyllic version or a nightmarish mutation of Sam Clemens's life? Some caution is required before any conclusions are reached. Sam Clemens as Mark Twain is, after all, a writer of fiction. He is an embellisher of fact. As he warns us, "I am not one of those who in expressing opinions confine themselves to facts. I don't know anything that mars good literature so completely as too much truth" ("Dinner Speech" 574). Even if he tried to restrain himself to telling the truth about his youth, his memory is not always trustworthy enough to do it (or so Clemens claims, in a statement that may be its own embellishment). "It isn't so astonishing, the number of things that I can remember, as the number of things I can remember that aren't so" (Paine 1269).

Growing Up at a Dangerous Time

Despite Clemens's professed memory lapses, his own boyhood was the foundation for Tom Sawyer's story, and one thing is certain: Samuel Clemens grew up at a dangerous time for children. He observed that it was typical for one or two Hannibal boys to drown every year, and he reports that he had to be "pulled out in a 2/3 drowned condition" on nine different occasions before he could swim (Leary 115). No one drowns in *Tom Sawyer*, though Tom plays the town's worry about his drowning to add to his own amusement.

Infections were another common cause of death, at a time when bacteria were yet to be identified and antibiotics did not exist. In 1847, in Sam Clemens's twelfth year of life, the Hannibal *Gazette* reported the chilling statistic that half of the children born in that era died before their twenty-first birthday. This pervasive worry about childhood death in Sam Clemens's day spills over into the pages of *Tom Sawyer*, where it begins to affect Tom's mood after Becky stops coming to school. At first, he tries to shut her out of his mind ("whistle her down the wind"), but Tom is not able to repress his thoughts about the possibility of Becky's death. "He began to find himself hanging around her father's house, nights, and feeling very miserable. She was ill. What if she should die!" (chapter 12). The nightmare of seeing the death of another child was a reality of Sam Clemens's youth; his sister Margaret died when he was three years old, and his brother Benjamin died when he was six. Clemens was kinder in creating Tom Sawyer's boyhood. No children die in *Tom Sawyer*.

The risk of childhood death in Clemens's youth is exemplified by a virulent measles epidemic that struck Hannibal in the spring of 1844. The epidemic "made a most alarming slaughter among the little people," Clemens remembered. "There was a funeral almost daily, and the mothers of the town were nearly demented with fright" (*Autobiography* 420). The maternal anxiety spilled over to affect the children. Clemens recalls that "no romping was allowed, no noise, no laughter, the family moved spectrally about on tiptoe, in a ghostly hush . . . My soul was steeped in this awful dreariness—and in fear" ("Turning Point" 458). Sam Clemens lived in a real nightmare.

Measles plays a far gentler role in *Tom Sawyer*. Tom comes down with an uneventful bout of the disease. It keeps him out of commission for several weeks, but there is no worry about his possible demise. While Tom is restricted to home and bed, all his friends (including Huck Finn) discover religion. When he rejoins them after his recuperation, Tom finds their new religious interests have rendered them painfully dull and uninteresting companions. Tom has a relapse of measles that puts him back in bed for a couple more weeks. On recovering, he is gratified to find that his comrades have also relapsed (from their religious pursuits). Life is back to normal, or even a bit better. No one dies. Tom's bout with measles is, thus, almost idyllic, not nightmarish. It gives him a chance to see his friends become afflicted with religious obsessions from a revival passing through town, without getting afflicted himself. It lets him ponder the transient nature of his comrades' religious fervor. In *Tom Sawyer*, measles is a useful disease, if not even an entertaining one—not at all the nightmare it had been for Sam Clemens.

Cholera was another nightmarish infection of Clemens's youth. Clemens never forgot Hannibal's "cholera days of '49" and the panic it created. "The people along the Mississippi were paralyzed with fright. Those who could run away, did it," he remembered. "And many died of fright in the flight. Fright killed three persons where the cholera killed one." Not everyone ran away. The Clemens family stayed put, but Sam Clemens's mother, Jane, was not about to let her children become passive victims. She was a woman of action. "Those who couldn't flee kept themselves drenched with cholera preventives," Sam recalled, "and my mother chose Perry Davis's Pain-Killer for me" (*Autobiography* 352). The Pain-Killer was an alcohol-heavy preventative patent medicine, laced with capsaicin (the chemical that creates the heat in hot peppers) and further enlivened by the malodorous scent of camphor.

Aunt Polly forces Tom to drink "Pain-killer" in *Tom Sawyer*, but Clemens does not set up the experience by threatening Tom's life during a cholera epidemic. Instead, he gives Tom a far less life-threatening affliction. Tom is love-sick and worried about Becky's absence from school, and he further feels guilty for not reporting

Muff Potter's innocence. Aunt Polly is not aware of the basis of Tom's despondency; it is part of his boy-world that he hides from her adult-world. Polly gives Tom the Pain-killer to cure his undiagnosed blues. She is pleased that it seems to work (in a way). "The boy could not have shown a wilder, heartier interest, if she had built a fire under him" (chapter 12).

To write a story in which Tom Sawyer becomes a hero, Clemens needed a villain less abstract than a fear of infection by measles or cholera. He needed a more tangible representation of evil, and that is where Injun Joe comes in. With Tom as the hero, and Injun Joe as evil personified, Clemens had to find feasible locations for Tom and Joe to cross paths. He settled for two ideal places, the town cemetery and the cave. The cemetery and the cave share a crucial element that is never mentioned in the book. The pernicious influence of a real-life St. Louis doctor named Joseph Nash McDowell weighs heavily over the events in both the cemetery and the cave.

The Eccentric Dr. McDowell—the Unseen Influence in *Tom Sawyer*

A gloomy cemetery at midnight is a perfect setting in which to introduce a sense of evil. The novel's macabre grave-robbing episode is a central part of the story, and yet the essential underlying question about the scene is never answered in *Tom Sawyer*. The question is not even asked, for that matter. *Why* is the grave of Hoss Williams being dug up? And why has Dr. Robinson, presumably a respectable adult member of the community, organized the grave-robbing expedition? And why is he paying Injun Joe and Muff Potter to help him? Robinson's murder quickly makes those questions seem less important as the threat of Injun Joe begins to loom as a greater concern. The basic question still remains, though. Would not Tom and Huck have wondered about the purpose of the grave robbery? After all, they have questions and opinions about almost everything else they encounter, from stump water to dead cats.

In the Missouri of Sam Clemens's boyhood, grave-robbing activity was traceable to Dr. Joseph Nash McDowell in St. Louis. McDowell founded the first medical school west of the Mississippi

River in 1840. The Missouri Medical College was often referred to as "McDowell's Medical College." Medical education of the era predominantly involved anatomic study, and McDowell was renowned for his expertise and enthusiasm as an anatomy teacher. According to Dr. E. B. Outten, a St. Louis surgeon who trained under McDowell, "students from his college were better and more enthusiastically instructed in anatomy than almost any college in the land. Anatomy here became almost a mania" (Outten 146). McDowell constantly needed study material (human bodies) for dissection by his students. Human dissection was illegal in most places, and procurement of cadavers was a challenge. McDowell stole bodies from St. Louis cemeteries, and he often enlisted medical students to help him. McDowell also employed professional grave robbers, who were known as "resurrectionists." When Tom and Huck discover Dr. Robinson, Muff Potter, and Injun Joe in the cemetery, they are watching an example of Dr. McDowell's resurrectionists at work.

Sam Clemens learned about the workings of McDowell's medical school from an uncle, Jim Lampton, who attended McDowell's college in the 1840s. He jotted the phrase "Jim Lampton & the dead man in Dr. McDowell's College" in his notebook of 1866 (*Notebooks and Journals* 136). In his *Autobiography*, Clemens characterized McDowell as "a St. Louis surgeon of extraordinary ability and wide celebrity. He was an eccentric man and did many strange things" (*Autobiography* 214). Some of the strangest things McDowell did took place in the cave in Hannibal that Sam Clemens knew so well. In fact, the "McDougal's cave" in *Tom Sawyer* was "McDowell's cave" in Clemens's youth, and McDowell's activities in the cave made it a nightmarish location when Clemens was a boy.

Fearful Findings in the Cave

Why did McDowell want to own a cave in Hannibal? Shortly after buying the cave in the late 1840s, he sealed the entrance with a stone wall. The citizens of Hannibal were suddenly barred from entering the cave, a popular recreational site, without explanation. The closure of the cave entrance by McDowell triggered local curiosity. Boys found crevices on the hillside that gave them new ways of getting into the cave. (In years to come, Sam Clemens would use one of those crevices to help Tom Sawyer find his way out.) The boys of Hannibal crawled into the cave through the side passages and returned with stories of some unusual findings in the cave. Adults eventually broke down McDowell's barrier of the main entrance to check things out for themselves. They discovered that McDowell was using the cave for nefarious purposes. He was conducting experiments on the preservation of bodies. According to Dr. Outten of St. Louis, McDowell "took a copper vase containing the body of one of his children and suspended it from the roof of the cave" (Outten 145). In his 1883 book *Life on the Mississippi*, Clemens provides details about this ghoulish activity, noting that the owner of the cave "turned it into a mausoleum for his daughter, aged fourteen," and explains that "this poor child was put into a copper cylinder filled with alcohol, and it was suspended in one of the dismal avenues of the cave" (*Life on the Mississippi*, chapter 55). Clemens could never get this memory out of his mind, and he repeated the details in his *Autobiography* (213–14).

McDowell believed in spiritualism and hoped to communicate with his family members after their deaths. He believed that traditional burials of bodies stifled the ability of the deceased to communicate with the living, and he hoped to find methods to make his relatives more accessible to him after their death. After he learned that his daughter's cylinder had been vandalized by the people of Hannibal, he removed her body from the cave and moved it back to St. Louis. The identities of those who interfered with the girl's body have always been reported in vague terms, and the descriptions of their means of entry are inconsistent. Outten blamed "some evil disposed and mischievous town loafers" for breaking down the barrier sealing the cave entry and opening the copper coffin. (Outten 145) Clemens does not use any of this in *Tom Sawyer*, but in *Life on the Mississippi* (chapter 55), he describes how unnamed culprits—he calls them "the baser order of tourists"—were able to get into the cave, remove the top of the cylinder, and then "drag the dead face into view and examine it and comment upon it." In his *Autobiography*, Clemens implies that he had no personal knowledge of such desecration, but reports "it was said" that "loafers and rowdies" were responsible, and he again describes how they "used to drag it up by the hair and look at the dead face" (214).

Clemens would have been almost twelve years old on November 4, 1847, when a reporter for the Hannibal *Gazette* reported seeing the cylinder on a recent trip into the cave. Was Sam Clemens among the curious boys who found alternate entrances to the cave after the main passage was blocked? Did he join the group of boys who scrambled in and out of the cave? Was he among the "loafers and rowdies" or "baser order of tourists" who interfered with the dangling body? He knew a lot of details about the dead girl, at the very least. In comparison to the discovery of the dead girl's body in the cave in Sam Clemens's day, the discovery of Injun Joe's presence in the cave by Tom Sawyer seems far less terrifying, and Wolff's criticism of *Tom Sawyer* as a "nightmare vision of American boyhood" begins to pale.

Whether his information about the suspended girl was firsthand or secondhand, Sam Clemens's knowledge of the cave's complex corridors became the foundation for one of book's important experiences of Tom and Becky: "It was an easy place to get lost in . . . I got lost in it myself, along with a lady, and our last candle burned down to almost nothing before we glimpsed the search party's lights winding about in the distance" (*Autobiography* 213). McDowell's activities provided further assistance with the book's details. McDowell's closure of the main entrance to keep the people of Hannibal out of the cave also gave Clemens a way to trap Injun Joe inside the cave until he died of starvation. When McDowell's blockade forced the boys of Hannibal to find new entrances into the cave, their discoveries suggested an exit route for getting Tom and Becky out of the cave.

Even if he never encountered McDowell's dead daughter face-to-face in the cave, Sam Clemens had a comparable gruesome childhood exposure to a corpse that created nightmare visions for him. In September of 1843, before he was eight years old, he sneaked into his father's office at night to avoid punishment for skipping

Fig. 3. Eight-year-old Sam Clemens's discovery of a corpse in his father's office. *The Innocents Abroad*, 1869, p. 176. [Public domain.]

school. In the moonlight he discovered that he was sharing the room with a dead man with a "ghastly stab" in his chest. He promptly exited through the window, suddenly willing to take any punishment that might await him at home. The dead man became a nightmare he could not forget. "I have slept in the same room with him often, since then—in my dreams" (*Innocents Abroad*, chapter 18).

Old Memories, Shifting Perspectives, and New Dreams

The experiences of boyhood fade over time, only to be reactivated (and perhaps distorted) in the dreams of adulthood. Old memories blur together to create new dreams, as Clemens discovered when he visited Hannibal as an adult. "During my three days stay in the town, I woke up every morning with the impression that I was a boy—for in my dreams the faces were all young again, and looked as they had looked in the old times" (*Life on the Mississippi*, chapter 55).

His boyhood memories kindled dreamlike sensations. "The things about me and before me made me feel like a boy again—convinced me that I was a boy again, and that I had simply been dreaming an unusually long dream" (*Life on the Mississippi*, chapter 53). Dreams and reality, at times, can be indistinguishable.

This leads to reconsideration of the question of whether *Tom Sawyer* is an idyllic dream or a nightmare. The answer, by necessity, is a matter of perspective. The question must be answered by considering the vantage point of the individual reader. Is the reading a first-time encounter (as it will be for most childhood readers) or is the reader an adult who has "been there" and shared Tom's experiences several times before? Does the first reading create any distortions of reality in the mind of the reader? (In childhood, unfamiliar details are often magnified when they are first encountered, only to shrink back toward reality with later experiences during adult life.) Misperceptions are rampant in childhood. A sense of proportionality is impossible to achieve in the absence of prior exposure and experience. Childhood is loaded with novel events. Tom Sawyer provides a prime example of youthful lack of perspective and proportion. Tom has a tendency to magnify the significance of every event of his life, and this behavior provides much of his appeal. For Tom, whitewashing the fence is a formidable task: "Thirty yards of board fence nine feet high." With no other options, "he dipped his brush and passed it along the topmost plank . . ." (chapter 2). Is the topmost plank *really* nine feet high? Or does it just seem that way to Tom when the fence looms as an insurmountable barrier to his freedom? Or is Tom following the lead of his creator, Sam Clemens, who does not feel compelled to confine himself to the facts when telling a story?

The adult/child contrast is essential to any consideration of a reader's reaction to *Tom Sawyer*. Each reading of the book generates a different response, and for good reason. We all change. The world changes. Our perceptions of the world change. No man can step in the same river twice, the ancient Greek philosopher Heraclitus observes, and the reason is simple. The river is never the same river; the man is never the same man (Taylor 90). Novelist E. L. Doctorow reminds us that Tom Sawyer lives "in the world of two distinct and, for the most part, irreconcilable life forms, the Child and the Adult," living as "separate species" within "separate cultures which continually clash and cause trouble between them." This conflict in viewpoint allows the book to work both ways, as a child's book or as an adult's book. Each reader will enter into *Tom Sawyer* from one of these two possible perspectives, and each one leads to a different conclusion. "We can read with a child's eye or an adult's," Doctorow suggests, "and with a different focal resolution for each" (Doctorow xxxiii–xxxiv). In discussing the same critical question, R. Kent Rasmussen agrees that each reader brings a personal perspective to the reading of *Tom Sawyer*. This is no small matter. The differences are so profound, Rasmussen advises that it is fair to ask "whether children and adults are reading the *same* book" (Rasmussen xxi). We thus need to read the book both ways if we really want to understand it.

Sam Clemens had his own explanation for the manner in which events from the past seem so different when they are revisited at later times in our life. Our reactions to any event are driven by the context of the event and the associations we make around it. It differs with every inspection. "We simply take a lot of old ideas and put them into a sort of mental kaleidoscope," Clemens suggests. "We give them a turn and they make new and curious combinations. We keep on turning and making new combinations indefinitely; but they are the same old pieces of colored glass . . ." (Paine 1343). The primary experiences of life (the "old pieces of colored glass") do not change, but their context and significance are altered by the twists and turns of our subsequent experiences. The original "pieces of colored glass" will never look the same as they did when we first encountered them. Each reading of *Tom Sawyer* puts the same words in front of us. The events in the book remain the same. Our reactions are never quite the same. Each reading is altered by the latest twist of our personal kaleidoscope, and we see a different pattern each time.

Is *Tom Sawyer* an idyllic dream or a nightmare? Is it a book for children or a book for adults? Are those, perhaps, one and the same question? Sam Clemens understood the differences between children and adults as well as anyone, and he also understood the value of reconnecting the adult of the present with the forgotten child of the past. One of his goals in writing *Tom Sawyer* was to "remind adults of what they once were themselves, and of how they felt and thought and talked, and what queer enterprises they sometimes engaged in" (preface). He blended his own childhood memories into his story of Tom Sawyer's boyhood, but he was cautiously selective in his choices. As he wrote *Tom Sawyer*, Clemens steered clear of the most troubling experiences of his own youth, such as his discovery of the dead man in his father's office or his misdirected self-blame for immolating the drunkard in the jailhouse. He made no references to the ghoulish reports of the dead girl suspended in the cave's copper casket. He kept the real nightmares—his own nightmares—out of Tom Sawyer's story. In telling Tom's story, Sam Clemens left some space open for the insertion of personal nightmares by each reader, if the reader chooses to supply them. The nightmares are not obligatory, though, and the book can be read without terror. *Tom Sawyer* is a book about innocence prevailing over maliciousness, humor prevailing over gloom, and goodness prevailing over evil. It may be an uneasy idyll for some, but *Tom Sawyer* is anything but a nightmare.

Works Cited

Doctorow, E. L. Introduction. *The Adventures of Tom Sawyer* by Mark Twain. Oxford UP, 1996, xxxi–xxxviii.

Leary, Lewis, editor. *Mark Twain's Correspondence with Henry Huttleston Rogers, 1893–1909*. U California P, 1969.

Outten, W. B. "Glimpses of Early St. Louis Medical History." *The Medical Fortnightly*, vol. 33, no. 6, 25 Mar. 1908, pp. 143–48.

Paine, Albert Bigelow. *Mark Twain, A Biography*. Three Volumes. Harper & Brothers, 1912.

Rasmussen, R. Kent. Introduction to *The Adventures of Tom Sawyer* by Mark Twain. Penguin Books, 2014.

Taylor, C. C. W., editor. *Routledge History of Philosophy,* Vol. 1: *From the Beginning to Plato*. Taylor & Francis Group, 1997.

Twain, Mark. *The Adventures of Tom Sawyer*. 1876. Oxford UP, 1996.

_____. *Autobiography of Mark Twain.* Vol. 1: The Complete and Authoritative Edition. Edited by Harriet Elinor Smith, U of California P, 2010.

_____. "Dinner Speech." Savage Club Dinner, London, 6 July 1907. *Mark Twain Speaking.* Edited by Paul Fatout, U of Iowa P, 1976.

_____. *The Innocents Abroad.* 1869. Oxford UP, 1996.

_____. *Life on the Mississippi.* 1883. Oxford UP, 1996.

_____. *Mark Twain's Notebooks & Journals.* Vol. 1, 1855–1873. Edited by Frederick Anderson, et al., U of California P, 1975.

_____. "The Turning Point of My Life." In *What Is Man? and Other Philosophical Writings.* Edited by Paul Baender, U of California P, 1973.

Wolff, Cynthia Griffin, "*The Adventures of Tom Sawyer*: A Nightmare Vision of American Boyhood," *Massachusetts Review*, vol. 21, no. 4, Winter 1980, pp. 637–52.

Becky Thatcher and Aunt Polly in Three Dimensions_____

Linda Morris

Across the course of his career, Mark Twain created a wide range of female characters. Among his earlier creations some, such as Becky Thatcher, tend to be dismissed by critics as relatively stereotypical, flat characters, and are routinely glossed over. By contrast others, such as Roxy in Twain's 1894 novel *Pudd'nhead Wilson,* are celebrated for being highly original, for the strength and uniqueness of their representation. Thus, to write focusing on Becky and Aunt Polly in *The Adventures of Tom Sawyer* is to read against the grain of traditional interpretations of the novel. It is to ask that we understand that this young girl and older woman are more interesting and more complex than ordinarily credited, and they are among the first such characters in whom Twain, in fact, invested a good bit of creative energy and originality.

Such a focus in no way alters the fact that Tom is the center of the novel, as the opening line makes abundantly clear: "Tom!" It is his novel, his story, his book, regarded by many as the ultimate "boy's book." Even his male companions, interesting though they become at times, (especially Huck Finn) are always and ever secondary to Tom. If the attention is not on him, he makes sure to draw it to him. So, what chances do a young girl, a newcomer to town, and a maiden aunt have when up against Tom?

Don't Sell Becky Short

If a reader is willing to avoid the tendency to dismiss Becky Thatcher as critics so often have as "boring," "a cipher," "helpless," as "the Angel in the house," Becky instead emerges as a worthy counterpart to Tom, a true match for him. It is not very far into the novel before Becky is introduced to the reader at the same moment Tom sees her for the first time. However, the language is wholly the narrator's, not Tom's: "A lovely little blue-eyed creature with yellow hair plaited into two long tails, white summer frock and embroidered pantalettes." The language that describes Tom's attempts to capture Becky's attention continues to be the narrator's: He "began to 'show off' in all sorts of absurd boyish ways in order to win her admiration. He kept up this grotesque foolishness for some time" (chapter 3). It is three chapters later before Becky appears again, and when she does and the readers truly sees her and hears her for the first time, she begins to emerge as a romantic match for Tom.

Fig. 1. True Williams's depiction of the "lovely little blue-eyed creature with yellow hair plaited into two long tails, white summer frock and embroidered pantalettes" whom Tom first sees in chapter 3. *Tom Sawyer*, 1876, p. 33. [Public domain.]

In fact, Becky quickly accepts her role as Tom's girlfriend, and she is given no other in *Tom Sawyer*. Further, that role is initially reinforced by her being referred to only as "the girl." Neither Becky nor Tom ever moves beyond their pre-assigned gender roles in their youthful courtship as it waxes and wanes. But within that role, Becky surprisingly holds her own against Tom. She may be the "archetypal" girl in nineteenth-century American terms (Cooley xi), but she is no slouch, and she gives as well as she gets, as their first real interaction demonstrates: "Presently the boy began to steal furtive glances at the girl. She observed it, 'made a mouth' at him and gave him the back of her head for the space of a minute" (chapter 6).

Moving very quickly, Tom persuades Becky to say she loves him even in their first time together alone, but as soon as she does so, she immediately "springs away." Things go smoothly between them until Tom blunders and lets it slip that he was once "engaged" to Amy Lawrence. Becky retaliates in the only way she can; she shuns him, and she sticks with this response. Consequently, she very effectively sends Tom off literally on his own in his disappointment that he is unable to regain control of the situation. This, in turn, sets into motion a series of events wholly separate from the courtship rituals, events that lead to Tom, Joe Harper, and Huck's famous escapades on Jackson's Island and Tom's engineering the boys' triumphal return to the village to march down the aisle at their own funeral.

Another eleven chapters elapse before Becky reappears in the novel, and this particular meeting between Becky and Tom represents the fullest, most balanced, standoff between the two of them. Tom has decided that he *could* become independent of Becky, and he attempts to prove that to himself and to her. It is one of the more delightful scenes between them precisely because of their equality. Becky announces to a group of friends that her mother is letting her have a picnic, and she begins to invite people in Tom's presence. Tom, for his part, shows no interest in the picnic and focuses his attention on Amy Lawrence.

When Tom deliberately ignores her, Becky "got away as soon as she could and hid herself and had what her sex called 'a good cry.' Then she sat moody, with wounded pride till the bell rang. She roused up, now, with a vindictive cast in her eye and gave her plaited tails a shake and said she knew what *she'd* do" (chapter 18). So, she sits with Alfred Temple and not only makes Tom jealous but makes him second guess himself for having thrown away a chance "for a reconciliation." It is manipulative on Becky's part, but she works with the material she has, and it is ultimately effective. Once again, Tom responds to her clear sign of indifference to him by literally leaving the scene: "he fled home at noon." Although her actions are a triumph of sorts, they bring Becky no real satisfaction.

Given how the novel is constructed, it is some time again before Becky is back in the scene, and for the only brief time she is wholly on her own. The sparring between Becky and Tom is interrupted by a more serious incident in which Becky shows a surprising boldness in a brief incident. The narration reveals that the schoolmaster, Mr. Dobbins, has a habit of pulling a particular book out of his locked desk when things get a bit dull in the classroom. Finding herself alone there, and spying the key in Dobbins's locked desk, Becky boldly unlocks the desk and takes out the book. This is not the action of a passive, timid "girl." Further, she is not shown to register any particular shock when she discovers the subject of the book: human anatomy with "a handsomely engraved and colored frontispiece—a human figure, stark naked" (chapter 20). What she does react to is being caught in the act by none other than Tom, and she accidentally rips the page in question. Becky understands instantly that she has set herself up to be severely punished for her action by the schoolmaster, and she fears receiving a beating.

The excuse offered in the novel for Dobbins reading such a book is that he was thwarted in his ambition to be a doctor, but the way he keeps the book locked up, and especially the fact that the children all speculate about the subject of the book, indicates that the subject matter is likely inappropriate for the children's classroom. It is surprising for the reader that the novel glosses over "the explicit sexual reference to sexuality in Tom Sawyer" (Stone 12). Apparently, Twain's earlier manuscript made a bit more out of children's natural sexual curiosity in this scene, with Tom wondering what would have happened if "Mary and Alf Temple had caught her looking at such a picture and went around telling" (Stone 12). The finished version of the text, however, turns to an emphasis on Becky's fear of being beaten and Tom marveling at "'what a curious kind of a fool a girl is . . . never been licked in school. Shucks. What's a licking!'" "The episode thus turns toward corporal punishment and away from young people's sexual curiosity" (Stone 12). The severity of the beating Tom receives when he heroically confesses that *he* is the one who tore the book only confirms how inappropriate Dobbins's secret is, for Tom "took without an outcry the most merciless flaying that even Mr. Dobbins had ever administered" (chapter 20). Ironically, the scene cements for the duration of the novel Tom and Becky's relationship as boyfriend and girlfriend.

The strength of Becky's character is once more on display in the novel when Tom and Becky get lost together in McDougal's cave, a terrifying experience that initially reinforces the relative equality of character between the two. Granted Tom takes the lead as the two of them begin to explore the cave, even as other pairs of children set out in separate directions into the vast network of tunnels and varying depths in the cave. His taking the lead seems only natural, and being a newcomer to the village it is likely the first time Becky has been in the cave at all.

What is a bit surprising is that as Tom and Becky continue to explore, Becky seems no more anxious than Tom for their safety, although they, like the others are guided only by their own candle lights (chapter 31). Confronted by a new area to explore, "at once the ambition to be a discoverer seized him, Becky responded to his call. . . ." All their exploration for some time after that is attributed to the two of them together as signaled by the repeated use of the word "they." Even when they come upon a mass of thousands of bats Becky shows no specific fright at being surrounded by the flying creatures, as might be expected in a stereotypic portrayal of a young girl. When they escape from the bats and rest for a while and the "deep stillness of the place laid a clammy hand upon the spirit of the children," Tom finally admits to Becky and himself that he cannot find the way back. Then, and only then, do the differences in their reactions emerge.

Becky begins to cry, although she does not blame Tom for getting them lost, and the differences between them become more pronounced. Increasingly Tom tries to sooth Becky, and reassure her, and Becky cries more and more as the helplessness of their situation intensifies. Even here she does not fulfill the expected role of an archetypal good girl of her time, for she does not turn to prayer and religion in her despair (Tindol 125). In the end, as readers know, as Becky gets weaker and more resigned, it falls to Tom to lead them out of the cave, a full three days and nights after they become lost. Tom emerges as Becky's savior and the clear hero of the day. From this point on, Becky fades from the scene with her status as the hero's girlfriend secure, but with no other role to play.

Although Becky all but disappears in the final pages of the novel, she has nonetheless fulfilled her role as a near-equal to Tom. She will be followed in Twain's career by other young girls who are granted greater freedoms to express themselves outside of any courtship role. These include, for example, Cathy Allison in "The Horse's Tale" and Rachael Hotchkiss in "Hellfire Hotchkiss." Becky made her mark.

"Original Compositions by Young Ladies"

No focus on the role of women in the novel would be complete without attempting to come to terms with the puzzling extended scene in which the narrator satirizes what he describes as the predictable sentimentality and sermonizing in compositions by the girls and young women of St. Petersburg and beyond. The occasion for this diversion from the main story in chapter 21 is "Examination Day" at the end of the school year. Initially focusing on the brutality of Mr. Dobbins as he "lashes" out at the younger students while they prepare to make their recitations, followed by a few examples of students failing to perform to Dobbins's standard, the narrator unexpectedly focuses on what he calls the main event of the evening, "original compositions by the young ladies."

> A prevalent feature in these compositions was a nursed and petted melancholy; another was a wasteful and opulent gush of 'fine language;' another was a tendency to lug in by the ears particularly prized words and phrases until they were worn entirely out; and a peculiarity that conspicuously marked and marred them was the inveterate and intolerable sermon that wagged its crippled tail at the end of each and every one of them (chapter 21).

If this were not enough, the narrator goes on to quote at length samples from offending compositions, especially those prone to sermonizing and sentimentality, with the final composition of the evening described as a "nightmare" that "wound up so destructive of all hope to non-Presbyterians that it took the first prize." Why such a marked digression from the main story as it nears its end? If,

---

as one critic suggests, it shows Twain's concerns for "unliberated femininity" and "unliberated humanity," is it a successful critique? (Georgoudaki 71). Unfortunately, it is hard to make that argument stick. At best, one can argue that it is a sincere attempt to satirize the worst of small-town artificiality and insincerity that young women were required to exhibit—the fate, perhaps, that awaited even Becky, even though she exhibited no such sentimentality even when facing possible death in the cave. At worst, it is a digression, unlinked from St. Petersburg and Tom's story and the extravagant prank that ends the evening—a cat lowered on a string that snatches Schoolmaster Dobbins's wig from his head in full view of the audience—conceived of as an act of revenge by the students for the way he has terrorized them in the schoolroom.

Aunt Polly's Thankless Job

Aunt Polly, whose voice (and responsibilities) launch the novel that centers on the young Tom and bears his name, is cast in a role not of her choosing. That is to say, as an unmarried woman of indeterminate age—more on that later—she finds herself in the relatively thankless position of raising two orphaned boys, at least one of whom (Tom) is the son of her dead sister. Furthermore, no father figures appear in the text, so all the adult parental responsibility falls to Aunt Polly. Hence it is not a stretch to refer to the town in which Tom claims most of the attention as a matriarchy, a world run by women according to the critic Cynthia Griffin Wolff, who also argues that Aunt Polly's "demanding tone permeates the novel" (Wolff 641–42). From Wolff's perspective, the world of St. Petersburg that "holds small boys in bondage" is a town "saturated with gentility, that is with women's notions." Other critics have taken up Wolff's characterization of the town as a "genteel," society. Trygve Thoreson, for example, identifies *Tom Sawyer* as Twain's "prime example of male escape from female-dominated society" (Thoreson 17). Nonetheless, Thoreson correctly argues that Aunt Polly's role is "somewhat more problematic than this one-dimensional view would have us believe." Aunt Polly, with her relative complexity as a secondary character, is worth a closer look.

Consider, for example, Aunt Polly's status in the community separate from her role in relationship to Tom. She clearly is not married; in the parlance of the day, she is an "old maid." We know this in part because of the obvious fact that there is no adult male in her household. The titles given to two other adult women in the novel also point in that direction. Joe Harper's mother, even with no father making an appearance in the novel, is known as "Mrs. Harper." That is, she is identified by her status as a married woman. Then there is the Widow Douglas, whose status is made obvious by her title. Further, there is explicit reference to her deceased husband, the would-be object of Injun Joe's revenge, which he intends to enact upon his widow until thwarted by Huck. So, Aunt Polly is a spinster, an "old maid."

Just how old is Aunt Polly? It is impossible to be sure, but she is sure to be younger than she is represented in the original illustrations for the novel by True Williams. Assuming she was relatively near in age to her sister, Tom's deceased mother, and likewise of the same approximate generation/age as her one other sister, Aunt Sally, who is featured toward the end of *Adventures of Huckleberry Finn* (1885), it is likely that she is no older than in her mid-forties. She is identified near the end of the novel as having gray hair (made grayer by Tom's antics), but that still puts her within that age range. Further, she seems to have remarkable energy to keep up with Tom, and at times keep ahead of him. Nevertheless, at that age, she would be a confirmed old maid, and so she would remain.

From the beginning, Tom and Aunt Polly engage in a game of wits that becomes a stand-off. Tom appears first only through Aunt Polly's perspective and in her voice, and there is nothing "demanding" about her tone. In fact, there is something quite charming about her looking over her spectacles, poking a broom under the bed to try to find Tom, and then hauling him up by "the slack of his roundabout" when he bolts out of the closet. No doubt Aunt Polly's charm owes something to her character's having been partly based on Twain's memory of his own mother, Jane Lampton Clemens. Of Aunt Polly's debt to Jane Clemens, Twain later said that he "fitted her out with a dialect, and tried to think up other improvements for her, but did not find any" (Twain 212). Aunt Polly does indeed speak in vivid vernacular English, uttering such phrases in chapter 1 as "seeing the beat of that boy," "what is that truck?," and "forty times I've said if you didn't let that jam alone I'd skin you." What is her response when Tom escapes over the fence in their first encounter in the novel? She laughs. This is an unexpected and defining characteristic of Aunt Polly.

Fig. 2. Mark Twain's mother, Jane Lampton Clemens, around 1870, and True Williams's portrait of her fictional counterpart, Aunt Polly. (Jane Clemens) A. B. Paine, *Mark Twain: A Biography*, 1912, vol. 1; (Polly) *Tom Sawyer*, 1876, p. 158. [Public domain.]

All feisty young boys should be so lucky. Aunt Polly has a duty to perform, and she is going to do her best by Tom and the community to do just that. Further, she does so with grace and dignity, not the kind of malice and would-be dominance shown by a character such as Schoolmaster Dobbins. She is fully conscious of her duty, and she recognizes that Tom outwits her time and again, which she actually begrudgingly admires. Her role is laid out at the beginning, with a good deal of self-awareness and a generous dose of genuine love for Tom. It is worth considering in some detail how that insight is relayed, for it tells us volumes about Aunt Polly:

> "Hang the boy, can't I never learn anything? Ain't he played me tricks enough like that for me to be looking out for him by this time? . . . But my goodness, he never plays them alike, two days, and how is a body to know what's coming? He 'pears to know just how long he can torment me before I get my dander up, and he knows if he can make out to put me off for a minute or make me laugh, it's all down again and I can't hit him a lick" (chapter 1).

This is a culture in which corporal punishment is not only allowed but encouraged, and as readers all know, the schoolmaster metes it out liberally to boys and girls alike. The narrator uses such terms as "flaying" and "beatings," and even Aunt Polly imagines she should be "lashing" Tom, but she never does. The most physical punishment she administers is unexpected when she knocks him to the floor, thinking him responsible for breaking her sugar bowl in chapter 3. More often, she just cracks him on the head with her thimble.

On the whole, however, punishing Tom costs Aunt Polly more than it costs Tom. If she punishes him, and she does both in terms of the occasional flick on the head or yanking on his ear, she is repeatedly bothered by having to do so. She is torn between her sense of duty toward Tom and her remorse for punishing him, with "a troubled heart" (chapter 3). One of the key scenes that reveals the complexity of Aunt Polly's predicament, charged as she is to restrain and guide her imaginative, indeed impulsive, nephew, is the comic episode featuring Tom, Peter the Cat, and Pain-killer medication. After Tom mischievously administers the medicine to the cat and Peter prances around the room then leaps through an open window, Aunt Polly enters the room "petrified with astonishment" and asks Tom to explain what in the world has just happened:

> "Now, sir, what did you want to treat that poor dumb beast so, for?"
> "I done it out of pity for him—because he hadn't any aunt."
> "Hadn't any aunt!—you numscull. What has that got to do with it?"

"Heaps. Because if he'd a had one she'd a burnt him out herself! She'd a roasted his bowels out of him 'thout any more feeling than if he was a human!"

Aunt Polly felt a sudden pang of remorse. This was putting the thing in a new light; what was cruelty to a cat *might* be cruelty to a boy, too. She began to soften; she felt sorry. Her eyes watered a little, and she put her hand on Tom's head and said gently:

"I was meaning for the best, Tom. And Tom, it *did* do you good"(chapter 12).

While it may appear that Tom gets the upper hand at the end of this exchange, Polly and Tom end with a kind of truce, or as one critic puts it, "they reach a tentative understanding" (Thoreson 20). Likewise, the reader reaches a new understanding, likely surprised by how quickly Aunt Polly understands what Tom is trying to tell her without turning defensive or bearing down on him to reinforce her role. Almost immediately she shows remorse, and she backs off. Tom, meanwhile, has pulled off one of the more spontaneous and quixotic scenes in the novel. It is more than a fitting conclusion to a satiric thrust at popular health cures, and those who like Aunt Polly are taken in by the "new-fangled methods of producing health or mending it . . . She was as simple-hearted and honest as the day was long, and so she was an easy victim."

A second scene in chapter 15 highlights Aunt Polly's kindheartedness as well as the depth of her understanding about Tom's true character. It occurs during the period when Tom and Joe Harper have been missing on the island and are feared by the townspeople to be dead. Aunt Polly and Mrs. Harper are consoling one another as best they can:

"But as I was saying," said Aunt Polly, "he warn't *bad*, so to say— only misch*ee*vous. Only just giddy, and harum-scarum, you know. He warn't any more responsible than a colt. *He* never meant any harm, and he was the best-hearted boy that ever was"—and she began to cry. . . . "Oh, Mrs. Harper, I don't know how to give him up, I don't know how to give him up! He was such a comfort to me, although he tormented my old heart out of me, 'most'" (chapter 15).

This is not the last time Aunt Polly will have to face the prospect of Tom being dead, and it is not the last time she will show the depth of her love for Tom through her sorrow. It is, however, the last time she will articulate so clearly her understanding of the internal conflicts inherent in her role as his aunt. When the town believes Tom and Becky are hopelessly lost in the cave, Aunt Polly's primary response is to fall "to crying and wringing her hands" (chapter 30). As more time goes by, "Aunt Polly had dropped into a settled melancholy, and her gray hair had grown almost white" (chapter 32). When the children are found alive, the narrator delivers the final word about Aunt Polly, which says volumes about her: "Aunt Polly's happiness was complete."

Aunt Polly as an Archetypal Strong Woman

If Aunt Polly were a character who might be seen as fulfilling a stereotype—the old maid enforcer of genteel values—she's a remarkably interesting stereotype. She has nuance, she speaks in lively, vernacular English, she sees the good-heartedness behind her nephew's need to capture the center of attention, and she has a great deal of self-knowledge. Instead of being dismissed as a stereotypical controlling woman, she should be understood to be one of Twain's first relatively lively and strong women characters.

Over the years Twain created a range of strong girls and powerful women who clearly push beyond any cultural or gender stereotypes. These include minor characters, such as the adolescent tomboy Rachel (Hellfire) Hotchkiss who pushes the limits of how girls were represented in nineteenth-century American literature. She was, in fact, described by one of her neighbors as "the only genuwyne male in this town . . . if you leave out sex and just consider the business facts" (Cooley 56). They include as well some remarkably strong and gender defiant women who are at the center of full-length novels. Some would argue that Twain's representation of Joan of Arc was his greatest departure from a gender conforming woman. An illiterate peasant girl, Joan cross-dressed in men's clothing, donned armor and led the French forces to overthrow the occupying forces. She was imprisoned by the Roman Catholic church and ultimately condemned to death and burned at the stake. In regard to another Twain novel, other critics might argue, with good reason, that there was no more original non-conforming woman character than Twain's Roxy in *Pudd'nhead Wilson*. As a slave she takes her fate into her own hands, liberates her natural son from slavery by exchanging him in the cradle with a white baby, and ultimately escapes from re enslavement in the Deep South by fleeing from a cruel plantation overseer and cross-dressing as a man.

But for all the power and originality of these heroines Twain would create, none had the sense of humor and selfless love shown by Aunt Polly. When she appears again, briefly and unexpectedly at the end *of Adventures of Huckleberry Finn,* she is as appealing and as forceful as she is throughout *Tom Sawyer.* As a matter of fact, she can be counted on to her put everything into perspective as she travels eleven hundred miles down the Mississippi River to discover what latest mischief Tom is up to, and that is exactly what she does. She is a force.

Works Cited

Cooley, John, editor. *How Nancy Jackson Married Kate Wilson and Other Tales of Rebellious Girls and Daring Young Women,* by Mark Twain. U of Nebraska P, 2001.

Georgoudaki, Catherine. "Women's Original Compositions." *The Adventures of Tom Sawyer, Life on the Mississippi,* and *Adventures of Huckleberry Finn. AAA. Arbeiten aus Anglistik und Amerikanistik,* vol. 4, no. 1, 1979, pp. 71–78.

Stone, Albert. Afterword to *The Adventures of Tom Sawyer,* by Mark Twain. Oxford UP, 1996.

Thoreson, Trygive. "Aunt Polly's Predicament." *Studies in American Humor,* vol. 5, no. 1, Spring 1986, pp. 17–26.

Tindol, Robert. "Tom Sawyer and Becky Thatcher in the Cave: An Anti-captivity Narrative." *The Mark Twain Annual,* vol. 7, 2009, pp. 118–26.

Twain, Mark. *Autobiography of Mark Twain, Vol. 1: The Complete and Authoritative Edition.* Edited by Harriet Elinor Smith, et al., U of California P, 2010.

Wolff, Cynthia Griffin. "*The Adventures of Tom Sawyer*: A Nightmare Vision of American Boyhood." *The Massachusetts Review*, vol. 21, no. 4, Winter 1980, pp. 637–52.

Fig. 3. True Williams's depiction of Tom escaping from Aunt Polly in the first chapter of *Tom Sawyer*, 1876, p. 18. [Public domain.]

Republican Motherhood and Tom Sawyer's Political Education

Hannah J. D. Wells

During the two years Samuel Clemens spent writing *The Adventures of Tom Sawyer*—from approximately June 1874 to its publication in June 1876—his home was filled with joy, as he and Livy relished the growth of their daughters, Susy and Clara, through their infancy and toddlerhood. On the title page of "A Record of the Small Foolishnesses of Susie and 'Bay' Clemens (Infants)," the journal he kept detailing his daughters' antics, he inscribed, "And Mary treasured these sayings in her heart," a paraphrase of Luke 2:19 referencing the mother of Jesus and her delight in the remarkable events surrounding her son's birth (Griffin 51). This epigraph conveys a sense of sanctity inherent in the parent-child relationship, especially in motherhood, a role Clemens ranked higher and holier than his own role as father. It comes as no surprise, then, that *Tom Sawyer* celebrates, alongside American childhood, American motherhood. The novel peers into the past, giving life on the page to Clemens's memories of his own boyhood in Hannibal, Missouri, in which his mother Jane Lampton Clemens played a central role. Nevertheless, the novel is not merely nostalgic; in it, Mark Twain questions the traditional family idyll in more ways than one. While he displays the value Americans placed on the family as the fundamental building block of society, he does so in a roundabout way, by positioning main characters who lack traditional familial bonds against a background of nuclear families. At the same time, he compels his readers to face the limits of St. Petersburg's conception of family life, especially concerning the moral formation of children. Viewed through this lens, a more critical look at the American family of the past emerges.

In the West, family symbolizes civilization. A household unit can be thought of as a microcosm of a political regime, as Aristotle suggested long ago in his *Politics*. Within this framework, a family-less individual may automatically be viewed as a threat; living alone is tantamount to a crime. Conversely, a person bound by familial ties and duties thus signals his commitment to political harmony, as well. A good family man is a good citizen, especially in a republic like the United States, where citizens are expected to participate in political decisions. Moreover, in early America, with its foundational commitment to democracy, the makeup of the family became less hierarchical than in aristocratic Europe. The equalization that occurred in both the domestic and political realms delineated a new role for women in eighteenth- and nineteenth-century America, since for much of those centuries, social and legal conventions still precluded women from joining the public sphere. An indirect mode of political participation reserved for women in early America is known as "republican motherhood," that is, the common-sensical idea that because mothers play a large role in rearing children, they are primarily responsible for molding their sons and daughters into good citizens. Proponents of this idea, writing around the turn of the nineteenth century, argued for a public education in republican virtue for male and female citizens alike, in order to prepare men for direct participation in politics and women for indirect participation as educators of their children. In *The Adventures of Tom Sawyer*, the women of St. Petersburg generally subscribe to this understanding of motherhood. The energy they devote to the task of child rearing is a constant force, one that predominates over other formative elements of children's lives. In part an affirmation of the power of a mother's influence, the novel also displays the significant gaps that plague St. Petersburg's approach to education, gaps through which children like Tom Sawyer are apt to fall.

The "Sawyer" Household

Tom Sawyer's "family" is not a nuclear unit: biologically speaking, it includes no true mother, father, son, or daughter. Nevertheless, the people who make up this patchwork group experience the full range of traditional familial sentiments, from love to rivalry to despair, that are emphasized far more than their biological relations, or lack thereof. In fact, the extended family tree that connects them is never fully revealed. Aunt Polly is Tom's aunt, his late mother's sister.

Sidney, or Sid, the other young boy of the household, is Tom's half-brother; by which parent readers are not told. Since both live with Polly, it may be reasonable to conclude that they are related through a common mother, Polly's sister, and have different fathers who are out of the picture for undisclosed reasons. On the other hand, in *Adventures of Huckleberry Finn*, Tom refers to his half-brother as "Sid Sawyer," raising the possibility that they share a father with that surname, in which case Sid, with a different mother, would not be related to Polly at all. Another possibility is that the surname Sawyer is Polly's own, and the children have all adopted it after moving in with her. In the stage play Mark Twain began shortly after finishing the novel, he does call her "Polly Sawyer." Assuming he maintained a firm grasp on the Sawyer family tree throughout the works in which the characters appear, that lends credence to this last possibility ("Tom Sawyer: A Play in Four Acts" 280). In any event, Polly's home makes a likely improvement over whatever unstable, perhaps traumatic, home life Tom and Sid experienced—together or separately, and, depending on their undisclosed ages, for weeks, months, or years—before their aunt took them in.

Tom's cousin Mary is the final member of this unconventional household. As a cousin, Mary might be Polly's biological daughter, although again, no mention is made of her father. More curiously, Mary herself refers to Polly as "auntie" (chapter 18), so it's possible that Polly took in children from two dead or indisposed siblings, perhaps while having no husband or children of her own, or perhaps after losing them, too. Throughout his fiction, Mark Twain habitually depicts and attempts to generate sympathy for characters whose home life has been disrupted, as James Grove observes. Often misanthropic about the human race in the abstract, Mark Twain nevertheless easily romanticizes the family, which becomes in his fiction "a force which raises our esteem of human beings" by displaying the depth of their capacity for self-sacrificial love (Grove 382). To consider the various misfortunes that brought Tom, Sid, and Mary into Polly's sole care should lead to an appreciation of her sense of duty and her desire to do right by them. Polly's ragtag group of relations is considered a real family by the people of St.

Petersburg, due to her respectability within the community and her assent to its standards of parental discipline.

With Sid and Mary, Polly's conventional approach to guardianship pays off. They are "isolated and incorruptible rocks" of obedience, much to the chagrin of unruly Tom (chapter 4). Sid's first words in the novel undermine Tom's attempts to escape Aunt Polly's punishments for going swimming instead of attending school. Tom's mischievousness often stands out more starkly against Sid's docility, but so does his waggishness, for Sid seems devoid of all humor. Aunt Polly justifies her harsh reactions to Tom's disobedience by telling him that "Sid don't torment a body the way you do" (chapter 3). Neither, however, does Sid make her laugh, while Tom, she confesses to herself, plays expertly on her emotions: "He 'pears to know just how long he can torment me before I get my dander up, and he knows if he can . . . make me laugh, it's all down again" (chapter 1). Polly's sense of humor is a trait she shares with Jane Clemens, and Tom certainly mirrors the boyish charm of young Samuel Clemens. As Sam's childhood sweetheart, Laura Frazer Hawkins, recalled, "Sam was always full of mischief . . . and liked to tease his mother. For this she often reprimanded him. She never knew what he was going to do next. However, he must have been a child after her own heart, for she, too, was a great lover of fun" (Watts 85). Beneath her affectation of strictness, Polly harbors a fondness for Tom at his most mischievous, the like of which she never displays toward Sid. The difference between the boys' characters and the difference in Polly's treatment of them both contribute to their long-standing rivalry.

Cousin Mary is several years older than the boys, and although she shares with Sid a fundamentally well-behaved disposition, her age and gender give her a different role in the household. It is Mary's duty to quiz Tom on the Bible verses he is to memorize for Sunday school. She is especially fit for this job, since her own biblical knowledge has yielded her two of the coveted Bibles, prizes for memorizing two thousand verses. She also oversees Tom's agonized washing and dressing for church. Throughout this Sunday morning ritual, Mary emerges as a mother figure for Tom. This was a common role for older daughters to take on in early America, including the household of John and Jane Clemens, where second-born Pamela often cared for younger brothers Benjamin, Samuel, and Henry (Sweets 48). In a single-parent household like Aunt Polly's, the responsibility would be even greater. In most cases, this role would have been part of the daughter's own education toward marriage and motherhood: a domestic apprenticeship.

Strikingly, Mary's approach to 'mothering' Tom does not mimic Polly's. Their philosophies of discipline are like night and day. Aunt Polly's approach is governed by the Bible verse she quotes: "Spare the rod and spile the child, as the Good Book says" (chapter 1, cf. Proverbs 13:24). Although this biblical belief in corporal punishment accords with the practices of most adults in St. Petersburg, it brings Polly's conscience, which believes in the corrective power of corporal punishment, in conflict with her heart, which she says "most breaks" "every time I hit him." Polly's vacillation on this issue signals, as Peter Messent argues, a wider cultural shift regarding discipline in the 1830s and 1840s, when "home-management manuals and educational theory [proposed] that the rod is not the most effective form of discipline for a child" (Messent 227).

The emerging philosophy of responding compassionately to disobedience is embodied by Mary. If Aunt Polly rules by the stick, Mary rules by the carrot, using positive reinforcement to encourage good behavior. Thus, when Tom fails to learn his Bible verses on the first attempt, Mary does not tease, shame, or get angry, but instead promises him "something ever so nice" if he manages it the next time. This tradeoff works marvelously well, for it pushes Tom to work "under the double pressure of curiosity and prospective gain" (chapter 5). She is similarly encouraging, but firm, with his attempts to shirk washing his face and neck for church, and when he loses his temper at the thought of being forced to wear shoes, she talks him into it calmly and "persuasively."

The shift in child-rearing in the early nineteenth century captured in *Tom Sawyer* is confirmed through the disciplinary practices of Olivia Clemens, raising her daughters in the 1870s. In "A Record of the Small Foolishnesses," her husband praises her mothering as "a master-work of good sense, sound judgement, loving consideration, and steady, even-handed justice." He goes on to contrast her with his view of the typical mother, "who thrashes for a misdemeanor to-day which she will allow to pass tomorrow, who requires obedience by fits and starts, and puts up with the opposite between times" (Griffin 69–70). This description of motherly inconsistency corresponds with Aunt Polly's practices in *Tom Sawyer*. The greater success of Mary's—and Livy's—method of firm encouragement and loving care is manifest. Tom's response to Mary's method is reliably stronger, albeit no more permanent, than his response to Polly's attempts at corporal punishment, as Polly later recognizes, too.

When Tom sleeps in after sneaking out at night, Polly takes him aside after his late breakfast and "Tom almost brightened in the hope that he was going to be flogged" (chapter 10). What she does instead is much worse, from his perspective, weeping and telling him "to go on, and ruin himself and bring her gray hairs with sorrow to the grave." Her posture of despair cuts straight to Tom's heart and pains him "worse than a thousand whippings," prompting him to promise his reform. Unbeknownst to either Polly or Tom, the dynamic between them in this and related scenes is part of Tom's political education. Rather than behaving well for his own interest—not being whipped—he does so for Polly's interest, in a touching moment of empathy. According to the model of republican

Fig. 1. At the end of chapter 10, Tom sincerely repents when he realizes how much trouble he has caused Aunt Polly. True Williams, *Tom Sawyer*, 1876, p. 100. [Public domain.]

motherhood, this emotional bond between the boy and his mother lays the first foundation for his ideal future as a citizen.

Mothers in St. Petersburg

Beyond Aunt Polly's home, the households that make up St. Petersburg never gain much depth or dimension in the novel. The townspeople are more often treated as a unit than as individuals, and they are collectively suspicious of outsiders. Many scholars have pointed out this "faceless generality"; some, like Cynthia Griffin Wolff, construe the population as ghostly, empty shadows (Wolff 166–67). One could also construe them to be mechanistic, empty automata. On this reading, St. Petersburg's collectivist mindset exemplifies one of the more unsavory features of republican education. Benjamin Rush, one of the leading proponents of republican motherhood, wrote in 1798, "I consider it possible to convert men into republican machines. This must be done, if we expect them to perform their parts properly, in the great machine of the government of the state" (Rush 14–15). In other words, part of the goal of republican education is to render the population intellectually homogeneous, with the explicit goal of subservience to the government. The dangerous extreme of such uniformity is hinted at when the village of St. Petersburg unanimously, and erroneously, condemns Muff Potter for the murder of Dr. Robinson, for, as the narrator quips, "the public are not slow in the matter of sifting evidence and arriving at a verdict" (chapter 11). With an overwhelming consensus holding everyone to identical opinions, however wrongheaded, the townspeople's harsh treatment of dissenters and outcasts like Muff is unsurprising.

Huckleberry Finn is another conspicuous outsider. Regarded as an orphan, Huck actually has a larger immediate family than Tom, although readers do not meet his abominable father in this novel. Huck also shares memories of his mother, although from this brief mention, it remains unclear whether she and Pap have separated or if she has died (in *Adventures of Huckleberry Finn*, she is confirmed to be dead). Huck's memories of his family life are far from pleasant. He brings up his mother in order to object to Tom's desire to get married, saying, "Well that's the foolishest thing you could do, Tom.

Look at pap and my mother. Fight? Why they used to fight all the time. I remember, mighty well" (chapter 25). Huck's rueful tone regarding his past family life helps explain why, at the end of the novel, he is so recalcitrant to entering society, which means entering a more traditional family arrangement. It is not the person of Widow Douglas to whom Huck objects, but the mothering role she ends up playing, compelling him to do things like wash, dress, and live according to a schedule. Yet, even as he rejects the constraints of family here, Huck's continued journey in *Adventures of Huckleberry Finn* is, as John Bird claims, a search for both freedom and a family, which he finds intertwined on his river raft home, with Jim for a surrogate father (Bird 220–22). In both novels, Huck remains equally averse to civilized society *and* desirous of familial affection.

Unfortunately, in St. Petersburg, families are understood to be inextricable from civil society, so Huck's lack of the former means he is not fit for the latter. He "was cordially hated and dreaded by all the mothers of the town, because he was idle, and lawless, and vulgar and bad—and because all their children admired him so, and delighted in his forbidden society, and wished they dared to be like him" (chapter 6). Despite the opinion of the collective mothers of St. Petersburg, Huck is not particularly vicious—idle, yes, and perhaps vulgar, but not lawless or bad at heart. Rather, the unspoken root of their hate and dread is that he is not part of a family structure; in other words, he is motherless, and, therefore, an image of what their children might look like without their maternal influence. This fear is compounded by their children's collective admiration of Huck's uncivilized lifestyle, which could be construed as a rejection of their own families and of polite society to boot. For most of the children, however, this is simply not the case. The boys may have wide imaginations for freedom from maternal supervision, but even the biggest braggarts among them secretly cherish the comfort and consistency of home and hearth.

At the end of the pirate escapade, Tom, Joe Harper, and even Huck all feel homesick, but Joe is the first to admit it, retorting to Tom, "Yes, I *do* want to see my mother—and you would too, if you had one" (chapter 16). Joe shows the emotional courage to stand up to Tom's teasing, taking advantage of Tom's orphanhood to justify his own affection for his mother—even though it was an unjustified punishment from her that spurred Joe to go pirating in the first place. Huck is next to acquiesce going home, even without an established home to go to, intimating that society has its charms even for "lawless" Huck. The boys trudge home the next day, entering the full village church in the midst of their own funeral, to the joy of "Aunt Polly, Mary, and the Harpers." Huck, however, is left out of the celebration, standing "abashed and uncomfortable, not knowing exactly what to do or where to hide from so many unwelcoming eyes" (chapter 17). Before he can escape the discomfort, Tom points out, "Aunt Polly, it ain't fair. Somebody's got to be glad to see Huck." Aunt Polly sympathizes, declaring, "I'm glad to see him, poor motherless thing!"

Though the narrator emphasizes that Huck's discomfort only increases at that, nothing suggests that he is ungrateful to receive this makeshift familial affection, only embarrassed to receive it publicly. The scene proves that before Huck can be accepted into St. Petersburg society, he must be accepted into a family structure, which, at this moment, only Aunt Polly is willing to provide, although later Widow Douglas will do so. Both Tom and Huck are technically motherless, as Joe spitefully points out, but it is clear that Polly does not think of Tom as an orphan to whom she has a duty, but a child whom she loves. Her ease in spreading that love out to embrace Huck sets her apart from those who have "unwelcoming eyes" turned toward Huck, perhaps including the Harpers and even Mary. Aunt Polly's unique familial circumstances have given her an ability to extend maternal affection beyond natural boundaries and show warmth to those the community has cast out. Although old-fashioned and inconsistent in her discipline, she is a mother figure worthy of admiration for the moments when she breaks from the town's unanimous consensus about parenting to follow the maternal instincts of her heart instead.

Fathers in St. Petersburg

Aunt Polly's pitying exclamation calling Huck a "poor motherless thing" glosses over the fact that one member of the community, Huck's father, *should* be there to welcome his son home. Tragically, Pap's alcoholism has led to egregious absentee parenting. This neglect, if to a lesser extent, seems typical of St. Petersburg father-son relationships. Discounting social pariahs like Injun Joe, the few community-minded men are subsumed in their careers—Mr. Walters's role as the Sunday school superintendent is his whole identity, just as Old Dobbins's is schoolmaster—and are not seen as husbands or fathers. At home, only the mothers stand out, often through their acts of discipline. When Tom chases the strange new boy, Alfred Temple, home, Alfred's mother chastises Tom from her house. Sereny Harper is introduced through the whipping she's given Joe for something he did not do. It is reasonable to suppose that both boys have fathers, too, but they are never singled out in the narrative and never seen interacting with their sons. In effect, every father in St. Petersburg is as absent from family life as Huck's drunken, neglectful father and Tom's and Sid's unheard-of father . . . or fathers.

Many scholars have noted this paternal absence, a detail that leads Wolff, for example, to refer to St. Petersburg as a "matriarchy," a place "saturated with gentility, that is, with women's notions" of "'duty' or 'morality'" (168). Republican motherhood emphasized the early formation of political morality in children through the mother's influence at home. However, for male children of this time, the completion of that education depended upon leaving the mother's domestic sphere and entering public life, by means of an apprenticeship for a career, a pursuit of higher education, or a related path open primarily to men. No boy in St. Petersburg has an obvious mentor to guide him through this stage of his formation, with the peripheral exception of Jeff Thatcher, nephew to Judge Thatcher and son of the village lawyer. Following the understanding of family life as a child's first political education, St. Petersburg's imbalance between male and female influence in the home signals a large pedagogical gap that is borne out by the boys' antisocial, anti-civilized behavior.

Judge Thatcher is perhaps the most positive adult male influence in the novel. Not coincidentally, he is also the only man shown in the role of father. He is Becky's biological father, but he also plays a paternal role for Tom. The judge visits Sunday school on the day that Tom presents his tickets in exchange for a Bible, and Tom is paralyzed. In part because the judge is Becky's father and in part because of his elevated position in the community, Tom "would have liked to fall down and worship him" (chapter 4). The judge later gains a high opinion of Tom, as well, after Tom's dramatic escape from McDougal's cave, claiming that "no commonplace boy would ever have got his daughter out of the cave"; moreover, when Becky confides in her father that Tom took a whipping at school that she deserved and lied to shift the blame onto himself, "the Judge said with a fine outburst that it was a noble, a generous, a magnanimous lie" (chapter 35). Apparently with no son of his own, Judge Thatcher imagines a future for Tom compatible with his view of manly excellence, picturing him as "a great lawyer or a great soldier some day." This expectation all but adopts Tom into the Thatcher family, known for its lawyers. It is a first step, albeit premature, towards blessing an eventual marriage between Tom and Becky, which would enmesh Tom fully in the fabric of the community. Finally, Judge Thatcher's wish also adopts Tom into the service of the nation, for both lawyers and military officers were distinguished as members of elite professions guarding the liberty and security of the republic. A father with such high hopes for his sons was widely regarded as a guarantor of the sons' successful integration into society.

Judge Thatcher is not, however, Tom's father, and his dreams for Tom's future do not hold the weight they might have if he were. Tom's own dreams tend towards the opposite end of the spectrum of political involvement. His veneration of the judge to the contrary, his imagination is full of great anti-citizens, that is, of men beyond the grasp of political society. Rather than the patriot soldier, Tom admires Robin Hood, who rejects his national and political loyalties in favor of a greater good—a noble figure, to be sure, but not a dependable soldier. Rather than upholding the law in the courts, Tom daydreams about breaking the law as a pirate and a robber.

Tom's attraction to such capers is a part of his natural desire for honor, the same desire that makes him yearn for "the glory and the éclat" that came with winning a Bible (chapter 4). Representative republican politics leaves little room for those naturally ambitious after honor, as Abraham Lincoln famously perceived in his 1838 Lyceum Address: "Many great and good men sufficiently qualified for any task they should undertake, may ever be found, whose ambition would aspire to nothing beyond a seat in Congress, a gubernatorial or a presidential chair, *but such belong not to the family of the lion, or the tribe of the eagle*" (Lincoln 82–83). While the village of St. Petersburg categorizes Tom with the former class and "believed he would be President, yet" (chapter 24), Tom himself echoes Lincoln's leonine spirit and claims that he "would rather be [an outlaw] a year in Sherwood Forest than President of the United States forever" (chapter 8). In the end, all the judge's high-minded rhetoric about Tom's future in a nation-building profession has no effect. The novel concludes with Tom still believing that robbers are "awful high up in the nobility" of most countries, "dukes and such," and that he can rise in the ranks of American nobility the same way (chapter 35).

Family, School, Church, and Nation

Two problems inherent in Tom Sawyer's political education point toward its potential failure. Aunt Polly's well-meaning attempts to be both mother and father to the orphaned boy stunts his political education. Although the seeds are there, they are not consistently nurtured in his home life so as to impress upon Tom the gravity of his future role as a citizen of the republic. Judge Thatcher is shown to have the potential to fill this gap in Tom's education, but in the course of this novel, his influence is too little, too late. Two additional loci of education of St. Petersburg's youth might fill the gap: the church and the school. These institutions can be seen as attempts to outsource the completion of children's moral formation. The St. Petersburg village schoolhouse, however, has little hope of fulfilling this great demand. It is a site associated with both mental and physical anguish for the children of the town, the former arising from the ennui of study, made more tedious by the schoolmaster's lack of engagement—readers first meet him dozing at the front of the classroom in the middle of the school day—and the latter from the master's reliance upon corporal punishment, for "he seemed to take a vindictive pleasure in punishing the least shortcomings" with "his rod and his ferule" (chapter 21). No positive model for citizenship is to be found at school.

Sunday school and church offer a more promising opportunity for moral development, but just barely. Mr. Walters, the stiff and distant superintendent, speaks in platitudes about "learning to do right and be good," but in front of a fighting and fidgeting audience, his words ring as hollow as the Bible verses meant to be memorized rather than

TOM AS A SUNDAY-SCHOOL HERO.

Fig. 2. Judge Thatcher, who demonstrates a growing fatherly affection for Tom, when they first meet in Sunday school. (Note how young True Williams makes Tom look in this scene.) *Tom Sawyer*, 1876, p. 51. [Public domain.]

comprehended (chapter 4). Just as the town of St. Petersburg has one collective character, both of these institutions attempt to complete an education of the town's children *en masse*, as "republican machines," to bring them as one into the communal fold. It remains unclear how successful this attempt will prove to be by the end of the children's formal schooling. On the other hand, even if it is perfectly successful, such an education leaves much to be desired in terms of fostering individuality and independence in the children as they mature.

An exceptional child like Tom, who seeks distinction from his peers at every turn, has the potential to see through these institutionalized educational efforts and reject them as belittling and dehumanizing practices. However, scores of scholars have suggested that the end of the novel reveals a chastened, socialized Tom, pitted against a still antisocial Huckleberry Finn. Often cited as evidence is Mark Twain's letter to William Dean Howells, written just after completing the *Tom Sawyer* manuscript, in which he claims that as an adult, Tom "would just be like all the one-horse men in literature & the reader would conceive a hearty contempt for him" (*Mark Twain's Letters* 503). That may be so, but within the confines of the finished novel, Tom remains a boy and remains divided about the benefits of civilized life. Even while he urges Huck to suffer the "bars and shackles of civilization" just as everyone else does, he simultaneously fantasizes about "turning robber," as if the great advantage of joining society is merely to enhance the thrill of subverting it (chapter 35).

In short, *The Adventures of Tom Sawyer* names no certain victor in the struggle between Tom's spirited nature and his enervating education, but if his educators at school, church, and home manage to reform him, they will have failed him, for their idea of reform is full of contradictions. Walters, Dobbins, and the other mechanical adults of the town will undoubtedly view Tom's dispiriting as a societal success story. One glimmer of hope remains: it is possible that Aunt Polly will come to regret the change in Tom's character, because in her heart she knows that the acceptable method of child-rearing is ill-matched for him. Polly's maternal instinct that every child has unique needs to which his education must be tailored is not a dominant trait in her character, yet because of it, she stands out from the faceless background of St. Petersburg as an advocate of genuine family feeling.

In his own life, Samuel Clemens, too, was a warm advocate of the family, at the heart of which was the loving mother. His writings attest his affection for his own "fine and striking and lovable" mother ("Jane Lampton Clemens" 82), on whom Aunt Polly is partially modeled, and for the mother of his children, whom he calls the "best and dearest mother that lives—and by a long, long, way the wisest" ("What Ought He to Have Done?" 4). And in his fiction, Mark Twain finds in the family structure the best hope for the human race, for he affirms that it is at home, through the devoted influence of fathers and especially of mothers, that children can be educated for good.

Works Cited

Bird, John. "Huck Finn, He Hain't Got No Family: Home, Family and Parenting in *Huckleberry Finn*." *Critical Insights: Adventures of Huckleberry Finn*. Edited by R. Kent Rasmussen, Salem Press, 2017, pp. 211–23.

Griffin, Benjamin, editor. *A Family Sketch and Other Private Writings*, by Mark Twain, Livy Clemens and Susy Clemens, U of California P, 2014.

Grove, James. "Mark Twain and the Endangered Family." *American Literature*, vol. 57, no. 3, 1985, pp. 377–94.

Lincoln, Abraham. "The Perpetuation of our Political Institutions: Address before the Young Men's Lyceum of Springfield, Illinois, 27 Jan. 1838." *Abraham Lincoln: His Speeches and Writings*. Edited by Roy P. Basler, World Publishing, 1946, pp. 76–85.

Messent, Peter. "Discipline and Punishment in *The Adventures of Tom Sawyer*." *Journal of American Studies*, vol. 32, no. 2, Aug. 1998, pp. 219–35.

Rush, Benjamin. *Essays, Literary, Moral, & Philosophical*. Philadelphia: Thomas & Samuel F. Bradford, 1798.

Sweets, Henry. "Sam and His Siblings." *Mark Twain and Youth: Studies in His Life and Writings*. Edited by Kevin Mac Donnell and R. Kent Rasmussen, Bloomsbury, 2016, pp. 47–54.

Twain, Mark. "Jane Lampton Clemens." *Huck Finn and Tom Sawyer Among the Indians: And Other Unfinished Stories*. Edited by Dahlia Armon and Walter Blair, U of California P, 1989.

_____. *Mark Twain's Letters*. Volume 6, 1874–1875. Edited by Michael B. Frank and Harriet Elinor Smith, U of California P, 2002.

_____. "Tom Sawyer: A Play in Four Acts." *Mark Twain's Hannibal, Huck & Tom*. Edited by Walter Blair, U California P, 1969.

_____. "What Ought He to Have Done? Mark Twain's Opinion." New York: *Christian Union*, vol. 32, no. 3, 16 July 1885, p. 4.

Watts, Aretta L. "Mark Twain's Gay Mother: 'Becky Thatcher' Describes the Woman from Whom He Inherited His Sense of Humor." *The New York Times,* 5 Feb. 1928, p. 85.

Wolff, Cynthia Griffin. "*The Adventures of Tom Sawyer*: A Nightmare Vision of American Boyhood." *Critical Insights: Mark Twain.* Edited by R. Kent Rasmussen, Salem Press, 2011, pp. 164–79.

Fig. 3. Aunt Polly reacting to Tom's dosing Peter the cat with "Pain-killer" in the first French edition of *Tom Sawyer*. Achille Sirouy, *Les Aventures de Tom Sawyer*, ca. 1880, p. 89. [Public domain.]

Injun Joe and Mark Twain's Attitudes toward Native Americans_____

Kerry Driscoll

The first American edition of *The Adventures of Tom Sawyer* was published in December 1876, less than six months after the Battle of the Little Bighorn in Montana Territory, at which Lieutenant Colonel George Armstrong Custer and over two hundred members of the U.S. Seventh Cavalry were slaughtered by a combined force of several thousand Lakota, Northern Cheyenne, and Arapaho warriors. Public outrage ran high in the massacre's aftermath, with newspapers in both the East and West demanding the immediate destruction of these "red devils" and "screeching fiends of the plains" (Welch 192). On 12 July 1876, the Bismarck, North Dakota, *Tribune* urged "Wipe out all treaties, rout out all agencies and reservations, and treat the Indians as they are, criminals and paupers. . . . Let there be no captures, but send all caught with arms in their hands, whether professedly friendly or known to be hostile, to the happy hunting grounds of their fathers by a short cut." Within this highly charged racial atmosphere, it is perhaps not surprising that contemporary readers and reviewers of *Tom Sawyer* were unfazed by Mark Twain's harsh depiction of its central antagonist, Injun Joe. For many Americans in the 1870s, the perception of native peoples as dehumanized savages represented a cultural norm.

Tom Sawyer, however, does not explicitly concern the 1870s. As Mark Twain explains in the novel's preface, it is set "thirty or forty years ago," meaning that the plot unfolds during the 1830s and 1840s, a decade that coincides with the author's own childhood. The community of St. Petersburg is modeled on Clemens's hometown of Hannibal, Missouri. As such, the character of Injun Joe must be interpreted through a dual lens—the historical era of the writer's youth as well as the more recent backdrop of the Indian wars. Both eras were instrumental in shaping the portrayal of Mark Twain's villain.

Was There a Real Injun Joe in Hannibal?

In the preface to *Tom Sawyer*, Mark Twain famously states that its characters are "drawn from real life" and that "most of the adventures recorded . . . really occurred." For this reason, it has long been assumed that Injun Joe is based on an actual person, although his identity has never been ascertained. Thirty years after the book's publication, Mark Twain confirmed Joe's historical existence in an autobiographical dictation: His father, Judge John Marshall Clemens, he said, "once tried to reform Injun Joe. That . . . was a failure, and we boys were glad. For Injun Joe, drunk, was interesting and a benefaction to us, but Injun Joe, sober, was a dreary spectacle. We watched my father's experiments upon him with a good deal of anxiety but it came out all right, and we were satisfied. Injun Joe got drunk oftener than before, and became tolerably interesting" (*AutoMT* 1:397). His reminiscence continues:

> I think that in "Tom Sawyer" I starved Injun Joe to death in the cave. But that may have been to meet the exigencies of romantic literature. I can't remember whether he died in the cave or out of it, but I do remember that the news of his death reached me at a most unhappy time—that is to say, just at bedtime on a summer night when a prodigious storm of thunder and lightning accompanied by a deluging rain that turned the streets and lanes into rivers, [and] caused me to repent and resolve to lead a better life . . . By my teachings I perfectly well knew what all the wild riot was for—Satan had come to get Injun Joe. I had no shadow of doubt about it. It was the proper thing when a person like Injun Joe was required in the underworld, and I should have thought it strange and unaccountable if Satan had come for him in a less impressive way (*AutoMT* 1:397–98).

Following Mark Twain's lead, scholars have proposed several theories about Joe's identity. One of his early biographers claims that Joe was part Osage Indian, scalped by Pawnees in Oklahoma as a child. Brought to Hannibal in his teens by cattlemen, Joe allegedly "lived in a big hollow sycamore on Bear Creek . . . earned a little cash by toting carpetbags between the wharf and tavern, [and] wore a red wig to conceal his horrid scar" (Wecter 151). The most enduring story about Joe, however, is that he was found as an infant in an abandoned Indian camp and raised by an African American man named Douglass. He settled in Hannibal, married a woman of color, and bought a home in a neighborhood later christened "Douglassville" in his honor. Throughout his long life, Joe denied being the basis for Mark Twain's character, explaining that he was born in the 1840s and did not even arrive in Hannibal until 1862, about ten years after the writer had left. He was, moreover, a peaceful, law-abiding man, whose behavior bore no resemblance to Mark Twain's fictional "bloody-minded outcast" (chapter 33). Even so, when Joe Douglass died in 1923—not in a cave but comfortably at home—this myth became literally etched in stone, as evidenced by his grave marker at Hannibal's Mount Olivet Cemetery.

Fig. 1. Joe Douglass, whom Hannibal residents believed to be the model for Tom Sawyer's "Injun Joe." Clemens, however, could not have known Douglass before he wrote his novel. Image courtesy of the Mark Twain Boyhood Home and Museum, Hannibal, Missouri. [Used with permission.]

Indians in the Mississippi River Valley

When the University of Missouri awarded Mark Twain an honorary doctorate in 1902, he returned to his boyhood home one last time. During that brief visit, he took a boat ride on the Mississippi with a local journalist. As they sped past the mouth of the cave, where Injun Joe perishes toward the novel's conclusion (chapter 33), the reporter explained that he had recently conversed with Joe Douglass. Mark Twain's response to this information was telling "If this man you speak of is Injun Joe . . . he must be about 95 years old. The half-breed Indian who gave me the idea of the character was about 35 years old 60 years ago." By the author's own calculations, the mysterious figure who inspired his villain was born several decades before Joe Douglass, circa 1807—a significant date in early Missouri history.

Prior to the War of 1812, Missouri Territory was a "frontier of inclusion" in which the French and Spanish traders who established outposts along the Mississippi River lived peaceably among—and intermarried with—the local tribes, producing a sizable population of "half-breeds." After the war, a wave of English settlers flooded into the region, outnumbering and eventually displacing the earlier traders. These newcomers had much more antagonistic attitudes toward Indians and their mixed blood progeny, and soon established a "frontier of exclusion," enforcing a policy of strict separation and segregation (Faragher 305). Within three years of Missouri's admission to the Union as a slave state in 1821, senator Thomas Hart Benton—whom Tom Sawyer pronounces "the greatest man in the world" (chapter 22)—introduced legislation in Congress to extinguish Indian title to land within its boundaries arguing that the removal of Indians would make room for the spread of slaves. Between 1824 and 1837, the federal government negotiated a series of land cession treaties with Missouri tribes, forcing them to relinquish title to millions of acres. This process of ethnic cleansing was so thorough that no federally recognized tribes or reservations exist in Missouri today.

Legally dispossessed of their ancestral homeland, Missouri's native peoples were also prohibited from hunting or establishing seasonal encampments there. Nonetheless, some groups actively resisted their enforced exodus, meaning that during the years when the novel is set, Indians and whites co-existed uneasily in and around Hannibal. Largely invisible, living on the margins of villages and towns, the Indians were reduced to the status of vagrants— itinerant beggars with no visible means of support. Vagrancy was a crime in the nineteenth century, often resulting in incarceration. Although the character of Injun Joe is largely a mystery—the novel never specifies his surname, tribal affiliation, place of origin, or the existence of any family ties—Mark Twain does emphasize that he is a vagrant. He is apparently the last sole remaining native inhabitant of the civilized, post-frontier community of St. Petersburg—and as such, an unwelcome, menacing presence.

"That murderin' half-breed"

Since the existence of Injun Joe's historical prototype cannot be verified, the character must be understood as a symbolic creation who represents Mark Twain's negative attitudes toward American Indians as well as the social stigma of racial intermarriage and perceived "taint" of Indian blood in nineteenth-century culture. In *The Oregon Trail* (1847), Francis Parkman famously described half-breeds as "a race of rather extraordinary composition, being according to the common saying, half Indian, half white man, and half devil"—in other words, monstrous beings who were more than the sum of their two biological parts (Parkman 362). Unlike full-blooded Indians who could be safely relegated to the nation's past, the mixed-blood—an inevitable product of western migration and colonization—were very much part of its present and therefore a threat to the dominant social order. The "half-breed" is a familiar stereotype in popular nineteenth-century American literature—a "malicious creature" who exists in a shadow world between the enlightenment of civilization and the darkness of savagery and embodies the worst traits of both races (Scheick 18).

At two different points in *Tom Sawyer*, Mark Twain directly links Joe's criminal behavior with his native ancestry. In chapter 9, for example, Joe attempts to extort more money from Dr. Robinson as payment for stealing the freshly interred corpse of Hoss Williams by listing a series of past wrongs the physician committed against him:

> Five years ago you drove me away from your father's kitchen one night, when I come to ask for something to eat, and you said I warn't there for any good; and when I swore I'd get even with you if it took a hundred years, your father had me jailed for a vagrant. Did you think

I'd forget? The Injun blood ain't in me for nothing. And now I've *got* you, and you got to *settle*, you know!

This reference to "Injun blood" implies that Joe's vengefulness is a racial rather than personal trait. Similarly, when Huck informs the "Welchman," Jones, about the mysterious Spaniard's plan to disfigure the Widow Douglas in chapter 30, the older man initially doubts the truth of his story. But once Huck reveals the stranger's identity as Injun Joe, Jones "almost jumps out of his chair," exclaiming: "It's all plain enough, now. When you talked about notching ears and slitting noses, I judged that was your own embellishment, because *white men don't take that sort of revenge. But an Injun! That's a different matter, altogether*" (emphasis added). The disturbing details of Joe's revenge plot—tying the widow down in bed, mutilating her with a knife, and allowing her to bleed to death—imply a metaphorical rape. This threat of sexual defilement is a characteristic Mark Twain identified with Indians in a number of later works, such as "The Californian's Tale" and "Huck Finn and Tom Sawyer among the Indians," and serves to highlight Joe's depraved nature.

In his manuscript of *Tom Sawyer*, Mark Twain described the half-breed's plans even more graphically than in the published text: "When you want revenge on a woman you don't kill her—bosh! You go for her looks. You take her nose off—& her ears!" (Baender 714). Such horrific mutilations were widely reported in the popular press in relation to General George Crook's 1872–73 campaign against the Arizona Apache, during which he criminalized the practice of cutting the noses off of adulterous Apache women. Mark Twain no doubt read of this punishment as he was composing the novel and incorporated it into his plot as a generically savage trait, despite its inapplicability to both the offense for which Joe seeks redress and the fact that the Apache are a southwestern rather than Missouri tribe. Mark Twain's tendency to generalize about Indian character can be traced back to earlier works like his 1870 sketch "The Noble Red Man" and *Roughing It*, an 1872 travelogue about his years on the western frontier. In the latter work, for example, he describes the "Goshoots," a band of Western Shoshone who inhabit the desert between Nevada and Utah, as "a silent, sneaking, treacherous looking race . . . of prideless beggars . . . who produce nothing at all, and have no villages," then concludes: "Wherever one finds an Indian tribe he has only found Goshoots more or less modified by circumstances and surroundings—but Goshoots, after all" (chapter 19).

It is also significant that Joe's thirst for vengeance in *Tom Sawyer* can only be satisfied by proxy since the two individuals responsible for his imprisonment "five years ago" (chapter 9)— the doctor's father and Judge Douglas—are now deceased. When this date is set within the novel's fictional time frame, it means that Joe's arrest occurred in the late 1830s, at roughly the same time as President Martin Van Buren's 1837 proclamation declaring Indian title to Missouri land "entirely extinguished" (Kappler 479). As Joe tells the ragged man outside the widow's house, her husband "was rough on me—many times he was rough on me—and mainly he was the justice of the peace that jugged me for a vagrant. And that

Fig. 2. True Williams's depiction of Injun Joe's flight from the courtroom at the end of chapter 23. *Tom Sawyer*, 1876, p. 188. [Public domain.]

ain't all. It ain't the millionth part of it! He had me horsewhipped!—horse-whipped in front of the jail, like a nigger!—with all the town looking on! HORSEWHIPPED!—do you understand? He took advantage of me and died. But I'll take it out of her" (chapter 29). Joe's rage is thus rooted in both the unjust circumstances of his arrest and the humiliating public punishment he suffers at the Judge's behest. His pride is offended at being treated like chattel rather than an autonomous human being.

Mark Twain's emphasis on Joe's Indian blood as the source of his criminality is visually echoed in illustrator True Williams's depiction of Joe's dusky skin tone. When the half-breed frames his drunken companion Muff Potter for the murder of Dr. Robinson in chapter 11, Huck and Tom are so dumfounded at the ease with which "the stony-hearted liar reel[s] off his serene statement" to the sheriff that they dare not speak the truth in order to save "the poor betrayed prisoner's life," understanding that "plainly this miscreant had sold himself to Satan and it would be fatal to meddle with the property of such a power as that" (chapter 11). This moment is captured in "Injun Joe's Two Victims" (see fig. 1 in Schmidt essay); although Joe's western style clothing renders him indistinguishable from the rest of the men gawking at the physician's corpse in the graveyard, his identity as a racial Other is marked by the horizontal lines across his face that represent not only his dark complexion but evil nature. This trait is even more pronounced in "Tom Dreams" in chapter 29 (see fig. 1 in Ober essay). Joe's complexion is especially evident in Williams's dramatic illustration of his escape from the courtroom at the end of chapter 23.

Mark Twain, moreover, explicitly associates Joe with Satan in three other instances in the novel, referring to him as "that Injun devil" (chapter 10), "that half-breed devil" (chapter 23), and having "sold himself to the devil" (chapter 11). This epithet is reminiscent of one Sam Clemens himself used in a March 1862 letter to his mother soon after arriving in Nevada Territory: "Generally speaking, we call [the local tribes] sons of the devil, when we can't think of anything worse" (*Letters* 1:175), indicating that his personal views of native peoples play a role in his fictional representation of Injun Joe.

"This flitting human insect"

The gruesome death Mark Twain fashions for Injun Joe in McDougal's Cave in chapter 33—imprisoned in the darkness of his primitive humanity, debarred from the "light and . . . cheer" of the civilized world, and reduced to eating candle stubs and bats before succumbing to starvation—symbolizes the historical exclusion and eventual erasure of Indians from the American landscape. The half-breed ultimately dies not of hunger but thirst, unable to sustain himself by collecting the "precious drop that fell once in every three minutes with the dreary regularity of a clock-tick" from the cave's ceiling, amounting to a meager "dessert spoonful" each day. Twain's description of the agonizingly slow pace at which water seeps from the stalactite is both a meditation on the passage of time and poetic testament to the triumphant march of western civilization: "That drop was falling when the Pyramids were new; when Troy fell; when the foundations of Rome were laid; when Christ was crucified; when the Conqueror created the British empire; when Columbus sailed; when the massacre at Lexington was 'news.'" Each of the events named is a benchmark of progress—from ancient Egypt, Rome, and medieval Britain to the European conquest and colonization of the New World, culminating in the creation of the United States—suggesting that the very course of history makes Joe's doom inevitable. With his passing, the last vestige of Missouri's multiethnic "frontier of inclusion" disappears, replaced by the new order of Southern slave-holding society. Manifest Destiny—the nineteenth-century belief that it was the God-given right of whites to seize control of the North American continent from coast to coast, displacing and eradicating the Indigenous peoples who stood in their path—is implicitly asserted here on a local level.

Injun Joe's death elicits an "abounding sense of relief and security" not only in Tom and Huck but also the community of St. Petersburg as a whole. His funeral is a communal celebration: "People flocked [to the cave] in boats and wagons from the town and from all the farms and hamlets for seven miles around; they brought their children, and all sorts of provisions, and confessed that they had had almost as satisfactory a time at the funeral as they could have had at the hanging" (chapter 33). Another beneficial consequence of the half-breed's demise is that it stops a misguided pardon petition to the governor:

> The petition had been largely signed; many tearful and eloquent meetings had been held, and a committee of sappy women been appointed to go into deep mourning . . . and implore [the governor] to be a merciful ass and trample his duty under foot. Injun Joe was believed to have killed five citizens of the village, but what of that? If he had been Satan himself there would have been plenty of weaklings ready to scribble their names to a pardon-petition and drip a tear on it from their permanently impaired and leaky waterworks (chapter 33).

The sarcastic tone of this passage reflects Mark Twain's hostile attitude toward liberal female reformers who were sympathetic to the plight of American Indians and believed they could become productive members of mainstream society through education and Christianization—a stance the writer regarded as naïve and dangerous (Driscoll 229–31).

Playing Indian

Over the course of his long literary career, Mark Twain viewed Indians as a source of terror, repugnance, and fascination. This unresolved contradiction is evident in *Tom Sawyer* in the way that the novel demonizes the community's last remaining native inhabitant on the one hand, while simultaneously romanticizing the imaginative allure of "playing Indian" on the other. For Tom and his companions, "going native" represents an irresistible fantasy of freedom and escape. After being spurned by Becky Thatcher in chapter 7, Tom retreats to the woods and contemplates a series of glamorous alternatives to his humdrum village existence:

> What if he went away, into unknown countries beyond the seas— and never came back anymore! How would she feel then! The

idea of being a clown recurred to him now, only to fill him with disgust . . . No, he would be a soldier, and return, after long years, all war—worn and illustrious. No—better still, he would join the Indians, and hunt buffaloes and go on the warpath in the mountain ranges and the trackless great plains of the Far West, and away in the future come back a great chief, bristling with feathers, hideous with paint, and prance into Sunday-school, some drowsy summer morning, with a blood-curdling war-whoop, and sear the eyeballs of all his companions with unappeasable envy.

Several chapters later, returning to school after an extended illness, Tom seeks to re-ingratiate himself with Becky—not by running away, but showing off: "One more frock passed in at the gate, and Tom's heart gave a great bound. The next instant he was out, and 'going on' like an Indian; yelling, laughing, chasing boys, jumping over the fence at the risk of life and limb, throwing hand-springs, standing on his head—doing all the heroic things he could conceive of" (chapter 12). In this instance, Twain equates native identity with wildness, impulsivity, and reckless displays of athletic prowess. Tom's disruptive behavior escalates when Becky refuses to acknowledge him; he "war-whoops around," stealing one boy's cap and tossing it onto the schoolhouse roof, and aggressively knocking over others, "tumbling them in every direction" before sprawling headlong "under Becky's nose, almost upsetting her." Unfortunately, the strategy does not produce the desired effect.

Becky's second romantic rejection prompts Tom to take the bolder, more extreme step of "becoming" an Indian rather than simply fantasizing about living among them as a scout. Christening himself the "Black Avenger of the Spanish Main," he persuades Joe Harper (aka "The Terror of the Seas") and Huck Finn (the "Red-Handed") to join him on Jackson's Island where they will live as "pirates." After several days of swimming, exploring, and hunting for turtle eggs, Joe and Huck tire of the escapade and express a desire to return home; hoping to avert mutiny, Tom proposes that they "knock off being pirates, for a while, and be Indians for a change" (chapter 16). The boys eagerly agree to the new plan, and "it was not long before they were stripped, and striped from head to heel with black mud, like so many zebras—all of them chiefs, of course—and then they went tearing through the woods to attack an English settlement." They appropriate native identity through the medium of their naked bodies, exhilarated by their absolute freedom. And yet, Twain's diction subtly suggests that this playful transformation into racial Others also compromises the boys' humanity, reducing them to exotic wild animals. "By and by they separated into three hostile tribes, and darted upon each other from ambush with dreadful war-whoops, and killed and scalped each other by thousands. It was a gory day. Consequently it was an extremely satisfactory one." True Williams's illustration of this passage, captioned "Terrible Slaughter," reinforces the primitivism of the boys' behavior.

Fig. 3. (At left) Captioned "Terrible Slaughter," True Williams's original depiction of the boys playing Indians on the island highlights their pretend violence. *Tom Sawyer*, 1876, p. 143; (At right) The full-color cover of a 1908 Chatto & Windus edition modified the illustration to make the scene appear less menacing. Note the position of the knife blade in each version. [Public domain.]

Tom, Huck, and Joe later smoke a "pipe of peace," discovering to their great delight that tobacco no longer sickens them. "Behold," Mark Twain announces with mock solemnity, "they were glad they had gone into savagery, for they had gained something . . . They were prouder and happier in their new acquirement than they would have been in the scalping and skinning of the Six Nations" (chapter 16). This allusion to the centuries-old Iroquois Confederacy, an alliance of the Seneca, Cayuga, Onondaga, Oneida, Mohawk, and Tuscarora tribes in what is now upstate New York, is somewhat puzzling considering the novel's midwestern setting. It does, however, have direct—and timely—relevance to Elmira, New York, the hometown of Mark Twain's wife. The Clemens family summered there for more than twenty years. Elmira was also the site of a hilltop study built for him by Livy's sister where Mark Twain did much of his writing—including some of the composition of Tom Sawyer. In the mid-1870s, plans were underway to erect a monument commemorating the centenary of the one of the American Revolution's most decisive military engagements, the Battle of Newtown, which took place just a few miles east of Elmira. On 29 August 1779, colonial forces attacked an Iroquois settlement, torching the Indians' homes, orchards, and crops, then collected grisly trophies from their victims, scalping at least ten men and skinning two others to make chaps (Mann 205). Clemens likely heard this atrocity tale from his brother-in-law, Charley Langdon, a member of the Newtown Monument Association, the group spearheading the campaign to construct a stone obelisk at the battle site. In linking the boys' playful fantasy with the "scalping and skinning of the Six Nations," Mark Twain blurs the distinction between civilization and savagery and anticipates an observation he makes in a much later book, *Following the Equator* (1897): "There are many humorous things in the world; among them the white man's notion that he is less savage than the other savages" (chapter 21). Ultimately, the boys' game offers them a therapeutic, though necessarily temporary, release from the rules and restrictions of civilized society; after this exhilarating experience of freedom, they return to their rightful place in St. Petersburg just in time to attend—and dramatically upstage—the solemn ritual of their own funerals.

"Born for a Savage"

Tom Sawyer's unresolved contradiction between this youthful idealization of Indians and the racial loathing that characterizes the attitudes of St. Petersburg's adults toward Injun Joe in some respect mirrors Mark Twain's own deep ambivalence about native peoples. At times, he harshly characterizes Indians as "vermin," "reptiles," and even "desirable subject[s] for extermination" ("The Noble Red Man" 443–44), while at others, he depicts them as representations of his truest, natural self. This perplexing pattern persists throughout his career. When Livy accepted his proposal of marriage in 1868, for example, he exulted to a friend, "I am so happy I want to scalp somebody" (*Letters* 2:293); even more explicitly, in an 1881 speech called "Plymouth Rock and the Pilgrims," he claims: "My first American ancestor, gentlemen, was an Indian—an early Indian" (CTSSE 1:782). Similarly, in an 1898 story, "Conversations with Satan" published in 2009 in *Who Is Mark Twain?*, he writes: "by rights I was an Indian, though changed in the cradle through no fault of my own" (37). But perhaps most remarkably, in an autobiographical reminiscence about the honorary doctoral degree presented to him by Oxford University in June 1907, he states: "A university degree . . . is a prize which I would go far to get at any time. I take the same childlike delight in a new degree that an Indian does in a fresh scalp, and I take no more pains to conceal my joy than an Indian does" (*AutoMT* 3:53). This shocking analogy, comparing his parchment diploma from one of Europe's oldest, most prestigious institutions of higher learning with an iconic trophy of savage warfare, reveals the writer's perception of himself as fundamentally uncivilized. Oxford also honored Clemens with a set of traditional doctoral regalia—a scarlet and grey academic robe—that so enchanted him he took to wearing it on other special occasions, such as his daughter Clara's 1909 wedding. He donned it as well at the conclusion of a speech following a 1908 New York

City banquet given in his honor. Gazing down at its rich fabric, he mused aloud, almost more to himself than the assembled company:

> I like that gown. I was always did like red. The redder it is the better I like it. I was born for a savage. Now, whoever saw any red like this? There is no red outside the arteries of an archangel that could compare with this (Neider 320).

Despite this insistent metaphorical identification with Indians, Mark Twain avoided expressing sympathy for their plight, at least in print. In an unpublished 1902 dialogue entitled "The Dervish and the Offensive Stranger," he acknowledges that Anglo-American settlers "hunted and harried the original owners of the soil and robbed them, beggared them, drove them from their homes, and exterminated them, root and branch," but simultaneously absolves them of any responsibility for these wrongs by claiming: "There is no such thing . . . as an evil deed. There are good impulses, there are evil impulses, and that is all . . . No man can command the results, nor allot them . . . It is the law" (CTSS&E 2:547–48). Mark Twain's description of this relentless historical process closely parallels the fate of Injun Joe, who is also beggared, driven from his home, and ultimately exterminated, suggesting that the character is not so much an individual as an emblem of his race.

Works Cited

Baender, Paul, editor. *The Adventures of Tom Sawyer: A Facsimile of the Author's Holographic Manuscript.* Two vols. University Publications of America, 1982.

Driscoll, Kerry. *Mark Twain among the Indians and Other Indigenous Peoples.* U of California P, 2018.

Faragher, John Mack. "'More Motley than Mackinaw': From Ethnic Mixing to Ethnic Cleansing on the Frontier of the Lower Missouri, 1783–1833." *Contact Points: American Frontiers from the Mohawk Valley to the Mississippi, 1750–1830.* U of North Carolina P, 1998.

Mann, Barbara Alice. *George Washington's War on Native America.* U of Nebraska P, 2009.

Neider, Charles, editor. *Mark Twain: Plymouth Rock and the Pilgrims and Other Speeches*. Cooper Square Press, 2000.

Parkman, Francis. *The Oregon Trail*. Boston: Little, Brown, 1880.

Scheick, William J. *The Half-Blood: A Cultural Symbol in Nineteenth-Century American Fiction*. UP of Kentucky, 1979.

Twain, Mark. *Autobiography of Mark Twain*. Vol. 1: The Complete and Authoritative Edition. Edited by Harriet Elinor Smith, U of California P, 2010.

_____. *Autobiography of Mark Twain*. Vol. 3: The Complete and Authoritative Edition. Edited by Benjamin Griffin and Harriet Elinor Smith, U of California P, 2015.

_____. "The Dervish and the Offensive Stranger," in *Collected Tales, Sketches, Speeches & Essays*. Vol. 2: 1891–1910. Edited by Louis J. Budd, Library of America, 1992.

_____. *Following the Equator*. Harper, 1897.

_____. *Mark Twain's Letters*. Vol. 1, 1852–1866. Edited by Edgar Marquess Branch et al., U of California P, 1988.

_____. *Mark Twain's Letters*. Vol. 2, 1867–1868. Edited by Harriet Elinor Smith and Richard Bucci, U of California P, 1990.

_____. "The Noble Red Man" and "Plymouth Rock and the Pilgrims." *Collected Tales, Sketches, Speeches & Essays*. Vol. 1: 1852–1890. Edited by Louis J. Budd, Library of America, 1992.

_____. *Who Is Mark Twain?* Harper Studio, 2009.

Wecter, Dixon. *Sam Clemens of Hannibal*. Houghton Mifflin Company, 1952.

Welch, James, and Paul Stekler. *Killing Custer: The Battle of the Little Bighorn and the Fate of the Plains Indians*. Penguin, 1994.

Tom Sawyer as an Enduring Icon of Boyhood_____

John H. Davis and Hugh H. Davis

As the protagonist of one of literature's most famous books about a boy, Tom Sawyer is often offered as a model both of and for young boys. *The Adventures of Tom Sawyer* (1876) by Mark Twain (Samuel Clemens) tells the tale of Tom and his friends, whose appeal has prompted many rereadings and retellings. Tom has become an enduring icon of boyhood for readers and viewers alike. Ric Averill's 2008 *Tom Sawyer* play, for example, emphasizes the Sawyer gang's "rank rascalities" as boys. In his "Director's Note" for a 2016 production of the play, Jeffrey Emmerich emphasized Tom's appeal to him when he was a boy. He recalled thinking of Tom as his best friend and idol and mused, "What little boy doesn't have a bit of Tom Sawyer in him?" Tom's iconic status as the ideal boy has grown since the original novel was first published, making him a symbol of and for nostalgic views of boyhood. Tom is Everyboy.

Tom in Boy Culture

According to Clemens's preface to *Tom Sawyer*, Huckleberry Finn is modeled on a real person, while Tom Sawyer is a composite of three boys he knew in Hannibal, one likely being himself. This combination is appropriate, for Tom has become a representation of childhood. Tom's boyhood is an outgrowth of "Boy Culture"—as depicted in so-called "boy books" of the time—and largely reflects American culture, but Tom himself embodies universal aspects. As a universal representation of boyhood, Tom is given no age in the book. Sometimes, he seems to be no older than ten, at others, at least thirteen. As a result, although Huck may sometimes seem older than Tom in *Tom Sawyer*, and both may be about fourteen in *Adventures of Huckleberry Finn* (1885), Tom has become ageless. This view has made Tom representative of impish youth, as interpreted from the novel and its sequels and embellished throughout popular culture retellings. Whether in prose or personal performance, animation, or puppeteered, Tom Sawyer is the iconic boy of Americana. Closer examination, however, reveals contradictions, paradoxes, modifications, and distortions. The iconic Tom is often a distorted image of the original protagonist, the result of perceptions from rereadings and many adaptations.

Tom Sawyer was first published at a time of contrasting views and images of boys in books. Boy books were books *about* boys, their activities, behavior, and personalities—often with autobiographical elements—as opposed to books *for* boys, such as "Aladdin's Wonderful Lamp" (eighth century) and Alexandre Dumas's *The Three Musketeers* (1844), and distinct from those promoting the Model Boy (Willie Mufferson in *Tom Sawyer*), which exemplified what their protagonists should be and do according to adult standards of virtue for children. Clemens mocked these so-called "good boy" books in sketches such as "Advice for Good Little Boys" (1865) and "The Story of the Bad Little Boy Who Did Not Come to Grief" (1865). Contrasting these moralistic stories, "bad boy" books, originating with Thomas Bailey Aldrich's *The Story of a Bad Boy* (1869), focus on superficially bad youngsters, like Tom, who behave as real boys actually behave by being more mischievous than mean. Despite making clear that their "bad" protagonists will mature, books such as *Tom Sawyer* typically do not take their boy protagonists into adulthood. A difference is that Clemens ultimately rejects

Fig. 1. Cream of Wheat was one of many products evoking Tom Sawyer's name in advertisements during the early twentieth century. *Needlecraft Magazine*, June 1918. [Public domain.]

the adult role Tom seems headed for that other "bad boy" books endorse.

Clemens originally intended his novel for adults, until critic William Dean Howells advised him to aim it for children. Although generations have enjoyed the novel as *the* boy's book, adult elements appear throughout *Tom Sawyer*. Studies uncover darknesses and adult themes in a violent, narrow-minded town biased in church, home, and school. Lawrence Berkove, for example, notes that mid-story Tom changes as he begins accepting the community's values. By the final chapters, he fully identifies with society (Berkove 16–17). Although Clemens rejected adult roles for his boys in their stories, he often contemplated what those roles might be. In notebooks, conversations, and letters, he pondered possible sequels that would present grown-up Toms and Hucks reuniting, even taking them into old age and death. These imagined reunions are poignant. One has an elderly Tom tending an ill Huck; another has an insane Huck thinking he is a boy again, seeking Tom and Becky Thatcher in every face; recalling old days, their failed lives now empty, every beautiful thing they loved now gone, they die together (Anderson 606, 645; Smith and Gibson 88, 91, 173; Kipling 174–76). Clemens knew that such representations could never be icons.

Tom as an American Icon

Just as Clemens is an iconic American author, so, too, are his most famous characters iconic American boys. In 1983, the Effanbee toy company, maker of such doll-characters as Charlie McCarthy, launched a "Great Moments in Literature" line, featuring cloth-dressed figurines to complement their "American Icons" line. The icons represented Hollywood stars, such as John Wayne, and historical personas such as Abraham Lincoln. In contrast, except for a Sherlock Holmes doll, the company's entire literary line consisted of Mark Twain, Tom Sawyer, Huckleberry Finn, and Becky Thatcher. Effanbee's white-haired, mustachioed Clemens doll wears his trademark white suit; the Huck doll makes E.W. Kemble's *Huckleberry Finn* illustrations three-dimensional; the Tom and Becky dolls resemble True Williams's illustrations for *Tom Sawyer*.

The Becky doll, however, has pigtails, evoking other depictions of the heroine. The Effanbee line launched and concluded "Great Moments in Literature" with Clemens and his most famous children characters, offering Tom and his friends as *the* iconic American literary characters.

The use of Clemens's creations in a wave of American nostalgic marketing is not surprising. Often presented as two sides of the same nostalgic coin, Tom–resourceful, well-read, and mischievous within social norms–is the clever product of middle-American values. Huck–orphaned, independent, and with a social conscience–is the resilient rebel from outside society. They are presented as the ultimate children of Americana, representing boyish enthusiasm, adventurousness, and innocence (albeit with an impish streak challenging authority). Tom is the quick-witted and imaginative icon of a courageous and smart young man. Two nostalgia-driven 1970s television-series, *The Waltons* and *Little House on the Prairie*, name-drop *Tom Sawyer* and its whitewashing scene as important, linking them to small-town American life and family-centered entertainment.

During the early twentieth century, the cartoonist Clare Victor "Dwig" Dwiggins used Tom and Huck to expand his output. In 1918, he created, with the blessings of the Clemens estate, *Tom Sawyer and Huck Finn* as a Sunday companion to his daily comic strip *School Days*. He later merged this Clemens-inspired, but only loosely connected, strip with his own *Nipper*. *School Days* and *Nipper* were rural-kids comics, gag strips with "Our Gang"-type antics in small-town America. Dwig used Tom and Huck to evoke adventurous boys at play. In 1937, Dwig revived his version of them in a daily *Huckleberry Finn* strip, whose tone approximated that of Clemens's sequel novella *Tom Sawyer Abroad* (1894). With adventures from the Far West to Africa, one strip even included a giant robotic duck. Clemens's famous characters immediately linked nostalgic readers to "bygone days" of boys at play.

Jim Henson, the creator of the Muppets, said he spent his childhood as "a Mississippi Tom Sawyer" (Jones 13). That is cultural shorthand for a youth spent in the rural South, playing on riverbanks, catching frogs, and skipping rocks. His imaginative boyhood, of course, gave way to his creative adulthood, and his allusion to Tom links his childhood to an all-American upbringing. Henson alludes to Mark Twain and *Tom Sawyer* in various Muppet creations. A *Sesame Street* calendar, for example, featured Bert and Ernie raft-fishing as Tom and Huck; the *Muppet Babies* episode "Buckskin Babies" (1990) had characters named "Scoot Sawyer" and "Hucklebunny" whitewash a fence. Henson's calling himself Tom requires no explanation. His creative teams present bucolic scenes with overalls-clad Muppets on a raft or painting a fence

Fig. 2. In 1925, Clare Victor Dwiggins published some of his Tom and Huck comic strips in book form. Collection of R. Kent Rasmussen. [Used with permission.]

without exposition. Images of Tom and scenes from *Tom Sawyer* are enough by themselves to convey meaning.

Tom Sawyer often serves as cultural shorthand. His very name has even become a verb. Inspired by the novel's whitewashing sequence, "to Tom Sawyer" means to trick someone into completing an otherwise onerous task. It is used and understood without reading Clemens's novel, as the use of Tom the character itself is understood as a symbol for American youth and nostalgia outside the text. Being "Tom Sawyered" transformed into a positive value in "Work" (1996), the premiere episode of the moralistic program *Adventures from the Book of Virtues*. The segment titled "Tom Sawyer Gives Up the Brush" praised Tom not for being clever and escaping his own labor or for being crafty and claiming prizes in trade for others' sweat but for his gift in allowing his friends to find joy in work. As themes are reshaped to fit new frameworks, excerpted scenes and characters are appropriated to recall Clemens's novel.

Tom's Appeal

Tom appeals for many reasons to readers and others, many of whom expand his image beyond the Tom of the book. That Tom lives in a world that initially appears to be mostly sunshine and summertime, a childhood Eden, and a boyhood realm of never-ending imagination. The book projects a sense of timelessness that is supported by a summertime the novel stretches to hold its many events. Summers really do seem longer during childhood. Darkness, while present in *Tom Sawyer*, is mostly insidious and not initially obvious. Reminding readers of the ideal and idyllic nature of small-town life surrounding Tom, St. Petersburg–which can be read as "St. Peter's Town"—evokes a Heaven for boys. Girls are present as they relate to and are important to boys, but it is a boys' playground, with adults as easily evaded obstacles. Here, boys can live adventurous lives by reenacting characters in stories. Tom is apparently the most avid reader, interpreter, and authority of these tales. The boys create their own adventures by sneaking out at nights and spooking themselves by reciting superstitions and visiting scary places like graveyards, with the fright and thrills that appeal to children. Readers sense the same sensations during the episodes in the haunted house and cave and experience vicarious adventures by running away to live on an island, physically and psychologically far from adults and their rules. There, they are free of clothes, inhibitions, and any authority but their own and the books they recreate. They play games, fish, swim, fix their own meals, roam freely, lie looking at the stars wonder-filled by their domain. Off the island, they—particularly Tom—ignore adults and their requirements by completing such activities as playing with insects instead of doing schoolwork. Nostalgic readers recall this kind of fascination from their own childhoods. Time in school is a contest with authority. Even though he receives a whipping, Tom tricks schoolmaster Dobbins into seating him beside Becky by saying he was late to school because he stopped to talk to the outcast Huckleberry Finn (chapter 6).

On and off the boys' pirate island, Tom is likable, impulsive, imaginative, dramatic, adventurous, courageous, dominating, romantically literate, more clever than most (both adults and children), and resistant to authority (Aunt Polly, Mr. Dobbins) and societal obligations (school and church). He is also a liar, con man, manipulator, prankster, and show-off. While Tom has both positive and negative traits, his position as protagonist marks him as good overall, and his legacy is as a clever but impish boy who enjoys a respectable and respected place. Both residents of St. Petersburg and readers of the novel shape Tom into an important figure, as Everyboy. As Everyboy, Tom represents any and all boys but also serves through his actions and in his stories as the leader of the gang. By serving as the iconic boy, Tom claims and maintains status as the ideal boy.

Tom, Status, and Race

Tom's status is important to him. In play, his ego requires him to be Robin Hood, a nobleman robber, or a head pirate. He must set and control the rules of play. Although he may not realize it and even reject the assertion, class emerges as a major concern for Tom. Showing a selective compassion, he opens his heart to characters as diverse as Becky and Muff Potter, but not Aunt Polly. Tom knows she grieves for him but does not relieve her or his cousin Mary after finding them crying, feeling "more in pity of himself than anybody else" (chapter 15). While some say, and many believe, Huck is Tom's best friend, Tom's actual best friend is Joe Harper, a boy of his own social class. Tom is friendly with Huck but being friendly and being compassionate are not the same thing. Tom erects social and class barriers to Huck's joining the Sawyer gang, telling him, "we can't let you into the gang if you ain't respectable, you know." "Selfish" and "cruel" also describe Tom when "Huck's joy was quenched" (chapter 35). As readers elevate Tom and Huck's friendship to "best" status, they palliate Tom's crueler moments, finding enough in the end to redeem these brief instances. Middle-class mentalities give Tom a complicated, multi-faceted view of others, especially as they relate to class and status.

Perhaps because of his own near-death experience in McDougal's Cave in chapters 31–32 or the glory he feels in imagining his own death in chapter 8, Tom empathizes, albeit briefly, with the dead Injun Joe but demonstrates no sympathy for enslaved people. The only black character with whom Tom interacts directly is "the small colored boy" Jim. In the very first chapter, Tom and Jim are supposed to cut wood together. Jim, however, does all the chopping while Tom recounts his activities. Later, Tom tries to bribe Jim with a white marble to whitewash the fence, but white boys do the whitewashing (chapters 1–2), a subtle comment on white people's glossing over what they would rather ignore. Tom obscures his task with exaggeration: "Thirty yards of board fence nine feet high," his hyperbole iterated by "far-reaching continent of unwhitewashed fence." If it were so, he could not have "dipped his brush and passed it along the topmost plank" (chapter 2). Tom's fence description metaphorizes his expansive imagination.

The whitewashing in the novel is transparent. The word "slave" only appears twice, but the effects of slavery are present, such as references to "mulatto" indicating miscegenation in chapter 2, the absence of black people's last names in chapter 25, and horsewhipping slaves in chapter 24. The word "nigger" occurs far fewer times than it does in *Huckleberry Finn*. Racism is not a theme in Tom's book, but Tom is superior to all. Except for learning a new way to whistle from a black person and saying black people know things white people do not in chapter 10, Tom is non-committal on the issue. Tom's strongest dismissal of blacks as people occurs in the final chapters of *Huckleberry Finn* when he plays cruel games with Jim's freedom by not telling anyone that Jim is already legally free. Tom's adventures in his own book are those of boyhood, a nostalgic view of innocent childhood written perhaps with one lens rose-colored and the other darkened. Tom supports the status quo as it allows him to maintain his own status. Tom seeks to remain on top in a seemingly bright and white-washed world, but elements of darkness envelop the light there.

Tom's Boyish Antics

Tom's antics in St. Petersburg are captivating, cherished by both readers and by many who have never read the novel. The townspeople also covertly admire Tom and his antics as escape from the boredom of small-town life. That boredom conceals and symbolizes conformity, hypocrisy, and their own empty lives (Fetterley 120–24). In the 1946 film *It's a Wonderful Life*, a copy of the book even becomes a gift to a man for a life well lived. Linked in that film to a nostalgic view of American life and sentimentality, the novel exemplifies Clemens using Tom to idealize boyhood. Readers uphold Tom as a paragon of boyish acts and innocence. Because Clemens is a realist compelled to assert adulthood negativity, Tom's acceptance of adult ways is an inevitable betrayal of boyish idealism.

In his later stories featuring Tom and Huck, Clemens repeatedly avoids making them adults. Tom remains Everyboy throughout the author's completed and attempted sequels, bolstering readers' perceptions as the archetypal boy of American letters. Despite continued declarations, even decades after the novel, that he would show results of carrying Tom and Huck into adulthood, Clemens never finished such a story. In *Tom Sawyer Abroad* (1894), *Tom Sawyer, Detective* (1896), the incomplete "Huck Finn and Tom Sawyer among the Indians" (1884), the nearly finished *Tom Sawyer's*

Conspiracy (1897), and the unfinished "Schoolhouse Hill" (1898), they remain boys.

Adult Versions of Tom

Consciously or not, Clemens also created adult characters who evoke Tom Sawyer. Among them are Colonel Sellers, who first appears in *The Gilded Age* (1873) but is more fully realized as clone of Tom in *The American Claimant* (1892). Others include Hank Morgan, the title character of *A Connecticut Yankee in King Arthur's Court* (1889), and Philip Traum/Satan and No. 44 in the *Mysterious Stranger Manuscripts* (1897–1908). Sellers's exaggerated schemes suggest stretches of Tom's imaginings. Just as Tom convinces himself that his favorite fictional characters are real, Colonel Sellers cons himself into believing his own cons. Like Tom, Hank believes effect is more important than actuality. "Effect" (what one does) and "style" (how one does it) are almost synonyms in both novels and in *Huckleberry Finn*. Tom and Hank *must* show off. Traum and No. 44, despite appearing young, with adolescent earthly bodies, are mature beyond their apparent ages in knowledge, power, and divine insight, while still boyish in attitude and behavior. God-like Traum creates little clay people, amuses himself with them, then destroys them and their world. No. 44 plays supernatural tricks on everyone. Tom's flights of fantasy become their fantastic creations. Satan/Traum/44 is "a divine, omnipotent, playful Tom Sawyer . . . on a permanent holiday" (Michelson 47, 48). Tom's childish self-centeredness, selfishness, and cruelties are logically, if not inevitably, expanded in these stories. These child-adults are Tom Sawyers on steroids, providing a rationale for the author's not carrying Tom himself beyond childhood. Knowing how the adult world can corrupt what has seemed ideal, Clemens kept Tom himself a child, and, thereby, a more enduring icon.

Many artists have produced their own visions of adult Toms and Hucks, going where Clemens did not and staging reunions of them in adulthood. Meeting by chance in their twenties, Tom and Huck seek new adventures out west in *Sawyer and Finn* (1983), George Schenk's failed television pilot. Roy Johansen's television movie

---

Back to Hannibal: The Return of Tom Sawyer and Huckleberry Finn (1990) features novice lawyer Tom and budding reporter Huck helping unjustly charged Jim find justice. Dan Walker's *Huckleberry Finn in Love and War: The Lost Journals* (2007) places Clemens's characters in the Civil War. Phong Nguyen's novel *The Adventures of Joe Harper* (2016) rejoins Joe, a failed-pirate-turned-vagabond, with Tom, twenty years after *Tom Sawyer*. In E.E. Burke's novels *Taming Huck Finn* (2018) and *Tom Sawyer Returns* (2021), the adult characters navigate the world of historical romance novels, while Tom and Huck reunite as old men in Bernard Sabath's play *The Boys in Autumn* (1981).

With his incorporation into later adaptations, Tom continues to be molded to fit others' views. Two twenty-first-century films, *The League of Extraordinary Gentlemen* (2003) and *Band of Robbers* (2015), offer grown-up versions of the bad boy of the novel. Both films imagine Tom's having an adult career in law enforcement. Aaron and Adam Nee's modern-set *Band of Robbers* retells *Tom Sawyer* with Tom, Huck, and Becky as adults struggling to find their way. Tom is presented as an underachieving and corrupt police officer, frustrated that his youthful dreams were not met. To fit the novel in this contemporary setting, Tom is reshaped into a burnt-out, ineffective cop.

Filmmaker Stephen Norrington's *League of Extraordinary Gentlemen* reshapes Tom into a U.S. Secret Service agent who joins a super-team of literary figures. Based on a graphic novel, *League* adds Tom Sawyer to its roster of British and French characters. Playing off Clemens's *Tom Sawyer Abroad*, which offers exotic international adventure, and *Tom Sawyer, Detective*, which shows Tom solving mysteries, Norrington imagined Sawyer growing up to become a federal agent. In his film, Tom is a dashing superspy and sharpshooter who helps save the world. Clearly shaped to fit this saga of literary superheroes, Tom's horizons expand greatly from those in Clemens's original text.

Tom as Creator/Creative Force

Tom creates what he imagines. In his introduction to the Oxford Mark Twain edition of *Tom Sawyer*, novelist E. L. Doctorow argues that "a godlike power of realization is conferred upon Tom. . . ." (Doctorow xxxvi). Michelson agrees, "very early on [Clemens] had comprehended that any God who would bother with the petty affairs of mankind must do so as a cosmic Tom Sawyer, an all-powerful Player who amuses Himself recklessly at the world's expense" (Michelson 45). Like Tom Sawyer, who transforms his readings into reality, Tom Canty of Clemens's next novel, *The Prince and the Pauper* (1881), is another Twainian child reader who engages in imaginative play. This Tom imagines living in a royal court rather than "a foul little pocket called Offal Court" and briefly escapes to a real palace. In his own world, Tom Sawyer is what he wishes. To him, if not to Huck, the creation is real. Tom *becomes* a pirate or an Indian. To him, a Sunday-school picnic *becomes* a caravan to be robbed. Tom both creates his own world in which he is the

Fig. 3. Tom meditating on gaudy future careers in chapter 8. True Williams, *Tom Sawyer*, 1876, p. 81. [Public domain.]

hero and becomes an actual hero and the inspiration for heroism in other works.

Tom in Other Media

Tom Sawyer is a hero other writers use to bridge literary worlds. He is courageous in the original novel, but his heroism grows with his appearances in works by others. An entry in Jeff Rovin's *Adventure Heroes* (1994) lists Tom's appearances in a variety of media based on the original Clemens novels and equates Tom to such daring figures as James Bond, Sherlock Holmes, and D'Artagnan, (Rovin 265–66). Tom joins quite an illustrious company. His character is clearly larger than any one book can contain.

In Will Vinton's 1985 Claymation film, *The Adventures of Mark Twain*, Tom, Becky, and Huck accompany their literary creator on a flying steampunk adventure. Novelist Tim Champlin's *Adventures in Time–1849* trilogy teams Tom and Huck with a time-traveling twenty-first-century boy named Zane Rasmussen. *The New Adventures of Huckleberry Finn* (1968–1969), a prime-time television family series combining animation with live-action, has Tom, Huck, and Becky share fantastic adventures with characters and worlds from other literary classics. Although the show's title suggests it follows Clemens's Huck novel, its premise is actually based on *Tom Sawyer*. In this fantasy adventure, Injun Joe (Ted Cassidy) chases the three youthful protagonists in the cave, where they fall through a magical portal and are transported to other worlds. Each episode has Joe chase them into a new setting taken from folklore or fiction. During its single season, the children traveled to such imaginary places as Lilliput and Atlantis and encountered such legendary and mythic characters as Aladdin, Don Quixote, and Hercules.

Crossing Tom, Huck, and Becky with folklore and mythology has been another form of adaptation. In "Simpsons Tall Tales" (2001), an episode of the long-running animated *Simpsons* show, for example, the three child characters appear in a segment alongside spoofs of Paul Bunyan and Johnny Appleseed. Although that show acknowledged that *Tom Sawyer* is not a tall tale, the use of its title reveals how universal Tom has become, standing alongside folklore and mythology. The long-running children's video series *VeggieTales* adapted Clemens alongside biblical stories to present "Tomato Sawyer and Huckleberry Larry's Big River Rescue" (2008). *Adventures from the Book of Virtues* took its examples mainly from legends and myths, with *Tom Sawyer* and *A Christmas Carol* the sole adaptations from canonical literature, merging whitewashing with legends and myths. Clemens's work is often placed alongside classics from religion, mythology, and oral tradition.

Adaptations of *Tom Sawyer* often link classic literature with popular culture. The novel was, for example, the first work adapted on PBS-TV's *Wishbone* series in 1995. That show's "A Tail in Twain" episode implicitly promoted the significance of *Tom Sawyer* while explicitly presenting the novel as a text all should read. A 2001 episode of Matt Groening's animated television series *Futurama*, "The Day the Earth Stood Stupid," featured its main characters Fry and Leela defeating the Big Brain, an alien that assimilates all knowledge, by using and entering literary works. When the protagonists realize that thinking defeats the alien, they turn to such classics as Herman Melville's *Moby Dick* (1851), Jane Austen's *Pride and Prejudice* (1813), and *Tom Sawyer* to defeat the menace. Knowledge of Tom Sawyer the icon thus helps Fry in his quest.

Connecting Tom Sawyer with other literary characters has also conferred new life on Tom. Whereas the novel becomes a conduit for knowledge and victory on *Futurama*, the quick-witted Tom is back in school as a student at Storybrooke Elementary in "Strange Case" (2016), an episode of the fairy tale drama *Once Upon a Time*. Young Tom's appearance merges the stylized look of the series (Tom wears a school uniform sweater, replete with Storybrooke crest) with traditional views of the character (or perhaps of the common blurring of Tom with Huck). His red curly hair billows out under a straw hat, with an intended resemblance to True Williams's original illustrations. Like many of the characters in that fantasy series, Tom moves from literature into its town of Storybrooke. The series featured characters primarily from legends and fairy tales, such as Snow White. *Tom Sawyer* and a few L. Frank Baum Oz tales were the only canonical American literary works it adapted.

Tom Sawyer's St. Petersburg is also linked to Baum's land of Oz in Austin O'Toole's *On the Tip of My Tongue* (1980). In that play, boys who are mistaken for Tom and Huck fight Injun Joe, King Midas, and the Wicked Witch alongside Snow White and Oz's Dorothy. Tom Sawyer began with Clemens and remains rooted in his boyhood adventures, but he now clearly has a mythic status and belongs to a much broader audience.

Tom Sawyer's mythic status has enabled a shift from adventurous boy to action hero. This transition in turn has allowed the expansion from page to screen to video game console. Nintendo's *The Adventures of Tom Sawyer* and Square's *Tom Sawyer*, two 1980s video games, place Tom on adventures spurred by dreams but limit their scope to St. Petersburg. In 2015, a strategy game from Intelligent Systems moved Tom Sawyer beyond the novel's original narrative. Like *League of Extraordinary Gentlemen*, the video game *Code Name: S.T.E.A.M* assigns Tom to a team of literary icons defeating monsters. This time, the monsters are alien invaders, and Tom is an agent assigned to save the earth. He joins such characters as Queequeg (*Moby Dick*), Tiger Lily (*Peter Pan*), John Henry (folklore), Dorothy (*Oz*), and the game player in this quest. Far removed from St. Petersburg, the game speaks to a continued desire to keep Tom alive, albeit in forms fitting its creators' needs more than the dictates of logic.

Conclusion

When British author Rudyard Kipling met Clemens in 1889, his desire to keep alive beloved literary characters moved him to ask *Tom Sawyer*'s creator whether Tom would later marry Becky and if readers would ever hear about Tom as a man. Clemens responded with two possible scenarios: He could either make Tom a politician or hang him (Kipling 174). In offering that answer, he echoed what his novel's narrator says about Tom in chapter 24: "There were some that believed he would be President, yet, if he escaped hanging." When Kipling protested Clemens's suggestions, Clemens further stated, "Suppose we took the next four and twenty years of Tom Sawyer's life, and gave a little joggle to the circumstances that controlled him. He would, logically and according to the joggle, turn out a rip or an angel" (Kipling 174–75). Kipling's reaction partially explains resistance to a less ideal view of Tom: ". . . don't give him two joggles and show the result, because he isn't your property any more. He belongs to us" (Kipling 176). Like others, Kipling did not wish to see the adult result.

Tom and Huck have evolved beyond their origins and out of their author's grasp, having become public property. As public property, Tom and Huck are owned by readers of the novels as well as those who have encountered, imagined, and re-imagined the characters. Clemens, who initially intended, and succeeded in writing, a book for adults—and children—seems to have shared this reluctance, which clarifies his lack of success in maturing the characters. Tom Sawyer does belong to all of us, even those who have never read his story.

Works Cited

Anderson, Frederick, editor. *Mark Twain's Notebooks & Journals.* Vol. 3, 1883–1891. U California P, 1979.

Berkove, Lawrence. "'Some Damned Fools': Mark Twain and the Deceptive Promise of Youth." *Mark Twain and Youth: Studies in His Life and Writings.* Edited by Kevin Mac Donnell and R. Kent Rasmussen, Bloomsbury, 2016.

Doctorow, E. L. Introduction to *The Adventures of Tom Sawyer.* Oxford UP, 1996.

Fetterley, Judith. "The Sanctioned Rebel." *Critical Essays on The Adventures of Tom Sawyer.* Edited by Gary Scharnhorst, G. K. Hall, 1993.

Jones, Brian Jay. *Jim Henson: The Biography.* Random House, 2013.

Kipling, Rudyard. "An Interview with Mark Twain." *From Sea to Sea: Letters of Travel.* Doubleday, Page, 1913.

Michelson, Bruce. "*Deus Ludens*: The Shaping of Mark Twain's *Mysterious Stranger.*" *Novel: A Forum on Fiction.* vol. 14, no. 1, Autumn 1980, pp. 44–56.

Rovin, Jeff. *Adventure Heros: Legendary Characters from Odysseus to James Bond. Facts on File*, 1994.

Smith, Henry Nash, and William M. Gibson, editors. *Mark Twain-Howells Letters.* 2 vols. Belknap Press, 1960.

Tom Sawyer's Complicated Relationship with Mark Twain's Hometown_____

Cindy Lovell

Few literary works have had relationships with their creators' hometowns as close as that of the 1876 novel *The Adventures of Tom Sawyer* and Missouri's riverfront town of Hannibal, where author Samuel L. Clemens grew up. Better known by his pen name, Mark Twain, Clemens was actually born farther inland, in the tiny village of Florida, in 1835. He and his family moved to Hannibal in 1839, and from then until 1853, that town was the source of his entire formal education, as well as the home of the relatives and friends and many of the adventures he would later immortalize in *Tom Sawyer*. Although the novel's fictional town of St. Petersburg is clearly modeled on Hannibal—with touches of nearby Florida—

Fig. 1. Frederick Hibbard's statue of Tom and Huck, facing south, down Hannibal's Main Street, in 2017. Photo by Coalfather, via Wikimedia. [CC 4.0.]

it and Hannibal are not the same. The resemblance is, however, close enough for the town to be—for better or for worse—indelibly associated with the book and Tom Sawyer himself. Imposing statues of Mark Twain stand along Hannibal's riverfront and in its Riverview Park, but the town's most easily seen sculpture is Frederick Hibbert's bronze statue of Tom Sawyer and Huck Finn gazing over the city from above the north end of Main Street. It is a reminder that while Clemens may be Hannibal's most celebrated resident, Hannibal is not so much Mark Twain's town as it is Tom Sawyer's town.

Other American towns have experienced similarly intimate literary relationships. In 1996, for example, the village of North Tarrytown, New York, officially changed its name to "Sleepy Hollow," which it took from Washington Irving's famous 1820 story, "The Legend of Sleepy Hollow." Irving lived a mile away in Tarrytown, where his home—like that of Clemens in Hannibal—has been open for tours. Although the town's famed bridge, on which Ichabod Crane tries to escape from the Headless Horseman, rotted away years ago, visitors can still tour the Sleepy Hollow Cemetery by lantern light or plan an autumn around the village's annual "Sleepy Hollow"–themed Halloween events. Tarrytown residents have seemingly embraced the literary legacy bestowed by Irving. Fall tourism alone generates roughly $5 million annually in the region. One store owner compared the town's Halloween shopping season to Christmas. All this from one memorable little, short story. Imagine the impact an entire novel might have on a small town!

In the Midwest, fans of Laura Ingalls Wilder's *Little House* books are more likely to drive cars in her footsteps than walk in them, but many make the pilgrimage to "Little House" sites across several states. The actual "little houses" Wilder knew have long since succumbed to weather, but visitors can still explore a replica log cabin in Pepin, Wisconsin, the site of her first book, *Little House in the Big Woods* (1932). There is also a replica of the house in *Little House on the Prairie* (1935) in Walnut Grove, Minnesota. Pa Ingalls was a restless sort, so literary pilgrims must keep moving west. Iowa and South Dakota also offer Wilder sites and capping off the trek is the time-capsule home in Mansfield, Missouri, the not-so-little house where Wilder herself wrote most of the beloved series. Some 30,000 people tour that home each year.

There is more to many of these literary road trips than meets the eye. Some visitors want to indulge their imagination or satisfy a curiosity. Others seek authentic stories and experiences. After all, they may have felt the hot breath of Irving's headless horseman's mighty steed down their necks or spent cozy evenings by the Ingalls family hearth. Why should they not go out of their way to bring beloved books to life?

The most famous of literary American hometowns, however, is doubtless Hannibal, Missouri, the inspiration for Tom Sawyer's hometown of St. Petersburg. To a large extent, Hannibal's history and public image have been shaped by a fictional character created by its most famous resident. However, while Sam Clemens himself was free to adopt the pen name "Mark Twain," Hannibal had no say in becoming "St. Petersburg." Thanks to that moniker, an odd kind of fame was thrust upon the town in the late nineteenth century when *Tom Sawyer* debuted to an enthusiastic audience. Technologies such as Google did not yet exist, but readers did not need computer search engines to confirm that "St. Petersburg" was none other than Hannibal. That real town, which has embraced the nickname "America's Hometown"—may be the American city most inextricably connected with a single work of literature. That, in turn, raises the question of exactly what Tom Sawyer's legacy in Hannibal is. It is, however, not easy to provide a clear-cut answer.

In 1946, Mark Twain editor and biographer Bernard DeVoto wrote that "Hannibal is the most important single fact in the life of Samuel Clemens, the person, and Mark Twain, the writer" (DeVoto 6). "As the St. Petersburg of *Tom Sawyer*," DeVoto added, "Hannibal is one of the superb idyls of American literature, perhaps the supreme one" (DeVoto 8). There is no denying the palpable presence of setting in *Tom Sawyer*. While visitors to Hannibal cannot meet the novel's actual characters or whitewash a fence themselves, they happily settle for the chance to walk in the imaginary footsteps of those characters and take pictures of themselves pretending to whitewash a fence. Hannibal affords ample opportunities to blur the lines between fact and fiction.

An *Illinois Magazine* staff writer got it exactly right during the 1935 centennial celebration of Sam Clemens's birth when he wrote, "Hannibal, Missouri has done for Mark Twain exactly what Mark Twain did for Hannibal" (Patton 33). In other words, each helped immortalize the other. In *The Adventures of Tom Sawyer*, Mark Twain froze Hannibal in time, with its best foot forward in a hazy summer of boyhood antics, albeit with occasional dark undertones. Hannibal reciprocated by embracing ambassadors Tom and Huck whose identities were convoluted with Mark Twain the author, Sam Clemens the person, and Clemens's boyhood pals. The story was raveled from the outset. With characters based on real people and the settings based on real places, confusing fact and fiction seemed inevitable. Would anyone even care?

Fictional St. Petersburg vs. Real Hannibal

Although fact and fiction intersect almost indistinguishably in Hannibal, much of the story is a matter of public record. Who were the real people, and what were the actual places in Hannibal that appeared in St. Petersburg?

The starting point for any survey of St. Petersburg sites is clearly Tom's home, Aunt Polly's simple, two-story house that he shares with his half-brother Sid and cousin Mary. Almost everything about the fictional house matches Clemens's Boyhood Home, which has been preserved as a public museum. The novel has little to say about other characters' homes and other buildings in St. Petersburg, but other kinds of sites figure prominently in the story. The novel's "Cardiff Hill" closely matches the promontory known as "Holliday's Hill" during Clemens's time. It was named after Captain Richard Holliday, who built a large house atop it. Holliday's widow was the inspiration for the novel's prosperous Widow Douglas, who lives atop Cardiff Hill. So closely did the name "Cardiff Hill" become associated with Hannibal's real hill that the city eventually formally made it the hill's name.

The most prominent real-world geographical feature in the novel is the Mississippi River. Its presence is felt throughout the novel, but it is, curiously, mentioned by name only twice–in chapters 13 and 32. The river plays its largest role in chapters 13 through 18, when Tom and his pals Huck Finn and Joe Harper spend several days playing pirates and other games on Jackson's Island. As the site of some of the boys' merriest frolics, the island has been of great interest to tourists. There is a problem, however, in satisfying visitors' aspirations. In *Tom Sawyer*, Jackson's Island is "[t]hree miles below St. Petersburg, at a point where the Mississippi river was a trifle over a mile wide . . ." (chapter 13). There is no such island around that distance from Hannibal, and even if there were, it would not be an easy place for tourists to reach. By 1902, the city began identifying an island immediately across the river that broadly fit the novel's description of Jackson's Island. Originally called Glascock's Island, that island was later sliced in half by the uncooperative river. Maps made in the 2020s have given the shrinking fragments of Glascock's Island different names, but for about 120 years, Hannibal residents have been satisfied that Clemens himself would not have minded their moving his island up the river in the interest of literature. He himself, after all, had moved his uncle's Florida, Missouri, farm to Arkansas in *Adventures of Huckleberry Finn*. In any case, if the novel's depiction of Tom's escapades on Jackson's Island had anything to do with any island adventures Clemens himself had experienced as boy, those adventures probably occurred on Glascock's Island.

One more major site in the novel to consider is "McDougal's cave," just south of St. Petersburg, near the river. Clemens modeled it on McDowell's cave, just south of Hannibal, near the river. Originally named after its owner, Dr. Joseph Nash McDowell, the cave is now known as "Mark Twain Cave." Clemens explored it as a boy and later at least mentioned it in several of his books, including *Huckleberry Finn*.

Most of the principal characters in *Tom Sawyer* are based on real people whom Clemens knew as a boy, starting with himself, as Tom is clearly based partly on him, with elements of his boyhood friends John Briggs and Will Bowen. According to a story the *St. Louis Post-Dispatch* reporter Robertus Love wrote at the time Clemens was revisiting Hannibal, residents of the town claimed Tom was based solely on Clemens, and that it was Clemens himself who tricked his friends into whitewashing a fence. In contrast to Tom, Clemens modeled Huckleberry Finn solely on one boyhood friend—Tom Blankenship, a neighbor from an impoverished family. In his autobiography Clemens said Blankenship was

> ignorant, unwashed, insufficiently fed; but he had as good a heart as ever any boy had. His liberties were totally unrestricted. He was the only really independent person—boy or man—in the community, and by consequence he was tranquilly and continuously happy, and was envied by all the rest of us. . . . And as his society was forbidden us by our parents, the prohibition trebled and quadrupled its value, and therefore we sought and got more of his society than of any other boy (Twain 397).

Clemens openly acknowledged basing Sid, Tom Sawyer's annoying half-brother, on his own younger brother, Henry, but added, "Sid was not Henry. Henry was a very much finer and better boy than ever Sid was. I never knew Henry to do a vicious thing toward me, or toward any one else—but he frequently did righteous ones that cost me as heavily," as when Henry once "called my mother's attention to the fact that the thread with which she had sewed my collar together to keep me from going in swimming, had changed color" (Twain 350). Sid does exactly the same thing in the first chapter of *Tom Sawyer*. The novel's Aunt Polly is another character in the novel clearly based on a Clemens relative—Jane Lampton Clemens, Clemens's own mother.

Clemens modeled Becky Thatcher on his childhood sweetheart, Laura Hawkins, whose family lived directly across from the Clemenses on Hill Street, in a home now restored and open to the public as the "Becky Thatcher House." Hawkins spent her entire life in Hannibal and after *Tom Sawyer* was published confirmed that some of the novel's incidents involving Becky had happened to her. Getting lost in the cave with Clemens, however, was not one of them.

Jim, "the small colored boy," appears only briefly in the novel's first two chapters but is important to mention, as he appears to be a slave in Aunt Polly's household. Clemens explicitly acknowledged basing him on a slave boy named Sandy, whose services his family rented (Twain 212). The villain known as "Injun Joe" will be discussed below.

Hannibal, Mark Twain, and the Rise of Tourism

In early 1902, Sam Clemens made a three-day visit to his hometown while on his way to the University of Missouri in Columbia to accept an honorary degree. It was his seventh and final return visit there and first since 1890, when he had returned for his mother's funeral, and he seemed to sense it would be his last. Perhaps the town did, too. Boys and girls turned out to greet him dressed in attire they thought resembled the characters in *Tom Sawyer*. He was from their town, and he had made it big. They were proud and most likely had read his books—or at least knew about them. His fame mattered. The *St. Louis Post-Dispatch* reporter Love accompanied Clemens on his visit and documented the outpouring of love from Hannibal's residents and Clemens's own occasionally tearful feelings for his hometown. Hannibal had spent the previous quarter of a century welcoming—or at least tolerating—visitors who came in search of *Tom Sawyer* sites such as "Cardiff Hill" and "Jackson's Island." No doubt Clemens's visit reinforced their civic pride in a town that was rapidly becoming a bona fide tourist destination.

Love also noted the adults who felt compelled to assert their own hand in Sam's success story, or at least the story of Tom Sawyer. "Today Hannibal is full of Huck Finns, Tom Sawyers and Beckys. There are more 'originals' of Huck, Tom and Becky in this town since Mark Twain arrived than one would expect to meet in a staid old town with 23 respectable Sunday schools and a Salvation Army" (Love 1). The number of ladies claiming to have been Clemens's "first love" numbered eighteen. In 1902, at least, "Mark Twain" enjoyed something of a fan club in Hannibal.

Fig. 2. Buttons made for street fairs held in Hannibal in 1898 and 1899.
Images courtesy of Kevin Mac Donnell. [Used with permission.]

In 1902, seemingly everyone was weighing in. One old Native
American Hannibal resident named Joe Douglass, who was long
believed by townsfolk to have been the original for *Tom Sawyer*'s
evil "Injun Joe," shared a story about himself with the *St. Louis
Post-Dispatch* that contradicted that belief. He claimed his mother
had been Spanish and his father a Cherokee Indian, and that he had
been captured by American soldiers in Mexico in 1847. He added
that he had first come to Hannibal in 1862, fully nine years after
Clemens had left. "As long as I remember I have been called Indian
Jo," Douglass told a newspaper reporter. "When I first came the

Fig. 3. Photographer Anna Schnizlein's postcard view of another photographer and others watching Mark Twain pose in front of his boyhood home during his 1902 visit to Hannibal.
Collection of R. Kent Rasmussen. [Used with permission.]

negroes were afraid of me because I was an Indian. I tried to pass myself off as a colored person, but they would not let me stay with them at first. They used to lock me up in a room at night and guard me to keep me from harming them" ("Tom Sawyer Characters" 5). Despite the impossibility of Clemens's having even known this man, Hannibal had been burnishing the "Injun Joe" myth for the sake of literature. That myth is quite literally cast in stone: Not far from Clemens family gravesites in Hannibal's Mount Olivet Cemetery, Douglass's tombstone states that he provided the model for the evil Indian character in *Tom Sawyer*. The story was convenient, if not accurate.

A year after Clemens's last Missouri visit, a body called the National Mark Twain [A]ssociation, whose headquarters was in Hannibal, decided to host a convention at the 1904 St. Louis World's Fair. Its members submitted plans to the fair committee that included an open invitation of delegates from towns around the country. In fact, the fair committee designated June 3, 1904, as "Mark Twain

Day" at the exposition, in the hope that Clemens himself would attend. On that date, however, Clemens would be in Italy, where his wife died only two days later. Meanwhile, nearly one hundred newspaper writers covering the fair wanted to visit Hannibal to see its *Tom Sawyer* sights for themselves. Hannibal residents viewed the journalists' interest in their town as a boon signaling that other visitors would follow. The town considered offering special railroad rates to fair attenders who wanted to visit Hannibal, but it is not clear if the daily train between Hannibal and St. Louis actually reduced its rates. "The people of Hannibal, one and all, regard Mark Twain as the greatest man on earth," stated one newspaper in late 1903. "It is not unlikely that Hannibal, being only three hours' run from St. Louis, will become a Mecca for many world's fair visitors next year. Only a few weeks ago it was announced that Jackson's island is to be turned into a summer resort" ("Humorist's Boyhood Home" 5).

In 1916, Hannibal's postmaster Robert Blackwood provided an insight to the town's response to growing tourist interest. By then, Hannibal was increasingly promoting itself as the "boyhood home" of Mark Twain, and the city's Commercial Club (precursor to the Chamber of Commerce) created a tour that included *Tom Sawyer*-related sites, such as McDougal's Cave. Local photographers made and sold thousands of copies of photographs of both the Clemens and Blankenship homes, earning far more from their pictures than the homes themselves were worth. Postmaster Blackwood summed up what was happening in a single sentence: "Hannibal, Mo., has capitalized one big asset we used to think was a liability." He was talking about Mark Twain and *Tom Sawyer* and went on to describe the efforts of Hannibal boosters who "went to work getting Hannibal on the map as the home of Mark Twain" by naming a hotel for him and creating maps for visitors to find various sites from the book ("Mark Twain an Asset" 4).

While all this was going on, Tom Sawyer was becoming a universally beloved character. His image was even starting to appear in advertisements in national magazines. In 1924, for example, the Proctor & Gamble Company, which advertised its cleaning and other products in magazines with circulations in the millions, published an ad with a picture of "The Old Swimmin' Hole" at Hannibal. The ad even included the tag, "Hannibal is famous the world over as the home of Mark Twain and his two immortal boy heroes, Huck Finn and Tom Sawyer" ("Missouri Facts" 2). It is impossible to calculate what this kind of free advertising did for Hannibal, but it very likely reinforced the town's identity as the home of Tom Sawyer.

Hannibal's Evolving Self-Image

In 1911, the first year after Clemens's death, his boyhood home on Hill Street was scheduled to be torn down and replaced by apartments. A farsighted Hannibal attorney, George A. Mahan, saved the house by purchasing it and donating it to the city. A year later, the house officially opened to the public. This first tangible step in preserving Mark Twain's legacy in Hannibal would prove to be a mixed blessing. While the boyhood home would help draw tourist dollars to the town, it also placed a burden on the city, which thenceforth had the responsibility to tell the house's story and maintain the property as visitors wore it down. That kind of responsibility would eventually grow into a local industry of sorts.

Through the ensuing years, popular feature film adaptations of *Tom Sawyer* in 1917–18, 1930, and 1938, as well as productions of *The Adventures of Huckleberry Finn* in 1920, 1931, and 1939, helped keep alive public awareness of the novel *Tom Sawyer*. By the 1950s, Hannibal's downtown Orpheum Theater had been renamed the "Tom Sawyer Theater." Events often occurred in Hannibal to remind the town of its Mark Twain's legacy. In 1943, for example, while the Warner Brothers Studio was preparing to make its biopic *The Adventures of Mark Twain*, it purchased the old building in which Clemens's father had worked as a justice of the peace and ended up donating it to the city, which later moved it to a site on Hill Street across from the boyhood home and dubbed it the "John Marshall Clemens Justice of the Peace Building." There was no escaping Mark Twain, even if Hannibal residents wanted to, and here was one more aging building for the city to preserve and maintain.

Meanwhile, visitors continued arriving with questions about *Tom Sawyer*'s sites. To accommodate visitors, the city eventually even changed the name of Holliday's Hill to "Cardiff Hill," as in the novel. The gradual morphing of Hannibal to St. Petersburg continued for decades, although the town itself has yet to change its own name, as Washington Irving's West Tarrytown eventually did.

In 1927, one anonymous travel writer lauded Hannibal as a prime tourist destination, urging people to "take a look at what Hannibal has to offer" while specifically listing the sites from *Tom Sawyer*, such as "the cave in which Becky Thatcher and Tom Sawyer were supposed to have been lost." The writer bolstered Hannibal's image as a tourist town, writing "Mark Twain's boyhood life in Hannibal establishes that city as a mecca for thousands of tourists every year" ("River Scenery" 11). In this one brief passage, this writer seemed to capture the dual identity of Tom Sawyer's St. Petersburg and Sam Clemens's Hannibal as the merger between the two continued.

In early 1935, Hannibal received unprecedented national news coverage when President Franklin D. Roosevelt flipped a switch in the White House to light the newly installed lighthouse atop Cardiff Hill, officially launching the city's celebration of the centennial of Clemens's birth. The occasion was also feted by Clemens's only surviving child, Clara Clemens Gabrilowitsch, who joined the nationwide radio broadcast from her home in Detroit, along with Missouri governor Guy Park and Hannibal's George Mahan for a nationwide radio broadcast. Clara and her daughter, Nina (Clemens's only grandchild), visited Hannibal later that year. When they arrived aboard the "Mark Twain Zephyr" train, they were greeted by children dressed as Tom, Huck, and Becky—just as Hannibal children had welcomed Clemens himself in 1902.

These and other events further bolstered the reputation of both Hannibal and Mark Twain. Hannibal residents relished this national spotlight and went all out for the centennial. Newspapers around the country published regular updates. Even *National Geographic* weighed in, saying, "As the 'little white town drowsing in the sunshine,' described in the novels 'Huckleberry Finn' and 'Tom

Sawyer', Hannibal is perhaps the best-known small town in the United States" ("Hannibal" 12). The 1935 celebration included a pageant of episodes from Clemens's life and writings, including "Tom Sawyer's Day," which saw nearly 1,000 boys whitewashing, and a Tom-and-Huck look-alike contest. Centennial celebrations were also held in Elmira, New York; Hartford, Connecticut; New York City; and Bermuda that same year. By the end of 1935, Hannibal was firmly entrenched in Tom Sawyer tourism. During the following year, President Roosevelt himself came to Hannibal to dedicate the new Mark Twain Memorial Bridge across the Mississippi River.

In 1956, *National Geographic* published a long article by Mark Twain biographer Jerry Allen titled "Tom Sawyer's Town." The article featured a map and twenty-two photographs of the town and Mark Twain. Who were the folks of Hannibal to argue with *National Geographic*? If that esteemed publication called Hannibal "Tom Sawyer's Town," it would get no argument from them.

That same year, one thousand St. Louis school children traveled to Hannibal to explore Mark Twain sites under the sponsorship of a television station. Hannibal was ready for them. Its Chamber of Commerce sponsored a Tom-and-Becky contest for local seventh graders. Contestants were judged on how well their costumes reflected True Williams's illustrations in the novel's first edition, their personality traits, and their ability to present themselves as Tom and Becky. The two winners were designated "ambassadors" for the city, and they officially welcomed their peers from St. Louis and served as their hosts. That contest might have been a one-time event but instead became an annual tradition that has continued into the 2020s. Each year, Hannibal's seventh-graders study *Tom Sawyer*, and are encouraged to try out for the Tom-and-Becky ambassador program that runs from one fourth of July to the next. Entrants are required to know Hannibal history, Clemens family history, and the book itself.

Demand for Tom and Becky appearances grew so strong by the 1990s that five Toms and five Beckys were selected each year, with one pair being dubbed the "official" Tom and Becky. Requests for appearances have even come from out of state, and some of the luckier children have represented Hannibal as far away as Bermuda.

Slavery, Race, and *Tom Sawyer*

Tom Sawyer mentions slavery and a few minor African American characters, such as the boy Jim, but the novel does not confront issues of race and slavery. Those are subjects addressed more directly in Clemens's later novels *Adventures of Huckleberry Finn* (1885) and *Pudd'nhead Wilson* (1894). By the time Mark Twain delved into that type of social criticism, Hannibal's residents and tourists had already embraced Hannibal's identity as "Tom Sawyer's Town." It may be generous to say that the town's Tom Sawyer identity was cast in nostalgia. To be fair, *Tom Sawyer* is set squarely in Hannibal's fictional counterpart, St. Petersburg, whereas *Huckleberry Finn* merely begins in St. Petersburg and then moves far down the Mississippi River. By the time *Huckleberry Finn* was published, both tourists and residents were already busily interpreting Hannibal as Tom's St. Petersburg, not Huck's. A change in perspective would come slowly, if at all.

Slavery is not an issue in *Tom Sawyer* as it is in *Huckleberry Finn*. However, the horrors of slavery and the conditions of enslaved African Americans were real in Hannibal, which has had its own aversion to a full-throated discussion of the topic. Indeed, in 1934 one public sign unashamedly referred to *Huckleberry Finn*'s escaping slave, Jim, as "Niggar Jim." [sic] That was literally a sign of the times. It would be more than one hundred years after *Huckleberry Finn*'s publication for Hannibal residents and city leaders to begin seriously discussing Hannibal's slave-holding history. Slavery might have been banished, but racism still existed, and would continue to do so.

Pulitzer Prize-winning journalist and Mark Twain biographer Ron Powers was born in Hannibal and lived there through the 1940s and 1950s. In 1984, when the city was preparing for a major celebration of its 1985 sesquicentennial anniversary of Clemens's birth, Powers returned several times to observe developments and reflect on his own childhood there. In 1986, he published *White Town Drowsing: Journeys to Hannibal*, part-memoir, part-journalism. Powers's reflective prose examined both his boyhood years and the city's overreaching pageant, which ultimately failed to meet its lofty goal of bringing millions of dollars to the town. That vision did not materialize, and the perceived failure would haunt city leaders for decades.

Powers recalled having never observed incidents of racial violence in Hannibal during his boyhood there. The city's schools were desegregated a few years before he entered high school. He wrote that "blacks were few and mostly invisible in the town. Those who lived there knew, as the saying had it, their place. Their place was mostly in the fetid flood plain of Bear Creek, an area known as the Bottoms" (Powers 1986, 49–50). Not exactly a positive description, but an accurate portrait of many American towns. During the civil rights activities of the 1960s, some Hannibal African Americans spoke out as others were doing so around the country, even turning out in protest. Hannibal resident Faye Dant recalls when Alabama's segregationist governor George Wallace held a rally in Hannibal's Central Park as members of the Ku Klux Klan stood by (Poletti). She left Hannibal but returned a few decades later with a mission. One of the first serious attempts to call attention to Hannibal's diverse racial history and past record of slavery was her 2013 creation of a museum focusing on local African American history. Taking its name from *Huckleberry Finn*, Dant dubbed the museum "Jim's Journey: The Huck Finn Freedom Center." The museum documents, presents, and preserves the history of both enslaved and free African Americans in Hannibal. It is located on North Third Street, in what is believed to have been the site that inspired "the old Welchman's house" in *Tom Sawyer*—the place where Huck Finn raises an alarm about potential violence against the Widow Douglas. The museum is near the recently rebuilt "Huck Finn House" and other sites that make up the Mark Twain Boyhood Home complex. Although its admission is free, it receives far fewer visitors than those other sites.

In 1995, Shelley Fisher Fishkin, author of the provocative book *Was Huck Black: Mark Twain and African-American Voices* (1993) visited Hannibal to investigate how Clemens's hometown presented its African American experience, particularly in relation to Clemens himself. She visited the usual tourist attractions, interviewed both locals and visitors, and attended a performance at the Mark Twain Outdoor Theater. That performance included a scene from *Huckleberry Finn* in which Huck and Aunt Polly conversed; it upset Fishkin because it contained no mention of Jim. She subsequently published a robust exploration of this critical topic in *Lighting Out for the Territory: Reflections on Mark Twain and American Culture* (1996). In that book she criticized Hannibal's neglect of its past slavery and historical diversity and reminded readers that when Clemens visited Hannibal in 1882, he noticed that an African American family was living in his former boyhood home.

Since Fishkin's 1995 visit, the Mark Twain Boyhood Home and Museum complex has continued to evolve. In 2005, it installed panels in its Interpretive Center that discuss Clemens's experiences with slavery in Hannibal. The next year, the museum opened the replicated Huck Finn House, whose exhibits featured a more expansive presentation on slavery in Hannibal and the Blankenship family's experiences. On "Juneteenth" in 2010, slavery finally made itself known within the Boyhood Home itself in the form of a hand-woven rug to serve as a pallet for Sandy, the enslaved boy who served the Clemens family when Sam was a child. The rug is accompanied by text panels featuring Clemens's personal recollections of slavery within his home and hometown. Additional exhibits pertaining to slavery were displayed in the restored Becky Thatcher House when it reopened in 2013. Thus, by the 2010s, Hannibal was still "Tom Sawyer's Town," but its story was becoming more complex.

Tom Sawyer's Economic Impact on Hannibal

There can be no denying tourism has become a vigorous industry in Hannibal. It has brought considerable revenue into the town, and much of the tourist industry revolves around Mark Twain's legacy.

Moreover, Mark Twain has generated revenue for Hannibal in more subtle ways. During the 1960s, for example, an executive for Underwood Deviled Ham made Hannibal the site of its new pork-processing plant primarily because of his admiration for Mark Twain. By the 2020s, that plant was a General Mills facility employing more than four hundred people—few of whom were probably aware they owed their jobs to literature.

In 2019, Hannibal celebrated the bicentennial of its 1819 founding with more than two hundred events, only a few of which were Mark Twain- or Tom Sawyer-related. This was by design. Hannibal actually boasts a number of famous residents, such as the "unsinkable" *Titanic* survivor Molly Brown; the voice of "Jiminy Cricket," Cliff Edwards; artist James Carroll Beckwith; Learjet inventor William Lear; Baseball Hall of Famer Jake Beckley; Navy admiral Robert Coontz; and hurdler George Poage, the first African American to medal in the Olympics, in 1904. The bicentennial program was a year-long festival celebrating Hannibal history whose only Twain-related events were its annual National Tom Sawyer Days and Mark Twain birthday celebrations. City officials did, however, designate country singer Brad Paisley's "Huck Finn Blues" as the official song of the bicentennial. Its lyrics emphasize the friendship and midnight adventures of Tom and Huck. The specter of the financial fiasco and letdown of the 1985 Clemens sesquicentennial loomed over the bicentennial planning, but the year-long event was a success.

In 2019, artists began painting exterior walls of buildings with murals, many of which replicate old advertising, and one that features a riverboat, Molly Brown, Mark Twain, Huck Finn, and a last-minute addition of *Huckleberry Finn*'s Jim (who was relegated to the mural's background). That mural generated a great deal of discussion about race and representation during the fund-raising period.

Meanwhile, in 2011, the Mark Twain Museum held its inaugural "Clemens Conference," during which Mark Twain scholars from around the world converged to share research and visit the sites

Clemens made famous. Designed as a quadrennial event, the conference complements a similar quadrennial conference that has been held at New York's Elmira College since the early 1990s. The museum has also been hosting teacher workshops since 2006, guiding and supporting teachers who embrace the challenges of teaching Mark Twain in twenty-first-century classrooms.

Twenty-first-Century Attitudes

Modern Hannibalians fall into three categories: (1) People who dislike Mark Twain and claim he has done little to nothing positive for the town; (2) those who embrace Mark Twain and champion his legacy; and (3) those who are indifferent. The last constitute the largest group.

Perhaps this division has always been the case. In retrospect, the Tom Sawyer-Mark Twain legacy may have been inevitable with the success of the book. One wonders, however, if the town would have embraced *Tom Sawyer* as it has without such impetuses as Clemens's return visits, George Mahan's purchase of the boyhood home, and President Roosevelt's enthusiasm for Mark Twain. That is impossible to know, but the Tom Sawyer-Mark Twain legacy has never been stronger, and it extends well beyond the borders of the town. Will it continue? As in the past, occasional newsworthy events continue to draw attention to Hannibal and *Tom Sawyer.* In 2019, for example, the discovery of Clemens's own signature on a wall deep in the Mark Twain Cave was reported by news outlets in Germany, Japan, Bermuda, and elsewhere. Clemens immortalized the cave in *Tom Sawyer.* "In one place," according to the novel, "far from the section usually traversed by tourists, the names 'BECKY & TOM' had been found traced upon the rocky wall with candle-smoke" (chapter 30). Since the book's original publication, owners of the cave have identified dozens of smoked signatures of Sam Clemens's boyhood friends, but Clemens's own signature proved more elusive. The discovery reinvigorated interest in the novel.

Over the years, factories and other industries have closed their doors in Hannibal, but Mark Twain has always remained. As young people have left the town for college and found careers in other places, Tom Sawyer has stuck around. Before a levee was built, when Mississippi floods came and washed away buildings, Cardiff Hill stood tall, and what the town and tourists have come to embrace as Jackson's Island resurfaced as the waters receded. Since 1876, Tom Sawyer and Mark Twain have remained ubiquitous in Hannibal, Missouri. It is doubtful that either of them will be leaving any time soon.

Works Cited

Allen, Jerry. "Tom Sawyer's Town." *National Geographic,* July 1956.

DeVoto, Bernard, editor. *The Portable Mark Twain.* Viking Press, 1946.

"Hannibal, Missouri, Honors Mark Twain, A Famous Son." *Grand Daily Independent* [Grand Island, Nebraska], 1 Apr. 1935, p. 12.

"Humorist's Boyhood Home: Day Set Apart at the World's Fair and National Association of Humorists Will Make a Trip to Hannibal." *Nebraska State Journal,* 16 Nov. 1903, p. 5.

Love, R. "Mark Twain Sees the Home of His Boyhood." *St. Louis Post-Dispatch,* 30 May 1902, p. 1.

"Mark Twain an Asset Now: Hannibal, Mo. Residents Once Resented 'Tom Sawyer.'" Knoxville, Tennessee *Journal and Tribune,* 26 Aug. 1916, p. 4.

"Missouri Facts for Missourians." *Jefferson County Republican* [DeSoto, Missouri], 1 May 1924, p. 2.

"Nation Begins Year of Honors to Mark Twain." *The Herald-Press* [St. Joseph, Michigan], 15 Jan. 1935, p. 1.

Patton, J. S. "Mark Twain Fast Becoming a Legend of the Mississippi." *Illinois Herald and Review,* 15 Dec. 1935, p. 33.

Poletti, Mary. "Hannibal Woman Searches for Clues to Black History of America's Hometown." *Quincy Herald-Whig.* 15 Mar. 2011, www. whig.com/archive/article/hannibal-woman-searches-for-clues-to-black-history-of-americas-hometown/article_1e4bd934-ddb6-56f5-b298-49d24e247111.html.

Powers, Ron. *Tom and Huck Don't Live Here Anymore.* St. Martin's Press, 2001.

_____. *White Town Drowsing: Journeys to Hannibal.* Atlantic Monthly Press, 1986.

"River Scenery and Shades of Mark Twain's Heroes Brings Many Tourists to Hannibal." *Herald and Review* [Decatur, Ill.], 28 Aug. 1927, p. 11.

"Tom Sawyer Characters in Hannibal." *St. Louis Post-Dispatch*, 2 June 1902, p. 5.

Twain, Mark. *Autobiography of Mark Twain.* Vol. 1: *The Complete and Authoritative Edition.* Edited by Harriet Elinor Smith et al., U of California P, 2010.

Fig. 4. Hannibal's Tom Sawyer Theater in 1954. Courtesy of Cindy Lovell. [Used with permission.]

Illustrating *Tom Sawyer*

Barbara Schmidt

For almost 150 years, publishers worldwide have been issuing illustrated editions of *The Adventures of Tom Sawyer* targeting book buyers of all ages and economic classes. Youngsters identify with Tom; his story overlaid with Clemens's social and religious satire is one that adults recognize in themselves. A reader's purchase of the book often hinges on the fame of the illustrator and the appeal of an eye-catching book cover. In addition to attracting book buyers, the illustrator's primary job is to guide the reader and enhance the text. They give physical attributes to characters and settings when the text fails to do so.

Under his pen name Mark Twain, Samuel L. Clemens published *Tom Sawyer* in 1876, during an era when lavishly illustrated novels were commonplace. The book's first publisher, the American Publishing Company (APC) of Hartford, Connecticut, specialized in subscription books with independent canvassers going door to door taking orders. Buyers of subscription books expected hefty, decorative volumes for their money. With only 76,000 words of text *Tom Sawyer* is not a long book, and APC padded it with illustrations by artist True W. Williams who provided more than 160 pictures for the book. Williams's illustrations set the tone for how readers would visualize characters and settings in the novel for over twenty years. Williams, however, was merely the first of more than fifty artists who have illustrated American editions of the book to date. This essay will explore how some of these illustrators have interpreted the book and why their editions are noteworthy.

The First Illustrator—True W. Williams

Born Truman W. Williams in New York's Allegany County in 1839, True Williams (1839–97) worked on four of Clemens's earlier books and enjoyed a good working relationship with Clemens (Schmidt).

In early November 1875, he asked Clemens for the job of illustrating *Tom Sawyer*. Clemens said yes and instructed Elisha Bliss, APC's president, to lend Williams his original handwritten manuscript. A holographic edition of Clemens's manuscript published in 1982 by Georgetown University Library, owner of the original manuscript, reveals the notes made by Bliss and Williams that were written in the margins of Clemens's pages as they read and jotted down ideas for illustrations. The handwritten oath signed in blood by Huck Finn and Tom in chapter 10 was taken directly from Clemens's own handwritten pages.

The first scholar to study Clemens's original illustrators closely was Beverly David, author of the two-volume study, *Mark Twain and His Illustrators* (1986, 2001). With Ray Sapirstein, David also contributed an essay on Williams's illustrations to the 1996 Oxford edition of *Tom Sawyer*, a photo-facsimile reprint of the book's first edition with all the original pictures. Another scholar in this field is Susan Gannon, who contributed an original essay on Williams's illustrations to the *Norton Critical Edition of Tom Sawyer* (2007).

The text of *Tom Sawyer* says very little about its characters' ages and physical traits. Clemens describes Tom as having curly hair in chapter 4 and being young enough to lose a baby tooth in chapter 6. Without illustrations to guide them, readers can only imagine if Tom is tall or short, thin or fat, or even how old he is. With little textual guidance, Williams and other illustrators have been free to depict Tom almost any way they want. Williams himself, however, never settled on a single look for Tom. For example, for a Sunday school scene in chapter 4 he drew Tom to look like he could be six or seven years old. In chapter 10, he drew Tom towering over his seated aunt, making him look like an adolescent (see Wells essay for both illustrations). Future illustrators would each bring more consistency in their work to Tom's appearance, each having their own ideas of what the characters looked like.

One benchmark by which to measure the faithfulness of illustrators to the text is depictions of the fence that Tom cons his friends to whitewash in chapter 2. The novel describes the fence as it appears to Tom when he surveys the immense task Aunt Polly has given him: "Thirty yards of board fence, nine feet high. Life to him seemed hollow, and existence but a burden. Sighing, he dipped his brush and passed it along the topmost plank . . ." Is the fence really that tall and long? Or, do those dimensions exist only in Tom's imagination? The mention of a "topmost plank" suggests the fence is made up of horizontal boards, but only a few illustrators have ever drawn it that way or made it look nine feet high. Williams himself drew the fence with horizontal boards to look about as high as Tom's neck (see cover of this book). Page 24 of Clemens's original manuscript describes the fence as four feet high, but Clemens crossed out "four" and replaced it with "nine."

Whatever height Williams thought the fence should be when he illustrated the book, he had a different view fifteen years later. In 1891, he illustrated a book titled *Kings of the Platform and Pulpit* edited by Melville Landon. That book includes *Tom Sawyer's* fence-painting episode, for which Williams drew a much taller Tom painting an equally tall fence made of *vertical* pickets. One of the most famous scenes in American literature, *Tom Sawyer's* whitewashing episode has inspired illustrators to interpret it in many different ways.

Williams worked on *Tom Sawyer* shortly after illustrating *Mark Twain's Sketches New & Old* (1875) for APC. The covers for both books had identical blue cloth designs. Williams drew ornate headpiece designs for the openings of each chapter of *Tom Sawyer*, using characters, animals, symbols, and settings relevant to the chapters' contents. Chapter 1, for example, opens with a picture captioned "Tom at Home" showing Tom standing on a dirt road in front of Aunt Polly's house. The fence in that picture matches Williams's drawing of the fence Tom is painting in chapter 2.

Williams had a keen sense of humor that can be seen in several pictures. Tucked in the corner of his picture of the murdered Dr. Robinson in chapter 11, for example, is an easy-to-overlook grave marker labeled "Sacred to the Memory of T. W. Williams." Another easy-to-overlook detail can be seen in his schoolroom picture in chapter 21 (see fig. 2 in Pascal essay). Among the motivational slogans posted on the room's walls is this:

THE PEN IS
MIGHTIER
THAN THE
SWORD.

Clemens may have enjoyed Williams's jokes, according to scholar Allison Ensor, who pointed out that Clemens later used the line "The pen is mightier than the sword" in a bawdy burlesque poem (Ensor 26).

Fig. 1. True W. Williams playfully wrote his own name on the tombstone of his drawing depicting Muff Potter's arrest at the site where Dr. Robinson's murdered body is found. True Williams, *Tom Sawyer*, 1876, p. 103. [Public domain.]

Another subject in *Tom Sawyer* that has challenged illustrators concerns the "mysterious book" schoolmaster Dobbins reads when his pupils are busy doing lessons. He normally keeps it locked in a desk drawer, but when Becky Thatcher enters the empty schoolroom during a lunchtime break in chapter 20, she spots Dobbins's key in its lock. Using it to unlock the drawer, she removes the book, and browses through it until Tom's sudden appearance startles her into tearing a page. The book happens to be an anatomy book, and the page Becky tears is the frontispiece illustration of a naked man. Dobbins is infuriated when he discovers the torn page. Williams illustrates that moment in his headpiece to chapter 20. Captioned "The Discovery," the picture shows Dobbins glaring at the torn page featuring an unrevealing shadowy figure. The implication that Becky sees a picture of a naked man is a rare suggestion connecting a girl to sexuality. Clemens's strikeouts and revisions in his original manuscript pages 520 to 523 show how he struggled with how much to reveal about the book's frontispiece of a "human figure, stark naked."

A striking characteristic of Williams's work is its avoidance of overt violence. In chapter 9, for example, he illustrates only the aftermath of Dr. Robinson's graveyard murder–a picture of a dead body behind Muff Potter and Injun Joe. His most graphic depiction of violence is a picture in chapter 16 showing Tom, Huck, and Joe Harper playing Indians on Jackson's Island (see fig. 3 in Driscoll essay). One boy is holding a knife directly over another boy's head, as if ready to scalp him, while the third boy raises a club. This scene, however, is merely pretend violence.

Another characteristic of Williams's work is his reluctance to endow Injun Joe with distinctively Native American features–something later illustrators have been less hesitant to do. Only one of Williams's drawings strongly suggesting a Native American man is the frightening picture of Joe looming over a sleeping Tom with a knife, "Tom Dreams," at the end of chapter 24 (see fig. 1 in Ober essay). In contrast, one of Williams's few depictions of African American characters is his large headpiece opening chapter 2. It shows the "small colored boy" Jim as a cartoonish figure with exaggerated lips and large whites in his eyes. Uncle Jake in chapter 28 is the most sympathetic black character in the book although he is mentioned in only one paragraph as Huck tells Tom how circumstances occasionally required him to eat meals with a slave. The passage hints of Clemens's future masterpiece *Adventures of Huckleberry Finn* (1885). Huck's story inspired Williams to feature Uncle Jake as the bearded, gray-haired man tamping down a tobacco pipe in the chapter's opening illustration.

Fig. 2. True Williams's depictions of the only African American characters the novel mentions by name. *Tom Sawyer*, 1876, p. 26 and 121. [Public domain.]

John George Brown and Worth Brehm

By 1899, Clemens had written enough books to justify a uniform edition of his works. Uniform editions are sets of books in matching formats and bindings often displayed prominently in a home. APC, the original publisher of *Tom Sawyer*, acquired the first rights to issue a twenty-two-volume set. Previously most of Clemens's books had been profusely illustrated. For the uniform editions, however, each volume featured only a few full-page illustrations by well-known artists. A limited number of the editions also contained tipped-in autographs by both Clemens and the illustrators for sale to wealthy book buyers.

APC chose British-born artist John George Brown (1831–1913) to illustrate the uniform edition of *Tom Sawyer*. Noted for his pictures of New York City children, Brown contributed four full-page monotone oil paintings. His vertical-plank fence whitewashing scene for chapter 2 shows Tom seated on a barrel eating an apple with a sly grin on his face while Ben Rogers paints. Many later illustrators would draw very similar pictures. Brown's Tom is a straight-haired, chubby-faced boy dressed in clothes that seem more appropriate for New York street urchins than for rural Missouri boys. His picture of Huck with a dead cat in chapter 6 makes Huck a handsome boy in oversize clothes. Brown's most poignant illustration shows Aunt Polly seated, holding in her hand the piece of bark with Tom's message telling her he is alive in chapter 19. There is nothing controversial or striking about Brown's illustrations, which are essentially portraits of Tom, Huck, Becky, and Aunt Polly. After Harper & Brothers obtained the rights to publish the uniform editions in 1903, the firm continued to issue uniform editions with Brown's illustrations throughout the 1920s.

Meanwhile, in 1910, Harper decided to issue a separate new edition of *Tom Sawyer*, bound in plain red cloth, with fresh illustrations by Worth Brehm (1883–1928). A native Midwesterner, Brehm was the first of numerous illustrators to visit Clemens's boyhood hometown of Hannibal, Missouri, for inspiration. The fifteen full-page charcoal crayon drawings he drew for the novel are effective in conveying emotions through body language, as in his drawings showing Tom being overwhelmed by stage fright in chapter 21 and testifying at Muff Potter's trial in chapter 23. Brehm likely used child models for his work and action scenes are lacking. Brehm's 1910 edition did not sell well until the publisher decided to have Brehm provide a colored painting of the fence whitewashing scene that could be used on dust wrapper, binding, and as a frontispiece. Unsold copies bound in red cloth were rebound with the new colored pictorial cover resulting in immediate sales. "Here was a forerunner of the modern tendency to put more effort on the jacket than on the book" (Chappell). Both Brown's and Brehm's illustrations—major departures in style from those of Williams—were the pictures seen by most *Tom Sawyer* readers through the first three decades of the twentieth century.

The 1930s and a Flood of Editions

Although illustrated foreign editions flourished overseas soon after *Tom Sawyer* was first published, the American copyright to *Tom Sawyer*, owned by Clemens's daughter Clara, expired in 1931. In advance of that date, Harper & Brothers, who had exclusive rights to publish the book, made business deals with other publishers who wanted to get a head start on issuing their own editions. Harper provided its 1929 printing plates to Grosset & Dunlap, a firm specializing in licensed reprints, for a 1930 edition. This unillustrated edition was issued with two different colored jackets. A cover drawn by Alfred Skrenda (1897–1978) featured a fence-painting scene while a cover by Nathan Machtey (1907–86) shows Tom ready to fight the new boy in town—dueling jackets with one featuring Tom's mental agility and the other showcasing his physical ability. No sales figures are available to determine which cover sold the most copies.

Random House publishers also obtained permission to issue their own exclusive edition prior to copyright expiration. During the summer of 1929, illustrator Donald McKay (1895–1974), like Brehm before him, visited Hannibal to prepare for illustrating an expensive edition limited to 2,000 copies designed for upscale book collectors. McKay wrote an account of his visit to Clemens's boyhood home that appeared in various newspapers including the *Kansas City Times* in November 1929. Jokingly observing that Tom Sawyer's fence was "difficult to find," he remarked that perhaps "some literary liberty was taken" (McKay). McKay's simple drawings are similar in style to those of Williams. They support and decorate Clemens's text but add little more.

The end of the year 1931 marked a watershed era in *Tom Sawyer* illustrating. With the novel now in the public domain, at least a dozen more American publishers issued new editions during the 1930s. Some editions used film stills and historical photos. Subjects included fence-painting scenes, Huck Finn with his dead cat, the graveyard murder, Tom and his friends playing pirates, and Tom and Becky's adventure in the cave.

Grosset & Dunlap continued to publish new editions over the ensuing decades. In 1931, they issued another edition with full-page still photos from Paramount's 1930 *Tom Sawyer* film starring Hollywood's leading child actor, Jackie Coogan. Its stills include an almost obligatory whitewashing scene, Tom fighting the new boy, and Tom and Becky in the classroom. Yet another Grosset & Dunlap edition in 1938 used black-and-white stills from that year's David O. Selznick color production of *The Adventures of Tom Sawyer*, starring newcomer Tommy Kelly.

One of the most notable editions of that era was published in 1931 by John C. Winston, who commissioned well-known artist N. C. Wyeth (1882–1945) and his son-in-law Peter Hurd (1904–84), to illustrate the book. Wyeth had previously illustrated Harper's 1916 edition of *The Mysterious Stranger*, a posthumously published and greatly altered version of one of Clemens's unfinished stories. The much younger Hurd was just starting his own distinguished career as a painter of southwestern landscapes. Wyeth's sole contribution to the book was essentially a mural—a fence-painting scene used for the book's wraparound dust jacket. In contrast to most other illustrators, Wyeth followed the novel's fence description precisely with a nine-foot-high *horizontal* plank fence. The portion on the front cover shows Rogers working a long-handled brush while Tom sits on a barrel, holding an apple, with a look of smug satisfaction on his face. On the back cover, schoolmaster Dobbins, Injun Joe, Huckleberry Finn, and Joe Harper look on as Tom hoodwinks his victim—a gathering that never occurred in Clemens's text. Wyeth's "cast of characters" approach wrapped around the book is extremely effective as his characters' body language implies their reactions to Tom's accomplishment.

Hurd's contributions to the book were four full-page color illustrations, plus numerous line drawings. In stark contrast to Wyeth's cover, Hurd drew the fence with *vertical* planks. Like McKay's illustrations, Hurd's line drawings are also stylistically similar to those of Williams and include many of the same subjects that Williams illustrated.

Enter Norman Rockwell

In 1929, publisher George Macy launched a subscription book service called the Limited Editions Club. Each month, it issued a boxed edition of a classic literary work with original illustrations–mostly in full color–by a noted artist. Each book was numbered and signed by its artist. Limited to 1,500 copies per title and priced at twenty dollars each, the books were designed for comparatively affluent book collectors. At the same time, Macy also launched Heritage Press to publish much less expensive volumes in unlimited editions. In 1936, Heritage issued a *Tom Sawyer* edition with original illustrations drawn by one of America's most famous illustrators— Norman Rockwell (1894–1978). Rockwell was becoming legendary for the numerous covers he had drawn for the magazine *Saturday Evening Post* since 1916. His sentimentally evocative illustrations were deeply rooted in portraying small-town American values. Macy's business correspondence with Rockwell is archived at the Harry Ransom Center at the University of Texas. A letter from Macy's assistant Lillian Lustig to Rockwell dated August 20, 1936, bluntly stated the publisher's aim, "We are, as you know, in the business of making beautiful books. The beauty of the book is our merchandise, not the text."

Rockwell visited Hannibal and carried along his copy of Worth Brehm's *Tom Sawyer* making notes in the margins. Ironically, some of Rockwell's first-hand observations led him to disregard the novel's text. When he visited Hannibal's cave, he noticed no stalagmites or stalactites, so he drew neither in his cave picture for chapter 31, despite the fact that the novel's fictional cave has both. (See "Cave" appendix.) Rockwell purchased old clothes from Hannibal's residents that he took back to New York for his models Richard F. Gregory and Charles Schudy, two young boys from his New Rochelle neighborhood. Throughout the fall of 1936, newspaper stories reported on Rockwell's models and the possibility they might appear in Selznick's new *Tom Sawyer* movie but they did not get the roles.

Rockwell produced eight full-page color illustrations plus black-and-white line drawings for chapter headpieces. His frontispiece illustration shows Tom whitewashing a vertical-plank fence with Rogers leaning in closely to observe. His picture of the dog sniffing the pinch-bug in church in chapter 5 conveys the humor of the episode by showing an adult churchgoer sharing Tom's delight in the scene. Although Rockwell was occasionally criticized for the overly cheerful nature of much of his magazine work, his *Tom Sawyer* illustrations include a number of scenes depicting the humor in pain. Chapter 7, for example, contains an almost shocking illustration of the schoolmaster Dobbins savagely whipping Tom for being late to class. As Dobbins faces away from the reader while holding Tom under his left arm and beating him with a switch with his right arm, readers see Tom's startled face with its mouth wide open. Faces of other pupils indicate reactions of shock, sorrow, and amusement. The vivid image is actually an example of an artistic liberty, as nothing in the novel's text suggests how Tom reacts to his whipping.

In chapter 12, Rockwell combines humor and pain in his depiction of Aunt Polly filling an obviously unhappy Tom with a foul-tasting patent medication ("fire in a liquid form") while Peter the family cat placidly watches. Chapter 16 contains another depiction of Tom suffering, showing him and Joe Harper nauseated after smoking pipes for the first time. Meanwhile, a relaxed, pipe-smoking Huck grins with devilish satisfaction.

In October 1972, the U.S. Postal System used Rockwell's fence whitewashing scene on a first-class stamp in the American Folklore series. That moment served to focus national attention on *Tom Sawyer*. More than 135

Fig. 3. Tom Sawyer 1972 commemorative stamp. [Public domain.]

million of the stamps were distributed, and President Richard Nixon's daughter Patricia Nixon Cox attended the stamp dedication ceremony in Hannibal. The speech she delivered there echoed Clemens's sentiment that Tom and Huck serve to remind adults of their own childhoods.

The Next Famous Illustrator–Thomas Hart Benton

In 1939, George Macy's Limited Editions Club issued an edition of *Tom Sawyer* illustrated by another famous artist, Thomas Hart Benton (1880–1975). A native of Missouri, Benton was named after his father's great uncle, Missouri senator Thomas Hart Benton (1782–1858), who appears briefly in chapter 22 of *Tom Sawyer* as "an actual United States Senator." Regrettably, neither Williams nor Benton illustrated Senator Benton's visit to Tom's hometown.

By the mid-1930s, Benton was winning a reputation as a controversial muralist. His face appeared on the cover of *Time* magazine's December 24, 1934, issue, which contained an article discussing the regionalist art movement. Answering critics who thought his murals were "loud and disturbing," he was quoted as saying he was not a sentimentalist. "I know an ass and the dust of his kicking when I come across it." That quote appeared on the *Time* cover below Benton's self-portrait. In 1936, Benton completed a 45,000-square-foot mural in Missouri's state capitol building. One of its sections depicts a steamboat named *Samuel Clemens* sailing past figures who are clearly Huck and Jim from *Huckleberry Finn*. Other sections of the mural depicting slave auctions and lynchings provoked strong controversy. If a headline-making illustrator was what Macy wanted for his limited edition of *Tom Sawyer*, he could not have done better than Benton. Benton completed his work in October 1939, and Macy was ecstatic with it, regarding it as sensational. Never reprinted, the Limited Editions Club *Tom Sawyer* has become a valuable collector's item.

Benton drew seventy-one black-and-white pictures for *Tom Sawyer*. They consisted of small line drawings at the head of each chapter and full-page pictures illustrating a moment in each chapter. The first chapter's headpiece depicts Aunt Polly examining a thread on Tom's shirt collar, followed a few pages later by Tom fighting with the newcomer on the ground at the back of a wagon pulled by mules. (Mules are never mentioned in *Tom Sawyer*.)

Benton never shied away from depicting violence or other unpleasant realities. His illustration of Injun Joe stabbing Dr. Robinson in chapter 9 may be the most starkly graphic in any edition of the novel. Tom's nightmare image of Injun Joe in chapter 11 is truly demonic. In striving for realism, Benton's illustrations of Tom's bedroom in that same nightmare image picture and in chapter 24 include chamber pots—a detail reflecting the absence of indoor toilets that no other illustrator has dared to show.

In November 1939, the *Kansas City Times* published an interview with Benton in which he described *Tom Sawyer* as "a Missouri book, not a Hannibal book" (Weaver). Benton's father was a Missouri lawyer. For the Muff Potter trial scene in chapter 23, Benton drew from memory his father's own Missouri courtroom with posters scattered along the walls and simple board benches for judge and jury. Benton's scenes of the schoolhouse, church, homes, furniture, and the extensive vegetation in his illustrations were similarly based on his own boyhood Missouri surroundings.

New Editions of the 1940s and 1950s

The first comic book adaptation of *Tom Sawyer*, priced at a dime, was issued by Dell Publishing in May 1942, with illustrations by George F. Kerr (1869–1953), a veteran illustrator of newspaper editorials and children's books. Like stage plays and films, comic books are adaptations that generally depart from their sources by ignoring some episodes while expanding others–typically episodes with action scenes that lend themselves to exciting illustrations. Consequently, Clemens's satirical narrative on society and religion are often lost in the adaptation process. Dell's version of *Tom Sawyer* tends to emphasize the novel's macabre episodes, such as the graveyard murder, to which it devoted nine of its sixty-four pages. At the same time, it omits the famous fence whitewashing episode completely.

In 1948, the Gilberton Company published the first Classics Illustrated comic book edition of *Tom Sawyer* with illustrations by Aldo Rubano (1917–89). His flashy cover illustration is an energetic depiction of Tom beating up the town's newcomer. His vigorous illustrations feature some of his own sense of humor. For example, one of his fence-painting pictures is virtually a duplicate of Rockwell's famous illustration. His treatment of the graveyard murder is less extensive than that of Kerr, but it includes a more graphic depiction of Injun Joe stabbing Dr. Robinson than is found in most illustrated novels.

During the 1950s, psychiatrist Dr. Fredric Wertham, author of *Seduction of the Innocent* (1954), condemned comic book publishers for contributing to violence and juvenile delinquency. Wertham singled out Rubano's *Tom Sawyer* cover as a violent example. Televised congressional hearings were held in 1954 to determine whether the comic book industry should be reined in. The industry survived the public scrutiny, but Classics Illustrated began moving away from violent cover art. In 1957, they replaced Rubano's cover with a peaceful fence-painting scene by an unidentified artist; inside the cover, they retained all of Rubano's illustrations for the next several years (Mac Donnell).

Both major and minor book publishers continued to issue freshly illustrated *Tom Sawyer* editions throughout the 1940s and 1950s. In 1943, popular caricaturist Peggy Bacon (1895–1987) illustrated the novel for Peter Pauper Press. Like others, she brought some personal biases to her work. Shunning violence and horror, she illustrated neither the graveyard murder nor Tom and Becky's ordeal in the cave. As a professed cat lover, she inserted cats in a number of pictures, such as a fence whitewashing illustration, in which a cat perches atop the fence. For chapter 29, she concocted a scene in which a cat toys with an inchworm next to Huck, who is relaxing on a porch when he should be on the lookout for Injun Joe.

In 1946, McKay returned to *Tom Sawyer* to illustrate a new edition for Grosset & Dunlap. His color and black-and-white pictures look quite different from those he had drawn for Random House seventeen years earlier. Nevertheless, some Williams influence is still evident in his work, particularly in his depictions of the slave boy Jim, Becky's anatomy book incident, and Tom's nightmare vision of Injun Joe. Unlike Bacon, McKay did not shy away from depicting violence, as in his color illustration of Injun Joe looming over Dr. Robinson with a knife after killing him in the graveyard. Occasionally, however, McKay allowed his imagination to get the best of him, as in chapter 13 when he transformed Tom and his friends' crude "small log raft" into a magnificent raft that appears to be at least twenty-five feet long and fifteen feet wide, with three expertly mounted sweeps.

The year 1950 saw Dell Pocket Books, Jr.'s publication of the first mass-market paperback edition of *Tom Sawyer*. Unlike many later paperback editions, it was lavishly illustrated by Harold Minton, who also illustrated Dell's *Huckleberry Finn* Pocket Book edition the same year. Minton's cover features "bad boy" images of a freckled-face Tom surrounded by scenes from the novel including fighting with the newcomer and fishing under a "No Fishing" sign—a scene that never occurs in Clemens's text.

In 1956, Simon and Schuster issued one of the first non-comic adapted editions of *Tom Sawyer* for young readers. Illustrated by Danish-born Hans Helweg (1917–2008), it features more than 160 colored illustrations depicting almost all the episodes in the novel. A wholesome cover features three well-groomed boys fishing and frying bacon along the river. Interior illustrations depict violence and nudity.

Entering the Novel's Second Century: The 1960s–1990s

During the 1960s, John Falter (1910–82) was one of the most prominent illustrators in America with his work frequently on *Saturday Evening Post* covers. In 1962, the Macmillan Company published an edition of *Tom Sawyer* with full-page black-and-white drawings and a color cover by Falter showing Tom standing with a long-handled paintbrush. Falter's frontispiece of a handsome Tom Sawyer confronting the newcomer is posed against a background of a boarded sidewalk on a dirt street with a mule-drawn wagon in the background. Rockwell's influence can be seen in Falter's illustration of Tom getting whipped by the schoolmaster. In chapter 33, Falter offers one of the most wrenching illustrations of Injun Joe's death in the cave with a close up of a dead hand turned upward, a broken knife blade and an insect crawling along Joe's limp arm.

During the mid-1960s, mainstream publishers continued the trend of issuing illustrated abridged and adapted versions of *Tom Sawyer* aimed at younger readers. In 1973, for example, Pendulum

---

Press issued an adapted black-and-white comic book illustrated by Filipino artist E. R. Cruz (b. 1934) that included a "Note to the Teacher" encouraging the use of illustrated comics to facilitate reading among young students. Cruz's edition was reissued by Marvel Classics in a full-color edition in 1976.

In 1983, Rand McNally issued an abridged, full-color "Illustrated Classics" edition. Designed for young readers, it was illustrated by British artist Harry Bishop (1920–2015), who was known for his realistic drawings of nineteenth-century American West stories. Bishop's cover features a character who can easily be interpreted as a female in pants watching Tom whitewash the fence along with the other boys. Clemens never writes about a girl being present in that episode. Both Brehm and Rockwell are evident inspirations for Bishop's work.

Illustrator and book designer Barry Moser (b. 1940) who credits Classics Illustrated comics with helping him pass his English classes in school, established his own Pennyroyal Press in 1970 and quickly rose to prominence in the art world in the 1980s. In Moser's 2011 autobiographical essay, "A Bookwright's Tale," he explains his relationship to an author's text: "Despite an illustrator's marriage to a text, he or she can maneuver within that marriage to find new and provocative light. Indeed, I believe that this is the illustrator's job: to take the text from where it is to where it ain't—to appropriate Mark Twain" (Moser).

In 1989, Books of Wonder issued *Tom Sawyer* with Moser's full-page watercolors that carried the text's skimpy physical descriptions of characters to new heights. Ten illustrations are mesmerizing portraits. Moser portrays Tom Sawyer on the cover as a handsome youth holding a paintbrush and a second time in the text holding a stick with a barrel hoop—another example of artistic creativity, as the text says nothing about any character's doing that. Moser has the novel's apparently mild-mannered minister, Mr. Sprague, preach with one hand clinched tight and the other reaching powerfully up toward heaven, his eyes closed and mouth wide open. Moser's Injun Joe, holding a menacing knife, is pale skinned with scraggly whiskers, and smokes a corncob pipe. Muff Potter has pale blue eyes and is missing some front teeth. Clemens's text lacks any hint of the attributes Moser provides these characters.

Children's Classics also published a new *Tom Sawyer* edition in 1989 featuring a dozen Williams line drawings and eight original full-page color paintings by Troy Howell (b. 1953). The book also contains a note by Howell describing his lifelong love of the novel. He recalls memorizing portions of both the Bible and *Tom Sawyer*, "One taught me what was good, the other what was wickedly delightful." Howell depicts Injun Joe as a sober-looking and respectably dressed man whose only distinguishing attributes are his long black hair and headband. If Moser is correct in arguing that illustrators should "take the text from where it is to where it ain't," Howell succeeds admirably in his painting for chapter 1 that is captioned, "Jim did three-fourths of the work." It shows "the small colored boy" Jim splitting logs with a heavy axe, while Tom rests comfortably on a stump, as his half-brother, Sid, looks on. Howell's illustration extends Clemens's text in ways immeasurable by providing a visual interpretation of child slave labor—a topic Clemens only hinted at in his book.

In 1996, Viking published an edition illustrated by the prominent French artist Claude Lapointe (b. 1938). Originally published in France in 1995, Lapointe's illustrations have a distinctly European flavor. They depict Tom with a blond page-boy haircut and make Huck's long, untrimmed hair look frizzy. The dainty picket fence in Lapointe's fence-painting scene has such thin vertical boards it could be painted with an artist's brush. In contrast, despite the fact that the haunted house in chapter 26 must be made out of wooden planks, Lapointe's house looks like a medieval stone ruin. Lapointe's color drawings actually constitute only a small part of the Viking edition's illustrations. The book features other artwork and historical photographs alongside Lapointe's artwork that encourage use of the edition as a reference tool in classrooms.

An Outstanding Twenty-first-Century Edition

Chris Fox "C. F." Payne (b. 1956), one of the most prolific illustrators of the twenty-first century has established a high bar for future *Tom Sawyer* illustration. A university professor and free-lance illustrator, his work has appeared on numerous national magazine covers. In 2015, Creative Editions published *Tom Sawyer* with Payne's illustrations in a volume arranged by award-winning book designer Rita Marshall. In the video documentary about his work, "C. F. Payne: An American Illustrator," Payne explained that *Tom Sawyer* has the aspects of a journal covering a period of several months. He wanted to match Clemens's text to an artist's sketchbook that is spontaneous and not limited to any particular medium. He wanted to produce a book that would persuade people who already owned copies of *Tom Sawyer* want to buy copies of his version. Payne explained, "You have to understand how many times *Tom Sawyer* has been illustrated. Norman Rockwell did a *Tom Sawyer* and I don't know anybody who wants to get in a footrace with Norman Rockwell, because you're gonna lose" (Payne).

Payne produced an overall body of illustrations that are attention-grabbing and dramatic. His style shows Rockwell's influence by combining nostalgic Americana with a hint of caricature. His Tom is an impish curly-haired redhead, often depicted with an elongated neck and large ears giving the impression of a growing boy. Payne's dramatic illustration of the pinch-bug standoff in chapter 5 invites readers to look over the backside of the pinch-bug directly into the face of the wide-eyed poodle. Payne successfully depicts humor in the pain in the Peter and the pain-killer episode in chapter 12 with a full-page illustration featuring wide-eyed Peter leaping in pain over three other cats as one cat grins and winks at readers.

Payne's full-page illustration of the church in which Tom, Huck, and Joe Harper's funeral is held in chapter 17 presents a dramatic low-angle perspective from the front of the church toward the double doors at the back of the church, above which the boys peep down from a balcony as mourners stare forward from their pews. In chapter 20 schoolmaster Dobbins points directly at readers wanting to know who tore his anatomy book while his other hand points backward to something unseen. A collage of Tom's facial expressions as he testifies at Muff Potter's trial in chapter 23 features Tom pointing to the following page where Injun Joe makes his escape. Injun Joe's eyes haunting Tom's nightmares appear to move across the page in chapter 24 as Payne depicts them three times, drawing the reader deeper into the nightmare drama.

If there is a trend to be found in the history of *Tom Sawyer* illustration, it is that the story has continued to appeal to both children and adults throughout the decades. Publishers, pursuing profits, continue to issue new illustrated editions because the text is capable of rich and varied interpretation. In turn, the illustrated editions have helped cement the novel's role as an American classic.

Works Cited

Chappell, Warren. "Tom Sawyer and the Illustrators." *The Dolphin*, vol. 4, part 3, Spring 1941, pp. 249–54.

David, Beverly. *Mark Twain and His Illustrators,* Vol. 1, 1869–1875. Whitston, 1988.

_____. *Mark Twain and His Illustrators:* Vol. **2,** 1875–1883. Whitston, 2001.

Ensor, Allison. "'Mightier than the Sword': An Undetected Obscenity in the First Edition of *Tom Sawyer*." *Mark Twain Journal*, vol. 27, no. 1, Spring 1989, pp. 25–26.

Gannon, Susan R. "200 Rattling Pictures." *A Norton Critical Edition:* The Adventures of Tom Sawyer. Edited by Beverly Lyon Clark, Norton, 2007.

Mac Donnell, Kevin. Personal communication, 25 Oct. 2021.

McKay, Donald. "Hannibal, Mo., Today Not the Drowsy River Town Described in 'Tom Sawyer.'" *Kansas City Times*, 7 Nov. 1929, p. 24.

Moser, Barry. "A Bookwright's Tale." *Image*, No. 71, 2011, imagejournal. org/article/a-bookwrights-tale/.

Payne, C. F. "C. F. Payne: An American Illustrator." Video documentary. Tony Moorman, producer, 27 Sept. 2017, vimeo.com/ondemand/ cfpayne/109770885.

Schmidt, Barbara. "The Life and Art of True W. Williams." *Mark Twain Journal,* vol. 39, no. 2, Fall 2001, pp. 1–60.

Twain, Mark. *The Adventures of Tom Sawyer*. 1876. Edited by Shelley Fisher Fishkin; Introduction by E. L. Doctorow; Afterword by Albert E. Stone. Oxford UP, 1996.

Weaver, John Downing. "Benton Continues His Discovery of Old Missouri with Mark Twain." *Kansas City Times*, 13 Nov. 1939, p. 18.

Fig. 4. Mr. Dobbins discovering the torn page in his anatomy book. True Williams, *Tom Sawyer*, 1876, p. 161. [Public domain.]

The *Tom Sawyer* Movie That Hollywood Got (Almost) Right_____

R. Kent Rasmussen

Few people seriously interested in literature would argue that watching a film adaptation is an adequate substitute for reading an actual novel. Some might even argue that watching an adaptation can contribute little or nothing to one's understanding of the work on which it is based. There is, however, another way to regard adaptations—to see them as *interpretations* of literary works in much the same sense as one views any critical essay. What, after all, does an adaptation do but suggest answers to questions about matters such as which of a novel's themes and episodes are worthy of emphasis, how characters should be depicted, and what moods literary passages convey? Allowances, of course, must be made for the fact that studios produce films to make money, and they make money by producing films that entertain.

With more than a dozen feature film and television adaptations made from it, Mark Twain's novel *The Adventures of Tom Sawyer* (1876) offers an excellent case study of the nature of screen adaptations and what they contribute to readers' appreciation of the original work. Film adaptation is an important subject, as it is likely many more people have seen screen adaptations of *Tom Sawyer* films than have ever read the book—a distressing imbalance that grows stronger with each passing year.

Fig. 1. Cover of *The Adventures of Tom Sawyer* press book.
Selznick International. [Public domain.]

The Internet Movie Database (IMDb) lists close to two hundred film and television productions of all types and lengths that have been adapted from Mark Twain's life and writings. Four titles stand out with at least a dozen full-length adaptations each: *Tom Sawyer*, *Adventures of Huckleberry Finn* (1885), *The Prince and the Pauper* (1881), and *A Connecticut Yankee in King Arthur's Court* (1889). Those numbers are impressive, but an unhappy footnote must be affixed to them: Not one of those many adaptations has ever been acclaimed a cinematic masterpiece. In contrast, numerous adaptations of works by the great English novelist Charles Dickens have earned such recognition (Rasmussen & Dawidziak 277). Among them is producer David O. Selznick's 1935 film *David Copperfield* for Metro-Goldwyn-Mayer (MGM). Selznick was a great admirer of *Tom Sawyer*, which he regarded as "the closest thing we have to an American *David Copperfield* " (Haver 213). In 1938, he tried to recapture his *Copperfield* success with his independently produced *The Adventures of Tom Sawyer*. The result was a film still widely regarded as the best adaptation of *any* Mark Twain work, but one that still fell short of cinematic perfection.

Many films made from Mark Twain's works have been good enough to achieve commercial success and some have even found recognition as minor classics. Few, however, have come close to satisfying admirers of their literary sources. Paramount Pictures' 1949 adaptation of *A Connecticut Yankee in King Arthur's Court* is a notable example. Starring singer Bing Crosby, at that time Hollywood's number-one box-office draw, it is a colorful and cheerful comedy sprinkled with sprightly musical numbers that has pleased audiences for more than seven decades. As an adaptation of Mark Twain's complex and often dark novel about a nineteenth-century American's disastrous efforts to introduce modern technology and culture to sixth-century England, however, it is barely recognizable. Like most screen versions of Mark Twain's dystopian time-travel novel, it ignores its source's mood and central themes in favor of comedy and romance. How, then, has Mark Twain's far simpler and more innocent *Tom Sawyer*, fared on the screen?

Connecticut Yankee's protagonist, Hank Morgan, has often been compared to Tom Sawyer as an attention-seeking rabble-rouser, so perhaps it is not surprising that *Connecticut Yankee* and *Tom Sawyer* films have much in common. Both play up their protagonists' romantic interests and imaginative schemes. Tom's own book, however, is a vastly different kind of novel, starting with the fact that it tells a less complex and more realistic tale. *Tom Sawyer* is essentially a story of a young mid-nineteenth century boy's experiences through the waning months of a school year and the summer that follows. Little about the boy himself is exceptional, except for his active imagination, readiness to flout adult authority, and courage in the face of true perils. Unlike Hank, Tom does not travel through time, try to modernize an entire society, challenge the authority of an established church, or start a political revolution and an apocalyptic war. His adventures instead revolve around such mundane matters as dealing with family friction, avoiding chores, being punished by a sadistic schoolmaster, agonizing over girlfriend problems, playing pirates, and finding lost marbles–all of which are overshadowed by the real possibility that a cold-blooded murderer may be out to get him. Despite *Tom Sawyer*'s fundamental simplicity, however, most of its screen adaptations have been deficient in one way or another. The one adaptation that stands out as the most nearly fully satisfactory is Selznick's. Before examining that film, however, it is useful to comment on other major versions.

From Guerrilla Film Making to Gender-Bending

Since its first adaptation in 1907, *Tom Sawyer* has found its way to theater and television screens more than two dozen times, including animated versions and such loose adaptations as *The Modern Adventures of Tom Sawyer* (2000; see Filmography). That film borrows the names of the novel's main characters and a few iconic moments, including a fence-painting episode. More difficult to classify is a film such as *The Adventures of Thomasina Sawyer* (2018), which has a female "Tom," a female Sidney, and a Muff Potter who is a sober, black family man. It follows the broad outlines of Mark Twain's novel in a nineteenth-century setting and even

---

borrows some of the novel's dialogue but also makes other surprising changes, such as turning Tom's rival Alfred Temple into the priggish brother of Becky Thatcher and making Huck the Cherokee-speaking son of Injun Joe. Of more immediate interest here, however, are the most influential "straight" adaptations, particularly the earliest versions. The four films most likely to be seen by modern audiences are those made in 1917, 1930, and 1938 and a musical version made by Reader's Digest in 1973—the same year a rarely seen Canadian version was made for television.

"Guerrilla films" is a modern coinage for ultra-low-budget productions shot on the fly, but the term seems appropriate for the very first *Tom Sawyer* film made in mid-1907. So little is known about that long-lost production it is difficult to say more about it than that it really did exist. A silent short, it was the brainchild of the pioneering woman director Gene Gauntier when she was just starting to work for the brand-new Kalem Company, whose primitive production facility was based near Greenwich, Connecticut (not far from Mark Twain's future home in Redding). By her own account, Gauntier was asked to come up with a

> scenario which we could take in one day outdoors, omitting all difficult situations, river or rough stuff. That scene of whitewashing the fence was my inspiration, for I saw it in every detail just as it would appear in the picture. The scenario was pretty dreadful but it was what [Kalem co-owner Frank] Marion and [director Sidney] Olcott wanted and it gave me the knack of writing. Henceforth I was the mainstay of the Kalem scenario department.
>
> Tom Sawyer was the first of over three hundred which I wrote and produced or sold. . . . After Tom Sawyer I never had a scenario refused, nor wrote one that was not produced. The compensation for those earlier efforts was twenty dollars a reel—a fairly high figure when you remember the director received only ten dollars for directing it (Gauntier 183).

These skimpy details make it easy to imagine Gauntier and Olcott finding a suitable Greenwich fence in need of paint, rounding up neighborhood boys to play Tom and his friends, shooting a few ten-minute reels of film in a single afternoon, and calling it a "wrap." It would have been difficult to do much more on a total budget that may have been less than fifty dollars, even in 1907. Unreviewed and unadvertised, the resulting one-reel film probably played for only a few days in make-shift theaters and then disappeared. No wonder it is now lost.

The next silent adaptation of *Tom Sawyer*, released fully a decade later, was a vastly different kind of production. The film industry had greatly evolved since 1907, and the second *Tom Sawyer* film was in the hands of Paramount Pictures, a rapidly expanding studio that had recently made feature-length versions of Mark Twain's *The Prince and the Pauper* and *Pudd'nhead Wilson*. Paramount split its *Tom Sawyer* production into two separate films: *Tom Sawyer*, released in December 1917, and *Huck and Tom: The Further Adventures of Tom Sawyer*, released in March 1918. (The latter film had nothing to do with *Huckleberry Finn*, despite its title.) Although released as separate productions, the two films were made with the same lead cast and crew and were probably made at the same time. Although the studio shot both in Northern California, it falsely claimed to have shot them in Mark Twain's hometown of Hannibal, Missouri. Not only did contemporary film reviewers—including several in Missouri—not contradict that blatant lie, but many actually praised the film for its "authentic" locations. In any case, both films were well received and at least moderately profitable.

Like Gauntier's 1907 film, Paramount's *Huck and Tom* appears now to be forever lost, but its *Tom Sawyer* has survived unscathed. In 2022, it could be viewed on DVD and on YouTube. As was true for Gauntier's film, the scripts for both Paramount films were written by a versatile female film maker, Julia Crawford Ivers, who also later wrote the script for Paramount's 1920 *Huckleberry Finn*; William Desmond Taylor—who in 1922 would be mysteriously murdered—directed all three films. The first of Ivers's *Tom Sawyer* scripts follows the novel reasonably closely up to the moment when Tom and his companions appear at their own funeral, and much of the dialogue on its title cards comes directly from the novel. The lost *Huck and Tom* film, for which no script is known to have survived, is presumably similarly close to the second part of the novel. At present, there is little to go on apart from a story synopsis in the pressbook made for exhibitors and fragmentary descriptions in contemporary reviews. Nevertheless, it appears the two Paramount films together constituted an impressively complete adaptation of Mark Twain's novel. One aspect of the films, however, tarnished the whole: their casting.

A curious aspect of Mark Twain's novel is its failure to provide a physical description of Tom or make clear his approximate age. In some chapters he seems to be as young as nine, in others as old as twelve or thirteen—but certainly not much older. For its screen Tom, Paramount cast Jack Pickford, the brother of the wholesome and

Fig. 2. Tom (21-year-old Jack Pickford) flirting with Becky (13-year-old Clara Horton) in Paramount's 1917 production of *Tom Sawyer*. Image courtesy of Kevin Mac Donnell. [Used with permission.]

popular star Mary Pickford. Born in Toronto on August 18, 1895 (the same day Mark Twain's daughter Susy Clemens died), Pickford was more than twenty-one years old when he portrayed Tom. Robert Gordon, who played Huck Finn in both films, was five months older than Pickford. Born in 1904, Clara Horton, the films' Becky, was much closer to the apparent age of her literary counterpart. However, having a thirteen-year-old girl play opposite a twenty-one-year-old man even in innocent romantic scenes lent a creepy dimension to the films not lessened by Pickford's growing off-screen reputation as a hard-partying womanizer. Nevertheless, both critics and audiences appeared to approve his performance as Tom.

The next film version of *Tom Sawyer,* and the first with sound, was another Paramount production released in 1930. It featured established child star Jackie Coogan as Tom. Coogan was fifteen when he made the film but looked younger and had been beloved by audiences since his starring role in Charles Chaplin's *The Kid* in 1921—a fact emphasized in the film's promotion. Paramount's remake of *Tom Sawyer* was a looser adaptation than its paired predecessors but was such a crowd pleaser it became Hollywood's top-grossing film of 1930 despite being released late in the year. Among all 1930s films, it was the fifth-highest grossing, trailing only *Gone with the Wind* (1939), *Snow White and the Seven Dwarfs* (1937), *The Wizard of Oz* (1939), and *Frankenstein* (1931), and ahead of *King Kong* (1933) and an impressive array of other screen classics (Filmsite). Now, however, it is nearly forgotten. It has not aged gracefully, but contemporary critics and audiences loved it. Mordaunt Hall of *The New York Times*, for example, called Coogan "a splendid Tom Sawyer," described the film as a whole as "beyond one's sincerest expectations," and urged Paramount to film more of Mark Twain's stories (Hall). Paramount quickly complied. The following year it made *Huckleberry Finn* with the same juvenile leads. To capitalize on Coogan's popularity, it had Tom join Huck on his river voyage, with Jim (Clarence Muse) coming along almost as an afterthought. Perhaps that was the film Paramount should have titled *Huck and Tom.*

Enter David O. Selznick

By the mid-1930s, David O. Selznick had logged more than a dozen years as a film producer and was just coming off successful MGM productions of two Dickens classics, *David Copperfield* and *A Tale of Two Cities*. Apparently impressed by the success of Paramount's recent adaptation of *Tom Sawyer*—a novel he esteemed—he got the idea of independently producing a large-scale version of the story. It happened that around that same time, the Technicolor Company was perfecting its three-color process, making possible natural-color movies for the first time, so filming *Tom Sawyer* in color became a key part of Selznick's plan. Before he could proceed, however, he had to clear several hurdles. Paramount's registration of its film with the Motion Picture Association effectively forbade any other studio from releasing another *Tom Sawyer* film before 1938. Moreover, despite the fact that Mark Twain's novel had by then fallen into the public domain, allowing anyone to adapt it to the screen without permission from the Mark Twain Estate, the name "Mark Twain" itself was legally protected by a trademark. Releasing a *Tom Sawyer* film without mentioning Mark Twain's pen name would have been folly, so in mid-1936 Selznick paid the estate $50,000 to use the name. Then Selznick discovered that the estate had licensed Paramount to film Mark Twain's 1896 novella "Tom Sawyer, Detective." Fearing the damage that release of another "Tom Sawyer" film could have on his own film's success, Selznick negotiated a deal with Paramount to delay release of its film until after his own film was released. Paramount agreed but insisted on a strange condition: Selznick

Fig. 3. Producer David O. Selznick in 1941. Library of Congress (item/98513763). [Public domain.]

had to pay Paramount $10,000 for all rights to the screenplay of its 1930 *Tom Sawyer* film (Haver 213–14). Selznick's *The Adventures of Tom Sawyer* was eventually released in February 1938, and Paramount's *Tom Sawyer, Detective* came out in late December of the same year. Not surprisingly, Selznick's version of *Tom Sawyer* had some scenes remarkably similar to scenes in Paramount's version. In the meantime, however, Selznick's plans for his film were almost derailed by other problems.

Selznick's next challenge was finding a director. After three-time Oscar-nominated King Vidor turned him down, the equally distinguished William Wyler accepted the gig and even went with Selznick to Northern California to scout filming locations. Casting the film took so long, however, that Wyler eventually backed out. Selznick then turned to the relative novice Henry C. Potter. Meanwhile, John V. A. Weaver wrote a script that Selznick liked. With his director in place and master cinematographer James Wong Howe also signed, Selznick was ready to begin production. Now a new problem arose: Delays caused the production to miss its chance to hire the then-scarce equipment needed for Technicolor, so shooting began using black-and-white film. When a Technicolor unit unexpectedly became available two weeks later, Selznick stopped production for several days so sets, costumes, makeup, and lighting could be modified for color, and even the script was modified to accommodate special needs for color. Footage already shot was discarded, and production resumed from scratch. Once again, Selznick switched directors. This time he hired Norman Taurog, who was noted for working well with children. Taurog had won an Oscar for directing *Skippy*, a sentimental 1931 film about a boy (Jackie Cooper) struggling to save a dog from a dogcatcher. That same year, he also directed Paramount's *Huckleberry Finn*, which doubtless influenced his perceptions of *Tom Sawyer* (Haver, 214, 220).

Casting the Film

Paramount's 1930 version of *Tom Sawyer* cast *the* most famous child actor of the 1920s as Tom, giving the film a ready-made audience

---

draw. In contrast, Selznick's film cast a total unknown, twelve-year-old Tommy Kelly, who was discovered in a nationwide talent search. Coming from a down-on-its-luck family struggling to cope with the Depression, Kelly gave the studio an appealing back-story that helped promote the film. Headlines such as "Poor Boy from Bronx Is Chosen for Star Role of 'Tom Sawyer'" must have pleased Selznick, but he had hoped for an even more appealing back-story. In August 1937, before he settled on Kelly, he memoed story editor Katharine Brown about his original hopes:

> I FEEL THAT THE GREATEST PUBLICITY STORY AND HORATIO ALGER STORY IN THE HISTORY OF THE PICTURE BUSINESS WOULD BE OUR FINDING TOM SAWYER AND OR HUCK FINN IN AN ORPHAN ASYLUM, AND THAT THIS WOULD RECEIVE SUCH TREMENDOUS ATTENTION AND AROUSE SUCH A WARM PUBLIC FEELING THAT IT WOULD ADD ENORMOUSLY TO THE GROSS OF THE PICTURE. I DON'T WANT TO TIP OUR HAND ON THIS BECAUSE WE ALL FEEL THAT THE IDEA IS SO IMPORTANT THAT WE ARE AFRAID THAT SOME QUICKY PRODUCER MAY GET BUSY . . . ON THE SAME ANGLE IF IT LEAKS OUT, SO THEREFORE KEEP OUR INTENTIONS TO YOURSELF . . . UNTIL WE FIND OUT IF WE ACTUALLY CAN FIND ONE OR MORE ORPHANS THAT FIT THE BILL (Behlmer 121–22).

Selznick's search had begun in July 1936 when the studio announced it was seeking children to play the film's leads. It added that would-be Toms and Hucks had to "be able to walk on their hands, swim, dive, and otherwise be the all-around boys that Twain's characters are" ("Huckleberry Finn"). The ensuing search generated a great deal of publicity, and the studio eventually claimed to have seen 25,000 boys. Director Taurog himself said that 110 scouts "were on the road and had interviewed 25,000 boys" (Othman, "Tom Sawyer"). Really? Considering how much time would have been needed merely to interview that many candidates, even with 110 scouts, that figure should be viewed with some skepticism. As one would suspect, the vast majority of applicants were instantly rejected for faults such as being too homely, too tall or too short, too thin or too fat; having bad teeth, big ears, poor speaking voices, or other perceived defects, including the wrong ethnic look. Only a minuscule number made it to screen tests (Graham 8). According to a Selznick biographer, the studio spent months "searching through orphanages, reformatories, and public schools" before finding Kelly in a Bronx Catholic school (Haver 220).

Kelly was a true amateur as an actor, but the film's other juvenile leads were experienced professionals. They included fourteen-year-old Jackie Moran (who later played Buster Crabbe's sidekick in the 1939 *Buck Rogers* serial) as Huck; ten-year-old Ann Gillis (who starred in *Little Orphan Annie* the same year) as Becky; and ten-year-old David Holt as Sid. Adult leads included eighty-year-old May Robson as Aunt Polly; recent Oscar winner Walter Brennan as Muff Potter; and Victor Jory as Injun Joe. In a smaller role, Joe Harper's mother was played by Margaret Hamilton, who would soon be terrifying children as the Wicked Witch in MGM's *The Wizard of Oz*. In *The Adventures of Tom Sawyer,* Hamilton's Sereny Harper is a loving mother whose gentle hymn singing Joe misses when he becomes homesick on the boys' pirate island. Mrs. Harper does not actually sing in the film, but that is fitting, as Mark Twain's novel says nothing about her singing hymns anyway.

The Finished Film

After Tommy Kelly worked with a diction coach to fix the Bronx accent that made him pronounce a word such as "worse" as "woise," filming began in August 1937 (Othman, "Tom Sawyer"). By the last day of the year, everything, including retakes, was completed, and Technicolor processing was rushed to ensure the film would make its official February 11, 1938, release date at New York's Radio City Music Hall (Haver 220). On that same date, the film also opened at Hollywood's Grauman's Chinese theater. Among those in attendance there were Selznick and his special guest, Mark Twain's daughter Clara Clemens Gabrilowitsch. It was not the first time a film producer courted Clara seeking her blessing for a film. In 1920, Paramount treated her to a private screening of its *Huckleberry Finn* film. Afterward, she expressed her regret that her father could not have seen it, as it "would have satisfied him in every detail, I'm sure" (Rasmussen, "Film" 333). Selznick's *Tom Sawyer* reportedly "sent her away from the theater with tears—of pleasure—streaming down her still-youthful face." She called that film "a wonderful experience" that brought back memories of sitting on her father's lap as child, listening to him read *Tom Sawyer*. She added that "her father would have liked Hollywood, would have enjoyed writing for the movies and 'would have loved that little Tommy Kelly'" (Othman, "Twain's Daughter").

Whether Mark Twain would have liked Selznick's film is impossible to know, but there are reasons why he might not have objected to it strongly—unlike how he might have reacted to Paramount's 1920 *Huckleberry Finn*, despite Clara's lavish praise. That earlier film blatantly inverts one of its literary source's dominant themes—Huck's unrelenting quest to escape the strictures of adult authority and civilization—by returning him to the Widow Douglas's home with the explicit goal of becoming educated to make himself worthy of Mary Jane Wilks. (Paramount's 1931 *Huckleberry Finn* has a similar ending.) Selznick's *Adventures of Tom Sawyer* inflicts no comparable damage on its source, but it does make some significant changes.

Before its credits roll, the Selznick film opens with a colorful and pleasant montage of scenes, showing villagers going about their business, Aunt Polly calling for Tom (as in the novel's opening lines), Tom swimming with a boy named Jim in a river. After the credits, a card appears containing the last sentence of the novel's preface: "Part of my plan has been to try to pleasantly remind adults of what they once were themselves, and of how they felt and thought and talked, and what queer enterprises they sometimes engaged in.—Mark Twain" To drive home that message, a second card adds an excerpt from the author's autobiography: ". . . the beautiful past, the dear and lamented past . . ." (Twain 157). The film then shows Tom and Jim riding through the village on the rear of an ox cart, from which they slide off and race home. Within minutes, the film succeeds in establishing Tom as a free spirit and then quickly shows that he and his friend Jim are clever tricksters.

The next scene shows Aunty Polly preparing to serve dinner in her kitchen, in which Tom's half-brother, Sid, is seated reading a book, and his cousin Mary (Marcia Mae Jones, who was originally cast as Becky) appears to be writing something atop a counter. As Polly grumbles about Tom's being late, expository dialogue deftly explains the relationships among the characters. Moments later, Polly visits the woodshed, where Jim distracts her while Tom sneaks into the kitchen and seats himself. "Little Jim" (Philip Hurlic), as he is called, is the "small colored boy" of the novel who chops wood in chapter 1, fetches water in chapter 2, and then disappears from the rest of the book. The film's Jim, however, frequently reappears, though his status—as in the novel—is never explained: Is he a hired servant or Aunt Polly's chattel slave? A clue to Tom's relationship to Jim can be found in Mark Twain's autobiography, which describes his own friendships with slaves on his uncle John Quarles's farm when he was a boy:

> All the negroes were friends of ours, and with those of our own age we were in effect comrades. I say in effect, using the phrase as a modification. We were comrades, and yet not comrades; color and condition interposed a subtle line which both parties were conscious of, and which rendered complete fusion impossible (Twain 211).

The film's depiction of Tom's relationship with Jim goes well beyond what the novel says about the two of them but instead echoes Mark Twain's own boyhood relationship with slave children. The film's Tom and Jim are comrades, yet not comrades. They play and scheme together, but they do not eat meals or go to school and church together. When the funeral is later held for the boys believed to have drowned, Jim is shown crying *outside* the church, but he is never shown *inside* the church. Footage cut from the beginning of the film reveals still more about his relationship to Tom. In the original swimming scene in Weaver's shooting script, Jim reminds Tom he needs to "get home from school"—a hint that Tom has been playing hooky. After the boys don their clothes, Jim himself sews Tom's collar together so Aunt Polly will not suspect he has been swimming. Jim then points out to Tom that he has put his pants on backwards (Weaver 13–14). The ensuing dinner-table scene in the final film is much like that in the novel, with Sid's calling attention to Tom's collar having been sewn together with the wrong color thread, and Polly's punishing Tom for playing hooky by requiring him to whitewash her fence the next day.

The film's fence-painting episode, Tom's first encounter with Becky, and the Sunday school episode in which Tom trades loot he has collected from his friends for allowing them to paint the fence are all broadly similar to their literary counterparts. So, too, are other episodes, including Dr. Robinson's murder in the graveyard, Tom's being unfairly punished after Sid breaks Aunt Polly's sugar bowl, and Tom's pirate escapade with Huck and Joe Harper, and the boys' appearance at their own funeral. Tom testifies against Injun Joe at Muff Potter's murder trial, but the film then moves directly to the picnic that leads to Tom and Becky's getting lost in the cave. It omits the episodes in which Tom and Huck dig for buried pirate treasure and in which Huck gets the Welchman and his sons to save the Widow Douglas from Injun Joe's intended violence. When Tom finds pirate treasure in the cave, it has nothing to do with Injun Joe.

What the Film Gets Wrong

With a few exceptions, characters in the Selznick film are reasonably true to their literary counterparts in how one might expect them to look and behave. The most glaring exception is Tom's half-brother, Sid. The novel describes Sid as "a quiet boy [who] had no adventurous, troublesome ways" (chapter 1). His name frequently appears throughout the book, but he himself actually appears only rarely and does almost nothing after the first chapter, in which his calling attention to the fact that the wrong thread has been sewn on Tom's collar makes Sid responsible for Tom's having to whitewash the fence in the next chapter. Tom later repays Sid by pelting him with dirt clods, and he remains distrustful of him throughout rest of the novel.

Selznick's film, in contrast, transforms Sid (David Holt) into a persistently annoying presence in Tom's life who serves as the film's dominant comic relief. Far from being a nearly invisible "quiet boy," not only is this Sid a consistently obnoxious brat ready to torment

Tom at every opportunity, he is also ever ready to shriek "Aunt Polly!" the moment Tom retaliates—usually by throwing something in his face. Selznick's film clearly modeled Sid on Paramount's Sid (Jackie Searl), an equally annoying pest and whiner. So popular with audiences was that film's Sid that Paramount made him a significant character in the *Huckleberry Finn* sequel it released the following year, even though Sid's only appearance in Mark Twain's *Huckleberry Finn* is as one of the passengers briefly seen on a boat in chapter 8.

The Sid in both the Paramount and Selznick films is the kind of character audiences love to hate. By the end of each film, however, it is not merely audiences who are fed up with him. Both films end with Aunt Polly slapping him. In the fancy-picnic scene at the end of the Selznick film, Tom throws a gooey strawberry shortcake in Sid's face. Once again shrieking "AUNT POLLY!," Sid runs to Polly in search of succor. She, however, is busy praising Tom's virtues to other women. Without even glancing at Sid, she slaps him hard on the face as she rambles on. That is a powerful audience-pleasing moment but can scarcely be what Mark Twain had in mind when he admitted modeling Sid on his own younger brother, Henry, whom he called "a very much finer and better boy than ever Sid was" (Twain 350). While the slapping scenes are untrue to the novel, they are excellent cinematic moments that audiences love.

Exactly how members of Aunty Polly's household are related to one another is a general problem in adaptations of *Tom Sawyer*. How, for example, is Sid related to Polly? In the novel he is the "half-brother" of Tom, who is the son of Polly's dead sister. He calls Polly "Aunt," but can he also be a "Sawyer," which is what the film calls him? Even more problematic is how "cousin Mary" figures into the mix. The kitchen scene at the beginning of the film shows Mary writing something on a counter as Sid approaches. That scene was cut just before Sid seizes what Mary is writing and reads it aloud. It is a morbid poem, titled "TO MY LOST LOVE," which Mary has signed "Mary Wadsworth Sawyer" (Weaver 17). While it is likely that Mary herself has added a middle name in honor of the venerated poet Henry Wadsworth Longfellow, it seems certain the film regards her as a Sawyer. (In the Reader's Digest film, Mary can be heard addressing Polly as "Mother." That is consistent with her being Tom's cousin but also has no basis in the novel.) In a later scene in the Selznick film, Mary again calls herself "Mary Wadsworth Sawyer." The night Tom sneaks home from his pirating adventure to leave a message for his aunt, he eavesdrops on a conversation among Polly, Joe Harper's mother, Sid, and Mary about the presumed drownings of the missing boys. As the older women sob, Mary reads a poem she has written:

> "Our Drowned Boys"
> By Mary Wadsworth Sawyer
>
> Alack, our broken hearts are so sad!
> Alack, our sorrow, it is so hard to measure.
> For though oftimes they may have acted pretty bad,
> Boys will be boys!
> They were our fond treasure!

Weaver's inspiration for that scene can only have been Emmeline Grangerford, the deceased funerary poet of *Huckleberry Finn*. It is one of the largest liberties with Mark Twain's novel that the film takes, as nothing in the novel hints that Mary is a Sawyer, that she writes poetry, or that she is obsessed with death. Indeed, quite the opposite on that last point. In chapter 3, she is first introduced returning home after an absence; she dances in the door, "all alive with the joy of seeing home again . . .[bringing] song and sunshine . . ."

The film takes a more jarring departure from the novel in the way it handles Tom and Becky's romantic relationship. In the novel, Tom is quick to make clear to Becky that he loves her in their first encounter in school in chapter 7. Soon afterward, he persuades her to become "engaged," only to alienate her almost immediately by letting slip he was previously engaged to Amy Lawrence. Becky then spurns all his efforts to win back her affection until chapter 20, in which he saves her from a whipping for damaging the schoolmaster's anatomy book by falsely confessing to the crime himself. After Tom takes the most severe beating the master has ever administered, Becky praises his nobility and her devotion to him is never again in doubt. Selznick's film handles the affair differently. While it was in production scriptwriter Weaver said "we have not prolonged the puppy love affair of Tom and Becky. We end it and take it for granted in the middle of the story, as Twain did" (Keavy 5–2). That, however, is not what the film actually does. After several scenes in which Tom and Becky admire each other from a distance, they finally meet face-to-face in the first schoolroom scene. In a single sequence, Tom expresses his love, takes Becky's punishment for drawing a caricature of the teacher on her slate, wins her praise for his nobility, persuades her to be engaged, and then ruins everything by letting slip his past engagement to Amy. From that moment, Tom and Becky's "puppy love" cannot be taken for granted—even after Tom's miraculous reappearance at the funeral, where Becky turns her back on him. It is not until the cave episode, more than an hour into the film, that they appear to be reconciled. In the film's concluding picnic scene, Becky herself lets Tom know she is his in no uncertain terms: After gazing longingly at the chest of pirate gold Tom has found in the cave, she turns to him and softly says, "Don't forget . . . we're engaged!"

Liberties such as those the Selznick film takes with Sid, Mary, and Becky are trivial, however, compared to what it does with Injun Joe, the novel's central villain. Described as a "murderin' half-breed" by Huck, he first appears in chapter 9 when Tom and Huck visit the town graveyard at night to use a dead cat in an incantation to remove warts. The boys see Joe and Muff Potter helping Dr. Robinson dig up a fresh grave. Joe argues with the doctor, starting a struggle that knocks Muff unconscious, and then kills the doctor with Muff's knife. Afterward, he makes the drunken Muff think he has killed the doctor himself. The next day, Muff is arrested and is later tried for murder. In both the novel and the film, Tom and Huck vow to remain silent and then agonize over the likelihood Muff will be hanged because of their silence, but they are too afraid of Injun Joe to say anything.

The most explicitly violent event in the novel, the graveyard murder is reenacted in virtually every screen adaptation. From that moment in the novel, Tom and Huck's fear of Joe drives much of the action in later chapters. In chapter 23, Tom finally works up the courage to testify against Joe at Muff's trial. His surprise testimony exonerates Muff and makes Tom a "glittering hero" in the town, but Joe's sudden bolting from the courtroom transforms him into a fugitive whose unknown whereabouts make him seem even more menacing. Virtually every adaptation of *Tom Sawyer* plays up the boys' fear of Joe to increase dramatic tension. It should be kept in mind, however, that the novel never even hints that Joe wants to harm the boys. Even when he is hiding out with his unnamed partner in the haunted house and is growing irritated by the sight of the "infernal boys" digging for treasure nearby, he makes no move against them (chapter 26). Later, when Tom and Becky are lost in the cave, and Tom spots a human hand and instinctually shouts, all Joe does is merely "take to his heels and get himself out of sight" (chapter 31). He is never again seen alive.

Both Paramount's 1930 film and Selznick's film take the same enormous liberties in two separate scenes involving Injun Joe. Both films' trial scenes have Joe glower menacingly at Tom while he testifies, and at the moment Tom is about to name him as Dr. Robinson's true murderer, Joe hurls a knife at Tom before leaping out a window and fleeing. It is a cinematically exciting moment but has no basis in the novel. In both films' cave episodes, not only does Joe see and recognize Tom, he also runs after him with the clear intention of killing him. Because everyone knows Tom will survive, Joe's pursuit can lead to only one possible outcome: his death. In both films his end comes when he is close to grasping Tom, only to slip and fall down a deep chasm. In the Selznick film Joe's fall results directly from Tom's throwing his beloved brass knocker into Joe's face. Tom might thus be said to have killed Joe himself. After the film has been showing Tom throw things in his brother's face, it seems cruelly ironic for the film to show him kill Joe by throwing an object in his face. The scene is a seismic change from the novel, in which Joe quietly dies of thirst and starvation when a newly erected iron door at the cave's main entrance prevents him from getting out. Moreover, when Tom first learns about the caves new iron door, far from being gratified to know about Joe's terrible predicament, he himself turns "white as a sheet" at the realization of what that means (chapter 32).

The film's depiction of the cave itself is another major departure from the novel. The novel's cave is not a twin of the real cave near Hannibal that inspired Mark Twain's version (see appendix on cave). Changes in the film's cave go further still. It has many features not in the novel's cave, but the most important differences are in scale: Everything in the film's cave is vastly larger and grander. When the studio was planning the film, it considered filming cave scenes inside the real Hannibal cave but gave up that idea quickly after concluding that the cave "look[ed] like an oversized gopher hole and was by no means picturesque enough" (Harrison 18). Photographers then took pictures of New Mexico's Carlsbad Caverns that set designers used to construct an artificial cave on a studio lot with huge chambers, large and colorful stalactites and stalagmites, deep chasms, and even a gushing waterfall. To enhance the films drama, the studio went even further by having Tom and Becky cut off from rescuers by a big rockslide that would be a physical impossibility in a real limestone cave, such as the one near Hannibal. The design of the film's cave and Joe's desperate pursuit of Tom are both examples of concessions made to enhancing the film's purely cinematic qualities and, thus, part of the reason the film still entertains audiences. Compared to its colorful and truly "cavernous" cave, the more cramped cave in the 1930 Paramount film almost does resemble an oversized gopher hole.

What the Film Gets Right

An outstanding attribute of Mark Twain's Tom is his rich imagination. Ever ready to play as a bloodthirsty pirate, heroic robber, or savage Indian, he enjoys pretending to be literary characters such as Robin Hood and the Black Avenger of the Spanish Main. Never, however, does he close his eyes and imagine he really *is* one of those characters. In this regard, the 1938 Selznick film contrasts with the 1930 Paramount film. In the earlier film Tom actually does engage in vivid fantasies. In one fantasy sequence, for example, he (Jackie

Coogan) appears as a knight in shining armor rescuing Becky (Mitzi Green), who also is suitably attired and tied to a tree. In another, he appears quite literally armed to the teeth as a cutthroat pirate. Later, when he, Huck, and Joe Harper board a tiny raft to begin their pirating escapade, his companions see only plain boards with a crude sail, while Tom sees a full-masted pirate ship. Such moments are entertaining and successful at conveying the richness of Tom's imagination. Like the novel, the Selznick film has no such scenes, but succeeds in a different way to depict Tom as an imaginative boy. By that kind of measure, the question of which film is "truer" to the novel probably rests on the individual tastes of the films' viewers.

One measure of the "faithfulness" of any screen adaptation is how it depicts its source's characters. Audiences understand that films cannot compress complete novels into hour-and-a-half or two-hour productions without omitting or truncating some episodes. For that reason, they tend to be tolerant of plot alterations. Altering major characters, however, is a different matter. Disney's 1993 *The Adventures of Huck Finn*, for example, offends many readers of Mark Twain's novel by depicting Huck as a happy-go-lucky clone of Tom Sawyer and transforming the intelligent but uneducated slave Jim into an articulate civil rights advocate. One of the strengths of Selznick's *Tom Sawyer* film is that its characters feel true to their literary counterparts. Thirteen-year-old Tommy Kelly, for example, looks and behaves as many readers would imagine Mark Twain's Tom to look and behave. Not everyone would agree, of course, but that is because the novel's lack of description allows readers to form their own mental pictures of Tom. An anonymous reviewer for the *Hollywood Spectator*, for example, complained, "My Tom Sawyer . . . is not the boy I saw last night on the screen, not the freckle-faced, roughneck kid of a thousand sly adventures and gay flirtations; he is Dave's [Selznick's], not mine and I prefer my own." Regarding Kelly himself, the reviewer added, "To me he merely is not the Tom Sawyer type . . ." ("Selznick" 6–7). Granted Kelly's Tom does not come across as a "roughneck," but a scene (copied from the 1930 film) in which Tom beats up Joe Harper (not Alfred Temple, as in the novel) was cut from the film. The reviewer's imagination, incidentally, was at work, as there is nothing in the novel to suggest Tom Sawyer, or any other character, has freckles.

Selznick's *The Adventures of Tom Sawyer* is by any standard an entertaining film. It has pleased audiences for many decades and is likely to continue doing so in the future. The same, however, might also be said for films such as Bing Crosby's *Connecticut Yankee in King Arthur's Court* and Disney's *The Adventures of Huck Finn* (1993)—two audience-pleasing films, neither of which is regarded as a satisfying adaptation of its source. Selznick's *Tom Sawyer* film is far from completely satisfying in that regard itself, but little in it greatly offends the critical literary eye. It encompasses most of the novel's main episodes—whitewashing the fence, Tom's Sunday school embarrassment, Tom's taking Becky's whipping in school, the boys' pirate adventure and subsequent appearance at their own funeral, and Tom and Becky's dramatic adventures in the cave. The film alters details here and there, but apart from exaggerating Injun Joe's attempts to kill Tom in two scenes, it adds nothing major that lacks a basis in the novel. Most of its characters and sets look about as readers are likely to imagine them, and the film is especially good at capturing their emotions, from Tom's tearful reveries to the terrified faces of his schoolmates when their sadistic schoolmaster grills them. Indeed, one of the best things about the film is its success in conveying characters' emotions.

Perhaps the best way to describe the film is to say that it *feels* right as an interpretation of the novel. For that reason one's experience in viewing it is similar to what one experiences in reading the book. The film may not get *Tom Sawyer* completely right, but it *almost* does.

Works Cited

Abbott, Mary Allen. "A Guide to the Discussion of the Technicolor Photoplay Version of *The Adventures of Tom Sawyer* as produced by David O. Selznick." *Photoplay Studies*, vol. 4, no. 2, Feb. 1938, pp 29–30, ia801903.us.archive.org/19/items/photoplaystudies04nati/photoplaystudies04nati.pdf.

Behlmer, Rudy, editor. *Memo from David O. Selznick.* Viking Press, 1972.

Filmsite. *Box Office Hits by Decade and Year.* www.filmsite.org/boxoffice2. html.

Gauntier, Gene. "Blazing the Trail." *Woman's Home Companion.* Part 1, vol. 55, no. 10, Oct. 1928, pp. 7–8, 181–84, 186.

Graham, Sheilah. "Boy to Play Tom Sawyer Hard to Find: Norman Taurog . . . Tells Why Others Were Rejected." *Hartford Courant,* 12 Aug. 1937, p. 8.

Hall, Mordaunt. "Some Clever Pictures: Three Comedies and an Operetta—Fine Talking Film of 'Tom Sawyer.'" *The New York Times,* 28 Dec. 1930.

Harrison, Paul. "Gray Paint Spreads Gloom in Cave of 'Tom Sawyer.'" *Racine Journal-Times,* 22 Oct. 1937, p. 18.

Haver, Ronald. *David O. Selznick's Hollywood.* Knopf, 1980.

Keavy, Hubbard. "Brings Twain to Screen." *Indianapolis Sunday Star,* 4 July 1937, part 5, p. 2.

Othman, Frederick C. "Tom Sawyer Goes in Production" (United Press). *Tampa Tribune,* 16 Aug. 1937.

_____. "Twain's Daughter Praises 'Tom Sawyer' of Screen" (United Press). *Pittsburgh Press,* 11 Feb. 1938.

Rasmussen, R. Kent. "Film, Television, and Theater Adaptations." *Mark Twain in Context.* Edited by John Bird, Cambridge UP, 2020. pp. 329–40.

_____, and Mark Dawidziak. "Mark Twain on the Screen." *A Companion to Mark Twain.* Edited by Peter Messent and Louis J. Budd, Blackwell Publishing, 2005. pp. 274–90.

"Selznick and Mr. Sawyer . . ." *Hollywood Spectator,* 19 Feb. 1938, pp. 6–7.

Twain, Mark. *Autobiography of Mark Twain, Vol. 1: The Complete and Authoritative Edition.* Edited by Harriet Elinor Smith et al., U of California P, 2010.

Weaver, John V. A. *The Adventures of Tom Sawyer* (1938)—Full Transcript, subslikescript.com/movie/The_Adventures_of_Tom_Sawyer-29844.

Adventuring with Tom Sawyer in a Twenty-first Century Classroom_____

John R. Pascal

Since 2015, I have taught a year-long junior- and senior-level honors course on Mark Twain that I created at Seton Hall Preparatory School, a Catholic boys school in New Jersey. Each year the course has had a special focus on *The Adventures of Tom Sawyer.* At the same time, I have also taught a junior-level American literature course whose focused readings include *Adventures of Huckleberry Finn.* I would never claim there is a *single* best way to teach Mark Twain, but I have learned that an essential ingredient is to passionately convey the *relevance* of Mark Twain to the students' own lives. Drawing on my experience, I shall discuss methods of teaching *Tom Sawyer*, using questions I have posed to my own students to stimulate their critical thinking. Many of my questions emphasize the students' specifically twenty-first-century experiences.

New forms of technology and social media continuously surround and distract modern-day students, making it difficult for them to have the patience and powers of concentration to read and comprehend books. Virtually all my students over the years had heard of *Tom Sawyer* before they entered my classes, but none of them had actually read the book. To help prepare them for the challenge of reading a nineteenth-century text about life in a world largely alien to their own, I always began by posing questions about their lives that are relevant to episodes in Mark Twain's novel. After this year's class had spent two full months with *Tom Sawyer*, I asked them to explain what makes this nearly 150-year-old story still worth reading. The response of one student, Christian M., suggests that my approach to the novel has been working:

> [The book's] simplicity and relatability, Twain's amazing descriptions
> and the lovable characters. I loved how easy the book was to read,
> which truly enabled me to read it as an actual story, rather than a book

for school. Never before have I read an author who has made me feel like I was in the heat of the moment, going step by step with Tom, as if I could experience the same senses Tom was feeling back in the early 1800s. Tom, Becky, Huck, Aunt Polly, and the widow Douglas are all characters that are too cool and likeable to dislike. I do not know how Twain could write them to seem so natural and human, especially because they are going on children's adventures. Their growth makes readers feel as if they are watching real-life people come up from the ink.

Many teachers would doubtless agree that making an 1876 work about a young boy living on the western frontier interesting and meaningful to modern high school students is challenging. I have found, however, that questions such as these help meet that challenge:

- *Have your parents ever ruined your plans for Saturday fun by dumping unwelcome chores on you?* (My students usually respond with smirks as they raise their hands and then slap their desks loudly.)
- *Will you ever forget your first love?* ("Certainly not," is their blushing response.)
- *Do you like to show off on social media such as Instagram and TicTok?* (Of course, everyone does.)
- *Have you ever attended Sunday sermons that are boring in new ways each week?* (All hands are raised tiredly.)
- *Has a parent ever poured a foul-tasting medicine down your throat?* (All their mouths remember that nightmare.)
- *Have you ever had a teacher you hated so much you fantasized about taking revenge with a practical joke?* (All hands on deck, once again.)
- *Would you enjoy exploring a haunted house at the edge of your neighborhood?* (Once again, the vote is unanimous)

Now, after the students are warmed up, they are better prepared to enter a world without cars. televisions, radios, computers, cell phones, and social media.

Breathing Life into Tom's Adventures

Literature is traditionally taught in classrooms in which students sit at their desks, essentially motionless (aside from their taking notes or surreptitiously texting on their phones). I have found that having them *physically* act out things that Mark Twain's characters do greatly enhances their engagement with his text. For example, one of the first action scenes in chapter 1 of *Tom Sawyer* is Tom's challenging the town's new boy (whom readers later learn is Alfred Temple) to a fight—merely because the stranger is "too well dressed on a week-day." To bring this scene to life, I have pairs of boys step to the front of the classroom to confront each other in a similar manner. Not only do they relish challenging each other in increasingly belligerent language, they instinctively begin shoving each other . . . without any prompting from their teacher.

Because young people are taught that physical violence is wrong, I then ask my classes if Tom Sawyer's fighting the new boy makes him "bad." Christopher I.'s answer was "no": "Tom is envious of wealth. That's part of the human condition. There is nothing wrong being ashamed. Tom is barely twelve years old. Give him a break!"

Another, more complex action episode is the scene in chapter 2 in which Tom's Aunt Polly spoils his Saturday plans for swimming by ordering him to whitewash what seems to be an impossibly large fence. In one of the most famous turnarounds in American literature, not only does Tom manage to persuade his friends to paint the fence for him, but he also gets them to *pay* for the privilege. Inspired by the annual whitewashing competition staged in Mark Twain's hometown of Hannibal, Missouri, I had my school's maintenance department erect two five-by-five-foot sections of fence in a parking lot for a painting competition each school year before the pandemic. Divided into two groups, my students engaged in furious races to determine which groups could finish painting their sections first. My mock fences were mere microcosms compared to the nine-by-ninety-foot nightmare Tom Sawyer confronts in the novel, but the exercise proved to be a revelation to many students. In addition to the pure joy they experienced acting out a famous American tradition—not to mention getting out of the classroom to splash paint around—some of them had never even held paintbrushes before and were amazed to discover how heavy and difficult they were to use.

In the novel, Tom Sawyer's crew applies three coats of whitewash to the fence. My students were also amazed to discover that covering wooden boards adequately requires at least two coats. When Tom Sawyer's friend Ben Rogers watches Tom paint in chapter 2, he asks, "Why, ain't that work?" It is not difficult to guess how my students would answer that question! "No wonder Tom Sawyer had other kids paint for him," remarked Peter G., "it's *hard* to do this correctly!" Edward G. added that "Painting is hard work, and the job is fantastically competitive, but it shows the spirit we had!" Patrick D. seconded that sentiment, adding "We may not be the best, but we are efficient. It's called teamwork." One thing for certain–the painting exercise helped the students appreciate the irony of Tom's convincing his friends that hard work is actually play. In Julian S.'s opinion, "Tom's efforts bring a smile because of how well he executed them." To that, Brady D. added, "A great smile comes to my face because it really sets up the character of Tom for the whole book!"

Tom's ruse in the fence-painting episode also raises the question of whether his behavior may be regarded as morally defensible. According to Declan F.,

> It might not be morally right to do what he did; however, that doesn't mean Tom's reasoning for success isn't valid. Look at the facts: Tom resisted Ben's begging several times. This makes it Ben's own fault for falling into Tom's trap, not Tom's.

Joseph S. agreed, pointing out that "Ben is a real 'flathead.'" Not all my students concurred, however. Jack F., for example, thought "Tom's reasons for tricking his friends were valid, but he took it too far. Accepting the bribes from friends while tricking them was just not the right thing to do." Christian M. was more emphatic, "As a businessman, Tom is a raging success because he went 'from being a poverty-stricken boy' to 'literally rolling in wealth.' But morally, he's a complete failure. His willingness to plan 'the slaughter of more innocents' is terrible. Overall, his reasoning for success depends on the reader's values and morals."

In chapter 3, Tom and his friends stage mock army battles. What do today's children have in common with them? My students were quick to point out that modern paintball fights, Nerf-gun games, and laser tag are essentially the same thing as Tom's battles.

Spoonfuls of Sugar Help Aunt Polly's Medicine Go Down

One of the most popular *Tom Sawyer* activities in which my classes annually participated before the pandemic was inspired by a sidebar in R. Kent Rasmussen's book *Mark Twain for Kids*. Designed to illuminate what was behind the foul-tasting "pain-killer" medication with which Aunt Polly doses Tom in chapter 12 of *Tom Sawyer* (and which Mark Twain's mother gave him when he was a boy), Rasmussen's sidebar is an activity for readers titled "Market Your Own Patent Medicine" (Rasmussen 13). Raised in the confident knowledge that the medications they take are government-certified as safe and effective, my students were surprised to learn that most nineteenth-century patent medicines were fake. They were especially intrigued to learn that people who used patent medicines back then believed the bogus concoctions cured their maladies and were happy to provide endorsements, which in turn were used to sell more of the medically worthless products. Following instructions in Rasmussen's book, the students had field days inventing and bottling pretend patent medicines of their own. They especially enjoyed coining names for their imaginary products and writing mock advertisements filled with glowing endorsements. Because the class exercise forbade the use of any modern technology, students had to use their hands and the most powerful tool of all—their imaginations.

The passionate energy students invested in the patent medicine exercise far surpassed my expectations. Poster-size advertisements they drew included imaginary endorsements from some of the Twain scholars with whom they had held Skype meetings and Mark Twain's own characters. They also presented enthusiastic oral presentations endorsing their products, which were themselves highly imaginative. For example, instead of offering cures for such ordinary ailments such as colds, their patent medicines promised relief from such maladies as academic laziness, shyness, and ugliness–all at the good-humored expense of their appreciative classmates. As with the fence-painting exercise, what the students gained from this activity was an ability to connect more directly with *Tom Sawyer*. Moreover, like Mark Twain, they also used humor to appreciate and gain a better understanding of an earlier period of their country's history. Another, unexpected benefit was their gaining a greater appreciation of modern healthcare–though that is not the sort of subject literature classes typically address.

Remembering a First Love

Modern technology need not be entirely shunned. One of my classes conducted an online Zoom meeting with seventh-grade students in Hannibal who had been selected to serve as the town's official "Tom" and "Becky" goodwill ambassadors for a year. Thanks to the efforts of the Mark Twain Boyhood Home and Museum, members of the class were able to ask questions about Tom and Becky's relationship, which their younger counterparts answered flawlessly while staying completely within character!

When Tom sees Becky for the first time in chapter 3 of the novel, she nonchalantly tosses a pansy over a fence for him to pick up as she disappears from view. Smitten by Becky's beauty, Tom then carefully maneuvers to lift up the flower with his barefoot without being noticed. To my class, I posed the question of how realistic Tom's romantic behavior is. One student, Jack F., said he would have no problem picking up that flower to get the chance to simply say "Hi!" Larry C., however, argued that while Becky's action was "subtle, people today are oblivious to the world around them due to technology." Nick P. put in that he "would have 'Tom Sawyered' Becky by simply talking to her!," adding that he had "done the same thing many times!"

How does one get pity even after being rejected by a true love? One way is to "die *temporarily!*" Tom imagines himself doing exactly that in chapter 8, after Becky has spurned him at the end of the previous chapter, in which he lets slip the fact he was previously "engaged" to Amy Lawrence. I asked my students to comment on Tom's morose reaction. Christian M. explained, "Tom doesn't desire death, just attention, which is a very innocent point of view given his age, and despite his being so obviously in the wrong." Indeed, Larry C. noted, "Mark Twain shows the innocence of Tom. He enjoys life too much to go away permanently." Berkeley H. remarked wryly, "By dying 'temporarily' he will get peace and Becky's love, but he still wants to live his life above ground!"

Enter Huckleberry Finn

As I mentioned earlier, many seniors come to my Mark Twain classes after having read *Huckleberry Finn* in their junior-level American literature course. Encountering *Tom Sawyer* for the first time clears up a mystery that had puzzled them when they read that novel's sequel the previous year–namely, *who* exactly Huck is. *Huckleberry Finn* is such an immediate sequel to *Tom Sawyer* that its first few chapters would–apart from shifting from third-person to first-person narrators–fit seamlessly as the final chapters of *Tom Sawyer.* When my seniors read *Tom Sawyer* for the first time, the sparse summary of his background that Huck provides in his own book finally makes sense to them. They are happily surprised to discover that it is in *Tom Sawyer* that Huck is introduced. This revelation helps them more fully appreciate how much he changes in his own story.

One senior student, Declan F., said of Huck, "It is especially interesting to see him through Tom's and the town mothers' points of view. In *Huckleberry Finn,* readers get to know Huck only through his own eyes, so reading of his earlier reputation really opened *my* eyes." Larry C. thought that "Huck doesn't get a fair depiction of who he really is in *Tom Sawyer* because we won't see his view of the world until his own adventures." Willem A. added that "Huck suffered through a lot of pain in his book, yet the kids in *Tom Sawyer* only see the good side of him. This tells me that Huck has a real life apart from everyone else."

In chapter 17 of *Tom Sawyer*, when Huck appears in the church's funeral with Tom and Joe Harper, he wants to "hide from so many unwelcoming eyes." Christian M. thought this was "heart-wrenching because a young boy should be shown all the love he needs, yet Huck receives none from the town." Brady D. observed that "Huck must have had so much built-up excitement from hearing Tom talk about how enjoyable it will be walking into the church, that he must have been especially disappointed when no one moved to welcome him."

In chapter 28, Huck remarks on his past associations with the slave named "Uncle Jake," who likes Huck because he does not act superior to him. In a passage that may foreshadow Huck's relationship with the fleeing slave Jim in *Huckleberry Finn*, Huck explains, "Sometimes I've set right down and eat *with* him. But you needn't tell that. A body's got to do things when he's awful hungry he wouldn't want to do as a steady thing." In Christopher I.'s view, "Huck's an outcast so he and Uncle Jake can relate to each other because people looked upon slaves as outcasts, too." Brady D. said the passage makes Uncle Jake feel like a human instead of a slave. Andrew K. saw it as showing Huck taking "a step forward in humanity by being willing to treat everyone equal." According to Willem A., "They broke bread and ate together, something unheard of at that time. Huck has a twenty-first-century heart and way of thinking, even though he worries about being discovered violating a nineteenth-century norm."

How Realistic are Tom and Huck's Imaginative Adventures?

With Huck usually in tow, Tom is always searching for adventure. When they pay the spooky town graveyard a midnight visit on a quest to cure their warts with a dead cat in chapter 9, they get more than they have bargained for when they witness Injun Joe murder Dr. Robinson. How do modern boys react to this episode? Christian M. liked the fact that Mark Twain

> not only establishes an eerie atmosphere, but he also personifies the graveyard! This would be enough to make a grown man flee in terror, let alone two young boys. Although this may seem silly to us, back in

their time the fear of spirits seeking retribution was a commonly held idea, and combining that with Tom and Huck's age, their fear seems quite rational.

Quinn S. said of the boys, "Their innocent adventure to a graveyard at midnight in pitch darkness is normal to them, certainly not to us! They are also relevant to our sense of freedom. We can never do this!" Berkeley H. went a little further, saying that "once Tom and Huck finally get a real adventure, they are terrified." Declan F. made the perceptive observation that although "the boys expect to see the devil in the graveyard and are not scared by that, seeing a murder scares them more than a devil could."

During the boys' Jackson's Island interlude in chapter 16, Tom and Joe Harper have Huck teach them how to smoke pipes. Having no idea how tobacco smoking affects human bodies, they both become sick. Brady D. noted the relevance of that episode to our modern world: "It is very human to want to do something that your friend is very fond of." Joseph S. took a more somber view: "Boys are young and innocent, so they try smoking. It's sad to see modern underage kids still smoking when they know it's wrong." Jack F. offered a more cautionary view: "It's relevant to our lives by showing how we shouldn't get ahead of ourselves whether it's smoking or anything else. It won't end well for us just like what happened to Tom and Joe." Berkeley H. made the perceptive observation that "Tom finds more enjoyment in being known as a smoker than in the smoking itself. Kids today are like this, posting pictures of themselves smoking on social media to be known as 'cool' smokers."

Christian M. found great humor in the smoking scene because Huck realizes his friends are getting nauseous, "but lets Tom keep rambling on, making the scene ten times funnier." Christian added that he had had a similar kind of humbling experience when he was learning to drive a car: "Just as I was bragging to my father that driving was a lot easier than he had warned, he didn't say anything as I backed the family car into a bush."

Tom's Compassion and Growing Maturity

Although Tom often behaves thoughtlessly, my students have seen signs of his budding maturity in the sincerity of his remorse in chapter 10, when he senses Aunt Polly is giving up on him for sneaking out. He almost hopes she will flog him. Christopher I. suggested that "no child wants to think he has broken his guardian's heart." "Instead of flogging Tom," Willem A. remarked, "she simply expresses how tiredly disappointed she is with him and his actions. Tom actually cares about Aunt Polly since he feels miserable and begs her to forgive him, an action we would not have expected from Tom earlier in the novel." Nick P. added, "they both love and care for each other, but as a child, Tom doesn't mean to inflict pain on someone who isn't even his real mother. His actions are just out of his desire for adventure."

Willem A. identified another sign of Tom's growing maturity: his reaction when he sees no one welcoming Huck when the boys suddenly appear at their own funeral: "He tells Aunt Polly that someone should be glad that Huck is alive. Although her hugs make Huck more uncomfortable, this moment reveals Tom's caring nature; he loves his friends, including Huck." In chapter 19, Polly berates Tom for having lied to her about a dream he claimed to have had when he was on Jackson's Island. Because of that lie, Polly has made a fool of herself by telling Joe's mother, Sereny Harper, about the so-called dream. Tom responds to her chastisement with the words, "Auntie, I wish I hadn't done it—but I didn't think." All my students admitted to having spoken similar words to their own parents, making already embarrassing situations even worse.

My students have seen another example of Tom maturing in chapter 20, in which Becky accidentally tears a page in the anatomy book the schoolmaster, Mr. Dobbins, normally keeps locked in a drawer, when Tom's sudden entrance in the otherwise empty schoolroom startles her. Later, when Dobbins tries to find the culprit by angrily grilling pupils one by one, Tom looks upon Becky as "a hunted and helpless rabbit . . . with a gun leveled at its head." He knows she is terrified by the certainty of being whipped after Dobbins gets to her. Mark Twain's use of figurative language resonated with my students as an indication of Tom's compassion and growing maturity. Declan F. said, "Mr. Dobbins's questioning Becky is the gun." Brady D. pointed out that Becky "has nowhere to run to escape a beating." "A beating is nothing new to Tom," according to Nick P., "because he is almost immune to them, but for a girl like Becky, it is like death is staring at her." Tom eventually saves Becky by claiming responsibility for the torn page himself and taking her whipping. His selfless deed moved Christian M. to observe that "Tom shows true maturity as his sacrifice to take 'the most merciless flaying' proves that his love and care for Becky overpowers his need to be petty."

Fig. 1. Tom saves Becky from a whipping by shouting, "I done it!" just as Becky is about to confess to having torn the schoolmaster's book. True Williams, *Tom Sawyer*, 1876, p. 165. [Public domain.]

Another example of Tom's compassion and maturity is his concern for the plight of the town drunk, Muff Potter, who is facing trial for the murder of Dr. Robinson—which Tom knows was committed by Injun Joe. When Tom and Huck visit Muff and pass tobacco and matches to him through the bars of his jail cell window, Muff remarks that the boys' "little hands [are] weak but they've helped Muff Potter a power, and they'd help him more if they could." Given the boys' knowledge of Muff's innocence, the irony of his words is not lost on my students. Christian M., for example, observed:

> Muff truly believes in their goodness; however, the reader knows this isn't true. They're at the jail out of their guilty secret; their

valid fear of Injun Joe keeps them from testifying. While this isn't malicious, they're also lying straight to Muff Potter's face, and this isn't acceptable.

Berkeley H. took a different view: "Tom's hands are described as 'weak' because he's young, and it would be a challenge to convince the town that Potter is innocent. He does end up helping Potter more significantly than just 'gifts' of tobacco and matches when he finally testifies in court." Larry C. noted that "Huck didn't break the oath, but Tom's testifying shows his maturity once again when he realizes the right thing to do is to ignore the oath."

The Climactic Cave Episode

What is perhaps the novel's most dramatic episode occurs in chapters 31–32, in which Tom and Becky are lost in the cave. To help my students appreciate this episode, I showed them pictures I had taken of the real cave near Hannibal that inspired the novel's fictional version. How realistic, I asked my class, is Tom's handling of Becky's despair and fear they will die in the cave? After Tom's last candle burns out, and he faces the "the horror of utter darkness," he perseveres and finds a way out of the cave. Is that believable? My students responded first by praising Tom for his valor. Nick P., for example, noted that "Tom takes responsibility for getting lost and getting out, showing how much he has matured throughout the novel as our esteem for him rises." Quinn S. added, "Tom acts like a man would; he has no choice but to remain calm and confident. When he spots Injun Joe, he does a remarkable job of keeping his cool; otherwise, both he and Becky would be dead." According to Christian M.,

> Tom knows their only chance of survival must be through him. He keeps Becky calm because he loves her too much to see her go crazy. To find his way out with a kite line in complete darkness without falling is hard to believe. But it might have been more realistic back in his life, as children then were much more deft and aware of how they could manipulate their surroundings.

Later in the book, as Tom is recovering from his cave ordeal, he learns that Judge Thatcher has had the cave's entrance locked shut with an iron door. Knowing that Injun Joe is probably still inside the cave, he turns "as white as a sheet." Again, I ask the class how realistic his reaction is when one might expect him to be elated by the news of his mortal enemy's peril. In Christian M.'s view, "Injun Joe is a man who showed no hesitancy at all to murder people who stood in his way; however, Tom feels awful for him which shows his pure goodness." Declan F. recognized that "Tom has compassion to realize how close he himself and Becky were to dying." Willem A. went even further: "Despite thinking Injun Joe would try to kill him, Tom sees a man dangerously alone. This is a sign of maturity that he didn't have earlier."

Chapter 33 describes what Injun Joe's last hours must have been like before he dies in the cave: All he had to drink was the equivalent of a "dessert spoonful" of water that dripped from a stalactite. The text also asks a thought-provoking question:

> Has everything a purpose and a mission? Did this drop fall patiently during five thousand years to be ready for this flitting human insect's need? and has it another important object to accomplish ten thousand years to come? No matter.

Brady D. observed that "Twain seems almost mad that the water dripped during all these major historical events, but its only purpose was to save an insect like Injun Joe." Berkeley H., however, suggested that "Twain knows it doesn't matter because Injun Joe is dead anyway." Willem A. took a more sympathetic view, crediting Mark Twain's "imagination and creativity to come up with this idea for us to ponder."

Another scene revealing Tom's maturation occurs in the next chapter, 34, in which Tom berates his half-brother Sid for having revealed a secret concerning Huck's role in averting Injun Joe's plan to harm the Widow Douglas:

> Sid, there's only one person in this town mean enough to do that and that's you. If you had been in Huck's place, you'd a' sneaked down

the hill and never told anybody on the robbers. You can't do any but mean things, and you can't bear to see anybody praised for doing good ones. There—no thanks, as the widow says.

Berkeley H. noted "in the beginning of the book, it was always Sid ridiculing Tom for doing the wrong thing. Now that Tom has matured, the roles have reversed by Tom's consideration of others." Willem A. added that "Huck deserves praise for his actions, so Sid's actions are nothing but childish." Christopher A. made the interesting observation that when Tom "ends his rant with a 'no thanks,' it shows how his word choices have become more refined."

The novel ends with Huck having fled from the cloying attentions of the Widow Douglas, who wishes to adopt him. Tom talks him into returning to his new civilized life–so he will be respectable enough to join Tom's planned robber gang. Christopher A. made another interesting observation in pointing out that Tom uses "almost the same psychology on Huck he uses in the beginning of the novel to persuade his friends to whitewash the fence. This time, however, it is for someone else's good. In his new maturity he knows the widow is stressing out about Huck, who shouldn't be sleeping in barrels and eating trash."

Revenge

The novel's eighteenth chapter, in which Tom, Becky, and Alfred all look for ways to take revenge on one another, is one that my students have found particularly poignant. The book's first-edition contents list contains the subhead "Black Revenge," an apt description of Alfred's pouring of black ink on Tom's spelling book in retaliation for his resentment of Tom. Christian M. said, "The entire chapter is black with revenge." It actually begins with Tom's feigning interest in Amy Lawrence to make Becky jealous, followed by Becky's using Alfred the same way to make Tom jealous, and finally, Alfred's taking out his anger on Tom. Christian M. made the perceptive observation that Tom does not call himself the "'Black Avenger of the Spanish Main' for nothing." All my students recalled moments when their friends–and even they themselves–had played the same kinds of vengeful tricks—which usually backfired. Nick P. noted that "the way both Tom and Becky have zero regard for the persons they are manipulating is sadly true to real life. Also, Tom had a chance to get back with Becky, but his pride and thirst for glory got in his way." In the matter of the damage Alfred does to Tom's spelling book, Christian M. pointed out that "books were very scarce at that time and damaging one is like damaging someone's mobile phone today."

Chapter 21, which is about "Examination day" at Tom's village school, offers another striking example of revenge. To repay the schoolmaster, Mr. Dobbins, for his cruel tyranny over the previous year, Tom's classmates carry out an elaborate practical joke. While Dobbins half-drunkenly sketches a map on a blackboard to exercise his geography pupils, one of the boys lowers a cat over his head from the ceiling above. When the cat's claws pull off his wig, not only is his "bald pate" revealed to the audience, so, too, is the fact it had been gilded while he was napping earlier. "That broke up the meeting. The boys were avenged. Vacation had come." As a teacher

Fig. 2. Examination day at Tom's school. True Williams, *Tom Sawyer*, 1876, p. 168. [Public domain.]

myself, I was naturally curious whether my students could imagine doing something like that to a teacher. Nick P. said that "vengeance is satisfied for Dobbins's terrible teaching, cruel ways of punishing children, and lack of dedication." Another, Conall G., was more sympathetic toward the humiliated teacher: "If Dobbins feels the need to wear a wig in his daily life to cover his insecurity, then their actions are extremely immature, despite his own unnecessary cruelty." Larry C. expressed a more modern view: "Today we could secretly videotape his rampage, post it on the Internet . . . and send it to CNN."

Civic Duty

One of the novel's most amusing episodes unfolds in chapter 22, in which Tom joins the "Cadets of Temperance." Attracted by their "showy" regalia, he vows to abstain from smoking, swearing, and chewing tobacco in return for a chance to parade in a striking red sash on public occasions, such as funerals of civic leaders. The failure of an ailing, old justice of the peace to die when Tom expects him to, causes Tom to resign from the Cadets in disgust—only to miss out on a fine parade when the old man then suddenly dies. "Who would not enjoy dressing in colorful regalia and marching in a parade," I asked my students? Christian M. offered a thoughtful reply:

> Tom's attitude with the Cadets of Temperance shows Twain's humor. Tom only wants to be a member for the uniform and parades; this is such a Tom Sawyer thing to do and honestly, I love it. Tom's hope for Judge Frazer's death so he can parade himself at the funeral is both terrible and funny simultaneously; and it shows Tom's thirst for glory. It only becomes funnier when the judge ends up dying just after Tom quits!

Several other students were less sympathetic. Nick P. said simply, "Tom has zero loyalty for the Cadets' rules." Julian S. agreed: "I think you should join an organization like this if you truly care about its purposes to be a model citizen." Brady D. concurred: "I don't like Tom's attitude because he didn't really give it a chance, and it was very immature of him to quit." Declan F. took a middle position:

"Although Tom's reasons for joining were wrong, he still keeps his word on not drinking and swearing. He is maturing."

Conclusions

I am occasionally asked if teaching *Tom Sawyer* has changed how I view the book. Not really. It still brings me the same joy I felt as a boy, when I found a copy on my older brother's bookshelf and began reading about Tom and Becky's exciting adventure in the cave. In an unmailed letter he wrote in 1887, Mark Twain described *Tom Sawyer* as "simply a hymn, put into prose form to give it a worldly air" (Paine 477). The purpose of a hymn is to celebrate. The novel is a celebration of childhood that should not be forgotten. While *Huckleberry Finn* reminds readers that a boy must grow into a man, *Tom Sawyer* reminds readers not to forget the boy who always remains within the man. Judging by their comments, my students have been hearing that message.

Berkeley H. observed that "childhood and adventures are universal and don't diminish over time." Brady D. added, "You can relate to Tom, Huck, Becky, almost any character; you feel emotions similar to theirs, and that in itself is a wonderful feeling." Declan F. believed that "everyone who reads this story was or is a kid. So, it helps them feel that way again; young, full of hope, and irresponsible like Tom." Quinn S. agreed: "Readers can experience all the joys of being young no matter how old they are." Conall G. elaborated on that sentiment by saying, "From his mischievous nature to his developing moral compass, it is very easy for readers to find themselves in Tom Sawyer." Willem A. asked whether Tom is brave or foolish, and answered, "Neither! He is adventurous and now so are we. It's not just a set of adventures—it is all of life!"

I can think of no more apt way to conclude than quoting an ironic observation made by Dr. Cindy Lovell: "Tom Sawyer is always trying to get out of school. The last place he wants to be is *in* school!" That, however, is what any teacher avid about Mark Twain should be doing—bringing Tom Sawyer back into the classroom—to stay.

Works Cited

Paine, Albert Bigelow, editor. *Mark Twain's Letters*. Vol. 2. Harper & Brothers, 1917.

Rasmussen, R. Kent. *Mark Twain for Kids: His Life & Times*. Chicago Review Press, 2004.

Twain, Mark. *The Adventures of Tom Sawyer*. 135th Anniversary Edition. U of California P, 2010.

RESOURCES

Tom Sawyer's Cave: Fact vs. Fiction_____

Danny Norman

Late in his life, Mark Twain recalled how in *Adventures of Huckleberry Finn* (1885) he had moved his uncle's farm from Missouri to Arkansas. As for the "morality" of what he had done, he added, "I cared nothing for that; I would move a State if the exigencies of literature required it" (Twain 1:209). Given such a casual attitude toward geographical realities, we should not be surprised to know that "McDougal's Cave" in which Tom and Becky get lost in *The Adventures of Tom Sawyer* (1876) bears only a passing resemblance to the real-world cavern near Hannibal, Missouri, that was known as "McDowell's Cave" in Samuel Clemens's time and is now known as "Mark Twain Cave." We should also be even less surprised to learn how wildly different screen versions of the cave are from both Hannibal's real cave and the novel's fictional version. It is always a good idea, therefore, to keep in mind the "exigencies of literature"!

Like Sam Clemens, I grew up in Hannibal, and like him I explored the nearby cave many times when I was a boy. Unlike him, however, I did that not as an unsupervised child adventuring with friends, but as a participant in school and Boy Scout outings and during my eighth-grade year, when I served as an official "Tom Sawyer" ambassador for Hannibal. Little did I then imagine how much

Fig. 1. Danny Norman as an official "Tom Sawyer" during his middle-school years in Hannibal. (The Mississippi River and Mark Twain Bridge are visible in the background.) Photo courtesy of Danny Norman. [Used with permission.]

more familiar I would later become with the cave's fascinating lore and seemingly endless crooked aisles. I spent the summer of 2019 working at the cave as part of a University of Missouri internship program. During that summer, I served mainly as a tour guide but also did nearly every other kind of job the privately owned cave needed and spent some of my own time exploring the cave. During that summer alone, I must have spent more than one hundred hours inside the cave—more time than Tom and Becky spend in *Tom Sawyer*'s fictional version.

Tom Sawyer's Fictional Cave

If Clemens intended the fictional version of the cave he describes in *Tom Sawyer* to be a recreation of the real cave he had known as a boy, he certainly took some big liberties, but *Tom Sawyer* is, after all, a work of fiction. Whether Clemens consciously introduced discrepancies to enhance a sense of wonderment or merely forgot what the real cave was like we cannot say. Much of what the novel says about the fictional cave is, however, also true about the real one. For example, chapter 29 describes a small chamber that is "chilly as an ice-house, and walled by Nature with solid limestone that was dewy with a cold sweat." In chapter 31 Tom and Becky experience this moment: "Now, for the first time, the deep stillness of the place laid a clammy hand upon the spirits of the children." Phrases such as "deep stillness" and "clammy hand" are accurate descriptions of how one can feel walking through the real cave, especially when one is alone. The cave's unvarying temperature of 52 degrees Fahrenheit makes everything feel clammy and as chilly as an icebox.

Thanks to the cave's natural air-conditioning, Hannibal used to hold city council meetings inside the cave during hot summer months. The council convened in a chamber known as the "Parlor Room," the only place in the cave where tourists are encouraged to sit down on furniture-like rock formations. The chamber's natural limestone furniture provides cold seats, however, as it is always cool to the touch and often feels slick, despite not actually being wet. The chamber, incidentally, is near a place that tour guides fancifully say is the novel's "jumping-off" spot where Tom catches a glimpse of Injun Joe and runs back to Becky in chapter 31.

Fig. 2. Postcard made in 1910 showing well-dressed Hannibal residents gathered in the cave's spacious "Parlor Room." Note the "furniture-like" rock formation. Image courtesy of Kevin Mac Donnell.
[Used with permission.]

One of the novel's most precise descriptions matching a section of the real cave appears in chapter 33, in which Tom and Huck are searching for the place where Injun Joe has hidden the pirate treasure: "Tom went first, cutting rude steps in the clay hill as he descended. Huck followed. Four avenues opened out of the small cavern which the great rock stood in." The boys continue on, hoping to find the treasure "under the cross," though not sure exactly what that phrase means. Immediately after the drop-off, or "jumping-off" spot, in the real cave, a cross of sorts can be seen on the ceiling overhead where two "lifelines" of the cave intersect above a unique rock formation, presumably the "great rock" mentioned in the novel. This area also leads directly into a spot in the cave called "Five Points." Counting the "four avenues" that spider out from the drop-off, there are exactly five points from which to continue exploring the cave.

The silence inside the cave can be deafening when one is not near a tour group, or especially in dry sections where no water seeps down from lifelines—the incipient ceiling cracks that eventually grow large enough to admit the water that carves out limestone caverns. One can

---

almost hear one's own thoughts bouncing off the limestone walls as one wonders what may be lurking down the next dark corridor. I always knew that Injun Joe's ghost was not really waiting for me in places like "Injun Joe's Canoe"—the last natural landmark of the tour route. The cave does, however, sometimes exude an eerie aura when one is alone armed only with a flashlight. I suspect this may be because of one's thoughts of the many thousands of souls who have walked through the cave's glacial clay, signed their names on the limestone walls, and bumped their heads on the aptly named "Headache Rock."

An interesting side note: Mark Twain Cave is illuminated throughout with electric light bulbs controlled by an intricate system of switches carefully placed for tour guides to find and tourists not to see. Nearby Cameron Cave, which was not discovered until fifteen years after Clemens's 1910 death, is also open to tours. It, however, has been left in its natural state without electric lights. I've stood in the dark corridors in the well-lit Mark Twain Cave and felt like I was being watched. I've also accompanied training tours in complete darkness inside Cameron Cave— where I could easily have gotten lost—yet never had the same feelings of being watched or of encountering something fearful lurking behind a corner. Nothing plays better tricks than one's own mind—something to remember when trying to imagine what Tom and Becky are feeling when they are lost in the cave.

Another passage in the novel containing an accurate description of the real cave occurs in chapter 31, in which Tom and Becky are just beginning their exploration of the cave:

> they wandered down a sinuous avenue holding their candles aloft and reading the tangled web-work of names, dates, post-office addresses and mottoes with which the rocky walls had been frescoed (in candle smoke.) Still drifting along and talking, they scarcely noticed that they were now in a part of the cave whose walls were not frescoed. They smoked their own names under an overhanging shelf and moved on. Presently they came to a place where a little stream of water, trickling over a ledge and carrying a limestone sediment with it, had, in the slow-dragging ages, formed a laced and ruffled Niagara in gleaming and imperishable stone.

The real cave has several long passageways whose surrounding limestone was carved into shelf-like structures akin to natural ladders. Past visitors probably climbed those structures to write on the ceilings high above the tour routes below. Signatures all over the cave have been scrawled in pencil, ink, chalk, soot, and even berry juice that looks much like blood. After years of searching, Clemens's own signature was finally found in the so-called "Lemon Squeeze" during Hannibal's 2019 Bicentennial year. It is, incidentally, now a federal crime to write on the cave's walls.

Fictional Discrepancies

In contrast to the novel's cave, the real cave has no subterranean lakes or rows of stalactites the size of men's legs, and the Mississippi River cannot be seen from any of the cave's entrances. Also, no one would need to trek five miles through the cave to hide a treasure chest as Injun Joe does. Nevertheless, most of the novel's grandiose descriptions seem to be based on some sort of reality. For example, pools of water can be seen in several areas, including "Aladdin's Palace," the only spot in the cave whose name was taken from *Tom Sawyer.* A small reflecting pool, however, scarcely constitutes a lake like the one where Tom and Becky rest in chapter 31. Stalactites can be seen in the real cave, but they are minuscule in size and

Fig. 3. When Tom and Becky emerge from the cave in the novel they see "the broad Mississippi rolling by"—an impossible view from any opening in the real cave. True Williams, *Tom Sawyer*, 1876, p. 249. [Public domain.]

number compared to those in the novel, and there is nothing resembling the great stalactite slowly dripping water on to a slowly rising stalagmite on which Injun Joe has scooped a "cup" before dying of thirst (chapter 33). When Norman Rockwell visited the cave before illustrating an edition of *Tom Sawyer* during the 1930s, he didn't notice any stalactites or stalagmites at all, so he didn't include any in his illustrations for the book.)

The real cave is also much smaller than the fictional cave appears to be. A survey conducted in 1986 mapped every passage in the cave and measured a grand total of 2.82 miles of passageways. In the novel, Tom and Becky cover a distance of about five miles between where they enter and exit the cave, and that figure doesn't account for twists and turns in their route, leave alone the many passageways they don't traverse. The standard modern tour route in the Mark Twain Cave is essentially a loop measuring about three-eighths of a mile.

Movie Versions of the Cave

The novel's transformation of the real cave pales in comparison to what movies have done to the novel's cave. The most striking differences have been in the sheer size of the movie caves. When David O. Selznick's studio was planning to film *Tom Sawyer* during the 1930s, it considered shooting cave scenes in Hannibal's real cave. That idea was quickly abandoned, however, when scouts reported that the cave looked "like an oversized gopher hole and was by no means picturesque enough. The outer locale was disappointing, too, what with so many signboards and telephone wires" (Harrison 4). That description seems harsh but has elements of truth. Tours through the cave must often form single-file lines to traverse narrow passages. Passages widen in a few areas, but most are snug. In many places, one cannot fully extend one's arms from side to side. The narrowest area, called the Lemon Squeeze, is only sixteen inches wide at its tightest spot.

There are reasons no *Tom Sawyer* film has ever been shot in the Mark Twain Cave. It would simply be impossible to squeeze a film crew and actors inside. Any attempt to do so would likely result in busted cameras and bloody noses from overcrowding. Even the widest passage in the cave. "Grand Avenue," isn't a big enough space for what a film production would require. The 1930 and 1938 productions of *Tom Sawyer* solved that problem by building their own caves on studio lots. Reader's

Digest's 1973 musical film shot cave scenes in larger Missouri caves. The artificial cave constructed for the 1930 film starring Jackie Coogan had passageways plenty wide enough for lots of school children to roam about freely. Selznick's 1938 Technicolor film went even bigger. Modeling parts of its studio cave set on the huge chambers of New Mexico's spectacular Carlsbad Cavern, its cave episode opens with children and adults climbing down a long wooden staircase into a gargantuan chamber more reminiscent of a scene in *Raiders of the Lost Ark* than anything in Hannibal's real cave or in Mark Twain's novel.

The cave in the 1938 film also has other features totally unrelated to either the real cave or the novel's cave, such as a large gushing waterfall and a formation of boulders that collapses and traps Tom and Becky in the cave. While the rockslide looks great on film, no such thing could ever happen in the Mark Twain Cave. Because its solid limestone was carved out by water over millions of years, there are no loose rocks in the cave. The only damage to the inside of the cave caused by an external force of which I have ever heard was a stalactite breaking off when the cave's modern entrance was blasted open.

Another grossly unrealistic moment is enacted in the 1930, 1938, and 1973 *Tom Sawyer* films. All three films (and others) show Injun Joe falling to his death down a deep chasm. There are simply no drops inside the Mark Twain Cave remotely similar to the chasms in the films, and the novel doesn't even hint that they exist. There is, however, another feature in the 1930 and 1973 films and in the novel that does exist in the real cave: natural spring water. Like the 1930 version, the 1973 *Tom Sawyer* film has Tom (Johnny Whitaker) mention an "underground spring" before clarifying that it is actually a river, calling it the "best drinking water in the state of Missouri." There are several springs in the real cave, but there are certainly no rivers. Despite being discouraged from drinking water from one of the hidden springs, I once filled a water bottle to the brim with the hard-to-find liquid. I can attest that it was, in fact, some of the best drinking water in the state of Missouri, but I don't recommend anyone else repeat my experiment.

One final feature links the novel to films—the presence of bats in the cave. Both the novel and the 1938 *Tom Sawyer* have scenes in which Tom and Becky are swarmed by bats. There may have been many bats in Hannibal's cave during Clemens's time, but they are rarely seen in the cave anymore. White-Nose Syndrome devastated the Midwest's bat population during the first decades of the present century. During all the time I spent exploring and leading tours in the Mark Twain Cave, I can remember seeing only three bats.

As in almost all works of fiction, real-life aspects were incorporated into the material to make *Tom Sawyer* a more mystical tale. Mark Twain cannot be faulted for embellishing upon his childhood playground. Perhaps his childhood memories grew fonder as he grew older, and the adventures seemed larger in scale than they really were. It pleases me to share a sentiment expressed in this remark that has been attributed to him: "I seemed to tire of most everything I did. But I never tired of exploring the cave." Mark Twain may never have actually said those words, but it accurately describes my own lingering itch to grab a flashlight and dive back into the cave once more. Next time I do, I think I'll bring my own water.

Works Cited

Harrison, Paul. "They Spread the Gloom Out of Buckets in 'Tom Sawyer.'" *Bangor Daily News* [Maine], 16 Oct. 1937, p. 4.

Twain, Mark. *Autobiography of Mark Twain*. Vol. 1, Edited by Harriet Elinor Smith et al., U. of California P, 2010.

Chronology of Mark Twain's Life and Legacy___

Nov. 30, 1835	Samuel Langhorne Clemens (SLC)—better known as Mark Twain—is born in the Missouri village of Florida. The sixth of seven children of John Marshall and Jane Lampton Clemens, he will outlive all his siblings, his wife, and three of his own four children.
1836–1846	Approximate period within which *The Adventures of Tom Sawyer* is set, according to the novel's preface.
1839–1853	SLC lives in Missouri's Mississippi River town of Hannibal, on which he will later model the fictional St. Petersburg of *Tom Sawyer* and *Huckleberry Finn*. After leaving school at eleven, he does printing work for local newspapers, including his brother Orion's papers, and writes occasional sketches and essays.
1847	Ned Buntline (Edward Zane Carroll Judson) publishes *The Black Avenger of the Spanish Main*, whose title Tom Sawyer adopts.
Mar. 24, 1847	John Marshall Clemens's death leaves his family impoverished.
Mar. 1, 1852	Boston's *Carpet Bag* magazine publishes "The Dandy Frightening the Squatter," SLC's first publication in an eastern journal.
1853–1856	SLC leaves Missouri to work as a printer in St. Louis, Philadelphia, and New York; after returning to the Midwest, he does similar work for Orion in southern Iowa.
1857	Thomas Hughes publishes *Tom Brown's School Days*.

May 1857– Apr. 1861	SLC spends two years apprenticing as a steamboat pilot on the lower Mississippi, followed by two more years as a licensed pilot.
June 13, 1858	Steamboat *Pennsylvania* blows up near Memphis, Tennessee, severely injuring SLC's younger brother, Henry, who dies eight days later.
Apr. 12, 1861	Civil War begins when Confederates fire on Fort Sumter in Charleston, SC. SLC, who is in New Orleans, will soon end his piloting career when the war stops commercial steamboat traffic on the lower Mississippi.
June 1861	SLC drills for about two weeks with a Missouri militia unit called up by the state's pro-Confederate governor.
July 1861	SLC crosses the plains with his older brother Orion, who has been appointed secretary to the government of newly created Nevada Territory.
July 1861– Sept. 1862	SLC prospects and collects mining claims in western Nevada.
Sept. 1862– May 1864	SLC works as a reporter for the *Virginia City Territorial Enterprise*.
Feb. 3, 1863	SLC uses the pen name "Mark Twain" for the first time in a report written in Carson City for the *Enterprise*.
June 1864– Dec. 1866	After relocating to California, SLC briefly reports for the *San Francisco Morning Call*, does some prospecting in the depleted gold fields of Tuolumne and Calaveras counties, and writes for a variety of publications, including *The Californian*, for which he writes "The Story of the Bad Little Boy."

Nov. 18, 1865	Publication of SLC's jumping frog story in New York's *Saturday Press* helps build his national reputation.
Mar.–Aug. 1866	SLC visits the Hawaiian (Sandwich) Islands as a correspondent for the *Sacramento Union*. After returning to San Francisco, he launches what will become a long and successful lecturing career by speaking on the islands in Northern California and western Nevada.
May 14, 1867	SLC publishes his first book, *The Celebrated Jumping Frog of Calaveras County and Other Sketches*.
June–Nov. 1867	SLC tours Mediterranean Europe and the Holy Land with the *Quaker City* excursion; his travel letters to San Francisco and New York newspapers are widely reprinted, expanding his reputation. After his return, Elisha Bliss of the American Publishing Co. (APC) of Hartford, CT invites him to write the book about his travels that will become *The Innocents Abroad*.
c. late 1868	SLC writes story posthumously published as "Boy's Manuscript" that anticipates *Tom Sawyer*.
1868–1869	Louisa May Alcott publishes *Little Women*.
Mar.–July 1868	SLC visits California for the last time to secure the rights to his *Quaker City* letters from the *San Francisco Alta California*; while there, he finishes writing *The Innocents Abroad* with Bret Harte's help.
1869	Thomas Bailey Aldrich publishes *The Story of a Bad Boy*.

July 20, 1869	APC publishes *The Innocents Abroad, Or, The New Pilgrims' Progress*, the first of SLC's five travel books; it will be his best-selling book throughout his lifetime and the best-selling American travel book of the nineteenth century.
Aug. 1869	SLC buys an interest in the *Buffalo Express* and becomes one of the newspaper's editors. After settling in Buffalo, NY, he begins the first of several major eastern lecture tours.
1870–1871	SLC writes whimsical sketches and stories for *The Galaxy*, including "The Story of the Good Little Boy Who Did Not Prosper."
Feb. 2, 1870	SLC marries Olivia (Livy) Langdon, the daughter of a wealthy Elmira, NY, coal magnate. The newlyweds settle in a Buffalo house given to them by Livy's father.
Nov. 7, 1870	The couple's first child, a son named Langdon, is born; he will live only 22 months.
Feb. 1871	Isaac Sheldon publishes *Mark Twain's Burlesque Autobiography and First Romance*, the first part of which is essentially a farce about imaginary ancestors that SLC would later regret having published.
Mar. 1871	After a year of family misfortunes, SLC sells his Buffalo house and interest in the *Express* and relocates to Elmira, where his family stays on the Quarry Farm of Livy's sister, Susan Crane. Over the next two decades, his family will spend most of their summers on the farm, where Clemens will do much of his most important writing.

Oct. 1871	SLC's family settles in Hartford, CT, before he starts another long lecture tour. His first daughter, Susy, is born the following March. In September 1874, the family will move into a magnificent new house that will be their home until 1891.
Feb. 29, 1872	APC publishes *Roughing It*, an embellished account of SLC's years in the Far West and Hawaii.
Aug.–Nov. 1872	SLC makes his first visit to England, to which he will soon return with his family.
Dec. 1873	APC publishes *The Gilded Age*, a novel by SLC and his Hartford neighbor Charles Dudley Warner. SLC's portions of the novel revolve around events modeled on his own family's history.
June 1874	SLC begins writing *Tom Sawyer* in earnest during the same month his second daughter, Clara, is born.
Jan.–Aug. 1875	The *Atlantic Monthly* publishes "Old Times on the Mississippi," SLC's first extended work about steamboating, in a seven-part series.
July 5, 1875	SLC tells William Dean Howells he has finished writing *Tom Sawyer* and turns to dramatizing the story in a play that will never be produced.
July 21, 1875	APC publishes *Mark Twain's Sketches New & Old*.
Nov. 5, 1875	SLC delivers manuscript of *Tom Sawyer* to APC.
June 9, 1876	Chatto & Windus issues the first edition of *The Adventures of Tom Sawyer* in England, as American publication is delayed.

June 28, 1876	Belford Brothers in Canada publishes a cheap pirated edition of *Tom Sawyer* that floods American markets.
c. Dec. 8, 1876	APC publishes the first American edition of *Tom Sawyer*.
Dec. 17, 1877	SLC delivers burlesque speech at a Boston birthday banquet for poet John Greenleaf Whittier that afterward causes him great embarrassment.
Apr. 1878– Aug. 1879	SLC travels to western Europe with his family.
Nov. 12, 1879	SLC delivers triumphant speech honoring Gen. Ulysses S. Grant at a Union Army reunion in Chicago.
Mar. 13, 1880	APC publishes *A Tramp Abroad*, a fictionalized account of episodes from SLC's recent European travels.
July 26, 1880	SLC's third daughter, Jean, is born.
Dec. 12, 1881	James Osgood of Boston publishes *The Prince and the Pauper*, SLC's novel about boys switching places in sixteenth-century England. Like Tom Sawyer, the pauper boy is named "Tom."
Apr.–May 1882	SLC travels by steamboat from St. Louis, MO, to New Orleans, and then upriver to St. Paul, MN, to gather material for the book to be called *Life on the Mississippi*.
May 17, 1883	Osgood publishes *Life on the Mississippi*, which expands SLC's 1875 "Old Times on the Mississippi" articles and adds new material from his 1882 return to the river.

May 1, 1884	SLC founds his own publishing house, Charles L. Webster & Co., with Charles Webster, his nephew by marriage, as company president.
July 1884	SLC begins writing unfinished sequel to *Huckleberry Finn* that will be first published in 1968 as "Huck Finn and Tom Sawyer Among the Indians." Tom is the dominant character in this story narrated by Huck.
Feb. 18, 1885	Webster Co. publishes *Adventures of Huckleberry Finn* in America, two months after Chatto & Windus publishes the English edition in London.
May 1885	Mollie Ravel stars in stage production based on *Tom Sawyer* in Yonkers and Hartford.
early 1888	Kitty Rhoades's theater company tours a stage production of *Tom Sawyer* in the American East.
Dec. 10, 1889	Webster Co. publishes *A Connecticut Yankee in King Arthur's Court*, SLC's novel about a contemporary American thrust back to sixth-century England.
Oct. 27, 1890	Jane Lampton Clemens, SLC's mother, dies in Keokuk, IA, at the age of 87.
June 1891– May 1895	Clemens family closes down the Hartford house—to which they will never return—and goes to Europe to live to cut down living expenses. As they move around in western Europe, SLC makes numerous quick trips to the United States to look after his failing business interests.
May 1892	Webster Co. publishes *The American Claimant*, SLC's novel about an American who claims to be heir to an English earldom.

1893–1894	SLC publishes *Tom Sawyer Abroad*, first as a serial in *St. Nicholas* magazine, then as the last book issued by his firm Webster Co., which goes into bankruptcy in April 1894.
Nov. 28, 1894	APC publishes *Pudd'nhead Wilson*, SLC's novel about slavery and miscegenation set in another fictional Missouri town modeled on Hannibal.
Apr. 1895– Apr. 1896	*Harper's Magazine* serializes SLC's novel *The Personal Recollections of Joan of Arc*, which afterward is issued in book form by Harper & Brothers, SLC's new authorized American publisher. Harper will soon begin reissuing all his books in uniform editions.
May 1895– July 1896	SLC leaves England with his family, beginning a round-the-world lecturing trip. After summering at Elmira, he, Livy, and daughter Clara travel cross-country to British Columbia, whence they cross the Pacific to Hawaii, Fiji, Australia, and New Zealand, and then cross the Indian Ocean to Ceylon, India, and South Africa, before returning to England. Meanwhile, SLC's daughters Susy and Jean remain behind in Elmira. Profits from the lecturing tour will pay off debts from his publishing firm's bankruptcy, and SLC returns to America hailed as a triumphant hero.
Aug. 18, 1896	Daughter Susy dies of spinal meningitis while SLC is in England. Jack Pickford, the first feature film "Tom Sawyer," is born in Toronto.
Aug.–Sept. 1896	*Harper's New Monthly Magazine* publishes *Tom Sawyer, Detective* as a serial.
1897	While in Switzerland, SLC begins writing "Tom Sawyer's Conspiracy," which he never quite finishes. It will be published in 1969.

Nov. 13, 1897	Harper and APC publish SLC's fifth travel book, *Following the Equator*, a relatively sober account of his round-the-world trip.
Dec. 11, 1897	SLC's brother Orion Clemens dies in Keokuk, IA.
Nov.–Dec. 1898	SLC begins writing a story first published as "Schoolhouse Hill," a variation of his "Mysterious Stranger" stories set in Tom and Huck's town.
May 29, 1900	Paul and Vaughan Kester sign agreement with SLC to dramatize *Tom Sawyer*.
Oct. 15, 1900	After an unbroken absence of five years, SLC returns to the United States with his family and rents a house in New York City.
Apr. 10, 1902	Harper publishes SLC's *A Double-Barrelled Detective Story*, a novella that features Sherlock Holmes as a bumbling detective.
May 1902	SLC pays his last visit to Hannibal and the Mississippi River during a trip to Columbia to accept an honorary degree from the University of Missouri.
Nov. 1903– June 1904	SLC takes his family to Florence, Italy, hoping the mild climate will help his wife Livy's failing health.
1903	Harper & Brothers becomes SLC's sole authorized American publisher.
Jan. 14, 1904	SLC begins dictating his autobiography to his family secretary, Isabel Lyon.
June 3, 1904	St. Louis World's Fair committee declares the date "Mark Twain Day" at the fair.

June 5, 1904	Livy dies in Florence; the rest of the family soon returns to the United States.
Aug. 31, 1904	Pamela Clemens Moffett, SLC's last surviving sibling, dies in Connecticut.
Sept. 1904–June 1908	SLC takes up residence on Fifth Avenue in New York City, where he is lionized as a public speaker and banquet guest.
Dec. 5, 1905	Col. George Harvey, president of Harper & Brothers and editor of *Harper's Weekly*, hosts a grand 70th birthday banquet for SLC at New York's Delmonico's restaurant.
Jan. 1906	Albert Bigelow Paine moves into SLC's home to begin work as SLC's authorized biographer.
1907	Gene Gauntier directs the first, one-reel, film adaptation of *Tom Sawyer*.
June–July 1907	SLC makes last trans-Atlantic voyage, to accept an honorary degree at Oxford University in England.
June 18, 1908	SLC moves into his last home, a newly built house outside Redding, CT.
Apr. 8, 1909	Harper publishes SLC's *Is Shakespeare Dead?*
Dec. 24, 1909	SLC's youngest daughter, Jean, dies of a heart attack suffered during a seizure, leaving Clara as SLC's sole remaining child.
Jan.–Apr. 1910	SLC visits Bermuda on his last trip outside the United States. When his health seriously declines, Paine goes to Bermuda to bring him home.

Apr. 21, 1910	Samuel Langhorne Clemens dies of heart failure in his Stormfield home at the age of seventy-four. Three days later, he is buried in Elmira's Woodlawn Cemetery, where all members of his family are eventually interred.
Aug. 18, 1910	SLC's only grandchild, Nina Gabrilowitsch, is born at Stormfield, on the fourteenth anniversary of Susy Clemens's death.
Sept. 1910	William Dean Howells publishes *My Mark Twain*, a personal tribute to his close friend.
1911–1912	Hannibal attorney George A. Mahan purchases SLC's boyhood home and donates it to the city, saving it from demolition.
Aug. 1912	SLC's literary executor, Paine, publishes his three-volume *Mark Twain: A Biography*. Over the next quarter-century, he will edit and publish numerous collections of SLC's previously unpublished writings.
1914	Paul Kester copyrights a play titled *The Adventures of Tom Sawyer*.
1917–1918	Silent film adaptation of *Tom Sawyer* is released in two parts: *Tom Sawyer* and *Huck and Tom; Or, The Further Adventures of Tom Sawyer*. Jack Pickford, the brother of "America's Sweetheart," film star Mary Pickford, plays Tom. Robert Gordon plays Huck, and Clara Horton plays Becky.
1918	*McClure* newspaper syndicate launches nearly two-decade run of "Tom Sawyer and Huck Finn" comic strip.

Feb. 1920	Silent film adaptation of *Huckleberry Finn* is released, with Lewis Sargent as Huck and Gordon Griffith as Tom Sawyer. This is the *Huckleberry Finn* film in which Tom has his largest role.
Dec. 1930	Paramount releases the first sound film adaptation of *Tom Sawyer*, with popular child star Jackie Coogan as Tom, Junior Durkin as Huck, Jackie Searl as Sid, and Mitzi Green as Becky. The production is the top grossing film released in the United States in 1930.
Aug. 1931	Paramount releases the first sound film adaptation of *Huckleberry Finn*. Hoping to repeat the success of the previous year's *Tom Sawyer*, the studio gives all that film's juvenile lead prominent parts and has Tom join Huck and Jim in their raft trip down the Mississippi River.
Dec. 1931	American copyright of *Tom Sawyer* expires; many unauthorized editions soon follow.
Dec. 25, 1931	Paul Kester's four-act *Tom Sawyer* play begins a six-performance run on Broadway.
1936	A Russian adaptation of *Tom Sawyer* filmed in the Ukraine is released.
Apr. 9, 1937	SLC biographer Albert Bigelow Paine dies in New Smyrna, FL; Bernard DeVoto succeeds him as editor of the Mark Twain Papers.
Dec. 21, 1937– Feb. 14, 1938	New York's Museum of Modern Art Film Library stages its first major exhibition, "The Making of a Contemporary Film," built around David O. Selznick's soon-to-be-released *The Adventures of Tom Sawyer*.

Feb. 1938	Selznick's production company releases first color film adaptation of *Tom Sawyer*, with Tommy Kelly as Tom, Jack Moran as Huck, and Anne Gillis as Becky.
Dec. 23, 1938	Paramount releases *Tom Sawyer, Detective*, with Billy Cook as Tom and Donald O'Connor as Huck.
1939	Clement Wood publishes *Tom Sawyer Grows Up*, a novel revisiting Tom and his friends several years after the events of *The Adventures of Tom Sawyer*.
Mar. 1939	MGM releases *The Adventures of Huckleberry Finn* with Mickey Rooney as Huck and Rex Ingram as Jim. Tom Sawyer does not appear in the film.
Feb. 13, 1940	U.S. Post Office issues ten-cent Samuel L. Clemens stamp in its "Famous Americans" series.
May 29, 1942	Dell Publishing copyrights the first comic book edition of *Tom Sawyer—The Complete Story of Tom Sawyer*, illustrated by George Kerr.
Jan. 1946	DeVoto resigns as editor of Mark Twain Papers. His successor, Dixon Wecter, will move the collection to the University of California at Berkeley three years later.
Aug. 1948	Classics Illustrated makes *The Adventures of Tom Sawyer* the fourth of its five Mark Twain titles and the fiftieth title overall in the series; the comic book is written by Harry Miller and illustrated by Aldo Rubano.
Jan. 1950	Pocket Books publishes first American paperback edition of *Tom Sawyer* with a cover describing the novel as "the greatest story of American boyhood ever told."

July 4, 1951	NBC–TV's Kraft Television Theatre broadcasts a one-hour production of *Tom Sawyer* with Charles Taylor as Tom, Tommy Rettig as Huck, Natalie Wood as Becky, and Mary Astor as Aunt Polly.
Feb. 10, 1952	*CBS Television Workshop* broadcasts excerpt from *Tom Sawyer* titled "Tom Sawyer, the Glorious Whitewasher."
May 21, 1954	Campbell Soup's *TV Soundstage* broadcasts adaptation of *Tom Sawyer*'s early chapters titled "A Little Child Shall Lead Them."
Nov. 21, 1956	CBS–TV's *United States Steel Hour* broadcasts musical production of *Tom Sawyer* with book and music by Frank Luther.
July 14–20, 1958	Kansas City's outdoor Starlight Theatre debuts new musical production of *Tom Sawyer* with Frank Luther's music and new book by Richard Berger, Edward Reveaux, and Peter Gurney. Folk singer Randy Sparks plays Tom. Noted actors in future productions in various cities include Joel Grey, Bobby Rydell, Davy Jones, Mickey Dolenz, and Kathleen Freeman.
1960	MGM releases first color film adaptation of *Huckleberry Finn* as *The Adventures of Huckleberry Finn*, with Eddie Hodges as Huck and boxer Archie Moore as Jim. Tom Sawyer does not appear in the film.
Nov. 19, 1962	Clara Clemens Samossoud, SLC's longest surviving child, dies in San Diego, CA.
Jan. 16, 1966	Nina Gabrilowitsch, SLC's only grandchild and last direct descendant, dies in Los Angeles.

Dec. 20, 1968	*Life* magazine publishes SLC's unfinished story "Huck Finn and Tom Sawyer among the Indians."
1969	University of California Press publishes *Hannibal, Huck & Tom,* edited by Walter Blair. Comprising most previously unfinished and unpublished SLC manuscripts, this collection includes "Huck Finn and Tom Sawyer among the Indians," "Doughface," "Tom Sawyer's Gang Plans a Naval Battle," "Tom Sawyer's Conspiracy," and "Tom Sawyer: A Play."
1970	Mark Twain scholar John Seelye publishes *The True Adventures of Huckleberry Finn,* a revision of SLC's novel that greatly reduces Tom Sawyer's role, removing him completely from the end of the novel.
Oct. 13, 1972	U.S. Post Office issues eight-cent "Tom Sawyer" stamp using the fence-painting illustration Norman Rockwell painted for the 1936 Heritage Club edition of the novel.
1973	Traumwald Press publishes *Tom Sawyer Comes Home,* a pastiche written during the 1950s by Missouri novelist Dorothy Langley (Dorothy Selma Richardson).
Feb. 25, 1973	The nineteenth episode of television's animated *Festival of Family Classics* broadcasts Tom Sawyer. Fifty-one-year-old Canadian actress Billie Mae Richards provides Tom's voice in the 30-minute adaptation.
Mar. 23, 1973	CBS–TV broadcast Canadian-made television adaptations of Tom Sawyer with Josh Albee as Tom, Jane Wyatt as Aunt Polly, and Buddy Ebsen as Muff Potter.

Apr. 1973	United Artists releases Reader's Digest's musical film adaptation of *Tom Sawyer* with Johnny Whitaker as Tom, Jeff East as Huck Finn, and Jodie Foster as Becky Thatcher.
Apr. 1974	United Artists releases Reader's Digest's musical adaptation of *Huckleberry Finn* with Jeff East returning as Huck and Paul Winfield playing Jim, but Tom Sawyer does not appear in the film.
Mar. 1975	Twenty-one-year-old Ron Howard plays Huck in television production of *Huckleberry Finn*, with Antonio Fargas as Jim and *Happy Days*'s Danny Most as Tom Sawyer.
Jan.–Dec. 1980	Japanese television broadcasts an animated adaptation of *The Adventures of Tom Sawyer* in 49 weekly half-hour installments; the production will later be shown in the United States and other countries and made available on DVD and streaming services.
1980	University of California Press publishes first corrected edition of *The Adventures of Tom Sawyer* based directly on original manuscript material and edited by the staff of the Mark Twain Papers.
1982	Georgetown University Library publishes two-volume facsimile edition of SLC's original handwritten manuscript of *Tom Sawyer*.
1983	Charles A. Norton publishes *Writing Tom Sawyer: The Adventures of a Classic*, the first full-length study of the novel.
1985	University of California Press publishes the first edition of *Huckleberry Finn* revised by the editors of the Mark Twain Papers.

Feb.–Mar. 1986	Public Broadcasting System (PBS) broadcasts four-hour adaptation *The Adventures of Huckleberry Finn* over four weeks, with Patrick Day as Huck, Eugene Oakes as Tom, and Samm-Art Williams as Jim.
1988–1989	HBO broadcasts an English-dubbed version of the 1980 Japanese *Adventures of Tom Sawyer* serial in early morning time slots.
Apr. 1993	Disney releases *The Adventures of Huck Finn*, starring future Hobbit Elijah Wood as Huck and Courtney B. Vance as Jim. Tom Sawyer is not a character in the film.
Oct. 13, 1993	U.S. Postal Service issues *Huckleberry Finn* stamp in its "Youth Classics" series.
Oct. 9, 1995	PBS–TV launches *Wishbone* series about a dog who fantasizes about being characters in classic literary works with "A Tail in Twain," with a two-part episode in which the dog imagines he is Tom Sawyer.
Dec. 22, 1995	Disney releases *Tom and Huck*, a new film adaptation of *Tom Sawyer* starring Jonathan Taylor Thomas as Tom and Brad Renfro as Huck.
Apr. 1996	Random House publishes first edition of *Huckleberry Finn* incorporating material from the long-missing first part of the manuscript rediscovered in 1991.
1998	Family Home Entertainment releases 51-minute video production of *The Animated Adventures of Tom Sawyer*, whose voice actors include Kirsten Dunst as Becky Thatcher and Christopher Lloyd as Judge Thatcher.

Mar. 21, 2000	*The Modern Adventures of Tom Sawyer* is released on video. Loosely based on the novel, the production stars Philip Van Dyke as Tom, Laraine Newman as Aunt Polly, and Erik Estrada as Joe.
Apr. 4, 2000	MGM Family Entertainment releases feature-length animated musical video of *Tom Sawyer* in which all the characters are animals. Tom (voiced by Rhett Akins) is a cat, and Huck (Mark Wills) is a fox. Betty White provides the voice of Aunt Polly.
2001	University of California Press publishes the first new edition of *Huckleberry Finn* fully integrating material from the manuscript found in 1991 in its Mark Twain Library series; a scholarly edition will follow two years later.
Apr. 26– May 13, 2001	Ken Ludwig's *The Adventures of Tom Sawyer* musical has twenty-one performances on Broadway.
Nov. 15, 2010	University of California Press publishes the first volume of *Autobiography of Mark Twain*, edited by Harriet Elinor Smith et al. of the Mark Twain Papers. The book will spend many weeks on *The New York Times* list of best-selling nonfiction.
2011	NewSouth Books in Alabama publishes editions of *Tom Sawyer* and *Huckleberry Finn* edited by Alan Gribben that substitutes "slave" for the "n" word and "Indian" for "Injun."
June 25, 2011	U.S. Postal Service issues a "forever" stamp depicting SLC with a river steamboat in the background.
Aug. 2011	Hannibal's Mark Twain Boyhood Home and Museum hosts its first quadrennial Clemens Conference, attended by Mark Twain scholars and aficionados.

Aug. 2, 2012	A German adaptation of *Tom Sawyer* titled *Tom und Haike*, set in post-World War II Germany, is released in Germany.
2013	Faye Dant opens Jim's Journey: The Huck Finn Freedom Centers.
Oct. 15, 2015	University of California Press completes publication of the three-volume *Autobiography of Mark Twain*.
Sept. 20, 2017	Novelist Tim Champlin publishes *Tom and Huck's Howling Adventure: The Further Adventures of Tom Sawyer and Huckleberry Finn*, the first volume of a trilogy in which a twenty-first-century boy named Zane Rasmussen travels back to Tom Sawyer's time.
2019	Hannibal, Missouri, celebrates the bicentennial of its 1819 platting.
Jan. 12–July 5, 2020	Animated twenty-six-episode French-Canadian *Tom Sawyer* series airs on French television. It is later broadcast in Finland, Italy, Canada, and Poland.
Nov. 10, 2020	USC student film production of *The Adventures of Thomasina Sawyer* is released, with Angelina Capozzoli as Thomasina ("Tom") and Patrick Donovan as Huck.
Jan. 6, 2021	Romance novelist E. E. Burke publishes *Tom Sawyer Returns: The New Adventures*, in which an adult Tom returns to St. Petersburg to help Becky Thatcher defend her father against treason charges.

Works by Mark Twain

Titles reprinted in these special editions are flagged: Library of America (LOA), Norton Critical Editions (NCE), Oxford Mark Twain (OMT), and the Mark Twain Project's University of California Press editions (UCP).

Original Editions of Novels, Travel Books, Sketches, Stories, Plays, and Essays

The Celebrated Jumping Frog of Calaveras Country and Other Sketches. C. H. Webb, 1867 (OMT).

The Innocents Abroad, or The New Pilgrims' Progress; Being Some Account of the Steamship Quaker City's Pleasure Excursion to Europe and the Holy Land. American Publishing Co., 1869 (LOA, OMT).

Mark Twain's (Burlesque) Autobiography and First Romance. Sheldon, 1871.

Roughing It. American Publishing Co., 1872 (LOA, OMT, UCP).

The Gilded Age: A Tale of To-day. Coauthored by Charles Dudley Warner. American Publishing Co., 1874 (LOA, OMT).

Old Times on the Mississippi. Belford Brothers, 1876.

The Adventures of Tom Sawyer. American Publishing Company, 1876 (LOA, NCE, OMT, UCP).

A True Story and the Recent Carnival of Crime. James R. Osgood, 1877.

Punch, Brothers, Punch! and Other Sketches. Slote, Woodman, 1878.

A Tramp Abroad. American Publishing Co., 1880 (OMT).

The Prince and the Pauper: A Tale for Young People of All Ages. James R. Osgood, 1881 (LOA, OMT, UCP).

The Stolen White Elephant, Etc. James R. Osgood, 1882 (OMT).

Life on the Mississippi. James R. Osgood, 1883 (LOA, OMT).

Adventures of Huckleberry Finn. Chatto & Windus, 1884; Charles L. Webster, 1885 (LOA, NCE, OMT, UCP).

A Connecticut Yankee in King Arthur's Court. Charles L. Webster, 1889 (LOA, NCE, OMT, UCP).

Merry Tales. Charles L. Webster, 1892 (OMT).

The American Claimant. Charles L. Webster, 1892 (LOA, OMT).

The £1,000,000 Bank-note and Other New Stories. Charles L. Webster, 1893 (OMT).

Tom Sawyer Abroad. Charles L. Webster, 1894 (LOA, OMT, UCP).

The Tragedy of Pudd'nhead Wilson and the Comedy Those Extraordinary Twins. American Publishing Co., 1894 (LOA, NCE, OMT).

Personal Recollections of Joan of Arc. Harper, 1896 (LOA, OMT).

Tom Sawyer Abroad; Tom Sawyer, Detective and Other Stories, etc., etc. Harper, 1896 (OMT, UCP).

Following the Equator: A Journey Around the World. American Publishing Co., 1897 (OMT).

How to Tell a Story and Other Essays. Harper, 1897 (OMT).

More Tramps Abroad. London: Chatto and Windus, 1897.

The Man that Corrupted Hadleyburg and Other Stories and Essays. Harper, 1900 (OMT).

English as She Is Taught. Mutual Book Co., 1900.

A Double-Barrelled Detective Story. Harper, 1902 (OMT).

My Début as a Literary Person and Other Essays and Stories. American Publishing Co., 1903.

A Dog's Tale. Harper, 1904.

Extracts from Adam's Diary. Harper, 1904 (OMT).

King Leopold's Soliloquy: A Defense of His Congo Rule. P. R. Warren, 1905 (OMT).

What Is Man? De Vinne Press, 1906 (OMT, UCP).

Eve's Diary: Translated from the Original Ms. Harper, 1906 (OMT).

The $30,000 Bequest and Other Stories. Harper, 1906 (OMT).

Christian Science. Harper, 1907 (OMT, UCP).

A Horse's Tale. Harper, 1907

Is Shakespeare Dead? From My Autobiography. Harper, 1909 (OMT).

Extract from Captain Stormfield's Visit to Heaven. Harper, 1909 (OMT).

Report from Paradise. Edited by Dixon Wecter, Harper, 1952.

Letters from the Earth. Edited by Bernard DeVoto, Harper, 1962

Simon Wheeler, Detective. Edited by Franklin R. Rogers, New York Public Library. 1963.

Mark Twain's Satires & Burlesques. Edited by Franklin R. Rogers, U of California P, 1967.

Mark Twain's Which Was the Dream? and Other Symbolic Writings of the Later Years. Edited by John S. Tuckey, U of California P, 1967.

Hannibal, Huck & Tom. Edited by Walter Blair, U of California P, 1969.

Mark Twain's Mysterious Stranger Manuscripts. Edited by William M. Gibson, U of California P, 1969.

Mark Twain's Fables of Man. Edited by John S. Tuckey, U of California P, 1972.

No. 44, The Mysterious Stranger. U of California P, 1982 (LOA).

A Murder, a Mystery, and a Marriage. W. W. Norton, 2001.

Is He Dead? A Comedy in Three Acts. Edited by Shelley Fisher Fishkin, U of California P, 2003.

Autobiography

Mark Twain's Autobiography. Edited by Albert Bigelow Paine, 2 vols, Harper, 1924.

Mark Twain in Eruption: Hitherto Unpublished Pages About Men and Events. Edited by Bernard DeVoto, Capricorn Books, 1940.

Chapters from My Autobiography. Oxford UP, 1996.

Autobiography of Mark Twain: The Complete and Authoritative Edition. 3 vols. Edited by Harriet Elinor Smith and Benjamin Griffin, U of California P, 2010, 2013, 2015.

Journalism

Sketches of the Sixties, by Mark Twain and Bret Harte, Being Forgotten Material Collected for the First Time from the Californian, 1864–1867. Edited by John Howell, John Howell, 1926.

The Adventures of Thomas Jefferson Snodgrass. Edited by Charles Honce, Pascal Covici, 1928.

Mark Twain's Letters from the Sandwich Islands. Edited by G. Ezra Dane, Stanford UP, 1937.

The Washoe Giant in San Francisco: Being Heretofore Uncollected Sketches by Mark Twain Published in the "Golden Era" in the Sixties. Edited by Franklin Walker, George Fields, 1938.

Mark Twain's Travels with Mr. Brown, Being Heretofore Uncollected Sketches. Edited by Franklin Walker and G. Ezra Dane, Alfred A. Knopf, 1940.

Mark Twain's Letters in the "Muscatine Journal." Edited by Edgar M. Branch, Mark Twain Association of America, 1942.

Mark Twain of the "Enterprise": Newspaper Articles & Other Documents, 1862–1864. Edited by Henry Nash Smith and Frederick Anderson, U of California P, 1957.

Traveling with the Innocents Abroad: Mark Twain's Original Reports from Europe and the Holy Land. Edited by Daniel Morley McKeithan, U of Oklahoma P, 1958.

Contributions to the "Galaxy," 1868–1871, by Mark Twain. Edited by Bruce R. McElderry, Jr., Scholars' Facsimiles and Reprints, 1961.

Mark Twain's San Francisco. Edited by Bernard Taper, McGraw-Hill, 1963.

Clemens of the "Call": Mark Twain in San Francisco. Edited by Edgar M. Branch, U of California P, 1969.

Mark Twain Speaks for Himself. Edited by Paul Fatout, Purdue UP, 1978.

Mark Twain at the "Buffalo Express": Articles and Sketches by America's Favorite Humorist. Edited by Joseph B. McCullough and Janice McIntire-Strasburg, Northern Illinois UP, 1999.

Letters, Speeches, and Miscellaneous Writings

Mark Twain's Speeches. Edited by Albert Bigelow Paine, Harper, 1910 (OMT); rev. ed., 1923.

Mark Twain's Letters. Edited by Albert Bigelow Paine, 2 vols. Harper, 1917.

Mark Twain's Speeches. Edited by Albert Bigelow Paine, Harper, 1923.

Mark Twain's Notebook. Edited by Albert Bigelow Paine, Harper, 1935.

The Love Letters of Mark Twain. Edited by Dixon Wecter, Harper, 1949.

Mark Twain to Mrs. Fairbanks. Edited by Dixon Wecter, Huntington Library, 1949.

Mark Twain-Howells Letters: The Correspondence of Samuel L. Clemens and William D. Howells, 1872–1910. Edited by Henry Nash Smith and William M. Gibson, 2 vols., Harvard UP, 1960.

Mark Twain's Letters to Mary. Edited by Lewis Leary, Columbia UP, 1961.

Mark Twain's Letters to His Publishers, 1867–1894. Edited by Hamlin Hill, U of California P, 1967.

Mark Twain's Correspondence with Henry Huttleston Rogers, 1893–1909. Edited by Lewis Leary, U of California P, 1969.

Mark Twain's Notebooks & Journals, 1855–1891. 3 vols. Edited by Frederick Anderson et al., U of California P, 1975, 1979.

Mark Twain Speaking. Edited by Paul Fatout, U of Iowa P, 1976.

Mark Twain's Letters. 6 vols. Edited by Edgar Marquess Branch et al., U of California P, 1988–2002.

Mark Twain: The Complete Interviews. Edited by Gary Scharnhorst, U of Alabama P, 2006.

Dear Mark Twain: Letters from His Readers. Edited by R. Kent Rasmussen, U of California P, 2013.

A Family Sketch and Other Private Writings, By Mark Twain, Livy Clemens, and Susy Clemens. Edited by Benjamin Griffin, U of California P, 2014.

Mark Twain on Potholes and Politics: Letters to the Editor. Edited by Gary Scharnhorst, U of Missouri P, 2014.

The Letters of Mark Twain and Joseph Hopkins Twichell. Edited by Harold K. Bush, Steve Courtney, and Peter Messent, U of Georgia P, 2017.

Posthumous Collections

What Is Man? and Other Essays. Edited by Albert Bigelow Paine, Harper, 1917.

The Curious Republic of Gondour and Other Whimsical Sketches. Boni and Liveright, 1919.

The Mysterious Stranger and Other Stories. Edited by Albert Bigelow Paine, Harper, 1922.

Europe and Elsewhere. Edited by Albert Bigelow Paine, Harper, 1923.

What Is Man? and Other Philosophical Writings. Edited by Paul Baender, U of California P, 1973.

Early Tales & Sketches. 2 vols. Edited by Edgar Marquess Branch and Robert H. Hirst, U of California P, 1979, 1981.

Collected Tales, Sketches, Speeches, & Essays, 1852–1890. Edited by Louis J. Budd, Library of America, 1992.

Collected Tales, Sketches, Speeches, & Essays, 1891–1910. Edited by Louis J. Budd, Library of America, 1992.

Bibliography

*Reference works and comprehensive studies of *Tom Sawyer* are asterisked. See also Works Cited lists following each essay

Aspiz, Harold. "Tom Sawyer's Games of Death." *Studies in the Novel*, vol. 27, no. 2, summer 1995, pp. 141–53.

Berkove, Lawrence. "'Some Damned Fools': Mark Twain and the Deceptive Promise of Youth." *Mark Twain and Youth: Studies in His Life and Writings*. Edited by Kevin Mac Donnell and R. Kent Rasmussen, Bloomsbury, 2016, pp. 12–20.

Blair, Walter. *Mark Twain and Huck Finn*. U of California P, 1960.

Bray, Robert. "*Tom Sawyer* Once and for All," *Review*, vol. 3, 1981, pp. 75–93.

Byers, John R., Jr. "A Hannibal Summer: The Framework of *The Adventures of Tom Sawyer*." *American Fiction*, vol. 8, Spring 1980, pp. 81–88.

*Camfield, Gregg. *The Oxford Companion to Mark Twain*. Oxford UP, 2002.

Cecil, L. Moffitt. "Tom Sawyer: Missouri Robin Hood." *Western American Literature*, vol. 4, Summer 1969, pp. 125–31.

Clark Beverly Lyon. "Editing Tom, Norton Critically." *Mark Twain Annual*, no. 5, 2007, pp. 15–24.

Csicsila, Joseph. "Langdon Clemens and *The Adventures of Tom Sawyer*." *Mark Twain and Youth: Studies in His Life and Writings*. Edited by Kevin Mac Donnell and R. Kent Rasmussen, Bloomsbury, 2016, pp. 64–74.

*De Koster, Katie, editor. *Readings on 'The Adventures of Tom Sawyer.'* Greenhaven Press, 1999.

Doctorow, E. L. "Sam Clemens's Two Boys." *Creationists: Selected Essays, 1993–2006*. Random House, 2006.

Evans, John D. *A Tom Sawyer Companion: An Autobiographical Guided Tour with Mark Twain*. UP of America, 1993.

Fetterley, Judith. "The Sanctioned Rebel." *Studies in the Novel*, vol. 3, Fall 1971, pp. 293–304.

*Gribben, Alan. *Mark Twain's Literary Resources*, vol. 1: *A Reconstruction of His Library and Reading* NewSouth Books, 2019.

_____. "Tom Sawyer, Tom Canty, and Huckleberry Finn: The Boy Book and Mark Twain." *Mark Twain Journal*, vol. 55, no. 1–2, Spring-Fall 2017.

Griffin, Benjamin. "'American Laughter': Nietzsche Reads Tom Sawyer." *New England Quarterly*, vol. 83, no. 1, Mar. 2010, pp. 129–41.

Hendler, Glenn. "Tom Sawyer's Masculinity." *Arizona Quarterly*, vol. 49, no. 4, winter 1993, pp. 33–59.

Hill, Hamlin. "The Composition and Structure of *Tom Sawyer*." *American Literature*, vol. 32, Jan. 1961, pp. 379–92.

Hirsch, Tim. "Banned by Neglect: *Tom Sawyer*—Teaching the Conflicts." *Censored Books I: Critical Viewpoints, 1985–2000.* Scarecrow Press, 2002, pp. 1–9.

*Hutchinson, Stuart, editor. *Mark Twain: Tom Sawyer and Huckleberry Finn*. Columbia UP, 1999.

Irwin, Robert. "The Failure of 'Tom Sawyer' and 'Huckleberry Finn' on Film." *Mark Twain Journal*, vol. 13, no. 4, Summer, 1967, pp. 9–11.

Lee, Fred G. "Tom Sawyer and Children's Literature." *Essays in Literature*, vol. 12, Fall 1985, pp. 251–71.

*LeMaster, J. R., and James D. Wilson, editors. *The Mark Twain Encyclopedia*. Garland, 1993.

Maik, Thomas A. "The Village in *Tom Sawyer*: Myth and Reality." *Arizona Quarterly*, vol. 42, Summer 1986, pp. 157–64.

Messent, Peter. "*The Adventures of Tom Sawyer*." *Mark Twain and Youth: Studies in His Life and Writings.* Edited by Kevin Mac Donnell and R. Kent Rasmussen, Bloomsbury, 2016, pp. 164–74.

_____. "Discipline and Punishment in *The Adventures of Tom Sawyer*." *Journal of American Studies* 32, no. 2, Aug. 1998, pp. 219–35.

Molson, Francis. "Mark Twain's *The Adventures of Tom Sawyer:* More Than a Warm Up." *Touchstones: Reflections on the Best in Children's Literature.* Edited by Perry Nodelman, Children's Literature Association, 1985, pp. 262–69.

Morris, Linda A. "*The Adventures of Tom Sawyer* and *The Prince and the Pauper* as Juvenile Literature." *A Companion to Mark Twain.* Edited by Peter Messent and Louis J. Budd, Blackwell, 2005, pp. 371–86.

*Norton, Charles A. *Writing 'Tom Sawyer': The Adventures of a Classic.* MacFarland, 1983.

Peck, Elizabeth G. "Tom Sawyer: Character in Search of an Audience." *American Transcendental Quarterly,* vol. 2, Sept. 1988, pp. 223–36.

Pinsker, Sanford. "*The Adventures of Tom Sawyer,* Play Theory, and the Critic's Job of Work." *Midwest Quarterly,* vol. 29, Spring 1988, pp. 357–65.

Prchal, Tim. "The Bad Boys and the New Man: The Role of Tom Sawyer and Similar Characters in the Reconstruction of Masculinity." *American Literary Realism,* vol. 36, no. 3, Spring, 2004, pp. 187–205.

Railton, Stephen. "Going Home: *Tom Sawyer.*" *Mark Twain: A Short Introduction.* Blackwell Publishing, 2004, pp. 32–49.

_____. *Mark Twain in His Times,* etext.virginia.edu/railton/index2. html (Includes full text of *Tom Sawyer* and numerous study aids).

*Rasmussen, R. Kent. "*The Adventures of Tom Sawyer.*" *Bloom's How to Write about Mark Twain.* Bloom's Literary Criticism, 2008, pp. 83–103.

_____, editor. *Dear Mark Twain: Letters from His Readers.* U of California P, 2013.

* _____. "*Tom Sawyer, The Adventures of.*" *Critical Companion to Mark Twain.* Facts on File, 2007, vol. 1, pp. 477–507.

Revard, Carter. "Why Mark Twain Murdered Injun Joe—and Will Never Be Indicted." *Massachusetts Review,* vol. 40, no. 4, Winter 1999/2000, pp. 643–70.

Robinson, Forrest G. "Social Play and Bad Faith in *The Adventures of Tom Sawyer.*" *Nineteenth-Century Fiction,* vol. 39, no. 1, June 1984, pp. 1–24.

Rubin, Louis D., Jr. "Tom Sawyer and the Use of Novels." *American Quarterly*, vol. 9, no. 2, Part 2, Summer 1957, pp. 209–16.

*Scharnhorst, Gary, editor. *Critical Essays on 'The Adventures of Tom Sawyer.'* G. K. Hall, 1993.

Seelye, John. "What's in a Name: Sounding the Depths of 'Tom Sawyer.'" *Sewanee Review*, vol. 90, no. 3, Summer 1982, pp. 408–29.

*Sloane, David E. E. *Student Companion to Mark Twain*. Greenwood Press, 2001.

Spengemann, William C. *Mark Twain and the Backwoods Angel: The Matter of Innocence in the Works of Samuel L. Clemens*. Kent State UP, 1966.

Steinbrink, Jeffrey. "Who Shot Tom Sawyer?" *American Literary Realism*, vol. 35, no. 1, Fall 2002, pp. 29–38.

Stone, Albert E., Jr. "Tom Sawyer and His Cousins." *The Innocent Eye: Childhood in Mark Twain's Imagination*. Yale UP, 1961, pp. 58–90.

Sweeney, Erin. "'A Far-off Speck that Looked Like Daylight': McDougal's Cave and the Vagaries of Discovery in *The Adventures of Tom Sawyer*." *Mark Twain Annual*, vol. 10, 2012, pp. 55–70.

Towers, Tom H. "'I Never Thought We Might Want to Come Back': Strategies of Transcendence in *Tom Sawyer*." *Modern Fiction Studies*, vol. 21, Winter 1975–1976, pp. 509–20.

Tracy, Robert. "Myth and Reality in *The Adventures of Tom Sawyer*." *Southern Review*, vol. 4, Apr. 1968, pp. 530–41.

Wolff, Cynthia Griffin. "*The Adventures of Tom Sawyer*: A Nightmare Vision of American Boyhood." *Massachusetts Review*, vol. 21, no. 4, Winter 1980, pp. 637–52.

Wuster, Tracy. *Mark Twain: American Humorist*. U Missouri P, 2016.

Zabeen, Saara. "The Introduction of *The Adventures of Tom Sawyer* to the Students of Independent University, Bangladesh, to Develop Their Reading Habit." *Mark Twain Annual*, vol. 13, 2015, pp. 167–75.

Notable American Editions of *The Adventures of Tom Sawyer*

For exhaustive lists of known American and foreign editions through the 1970s, see Robert M Rodney, ed., *Mark Twain International: A Bibliography and Interpretation of His Worldwide Popularity* (Greenwood Press, 1982).

Publisher, Year, Editor/Annotator	Special Features
Chatto & Windus (London), 1876 **Belford Bros. (Toronto)**, 1876 **American Publishing Co.**, 1876	First British, Canadian, and American editions, issued in that order
American Publishing Co., 1892	Publisher's "cheap" edition
Harper & Bros., 1903	First of about 17 authorized Harper editions
Harpers Modern Classics, 1920 Percy Boynton	Introduction
Gabriel Wells, 1922 **Harper & Bros. Stormfield ed.**, 1929 Booth Tarkington and Albert Bigelow Paine	Textually identical editions printed off the same plates, both with Tarkingon's "Appreciation" and Paine's introduction
Many publishers, 1930–	Beginning of unauthorized editions after book's copyright expired
Limited Editions Club, 1939 Bernard DeVoto (editor)	Illustrated by Thomas Hart Benton
Famous Stories Books, Dell Publishing, 1942 Oskar Lebeck (adaptor)	First comic book edition

Armed Services Editions, 1943	Number C-76 in a paperback series made specially for overseas troops
Classics Illustrated Comics, Gilberton Co., 1948 Harry Miller (adaptor)	First of several *Classics Illustrated* editions
Pocket Book, Jr., 1950	First modern mass-market paperback edition
Signet Classics, 1959 George P. Elliott	Afterword
Houghton Mifflin, 1962 Walter Blair and Frank H. Townson	Introduction by Blair, reading suggestions by Townson
Collier Books, 1962 Diana Trilling	Introduction
U. California Press, 1980 John C. Gerber, Paul Baender, and Terry Firkins (editors)	Omnibus edition that includes *Tom Sawyer Abroad* and *Tom Sawyer Detective* and has full scholarly editorial apparatus and extensive annotations
Mark Twain Library, U. of California P., 1981 John C. Gerber and Paul Baender (editors)	Scaled-down reader's edition with condensed introduction and annotations
Georgetown University Library, 1982 Paul Baender	2-vol. facsimile of the original holographic manuscript with introduction by Baender

Library of America, 1982 Guy Cardwell	*Mississippi Writings* collection that includes *Life on the Mississippi*, *Adventures of Huckleberry Finn*, and *Pudd'nhead Wilson*, with notes and chronology by Cardwell
Penguin Classics, 1986 John Seelye and Guy Cardwell	Introduction by Seelye and notes by Cardwell
Great Illustrated Classics, **Baronet Books**, 1989 Diedre S. Laiken (adaptor)	Widely read by young readers, this edition is a reprint of a 1979 paperback first published as a promotional item
First Edition Library, **Collectors Reprints, Inc.**, 1991	First full facsimile reprint of American first edition
Library of America, 1991 Russell Baker and Guy Cardwell	Introduction by Baker and notes and chronology by Cardwell
Project Gutenberg, 1993	Complete text of the first edition in multiple electronic formats, including facsimile pages, that can be read online or downloaded
Viking, 1996 Michel Fabre	Translation of Editions Gallimard's 1995 French edition with extensive illustrations by Claude Lapointe and notes by Fabre

Oxford UP, 1996
E.L. Doctorow, Albert E. Stone,
Beverly R. David, and
Ray Sapirstein

Part of Oxford Mark Twain
edited by Shelley Fisher Fishkin
with introduction by Doctorow,
afterword by Stone, and notes on
illustrations by David and
Sapirstein

Modern Library, 2001
Frank Conroy

Introduction

Broadview Press, 2006
Lucy Rollin (editor)

Norton Critical Editions, 2007
Beverly Lyon Clark (editor)

Full text plus c. 200 pages of
critical essays, supplemental
readings, and bibliography

NewSouth Books, 2012
Alan Gribben (editor)

Two otherwise matching editions,
with and without the words
"nigger" and "Injun"

Penguin Classics, 2014
R. Kent Rasmussen

Introduction, chronology,
bibliography, and annotations

Published Plays Adapted from *The Adventures of Tom Sawyer* and Its Characters_____

(List excludes most television and stage productions not published in books)

Tom Sawyer: A Play in Four Acts, Mark Twain, written in 1870s, published in 1969

Shadows of the Past [also a Broadway production], 1898

Huckleberry Finn [mostly adapted from Tom Sawyer], Lee Arthur, 1902

Tom Sawyer: A Play in Four Acts [also a Broadway production], Paul Kester, 1931

Tom Sawyer: A Play in Four Acts, Beatrice Odie, 1933

Tom Sawyer: A Play for Old & Young With or Without Music, Sara Spencer, 1935

The Adventures of Tom Sawyer: A Play in Three Acts, Charles George, 1936

Tom Sawyer: An Operetta in Three Acts Based on Mark Twain's Story, Tom Sawyer, Theodosia Paynter; music by G. A. Grant-Schaefer, 1936

Adventures of Tom Sawyer: A Play for the Marionette Theatre in Four Acts, Federal Theatre Project, c. 1936–39

Tom Sawyer Wins Out: A One-Act Play-Dramatization from incidents in Mark Twain's famous story, "The Adventures of Tom Sawyer," Pauline Phelps, 1936

Tom Sawyer's Morning, Regina Brown, 1947

Mississippi Melody: An Operetta in Two Acts Based on The Adventures of Tom Sawyer and Huckleberry Finn, Charles George, 1951

Tom Sawyer: A Musical Play in 1 Act & 7 Scenes, Jonathan Elkus, 1955

The Adventures of Tom Sawyer: A Comedy in Four Acts, Charlotte B. Chorpenning, 1956

Tom Sawyer: A Musical Play, Jack Urbont, 1958

Tom Sawyer: A Play, H. B. Sharp, 1958

The Adventures of Tom Sawyer: An Ageless Comedy for Children & Grown-ups Alike in Three Acts, Wilbur Braun, 1963

The Adventures of Tom Sawyer: A Play with Music, Robert A. Gibson, 1963

Tom Sawyer's Treasure Hunt in Four Acts, Charlotte B. Chorpenning, 1965

The Boys in Autumn, Bernard Sabath, 1974

Tom Sawyer, Sarah Marie Schlesinger and Michael Dansicker, 1975

Adventures of Tom Sawyer: Play, Derek Lomas, 1976

Tom Sawyer, John Charlesworth and Tony Brown (Eric Wayman, music), 1976

Tom Sawyer: An Operetta, Gwendolyn Skeens, 1977

The Adventures of Tom Sawyer, Samuel L. Rosen, 1978

The Trial of Tom Sawyer, Virginia Glasgow Koste, 1978

Tom Sawyer: A Comedy in Two Acts, Tim J. Kelly, 1983

Tom Sawyer: Opera in One Act, Richard Owen, 1989

The Adventures of Tom Sawyer, Dave Barton and Matt Bond, 1990

Tom Sawyer: A Musical Adaptation of the Mark Twain Classic, Mary Donnelly and George L. O. Strid, 1995

Adventures of Tom Sawyer, John Worth, 1997

The Adventures of Tom Sawyer [Broadway musical production], Ken Ludwig et al., 2001

The Adventures of Tom Sawyer, Timothy Mason, 2007

Reader's Theater Classics/ Mark Twain's The Adventures of Tom Sawyer/ Whitewashing the Fence, Jeanette Sanderson, 2007

Tom Sawyer, Ric Averill, 2008

Mark Twain Presents The Adventures of Tom Sawyer: A Stage Play, Mike Parker, 2013

The Adventures of Tom Sawyer, Laura Eason, 2013

Further Adventures of Tom and Huck and Other Plays, Don Nigro, 2014

Tom Sawyer & Company: A Mini-Musical Based on The Adventures of Tom Sawyer, Mark Cabaniss, 2014

Tom Sawyer: A Chamber Opera Vocal Score, Philip Martin, 2014

Illustrators of American Editions of
The Adventures of Tom Sawyer⎯⎯⎯⎯⎯⎯

Full-Text Editions

True Williams, American Publishing Company, 1876

John George Brown, American Publishing Company, 1899

Worth Brehm, Harper & Brothers, 1910

Alfred Skrenda (jacket only), Grosset & Dunlap, 1930

Nathan Machtey (jacket only), Grosset & Dunlap, 1930

Donald McKay, Random House, 1930

Paramount film stills, Grosset & Dunlap, 1931

1930 Paramount film stills (jacket only), Whitman, 1931

Peter Hurd & N. C. Wyeth (jacket), John C. Winston, 1931

Worth Brehm (jacket) & Paramount film stills, A. L. Burt, 1931

Corinne Ringel Bailey, Saalfield Publishing Company, 1931

James Daugherty, Blue Ribbon Books, 1932

Richard Rogers, Illustrated Editions Company, 1933

George Carlson, Noble & Noble, 1936

Norman Rockwell, Heritage Press, 1936

1938 Selznick film stills, Grosset & Dunlap, 1938

Thomas Hart Benton, Limited Editions Club, 1939

Peggy Bacon, Peter Pauper Press, 1943

Arthur Jameson, Whitman, 1944

Charles B. Falls, David McKay/Newbery Classics, 1945

Louis Slobodkin, World Publishing, 1946

Donald McKay, Grosset & Dunlap, 1946

Seymour Fleishman, Scott, Foresman, 1949

Harold Minton, Dell Pocket Books, Jr., 1950

Richard M. Powers, Junior Deluxe Editions, 1954

Paul Frame, Whitman, 1955

Walter Hodges, E. P. Dutton & Company, 1955

Edward F. Cortese & Peter Hurd (from 1931 ed.), Holt, Rinehart & Winston, 1961

John Falter, Macmillan Company, 1962

Jo Polseno, Grosset & Dunlap, 1963

Polly Bolian, Golden Press, 1965

Richard Loehle, Whitman/Western Publishing, 1971

Warren Chappell, Harper & Row, 1978

Paul Geiger, Reader's Digest, 1986

Luis Dominguez, Western Publishing Company, 1986

Barry Moser, Books of Wonder/HarperCollins, 1989

Troy Howell & True Williams, Children's Classics, 1989

Neil Reed & Gavin Dunn (cover), Puffin Classics, 1997

Claude Lapointe, Viking (translation of 1995 French edition), 1996

Scott McKowen, Sterling, 2004

Jim Rimmer, Pie Tree Press, 2008

Robert Ingpen, Sterling, 2010

Iacopo Bruno, Simon & Schuster Books for Young Readers, 2014

C. F. Payne, Creative Editions, 2015

Comic Book and Illustrated Abridged and Adapted Editions

True Williams & Milo Winter (cover), Rand McNally (abridgment), 1938

George F. Kerr, Dell (comic book), 1942

Aldo Rubano, Classics Illustrated (comic book), 1948

Floyd James Torbert, Pixie Books/John C. Winston (adaptation), 1952

Hans Helweg, Golden Picture Classic/Simon & Schuster (adaptation), 1956

Aldo Rubano & unidentified cover artist, Classics Illustrated (comic book), 1957

Frank Thorne, Dell Junior Treasury (comic book), 1957

unidentified artists, Classics Illustrated (comic book), 1961

John Philip Falter, Reader's Digest (abridgment), 1966

E. R. Cruz, Pendulum Press (B&W comic book), 1973

E. R. Cruz, Marvel Classics Comics (color comic book), 1976

Pablo Marcus Studio & Al Leiner (cover), Playmore, Inc. (adaptation), 1979

Harry Bishop, Illustrated Classics/Rand McNally (abridgment), 1983

John Falter, Reader's Digest (abridgment), 1989

Pablo Marcos Studios & Earl Norem (cover), Playmore, Inc. (adaptation), 1989

Michael Ploog, Classics Illustrated/Berkley/First (comic book), 1990

Aldo Rubano, Classics Illustrated/Acclaim (comic book), 1996

Ruth Palmer, Dalmation Press (adaptation), 2001

Ruth Palmer & Albert Slark (new cover), Dalmation Press (adaptation), 2004

Daniel Strickland, Stone Arch Books (adaptation), 2006

Rad Sechrist, Sterling (comic book), 2008

Severine Lefebvre, Classics Illustrated Deluxe/Papercutz (comic book; translation of 2007 French edition), 2009

Howard McWilliam, Calico Illustrated (adaptation), 2010

Alfredo Belli, QEB Publishing (adaptation), 2013

Filmography_____

This filmography lists feature film (F), television (TV), and video (V) productions adapted from both all and parts of *The Adventures of Tom Sawyer*. Some productions draw on both *Tom Sawyer* and *Adventures of Huckleberry Finn*. The list includes some very loose adaptations, such as *Band of Robbers* (2015), but not productions using Tom Sawyer as a character in stories unrelated to Mark Twain's novel, such as *The League of Extraordinary Gentlemen* (2003). Specific dates and other details for some listed titles may be found in the Chronology.

Symbols for special types: ♪ musical; ☺ animated; ✈ set in modern times; ✗ television series

Tom Sawyer, (1907, F, 10 min.?); Gene Gauntier, director and scriptwriter.

Tom Sawyer, (1917, F, 44 min.); William Desmond Taylor, director; Julia Crawford Ivers, scriptwriter. Performed by: Jack Pickford (Tom), Edythe Chapman (Aunt Polly), Robert Gordon (Huck), Clara Horton (Becky).

Huck and Tom; (1918, F, c. 45 min); William Desmond Taylor, director; Julia Crawford Ivers, scriptwriter. Performed by: Jack Pickford (Tom), Edythe Chapman (Polly), Robert Gordon (Huck), Clara Horton (Becky), Tom Bates (Muff), Frank Lanning (Injun Joe).

Tom Sawyer; (1930, F, 86 min); John Cromwell, director; Grover Jones and William Slavens McNutt, scriptwriters. Performed by: Jackie Coogan (Tom), Junior Durkin (Huck), Mitzi Green (Becky), Clara Blandick (Polly), Jane Darwell (Widow Douglas).

Tom Soier; (1936, F, 76 min); Lazar Frenkel and Gleb Zatvornitsky, directors; Nikolay Shestakov, scriptwriter. Performed by: Kotia Kul′chitskii (Tom), Kolia Katsovich (Huck), Klavdiia Polovikova (Polly).

The Adventures of Tom Sawyer; (1938, F, 93 min); Norman Taurog, director; John Weaver, scriptwriter. Performed by: Tommy Kelly (Tom), Jackie Moran (Huck), Ann Gillis (Becky), May Robson (Polly), Walter Brennan (Muff), Victor Jory (Injun Joe).

"The Adventures of Tom Sawyer"; (1951, TV, 60 min); Performed by: Charles Taylor (Tom), Tommy Rettig (Huck), Natalie Wood (Becky), Mary Astor (Polly), Joseph Walsh (Injun Joe).

"Tom Sawyer, the Glorious Whitewasher"; (1952, TV, 30 min); Performed by: Ken Walken (Tom?), Helen Carew (Polly?).

"A Little Child Shall Lead Them"; (1954, TV, 30 min); Garry Simpson, director; Performed by: Joey Fallon (Tom), Eileen Heckart (Polly).

"Tom Sawyer"; (1956, TV ♪, 60 min); John Haggott, director; Frank Luther, scriptwriter. Performed by: John Sharpe (Tom), Jimmy Boyd (Huck), Bennye Gatteys (Becky), Matt Mattox (Injun Joe).

"Tom and Huck"; (1960, TV, 60 min); Paul Nickell, director; Bruce Geller, scriptwriter. Performed by: David Ladd (Tom), Teddy Rooney (Huck), Ruthie Robinson (Becky), Janet Blair (Polly), Jackie Coogan, (Marshal Rogers), Dan Duryea (Muff Potter).

The Adventures of Tom Sawyer (French); (1968, TV ✗, 17×30 min?); Mihai Jacob and Wolfgang Liebenheimer, directors; Walter Ulbrich, scriptwriter. Performed by: Roland Demongeot (Tom), Marc Dinapoli (Huck), Lucia Ocrain (Becky), Lina Carstens (Polly), Otto Ambros (Muff).

Tom Sawyer, (1973, TV ☺, 30 min); Jules Bass and Arthur Rankin Jr., directors; Robert Littell, scriptwriter. Performed by: *voices:* Billie Mae Richards (Tom), Peggi Loder (Becky).

Tom Sawyer; (1973, F ♪, 100 min); Don Taylor, director; Robert B. and Richard M. Sherman, scriptwriters. Performed by: Johnny Whitaker (Tom), Jeff East (Huck), Jodie Foster (Becky), Celeste Holm (Polly), Warren Oates (Muff), Lucille Benson (Widow Douglas), Kunu Hank (Injun Joe).

Tom Sawyer; (1973, TV, 78 min); James Neilson, director; Jean Holloway, scriptwriter. Performed by: Josh Albee (Tom), Jeff Tyler (Huck), Buddy Ebsen (Muff), Jane Wyatt (Polly), Vic Morrow (Injun Joe).

Die Abenteuer von Tom Sawyer under Huckleberry Finn (German; shown in United States as Huckleberry Finn and His Friends); (1979, TV ✗, 26×60 min); Jack B. Hively and Ken Jubenvill, directors;

various, scriptwriters. Performed by: Sammy Snyders (Tom), Ian Tracey (Huck), Brigitte Horney (Polly), Holly Findlay (Becky), Blu Mankuma (Jim).

Tomu Sooyaa no bouken (Japanese; shown in United States as The Adventures of Tom Sawyer); (1980, TV ☺ ✗, 49×24 min);

Hiroshi Saitô, director; Tadahiko Isogai and Mei Katô, scriptwriters. Performed by: *voices (Japanese version):* Masako Nozawa (Tom), Kazuyo Aoki (Huck), Keiko Han (Becky).

Priklyucheniya Toma Soyera i Geklberri Finna (Russian production; released on video in United States in 1997 as Tom Sawyer); (1981, TV, 225 min); Stanislav Govorukhin, director and scriptwriter. Performed by: Fyodor Stukov (Tom), Vladislav Sukhachyov-Galkin (Huck), Mariya Mironova (Becky), Yekaterina Vasilyeva (Polly) (*actors' names are Americanized on American video release*).

The Adventures of Tom Sawyer; (1986, TV ☺, 60 min); Joel Kane, scriptwriter. Performed by: *voices* Simon Hinton (Tom), Scott Higgins (Huck), Jane Harders (Becky), Michael Pate (Injun Joe).

Tom and Huck; (1995, F, 97 min); Peter Hewitt, director; Stephen Sommers and David Loughery, scriptwriters. Performed by: Jonathan Taylor Thomas (Tom), Brad Renfro (Huck), Rachel Leigh Cook (Becky), Eric Schweig (Injun Joe), Michael McShane (Muff), Marian Seldes (Widow Douglas), Amy Wright (Polly).

The Modern Adventures of Tom Sawyer; (1998, F ✻, 92 min); Adam Weismann, director; Drew Daywalt and David Schneider, scriptwriters. Performed by: Phillip Van Dyke (Tom), Adam Dior (Chuck [Huck]), Bethany Richards (Becky), Laraine Newman (Polly), Erik Estrada (Joe).

Tom Sawyer; (2000, V ♪ ☺, 89 min); Phil Mendez and Paul Sabella, directors; Patricia Jones and Donald Reiker, scriptwriters. Performed by: *voices:* Rhett Akins (Tom), Mark Wills (Huck), Lee Ann Womack/ Hynden Walch (Becky), Betty White (Polly), Kevin Michael Richardson/Hank Williams Jr. (Injurin' Joe/Injun Joe), Don Knotts (Muff), Waylon Jennings (Judge Thatcher).

Tom Sawyer; (2011, F, 109 min); Hermine Huntgeburth, director; Sascha Arango, scriptwriter. Performed by: Louis Hofmann (Tom), Leon Seidel (Huck), Heike Makatsch (Polly), Benno Fürmann (Indianer Joe).

Tom und Hacke; (2012, F 🎯, 90 min); Norbert Lechner, director; Rudolf Herfurtner, scriptwriter. Performed by: Benedikt Weber (Tom), Xaver-Maria Brenner (Hacke).

Tom Sawyer and Huckleberry Finn; (2014, F, 90 min); Jo Kastner, director and scriptwriter. Performed by: Joel Courtney (Tom Sawyer), Jake T. Austin (Huck). Katherine McNamara (Becky), Christine Kaufmann (Aunt Polly), Val Kilmer (Mark Twain).

Band of Robbers; (2015, F 🎯, 95 min); Aaron and Adam Nee, directors and scriptwriters. Performed by: Adam Nee (Tom), Kyle Gallner (Huck), Melissa Benoist (Becky), Stephen Lang (Injun Joe).

Tom Sawyer; (2020, TV ☺ ✗, 26×22 min); *various*, directors and various scriptwriters. Performed by: *voices:* Daniel Brochu (Tom), Robert Naylor (Huck), Angela Galuppo (Becky).

The Adventures of Thomasina Sawyer; (2020, F, 90 min); *various*, directors and *various*, scriptwriters. Performed by: Angelina Capozzoli (Tom), Patrick Donovan (Huck), Shay Rudolph (Becky), Marianna Palka (Polly), Arthur Redcloud (Joe), Gary McDonald (Muff).

About the Editor

R. Kent Rasmussen traces his love of Mark Twain back to the age of eight, when his family inherited the Collier edition of Mark Twain books from a grandfather. Books were rare in his home, so those twenty-five volumes became very special to him—particularly since he shared his bedroom with them while growing up. The first of those books he read was, of course, *Tom Sawyer*. He still remembers the electric thrill he got in chapter 20. Like any misogynist nine-year-old boy of his time—he smugly waited for the prissy Becky Thatcher to be whipped for tearing a page in the schoolmaster's anatomy book, only to almost fall off his chair when Tom suddenly sprang up and shouted, "I done it!" That moment did not improve Kent's grammar education, but it certainly taught him the power of literature, and he has been hooked on Mark Twain ever since. So hooked, in fact, that the present volume is the thirteenth book on Mark Twain that he has written or edited, and he is not done yet. Were it not for his grandfather's books, he probably wouldn't be writing these lines now.

Despite his early conversion to literature, the doctorate he later earned at UCLA was in African history, not literature. After graduate school, he taught briefly, wrote five books about Africa, and went on to spend most of his working career as an editor—including a long stretch creating Salem Press reference books. Before that, however, while he was associate editor of the Marcus Garvey Papers at UCLA, he became curious about the source of Mark Twain's famous quip about the coldest winter he had ever spent being a summer in San Francisco. He looked for the answer in a library copy of *Roughing It*. He didn't find it there, or anywhere else, because Mark Twain never said that, but he found *Roughing It* such compelling reading he decided to make a hobby of reading "everything" Mark Twain published and compiling a collection of quotes in a modest book.

That was a little more than thirty years ago. To jump way ahead, Kent's little hobby eventually led to his publication of *The Quotable Mark Twain* (1997), but before that happened, an unlikely series of both unfortunate and fortunate events resulted in his writing *Mark Twain A to Z* (1995), the book for which he is still best known. Since then, each new Mark Twain book tended to lead to another. His list of titles now includes *Mark Twain for Kids* (2004), *Critical Companion to Mark Twain* (2007),

Bloom's How to Write about Mark Twain (2008), *Dear Mark Twain: Letters from His Readers* (2013), and *Mark Twain and Youth: Studies in His Life and Writings* (2016, co-edited with Kevin Mac Donnell), plus two other *Critical Insights* volumes. Kent also assembled the first Penguin Classics edition of *Mark Twain's Autobiographical Writings* (2012) and wrote introductions and notes for new Penguin editions of *Tom Sawyer* and *Huckleberry Finn* (both 2014). His other writings on Mark Twain include numerous articles in reference books, essay collections, and the *Mark Twain Journal*. In addition to his books on African history, he has also published books on African American history, Native Americans, and both world wars.

Kent's honors have included being profiled as a Legacy Scholar in the *Mark Twain Journal* in 2015 and receiving the Mark Twain Circle's Thomas A. Tenney Service award in 2017. He recently joined the editorial board of the *Mark Twain Journal* and is presently finishing a broad study of screen adaptations of Mark Twain's novels for the University of Missouri Press.

Contributors

Philip Bader earned his bachelor's degree at the University of Nebraska. While struggling to stay interested in his anthropology major there, he took some elective literature courses that introduced him to Mark Twain and Tom Sawyer. With the support of a delusional Spanish aristocrat, a cranky white whale, and others, Tom helped persuade Phil to change his major to English and begin a lifelong love affair with literature. Phil later wrote Facts on File's *African American Writers* (2004; rev. 2011), several travel books for young readers, and numerous book reviews and literary essays for a variety of journals and books, including *Critical Insights: Adventures of Huckleberry Finn*. Along the way, his world travels have included nearly a decade in Southeast Asia working as a reporter and editor for regional news agencies. Since returning to the United States, he has done writing and editing work for Sony Pictures Entertainment and an IT security firm while continuing to pursue his literary passion. He is currently finishing a book on George Orwell.

John Bird was introduced to *The Adventures of Tom Sawyer* in the fifth grade, when his teacher, Mrs. Hathcock, read the novel aloud to his class every Friday afternoon. Now, many, many Friday afternoons later, John is a past president of the Mark Twain Circle of America, the former editor and founder of *The Mark Twain Annual,* and emeritus professor of English at South Carolina's Winthrop University. He is also the author of *Mark Twain and Metaphor* (2007) and editor of *Mark Twain in Context* (2020), as well as the author of numerous articles on Mark Twain.

Hugh H. Davis has the good fortune to be the son of Mark Twain scholar John H. Davis. The summer he turned nine, he was introduced to *Tom Sawyer* by his father, with whom he read the novel aloud. Now Hugh is director of the Albemarle Regional Library in Winton, North Carolina. As the world pivoted in 2020 during the Covid-19 pandemic, he transitioned to library work after two decades of teaching high school English. Before then, he taught literature in both public and private schools, with his final position at C. S. Brown High School, where he was named 2014–2015 Teacher of the Year and served as the school's inaugural librarian. A former president of the Popular Culture Association in the South, he was named a member of the North Carolina Library Association Leadership Institute in 2022. As both teacher and librarian, he seeks ways to engage readers through inventive methods, often incorporating adaptations such as films into literary studies. He has previously written about *The Prince and the Pauper* in *Mark Twain and Youth* and in *The Mark Twain Annual* and about *Huckleberry Finn* in the *Mark Twain Journal* and *Critical Insights: Adventures of Huckleberry Finn*. He has also contributed chapters to *Shakespeare into Film, Past Watchful Dragons, Kermit Culture, Dickens Adapted*, and *Tantalizing Alice* and published articles in *Studies in Popular Culture, The Journal of American Culture, The Edgar Allan Poe Review*, and *Literature/Film Quarterly*.

John H. Davis, honored as distinguished professor emeritus of English by North Carolina's Chowan University, has retired from fifty-two years of college teaching. Forty of those years were at Chowan, which has named its annual symposium's keynote lecture after him. He himself delivered the very first such lecture, when the symposium's theme was Mark Twain, his favorite author since high school. *Tom Sawyer* wasn't assigned during his school years, and he doesn't recall exactly when he first encountered the novel. He does, however, remember reading it when writing his dissertation about Mark Twain's dream fiction and comparing Tom's "Injun Joe" nightmares to Huck's recurring dreams about Buck Grangerford's murder in *Huckleberry Finn*. Both stories capture juvenile feelings and adult memories. Their intensity, mixed with humor, impelled John to devote much of his later career to Mark Twain—teaching, presenting, and publishing in such journals as *Mississippi Quarterly, American Literary Realism, Mark Twain Journal*, and *The Mark Twain Annual*, and in Joseph A. Alvarez's *Mark Twain's Geographical Imagination* and R. Kent Rasmussen's *Critical Companion to Mark Twain* and *Critical Insights: Adventures of Huckleberry Finn*.

Kerry Driscoll, professor emerita of English at West Hartford, Connecticut's University of Saint Joseph, is currently an associate editor at the Mark Twain Papers and Project at the University of California, Berkeley. She is the author of *Mark Twain among the Indians and Other Indigenous Peoples* (2018), the first book-length study of Mark Twain's evolving views of the aboriginal inhabitants of North America and Australasia and his deeply conflicted representations of them in fiction, newspaper sketches, and speeches. Kerry is also a past president of the Mark Twain Circle of America and a long-time contributing editor to its journal, *The Mark Twain Annual*, and she serves on the Board of Trustees of the Mark Twain House and Museum in Hartford, Connecticut.

Joe B. Fulton is editor of the *Mark Twain Journal* and a professor of English at Waco, Texas's Baylor University, which has honored him as a Class of 1945 Centennial Professor. His interest in Mark Twain began early and was influenced by his growing up in a small, St. Petersburg-like town along the Midwest's Wabash River. There, his sister Susan gave him a copy of *Huckleberry Finn* on his eighth birthday. A year or two later, his other sister, Jane, read *Tom Sawyer* aloud to him, doing the voice of Aunt Polly especially convincingly. So far, that interest has led Joe to publish five thought-provoking books on Mark Twain: *Mark Twain's Ethical Realism: The Aesthetics of Race, Class, and Gender* (1997), *Mark Twain in the Margins: The Quarry Farm Marginalia and A Connecticut Yankee in King Arthur's Court* (2000), *The Reverend Mark Twain: Theological Burlesque, Form, & Content in Mark Twain's Works* (2006), the award-winning *Reconstruction of Mark Twain: How a Confederate Bushwhacker Became the Lincoln of Our Literature* (2010), and *Mark Twain Under Fire: Reception and Reputation, Criticism and Controversy, 1851–2015* (2018).

Alan Gribben was a young teenager when he discovered *Tom Sawyer* in his local library. He took the book home, read it twice, but could not have imagined what its author would mean to his own future. After earning a doctorate in English years later at the University of California, where he also worked for the Mark Twain Papers, he began a forty-five-year teaching career that included twenty years as department head at Auburn University at Montgomery, Alabama. Meanwhile, he converted his massive doctoral dissertation into the two-volume *Mark Twain's Library: A Reconstruction* in 1980. He has now expanded that exceptionally useful work into two larger volumes reflecting five decades of research as *Mark Twain's Literary Resources: A Reconstruction of His Library and Reading* (2019, 2022). Over the years, he has published scores of articles, a biography of library pioneer Harry Ransom, and *Mark Twain on the Move: A Travel*

Reader (2008), which he co-edited with Jeffrey Melton. For fifteen years, he reviewed books and articles about Mark Twain for the annual *American Literary Scholarship*. In 2011, his publication of six variant editions of *Tom Sawyer* and *Huckleberry Finn* for NewSouth Books ignited a national debate on Mark Twain's use of the notorious "n-word." More recently, he completed a twelve-year stint as Thomas A. Tenney's successor as editor and publisher of the *Mark Twain Journal: The Author and His Era* and turned the journal over to Joe B. Fulton.

Cindy Lovell first met Tom Sawyer at Newberry Elementary School in Etters, Pennsylvania, where each day her fourth-grade teacher, Ronald E. Riese, read a chapter from a different book to his class. One day, he read *Tom Sawyer*'s whitewashing chapter, hooking Cindy on the novel for life. Cindy went on to earn a doctorate in education at the University of Iowa and has since taught *Tom Sawyer* to hundreds of students, ranging from elementary school to college level. She has also served as executive director of both the Mark Twain Boyhood Home & Museum in Hannibal and the Mark Twain House & Museum in Hartford. Over the years, she has lectured about Mark Twain on Mississippi River cruises and at sites as far afield as England and Bermuda. She still regards Hannibal as her second home and is particularly proud of having written and produced the double album *Mark Twain: Words & Music*, whose profits all go to the town's museum foundation. In 2019, after twenty years of diligent searching, Cindy fulfilled a lifelong dream when she discovered Samuel Clemens's long-sought signature penciled on a wall deep inside the Mark Twain Cave.

Kevin Mac Donnell encountered *Tom Sawyer* for the first time around the age of ten, when he was addicted to biographies of famous people. Thinking that book a biography, he pulled a copy off a library shelf and soon discovered it was something even better. His early fondness for books and libraries eventually led to his earning a master's degree in library science at the University of Texas and building the world's largest privately owned collection of Mark Twain first editions, photographs, manuscripts, and artifacts. He has also become a successful rare-book dealer and earned recognition as a master researcher. In 2013, for example, *The Chronicle of Higher Education* cited his discovery of the probable source of Mark Twain's famous pen name as "research of note." His essays on librarianship, antiquarian bookselling, and authors ranging from Mark Twain to Herman Melville have appeared in numerous journals and books, including *The Mark Twain Encyclopedia* (1993), and he has reviewed more than fifty titles for the Mark Twain Forum. He has also co-edited *Mark Twain's Rubaiyat* (1983) with Alan Gribben and *Mark Twain and Youth* (2016) with R. Kent Rasmussen. He now serves on the editorial boards of both *Firsts Magazine* and the *Mark Twain Journal*, which honored him as a Mark Twain Legacy Scholar in 2016.

Peter Messent is emeritus professor of modern American literature at the University of Nottingham in England. His long-term interest in Mark Twain has led to six books and many essays touching, in one way or another, on the vast majority of Twain's works. *Mark Twain and Male Friendship* (2009) won him book-of-the-year awards from both the British and European Associations for American Studies. His most recent book, which he co-edited with Steve Courtney and Harold K. Bush, is *The Letters of Mark Twain and Joseph Hopkins Twichell* (2017). Pete has also written on a wide range of other American authors and has published both books and articles on his other specialty areas, Ernest Hemingway, crime fiction, and narrative theory. An honorary life member of the Mark Twain Circle, he now spends his time walking his dog, playing golf, and indulging in other gentle activities (not including fence-painting).

Linda Morris is distinguished professor emerita, University of California, Davis, who first encountered *Tom Sawyer* in graduate school. A former president of the Mark Twain Circle of America, she received that organization's Olivia Langdon Clemens Award in 2017 and the American Humor Studies Association's Charlie Award in 2018. Her many publications include *Gender Play in Mark Twain: Cross-Dressing and Transgression* (2007) and *Women's Humor in the Age of Gentility: The Life and Works of Frances Miriam Whitcher* (1992). She has also published numerous articles about such Mark Twain works as *Personal Recollections of Joan of Arc*, *Adventures of Huckleberry Finn*, and *Pudd'nhead Wilson*, as well as articles on the humor of Marietta Holley, Roz Chast, and Mary Lasswell. Linda's most recent writings include an article on the Cree artist Kent Monkman she coauthored with Kate Morris and a paper on "Continental Drift" for Elmira College's 2020 Conference on Humor and Empire.

Danny Norman is a true native son of Hannibal, where he was born, and where—like the young Sam Clemens—he grew up walking the same streets, swimming the same river, and exploring the same limestone cave. He recalls first reading *Tom Sawyer* around the time he was in fifth grade and read it again when it was assigned in middle school. That second reading led to his participation in the city's annual Tom-and-Becky competition. That, in turn, led to his selection as a "Tom Sawyer" ambassador in 2011–12 (when the editor of this volume first met him and was deeply impressed by his intelligence and interest in the world). Since then, Danny's fondness for Mark Twain has continued to grow. While an undergraduate at the University of Missouri, he bridged his past and his present by completing a capstone internship as a guide at the Mark Twain Cave, nearly every inch of whose limestone passages he carefully explored. Through his college years, he also worked as a graduate teaching assistant. During the summer of 2022, the university awarded him a master's degree in parks, recreation, and tourism.

K. Patrick Ober is a medical doctor and professor of internal medicine at the Wake Forest School of Medicine in Winston-Salem, NC. Several times recognized as a "best doctor in America," he has also been honored with the Association of American Medical Colleges' distinguished teacher award. His interest in Mark Twain goes back to when he was ten and was given a copy of *Huckleberry Finn*—the first book he ever owned. That novel's opening line made a deep impression: "You don't know about me, without you have read a book by the name of *The Adventures of Tom Sawyer* . . . " Inspired by Huck's personal recommendation, Pat tracked down and read *Tom Sawyer.* Years later, in 2003, he combined his medical expertise with his lifelong love of Mark Twain to publish his highly acclaimed *Mark Twain and Medicine: "Any Mummery Will Cure."* Since then, he has written numerous articles on aspects of Mark Twain's medical history and related subjects for both professional medical journals and the *Mark Twain Journal,* as well as other books. Pat's contributions to medical history and Mark Twain scholarship led to his being honored by the American Osler Society for modeling "Sir William Osler's interests in the interface between the humanities and the sciences—in particular, medicine, literature, philosophy, and history."

John R. Pascal discovered *Tom Sawyer* on his older brother's bookshelf at the age of eight. He immediately started reading about Tom and Becky's cave adventure and finished the story inside the hollow trunk of a huge fallen tree, imagining it to the cave. Years later, he graduated from Villanova University, earned master's degrees in English and business at Montclair State and Seton Hall University, and started a promising career in business. Eventually, however, his love of literature led him into teaching. Now in his twenty-first year of teaching English at New Jersey's Seton Hall Prep, he is recognized for his generosity and passion as an instructor and counselor and has received several awards. Among his classes is a year-long course devoted solely to Mark Twain whose students can earn college credits at Seton Hall University. (It is probably the only such high school course in the world.) John's publications include *Artemus Ward: The Gentle Humorist* (2008), articles in the *Mark Twain Journal* and several books, including Mac Donnell and Rasmussen's *Mark Twain and Youth*, and reviews for the Mark Twain Forum. He has also presented papers at the Hannibal and Elmira conferences, lectured at Hartford's Mark Twain House, and been a Quarry Farm Fellow.

Barbara Schmidt recalls reading *Tom Sawyer* for the first time as a child, when she found a copy of the novel in a care package of used books sent to her by wealthy cousins. Now she is a much appreciated independent Mark Twain researcher who has become legendary for the wealth of useful material she makes available on the web and generously shares with other scholars and Mark Twain admirers. A resident of Kingsland, Texas, Barb holds a degree in criminal justice and psychology from Tarleton State University, where she also spent years as head of the instructional media center. Her job helped make her become an innovative Internet pioneer. In 1997, she launched one of the earliest Mark Twain websites, *twainquotes.com*, devoted to accurately documenting Mark Twain quotations and biographical information. Since then, she has used the site to publish her own original research, as well as groundbreaking research of other scholars. She is also the first biographer of illustrator True W. Williams, whom Mark Twain selected to illustrate the first edition of *The Adventures of Tom Sawyer*. Meanwhile, Barb has also long served as book review editor for the Internet discussion group Mark Twain Forum. In 2017, the *Mark Twain Journal* honored her as a Mark Twain Legacy Scholar.

Hannah J. D. Wells, presently a doctoral student in English at Baylor University, studies nineteenth-century American fiction with a special interest in the history of science and political philosophy. Her dissertation examines the role of Baconian science and utopianism in the writings of such authors as Nathaniel Hawthorne, Herman Melville, Edgar Allan Poe, and Mark Twain. She has written articles for the *Eudora Welty Review* and *Cather Studies* and has also contributed "Stormfield Scholar" articles to the *Mark Twain Journal*, for which she is both book review editor and assistant editor. Hannah's first encounter with *Tom Sawyer* occurred at the age of eight, when her parents took her to a dinner-theater musical production of the story in Kansas City. She recalls being filled with terror at the idea of being lost in a cave. (She does, however, recommend the New Theatre's stellar garlic mashed potatoes.)

Index

Entries relating to Mark Twain may be found under "Clemens, Samuel Langhorne" (rendered as "SLC" elsewhere). *The Adventures of Tom Sawyer* and *Adventures of Huckleberry Finn* are listed under their full titles. Titles of SLC's other published works follow the "Clemens" entries. All fictional characters are listed under "characters, fictional." All film and television adaptations of both *Tom Sawyer* and *Huckleberry Finn* are listed under "film and television productions." Other screen productions are listed under their own titles. Numbers of pages with illustrations are boldfaced.

holographic manuscript 204
interpretability of xxxvii, 22, 166
length of 60
as a "Missouri book" 216
multimedia adaptations xxxvi, 167, 176, 178-80, 193, 216, 309-10, 315-18
narrative voice 27, 40, 41, 71, 79, 120, 129
as nightmare vision or idyllic dream 103-19
Oxford edition 60, 177, 204
paperback editions 218, 287
preface xix, xxx, 72, 85, 93, 151, 166, 236
publication history xxxi, 20, 94, 203-23, 279, 280, 286, 290
real-life models for characters 187
screen adaptations 193, 211, 224-46, 284-85, 290-91, 293, 315-18
sequels 71-86, 91, 99, 168, 174, 281
television productions xxxvi, 176, 224, 226-28, 288-90, 293, 316-18
time period of 3, 5, 150, 156, 275
writing of xx, xxviii, xxxix-xxx, 3, 6, 91, 134, 279
African Americans 174
and SLC 11
fictional characters 173, 196, 207

in Hannibal 196-99
Akins, Rhett 292
Albee, Josh 289, 316
Alcott, Louisa May 22, 23, 89, 277
Aldrich, Thomas Bailey viii, 23, 167, 277
and boy books 54, 55
boyhood experiences 25
SLC's opinion of 91
and *Tom Sawyer* 93
Allen, Jerry 195
American Publishing Company xxxi, 29, 203, 277
anti-modernism 9
Arthur, Lee 98
Astor, Mary 288, 316
Atlantic Monthly xxx, 63
Austen, Jane 51, 179
Australia xxxiv, 282
Averill, Ric 166

Bacon, Peggy 217
Bader, Philip ix, 321
balloon voyage. *See Tom Sawyer Abroad*
bats 14, 124, 158, 273, 274
Battle of Newtown (1779) 162
Baum, L. Frank 179
Beckley, Jake 199
Beckwith, James Carroll 199
Benson, Florence xix
Benton, Senator Thomas Hart 153, 214
Benton, Thomas Hart (artist) 214-16
Berger, Richard 288

film depictions 178, 242, 273
funeral 47, 158
illustrations of 157, 207, 215, 219
real-life models for 151, 152, 190, 191
symbolical twinning with Tom 12, 15, 16
Tom's empathy for 47, 48, 173, 243, 259
as a villain 14, 46-47, 111, 157, 190
Jake, Uncle 11, **208**, 254
Jim 10, 173, 174, **208**
film depictions 236-37
illustrations of 208, 217, 220
Jim (in *Huckleberry Finn*) xxviii, 9, 30, 78-81, 83-84, 96-97, 100, 196-99
film depictions 231, 244
illustrations of 215
Jones, Mr. (Welchman) xvii, 11, 107, 155, 197, 238
Lawrence, Amy xxxix, 122, 240, 241, 253, 260
Mary, cousin 134, 137-39, 142
and Emmeline Grangerford 240
film depictions 237, 239, 240
surname of xxxii, 136
and Tom 173
Morgan, Hank (in *Connecticut Yankee*) 175, 227
Mufferson, Willie 167

pastor. *See* Sprague, Mr.
Phelps, Sally (in *Huckleberry Finn*) xxxii, 127
Polly, Aunt 120-33, **128**, **139**, **149**
age 127
and Clemens, Jane Lampton xxxii, 127
and Harry Potter's Aunt Petunia 56, 57
in *Huckleberry Finn* 132
as mother figure 136, 138, 142, 145
illustrations of 127
surname of 136
and Tom 127-30, 137, 172, 173
Potter, Harry (Rowling character) 51-67
Potter, Muff 32, 105-07, 111, 140, 172, **206**, 257, 258
film depictions 227, 235, 241
illustrations of 220
Robinson, Dr. 111, 112, 153, 155, 205, 207, 215-17
film depictions 241
Rogers, Ben xxv, 6, 209, 212, 213, 250
Rogers, Billy (in "Boy's Manuscript") xxxix
Roxy (in *Pudd'nhead Wilson*) 120, 132
Sawyer, Tom **82**, **139**, **146**, **149**, **177**, **257**
age of 166

and Tom 144, 145
Voldemort, Lord (Rowling
character) 56, 63, 64
Walters, Mr. (Sunday school
superintendent 143, 146-47
Watson, Miss (in *Huckleberry
Finn*) 25, 79, 96, 97
Weasley, Ron (Rowling
character) 58, 59
Welchman (Welshman). *See*
Jones, Mr.
Wilks, Mary Jane (in
Huckleberry Finn) 95, 236
Williams, Hoss 153
Charles L. Webster & Co. xxxiv,
82, 281, 282
Chatto & Windus xxxi, 161, 279,,
281
Cherokee people 190, 228
cholera 110
Chronicles of Narnia, The (Lewis)
54
circuses xxv
Civil War, US xxvi, xxvii, 7, 11,
28, 276
Grant memoirs xxxiv
in fiction 176
Clark, Beverly Lyon 88
Classics Illustrated comic books
216-17, 219, 287
Clemens, Benjamin 109, 138
Clemens, Clara (SLC's daughter)
85, 134, 163, 194, 210, 235,
284
birth 279
death 288

Clemens, Henry (SLC's brother)
xxxii, 138, 188, 239, 276
Clemens, Jane Lampton (SLC's
mother) 26, 110, 134, 138, 147
and Aunt Polly xxxii, 127,
137, 188
death 281
funeral 189
Clemens, Jean (SLC's daughter)
128, 282, 284
Clemens, John Marshall (SLC's
father) 138
and Injun Joe 151
death 6, 275
law office 114, 118, 193
Clemens, Langdon (SLC's son)
93, 278
Clemens, Margaret (SLC's sister)
109
Clemens, Olivia (Livy; SLC's
wife) xxxix, xxxiv, 23, 134,
163
death 192, 284
disciplinary practices 138, 139
marriage 278
Clemens, Orion (SLC's brother)
xxvii, 275, 276, 283
Clemens, Pamela (SLC's sister)
xxxii, 138, 284
Clemens, Samuel Langhorne
(SLC) **xxiii, xxxvi, 190, 191**
and African Americans 11, 237
as character in *The Gilded Age*
xxx
birth xx, xxi, xxxviii, 5, 183,
186, 196, 275

grave robbing 74, 111, 241
    purpose of 111, 112
Green, Mitzi 286
Gregory, Richard F. 213
Grey, Joel 288
Gribben, Alan viii, 88, 292, 323, 324
Griffith, Gordon 286
Grosset & Dunlap 210, 211, 217
Grove, James 136
Gurney, Peter 288

Hall, Mordaunt 231
Hamilton, Margaret 235
Hank, Kunu 316
Hannibal, Huck & Tom (Blair) 289
Hannibal, Missouri 183-202, **183**, **190**, **191**
    ambassador program 188, 195-96, 198, 252, 267
    and fictional St. Petersburg xxii-xxiii, 3-5, 183, 185-87, 194
    as a film location 229
    Becky Thatcher House 188, 198
    bicentennial 199, 271, 293
    city council meetings in cave 268
    Clemens Conferences 292
    Huck Finn House 197, 198
    Mount Olivet Cemetery 152, 191
    Native American residents 151-53
    nineteenth-century perils 109
    slavery in 197-98
    and *Tom Sawyer* 60, 183-202
    Tom Sawyer Theater 193, **202**
    tourism xxiii, 187, 189, 192, 196, 198-99
Harper and Brothers 209-11, 282-84
Harry Potter books 51-67
Harte, Bret 277
Hartford, Connecticut xxx, xxxi, xxxiv, 34, 195, 279, 281
Harvey, George 284
haunted house 105, 220
Hawaiian Islands 277, 279, 282
Hawkins, Laura xxiii, xxxii, 137, 188
Helweg, Hans 218
Henry, O. xxi
Henson, Jim 169, 170
Heraclitus 116
Heritage Press 212
Heston, Charlton 52
Hibbard, Frederick 184
    Tom and Huck statue **183**
history and *Tom Sawyer* 3-19, 153, 158, 252
Hodges, Eddie 288
Holliday, Captain Richard 186
Holliday's Hill 4, 186, 194
    See also Cardiff Hill
Holm, Celeste 316
Holmes, Sherlock 168, 178, 283
Holt, David 235
homesickness 37, 141, 235
Horton, Clara **230**, 231, 285, 315
Hotchkiss, Hellfire 131

True Adventures of Huckleberry Finn, The (Seelye) 30, 289
turtle eggs **36**, 44, 160
Twain, Mark. *See* Clemens, Samuel Langhorne
Tyler, Jeff 316
typesetting machine xxxiv

Universal Studio parks 53
University of Missouri 152, 283

Van Buren, Martin 156
Van Dyke, Philip 292
Vance, Courtney B. 291
VeggieTales (TV program) 179
vengeance 49, 126, 127, 155, 156, 260-62
Verne, Jules xxxix
video games 180
Vidor, King 233
Viking Press 220
Vinton, Will 178
violence 16, 96, 168, 249
    and comic books 216, 217
    graveyard murder 25, 207, 216, 241
    in illustrations 207, 215, 217, 218
    racial 197
    and slavery 11

Walker, Dan 176
Wallace, George 197
Walsh, Joseph 316
Waltons, The (TV program) 169
Ward, Artemus 87
Ward, Edmund Franklin xxiii, xxxvi

Warner Brothers 193
Warner, Charles Dudley xxii, xxx, 27, 279
weather 43, 151
Weaver, John V. A. 233, 237, 240, 241, 315
Webster, Charles 281
Wecter, Dixon 287
Wells, H. G. xxxix
Wells, Hannah J. D. xi, 328
Wertham, Fredric 217
Whitaker, Johnny 273, 290, 316
White, Betty 292
White, Lynn 40
White, T. H. 51
Whittier, John Greenleaf 280
Wilder, Laura Ingalls 184, 185
Williams, Samm-Art 291
Williams, True W. xxxi, 16, 127, 203-08, 211-12, 217, 220
    sense of humor 205
    and violence 161
Winfield, Paul 290
Winston, John C. 211
Wishbone (TV series) 179, 291
witchcraft 55, 62
Wizard of Oz, The (film) 231, 235
Wolff, Cynthia Griffin x, 104, 105, 107, 108, 114, 126, 140, 143
Wood, Clement 287
Wood, Elijah 291
Wood, Natalie 288, 316
Wordsworth, William 89
Wyatt, Jane 289, 316
Wyeth, N. C. 211, 212
Wyler, William 233